"Dryden's stimulating volume helps us appreciate a wisdom hermeneutic for reading the Bible. Arguing that the sacred Scriptures were not primarily written to convey abstract doctrines or to create interesting historical-critical puzzles for us to solve, Dryden follows an older path, one far more promising. It was first trod by ancient authors and later advocated by the likes of Augustine in his hermeneutic of love. Following this approach, Dryden believes *the Bible is primarily meant for spiritual formation*, shaping us so that we might faithfully commune with God and neighbor. As we abide in Christ and he in us, we are shaped by his kingdom values and learn to flourish in God's world. There is so much wisdom and sanity in these pages! While this book is not written for laity—it is informed by top scholarship and argues with academic integrity—*its effect is to give Christian laity their Bible back*!"

—**Kelly M. Kapic**, Covenant College

"As Augustine suggested, the seeker needs wisdom in order to find more of it—to know what one is looking for. Augustine also taught that we need wise mentors to guide us into wisdom. What a help, then, is this treasury of prudential guidance in how to read the Bible, particularly the New Testament, to become wise. From Dryden's perspective, given God's communicative agenda, the entire Bible should be considered Wisdom literature that is composed of many subgenres. This book exemplifies 'formative literature' that seeks to impact the shape of the reader's character as well as the reader's mind."

—**Eric L. Johnson**, Southern Baptist Theological Seminary

"This book is a hermeneutically, theologically, and exegetically powerful way forward for reading New Testament texts as deeply formational and virtue inducing. Dryden helpfully culls insights from hermeneutics, philosophy, and genre analysis to present a vision of the embodied life and wisdom to which Christ calls his disciples. Dryden's specific readings of New Testament texts helpfully unite both theory and practice. I look forward to using this book with great profit in my own teaching of the New Testament."

—**Joshua Jipp**, Trinity Evangelical Divinity School

A HERMENEUTIC
OF WISDOM

A HERMENEUTIC OF WISDOM

RECOVERING
THE FORMATIVE AGENCY
OF SCRIPTURE

J. DE WAAL DRYDEN

Baker Academic

a division of Baker Publishing Group
Grand Rapids, Michigan

Published by Baker Academic
a division of Baker Publishing Group
PO Box 6287, Grand Rapids, MI 49516-6287
www.bakeracademic.com

Printed in the United States of America

Library of Congress Cataloging-in-Publication Data
Names: Dryden, J. de Waal, 1967– author.
Title: A hermeneutic of wisdom : recovering the formative agency of scripture / J. de Waal Dryden.
Description: Grand Rapids : Baker Publishing Group, 2018. | Includes bibliographical references and index.
Identifiers: LCCN 2018003749 | ISBN 9780801097935 (pbk. : alk. paper)
Subjects: LCSH: Bible. New Testament—Hermeneutics | Bible. New Testament—Criticism, interpretation, etc. | Wisdom—Biblical teaching.
Classification: LCC BS2331 .D79 2018 | DDC 225.601—dc23
LC record available at https://lccn.loc.gov/2018003749

18 19 20 21 22 23 24   7 6 5 4 3 2 1

To my NT Ethics students of the last decade,
with sincere gratitude and deep affection.

"There is a river in the Bible that carries us away—

once we have entrusted our destiny to it—

away from ourselves to the sea."

—Karl Barth

CONTENTS

ACKNOWLEDGMENTS

This book has been stirring around in my head since my doctoral studies, and in some ways it is my attempt to take my work there on 1 Peter and expand it into a methodology that covers the rest of the NT. In those dozen or so years I have had numerous conversation partners that have helped me formulate into words what started as a set of tacit exegetical instincts. The first discernible stage of development was a seminar I did on biblical hermeneutics with some of my students at the English L'Abri. They were my first guinea pigs and we learned a lot together, especially that the Bible can be wild, scary, and beautiful. So, my first debt of thanks belongs to them. They convinced me to continue on my methodological and pedagogical sojourn.

Much of the material substance of this book was developed subsequently in several iterations of a class I taught at Covenant College on NT Ethics. These were my real guinea pigs. Again, we all learned much together, and my small attempt to repay the immeasurable debt I owe to these students can be found in the dedication to this volume. Together we learned how the NT functions as wisdom to shape our lives, and we did our best to open ourselves to that process. It was a deep pleasure and genuine privilege to see students embrace the Bible as a source of wisdom for shaping their humanity and agency.

My colleagues helped me in innumerable conversations: encouraging, challenging, and clarifying my work along the way, both in my writing and in the classroom. For this I am especially thankful to Scott Jones, Kelly Kapic, Hans Madueme, and Jonathan Pennington. In addition, alongside these conversation partners were pastors and friends who were wrestling with what these ideas meant for practical exegesis, preaching, and the lives of their congregants. Eric Youngblood, Tim Hayes, and Robby Holt were all excellent sounding boards as well as skilled practitioners of the pastoral arts, with excellent instincts for both people and theological interpretation and what all this might mean for spiritual formation.

Covenant College has been my institutional home for the last decade and has supported me in the development of this material. I am especially thankful to the board, faculty, and administration of the college for two sabbaticals granted during the fall of 2012 and the spring of 2015. The support of the excellent library staff, especially Tad Mindeman†, John Holberg, and Tom Horner, was invaluable to me in researching this work over the course of many years.

My penultimate gratitude is for the sustaining fellowship of the *Schlupfwin-kelbrüderschaft*, apart from whom this book would never have been possible. This group of men has fostered my work with their keen interest, but more importantly, they have been the caretakers of my soul through many difficult days (including two back surgeries). In all this they encouraged and enjoyed me; they provided me a place of rest; they bound up my wounds and sent me back into the fight.

Final thanks, and my deepest debt of gratitude, belongs to Heather, my beautiful wife. She nurtured me and this project for more than a decade. She bore the weight of my discouragements and frustrations along the way, especially the ones that were too deep to verbalize. Despite all this, she still believes in me, and that has made all the difference.

ABBREVIATIONS

AB	Anchor Bible
ABD	*Anchor Bible Dictionary*. Edited by David Noel Freedman. 6 vols. New York: Doubleday, 1992
ABRL	Anchor Bible Reference Library
ACCSNT	Ancient Christian Commentary on Scripture: New Testament
AnBib	Analecta Biblica
ANRW	*Aufstieg und Niedergang der romischen Welt: Geschichte und Kultur Roms im Spiegel der neueren Forschung*. Part 2, *Principat*. Edited by Hildegard Temporini and Wolfgang Haase. Berlin: de Gruyter, 1972–
BBR	*Bulletin for Biblical Research*
BECNT	Baker Exegetical Commentary on the New Testament
BFCT	*Beitrage zur Forderung christlicher Theologie*
Bib	*Biblica*
BibInt	*Biblical Interpretation*
BNTC	Black's New Testament Commentaries
BZAW	Beihefte zur Zeitschrift für die alttestamentliche Wissenschaft
BZNW	Beihefte zur Zeitschrift für die neutestamentliche Wissenschaft
CBQ	*Catholic Biblical Quarterly*
CTJ	*Calvin Theological Journal*
CurBR	*Currents in Biblical Research*
DPL	*Dictionary of Paul and His Letters*. Edited by Gerald F. Hawthorne and Ralph P. Martin. Downers Grove, IL: InterVarsity Press, 1993
DSD	*Dead Sea Discoveries*
ETL	*Ephemerides Theologicae Lovanienses*
FFNT	Foundations and Facets: New Testament
ICC	International Critical Commentary
JBL	*Journal of Biblical Literature*
JRH	*Journal of Religious History*
JSNT	*Journal for the Study of the New Testament*
JSNTSup	Journal for the Study of the New Testament Supplement Series
JSOTSup	Journal for the Study of the Old Testament Supplement Series

JSPL	*Journal for the Study of Paul and His Letters*
JTC	*Journal for Theology and the Church*
JTI	*Journal for Theological Interpretation*
JTS	*Journal of Theological Studies*
LCL	Loeb Classical Library
LEC	Library of Early Christianity
LHBOTS	The Library of Hebrew Bible/Old Testament Studies
NIB	*The New Interpreter's Bible*. Edited by Leander E. Keck. 12 vols. Nashville: Abingdon, 1994–2004
NICNT	New International Commentary on the New Testament
NIDB	*New Interpreter's Dictionary of the Bible*. Edited by Katharine Doob Sakenfeld. 5 vols. Nashville: Abingdon, 2006–2009
NIGTC	New International Greek Testament Commentary
NovT	*Novum Testamentum*
NovTSup	Supplements to Novum Testamentum
NTL	New Testament Library
NTS	*New Testament Studies*
OTS	Old Testament Studies
PNTC	Pelican New Testament Commentaries
Presb	*Presbyterion*
SBT	Studies in Biblical Theology
SJT	*Scottish Journal of Theology*
SNTSMS	Society for New Testament Studies Monograph Series
STI	Studies in Theological Interpretation
VT	*Vetus Testamentum*
VTSup	Supplements to Vetus Testamentum
WBC	Word Biblical Commentary
WUNT	Wissenschaftliche Untersuchungen zum Neuen Testament
ZNW	*Zeitschrift für die neutestamentliche Wissenschaft und die Kunde der alteren Kirche*
ZTK	*Zeitschrift für Theologie und Kirche*

INTRODUCTION

Charles Taylor has aptly described our contemporary world as a "cross-pressured"[1] age, where the sacred and secular commingle and we often find ourselves defined by competing allegiances to antithetical (but strangely codependent) narratives. Faith is no longer understood in contradistinction to doubt but instead draws legitimacy from it. Only in its acceptance of doubt can faith be seen as authentic and distinguished from a naive faith that denies the resolute presence of doubt. At the same time, Taylor recognizes the deep longings for transcendence that mark the immanent secularism of our age. The secular is haunted by the chorus of the sacred, and the sacred is validated by its enmeshments with the secular.

My aim here is not to evaluate Taylor's description, although I do find it compelling. What interests me is how it translates into our habits for reading the Bible. Especially for those trained in biblical studies, whether biblical scholars or those with seminary training, there seems to be a cross-pressured tension between what could loosely be labeled "historical" readings of the Bible on the one hand and "theological" readings on the other. While some continue to argue for the strict compartmentalizing of these two modes of interpretation—and sometimes even argue against the validity or propriety of one or the other—I think just as many of us find ourselves in a cross-pressured space where we feel core allegiance to one side alongside the strong pull of the other. Some feel a core allegiance to the methods of historical and sociological research of the Bible but also a strong desire to see the Bible shape the lives of the communities we are a part of. Others come from a place of embracing the

1. Charles Taylor, *A Secular Age* (Cambridge, MA: Belknap Press of Harvard University Press, 2007), 594–617.

biblical text as God's self-revelation that effects communion with his people and fosters virtue in the believing community. At the same time, this group believes that historical and sociological research into the text is essential to ground the application of the text for the believing community.

Whether our cross-pressured age is an improvement over the previous modern dichotomist one is up for debate, and what it will produce has yet to be seen. But I want to suggest it affords us an opportunity for a rapprochement between historical and theological modes of reading. That said, the realization of this opportunity is far from inevitable; our cross-pressured age is equally defined by forces of sociological alterity—of communities that exist in incommensurable fields of discourse that are moving farther apart. So if we are going to resist this movement we need a compelling theological counternarrative, and I believe that counternarrative is found in the Bible when it is embraced as both historical witness and the creative self-revelation of God.[2] The category I will use to access this approach, rooted in the ancient world as well as biblical and ecclesial traditions, is "wisdom."

The central thesis of this book is at once commonsensical and controversial: the Bible is a wisdom text. Written by many authors and editors over a long period of time in diverse social, religious, and political environments, all of which were markedly different from our own moment in history, this diverse collection of texts seeks to shape the people of God in particular ways—to cultivate certain devotions, beliefs, desires, and actions—to prize some things and to despise others. The question of whether the Bible as a whole represents a *coherent* account of devotions, beliefs, and practices, while debatable, is (at this point in my argument) immaterial. All I mean to argue for now is a formative agenda per se, not necessarily a singular formative agenda. Even though the biblical authors adopted different genres and different modes of literary discourse, and even though there are tensions in the content they

---

2. Cf. John Webster, *Holy Scripture: A Dogmatic Sketch*, Current Issues in Theology (Cambridge: Cambridge University Press, 2003), 21,

> Both naturalism and supernaturalism are trapped, however, in a competitive understanding of the transcendent and the historical. Either the naturalness of the text is safeguarded by extracting it from any role in God's self-communication, or the relation of the text to revelation is affirmed by removing the text from the historical conditions of its production. Pure naturalism and pure supernaturalism are mirror images of each other; and both are fatally flawed by the lack of a thoroughly theological ontology of the biblical texts. . . . This frankly dualistic framework can only be broken by replacing the monistic and monergistic idea of divine causality with an understanding of God's continuing free presence and relation to the creation through the risen Son in the Spirit's power. In this continuing relation, creaturely activities and products can be made to serve the saving self-presentation of God without forfeiting their creaturely substance, and without compromise to the eschatological freedom of God.

present, there is a common intentionality of shaping devotions and moral agency at both the individual and corporate levels. In the ancient world the most common label given to this formative intentionality was that of "wisdom." In this sense, I mean to argue that the whole of the Bible is wisdom.[3]

For many this will seem commonsensical, especially given that this has been the majority opinion of the church throughout its history and was uncontroversial in all ages prior to the modern era. Where this proves controversial is in the recognition that the majority of our current reading strategies and critical methodologies, while very good at historical reconstructions, ignore and usually deconstruct this wisdom intentionality. The tools of NT research are designed to answer a set of questions about the origins of early Christianity: the evolution of certain beliefs and practices and the social forces that drove that evolution. These tools are adept at getting *behind* the text to formulate historical reconstructions—using the text as a window into struggling Christian communities working to justify and sustain their existence. This book breaks new ground in its attempts to develop in detail some reading strategies for the NT based on a recognition of the formative agendas that shape NT literature.

Traditional methodologies use detailed textual observations to answer a set of theological-historical questions, but they, by definition, exclude the intentionality of the text, because they separate textual observation from adherence to and sympathy with that intentionality.[4] This does not mean that all (or even most) biblical scholars reject readings of biblical texts that are deeply sympathetic to textual intentionality. It does mean, however, that historical and theological readings are methodologically distinguished as two separate and incommensurable types of reading. Since Johann Philipp Gabler,[5] critical readings have been (ideally)

3. This more general sense of "wisdom" is obviously not the same as the restricted sense that biblical scholars typically apply to the "Wisdom literature" of the OT and other early Jewish texts. I have addressed this issue in an appendix on the category of "Wisdom literature" in the history of biblical criticism that situates my use of the category of wisdom within recent discussions within the discipline.

4. Cf. Brevard S. Childs, *Biblical Theology of the Old and New Testaments: Theological Reflection on the Christian Bible* (Minneapolis: Fortress, 1993), 8, "Any new approach to the discipline must extend and indeed develop the Enlightenment's discovery that the task of the responsible exegete is to hear each testament's own voice, and both to recognize and pursue the nature of the Bible's diversity. However, an important post-Enlightenment correction is needed which rejects the widespread historicist's assumption that this historical goal is only objectively realized when the interpreter distances himself from all theology."

5. While he had his predecessors, most historians of biblical research would trace the formulation of this dichotomy back to the famous 1787 address of Gabler on "The Distinction between Biblical and Dogmatic Theology." See John Sandys-Wunsch and Laurence Eldridge, "J. P. Gabler and the Distinction between Biblical and Dogmatic Theology: Translation, Commentary, and Discussion of His Originality," *SJT* 33 (1980): 133–58. Gabler defined the rules for the discipline of biblical studies in terms of a division between historical research and theological

seen as foundational for theological readings, but these theological readings just as often simply sidestep the critical process.[6] As we will see below, this whole methodological scheme is inherently tied to modernist epistemological and metaphysical assumptions.[7] (This is why these tensions simply did not exist before modern biblical criticism and also why premodern exegetical practices often seem foreign to us in their naive lack of "objectivity" in approaching the Bible.)

Karl Barth put his finger on this tension in describing his fundamental hermeneutical conviction: "To understand an author means for me mainly to *stand with him*, to take each of his words in earnest, so long as it is not proven that he does not deserve this trust, to participate with him in the subject matter, in order to interpret him from the inside out." He contrasts his approach with what he labels the "dominant science of biblical exegesis," which he contends "does not stand with the prophets and the apostles; it does not side with them but rather with the modern reader and his prejudices; it does not take the prophets and apostles in earnest, instead, while it stands smiling sympathetically beside them or above them, it takes up a cool and indifferent distance from them; it critically and merrily examines the historical-psychological surface and misses its meaning."[8] Barth deftly describes the tension between historical and theological interpretations of the Bible.

While deeply sympathetic with Barth's formulations, my goal is actually to take a step beyond them and move past the modernist bifurcations of being/doing, meaning/significance, critical/confessional, fact/value, head/heart, indicative/imperative, and history/theology.[9] This means recognizing

---

application. Technically he distinguished "biblical theology" from "dogmatics," where the latter was understood as the theological application of biblical truths to the contemporary needs of the church. Within "biblical theology" he also drew a distinction between "true" biblical theology (historical description) and "pure" biblical theology (universal truths implicit in the Bible). Gabler's influence may not be due to either his originality or inherent genius but more likely his ability to define the discipline in a concise way that was amenable to Enlightenment rationality. Given the metaphysical and epistemological presuppositions of modernism, Gabler's formulation was not so much ingenious as inevitable.

6. This latter move is dependent on a construal of Barth's theological exegesis that fails to appreciate the central tensions that Barth struggled to resolve in recognizing the revelation of the Word of God in history.

7. As Brevard Childs opines, "The paradox of much of Biblical Theology was its attempt to pursue a theological discipline within a framework of Enlightenment's assumptions which necessarily resulted in its frustration and dissolution" (*Biblical Theology*, 9).

8. Quotation taken from Barth's second draft of his preface to the second edition of his *Römerbrief*. See Richard E. Burnett, *Karl Barth's Theological Exegesis: The Hermeneutical Principles of the Römerbrief Period* (Grand Rapids: Eerdmans, 2004), 284.

9. On the whole Barth's project still accepts these fundamental bifurcations. His distinction came in his methodological allegiance to beginning from the side of theological application, based on the foundational revelation of the saving Word of God, not on what human reason can surmise about God.

and embracing the function of biblical text as primarily defined by wisdom formation—and also recognizing that historical research is the path to embracing these texts as wisdom texts—and reading in a way that is sympathetic to their formative agendas. So we will see that the NT texts are not neutral texts that we derive significance from but texts possessing their own material agency that we can choose to reject or to accept in their agendas of shaping and sustaining our deepest convictions, desires, and practices.[10]

Road Map

This is only possible if we first look at the modernist foundations of our reading methodologies and question them (along with their postmodern cousins).[11] So the first two chapters take up the issues of epistemology (chap. 1) and the metaphysical bifurcation of being and action (chap. 2). Chapter 1 will give an account of our modern and postmodern epistemological heritage with a special focus on what this means for biblical hermeneutics. The purpose there will be to describe the relationship between the knower and the known along the lines of a fiduciary formative encounter with the biblical text. At the end of the chapter, I will use John 3 as a test case to contrast a wisdom reading with modern and postmodern readings. Chapter 2 addresses the dichotomy between being and doing that is a foundational component in our Western intellectual furniture and shows how the biblical text resists this dichotomy. Traditional categories of indicative/imperative or theology/ethics that cut the crucial link between gospel faith and gospel obedience make the biblical text opaque to us at this point. The chapter concludes with a reading of Philippians 2 in an attempt to restore this link.

These chapters are ground-clearing exercises, clarifying foundational issues that have historically inhibited our access to the Bible as wisdom. In the same

10. As Markus Bockmuehl argues, "Without facing the inalienably transformative and self-involving demands that these ecclesial writings place on a serious reader, it is impossible to make significant sense of them—or to understand why they were written or how they survived" (*Seeing the Word: Refocusing New Testament Study*, STI [Grand Rapids: Baker Academic, 2006], 46).

11. To my knowledge the only scholars who have done this with any consistency are Hans-Georg Gadamer, Sandra Schneiders, and Adolf Schlatter. So, for example, Schneiders's recognition of the need for hermeneutics to begin with a theological questioning of the foundation of Enlightenment metaphysics and epistemology: "In short, mainstream biblical criticism has been guided by its espousal of and fascination with a method, namely, historical criticism, rather than by a developed hermeneutical theory. It has not raised the ontological, epistemological, and methodological questions whose answers are integral to any such theory." Sandra M. Schneiders, *The Revelatory Text: Interpreting the New Testament as Sacred Scripture*, 2nd ed. (Collegeville, MN: Liturgical Press, 1999), 23.

vein, chapter 3 addresses another fundamental dichotomy that impairs our appropriation of the Bible as wisdom: the traditional antithesis between law and gospel, which sets the promises of the gospel over against its demands. We will need to rehearse the history of this dichotomy and its roots in the Reformation teaching on justification. Our goal will be to understand the message of salvation in the gospel as both gift and call, not driving a wedge between faith and repentance (i.e., not jettisoning the necessity of obedience nor disconnecting that obedience from the free gift of salvation). The chapter concludes with a study of John 15 and a brief excursus on the New Perspective on Paul.

After this ground-clearing activity of part 1, we move on to develop positive methodologies of how to read the NT as wisdom. Since different genres use different tools to implement wisdom agendas, we will need to examine separately the two primary genres of the NT: gospel and epistle. So part 2 will consist of two chapters on gospels (one theoretical and one exegetical) and two chapters on epistles (one theoretical and one exegetical). We will demonstrate that both of these genres were wisdom genres in the Greco-Roman world appropriated by the early church to realize the formation of young Christian churches in their devotions and practices. We will also develop some reading strategies particular to those genres that recognize their formative agendas. All this is followed by summary insights in a concluding chapter.

Actions, Reasons, and Motivations

To approach the Bible as wisdom presupposes that the redemption of human agency is constitutive of both the message of salvation and the teleology of the biblical text. Traditionally, at least since Aristotle, human agency has been understood through three coreferential lenses: action, reason, and motivation. We judge moral actions based on (1) the action itself, (2) our reason/justification for the action, and (3) our motivation for the action (i.e., what we desire to accomplish in performing it). So, good (or virtuous) actions are seen as an alignment of right actions with right reasons and right motivations. We commonly hear, "He did the right thing but for the wrong reason or with the wrong motivation." And when that happens, in most cases, we mean that what he did was actually not right, or possibly the right thing done poorly.

Right motivations and right reasons can be distinguished with reference to the traditional distinction between the faculties of reason and emotion. Right reason has to do with the question of what makes an action intelligible. How does this action correlate to my understanding of reality in relation to the good? Right motivation speaks to the desires bound up in the performance of an action. For example, how does my desire for relational significance motivate this action? Right motivation has to do with the energy behind the action, while right reason has to do with the context that legitimates that action.

Wisdom texts such as the Bible seek to inform and shape us in all three areas: actions, reasons, and motivations. While "ethics" in the Bible is often associated with commands and prohibitions (e.g., the Ten Commandments), the Bible also contextualizes commands in ways that make them intelligible and desirable. The Bible projects a "moral vision"[12] that renders injunctions to self-denial and love for God and neighbor both reasonable and attractive. When the Bible reorients our pictures of God, self, and world, it gives us a means to value what is truly worthy of our devotions and, conversely, shows what things are less worthy or altogether worthless. Augustine spoke about this in the language of "ordered loves."[13] In fostering wisdom, the Bible reveals the truth of who God is not merely to teach us "theology" but to inform our understanding and affections that we might orient ourselves toward him with a reverence that reflects both his glory and our dependence on that glory.

The idea of "ordered loves" presupposes the possibility of appropriate devotion to all kinds of things that call for our commitments and affections. Some objects of devotion are illegitimate recipients of our allegiance, which the Bible generally associates with idolatry in various forms. But if we remove these idols, we are still left with a vast array of goods worthy of our energies and devotion. The wisdom question is: Which ones should I esteem as most valuable? This is exactly the kind of question that Jesus is answering in his command to "seek first the kingdom of God" (Matt. 6:33). Jesus is prioritizing devotion to the rule of God over all other goods. This involves a relativizing, but not a negation, of other goods. "Seek *first*" does not mean "Seek *only*," but it does recognize that competing devotions can displace the kingdom of God as our primary orienting desire. So Jesus's command does challenge inordinate devotion to lesser goods and prioritizes allegiance to God and his kingdom over all other goods. When Jesus warns his disciples that only those prepared to sacrifice their familial ties are fit to be his disciples (Luke 14:26) does this mean that families are evil? No, but they are a competing devotion, and lesser goods sometimes need to be sacrificed for the sake of greater ones. A good becomes an idol when it receives inordinate devotion.

12. Richard B. Hays, *The Moral Vision of the New Testament: Community, Cross, New Creation, A Contemporary Introduction to New Testament Ethics* (San Francisco: HarperSanFrancisco, 1996).

13. Cf. David K. Naugle, *Reordered Love, Reordered Lives: Learning the Deep Meaning of Happiness* (Grand Rapids: Eerdmans, 2008).

Understanding the biblical text in terms of shaping wisdom through a category such as "ordered loves" will help us to see that biblical texts are doing more than simply teaching theology or giving us ethical principles.[14] One helpful shorthand way of accessing this will be to use the simple rubric of right actions, right reasons, and right motivations (hereafter abbreviated as Right ARM[15]). We will see that this rubric is a helpful orienting tool in reading biblical texts in a way that reveals their intentionality to form readers in an integrated act of wisdom formation. The goal of this kind of formation is a life marked by coherent desires, convictions, and actions. The Right ARM rubric is a simple exegetical tool that will help us to see how the biblical text marries these elements in formative ways. We will also discover that these elements are not confined to the corners of the Bible that are concerned with "ethics" but actually describe the material aims of the biblical text across the canon.

Three Clarifications

This book crosses numerous disciplinary boundaries. Such interdisciplinary studies are always open to the liability of oversimplifications, and there will necessarily be some cursory treatments in the pages that follow. While the academy generally approves of interdisciplinary ventures, there are also some interdisciplinary lines that are historically sacred, and their infringement is verboten. In what follows I will incorporate into my study of the NT insights from philosophy, hermeneutics, ethics, literary theory, and linguistics. While these disciplines are often considered ancillary to NT studies, they are also accepted areas of interdisciplinary discussion. But I will also venture into areas of moral psychology, practical theology, and spiritual formation in an effort to move toward what Sandra Schneiders labels "integral interpretation."[16] While these kinds of cross-disciplinary moves have typically been looked on as unsanctioned infiltrations of "edifying" interpretive agendas, I find that these interdisciplinary discussions are necessitated by the nature of the biblical text itself. Their exclusion is a historically conditioned employment of

14. Many readers will recognize here that the fundamental principles of speech-act theory are assumed in my approach.

15. I owe this abbreviation to my NT Ethics students Hannah Taylor and Morgan Crago.

16. Schneiders, *Revelatory Text*, 3, "Integral transformative interpretation is an interaction between a self-aware reader open to the truth claims of the text and the text in its integrity, that is, an interaction that adequately takes into account the complex nature and multiple dimensions of the text and the reader. Traditional historical critical exegesis, because it deals with the text only as an historical document, is necessary but not sufficient for integral interpretation."

certain beliefs foundational to modernist understandings of anthropology and epistemology, for which I can salvage only a mild allegiance.

Second, this book assumes that the redemption of human moral agency is an essential goal of the gospel proclamation as found in the NT. At the same time, I also assume that human moral agency cannot be circumscribed by what we have normally described as "ethics," especially when ethics is understood as moral casuistry within an idealist deontological (Kantian) framework, which is on the whole assumed in the discipline of NT studies when it ventures into ethics. In a way that is similar to virtue ethics (and its Aristotelian foundations), I understand ethics as describing not simply duties but the totality of moral agency entailed in the pursuit of true joy. So alongside moral responsibilities we will need to attend to the processes of moral formation. In a Christian context this also includes what today is loosely called spiritual formation—in that moral agency and moral formation only make sense in the context of how that agency is directed toward God as the giver of all things and whose glory is the proper τέλος of all human loves and actions. Consequently, this means that the categories of ethics, moral formation, and spiritual formation are all interdependent and not independent pursuits. These are all linked and overlapping, but each can still be properly distinguished. As we will see below, the traditions that sharply distinguish these spheres of life are founded on modernist assumptions.[17]

Finally, I owe an apology to every student of the Hebrew Bible: as they in particular will have noticed that I have, up to this point, spoken of the Bible and the NT interchangeably. This is not meant to imply that I believe they are synonymous. As a NT specialist the focus of this book will be on the primary genres of the NT—gospels and epistles—demonstrating how they function as wisdom genres. While my specialized knowledge ends there, my argument does not. I have outlined an argument, in an appendix, that *all* of the biblical genres of the OT and NT are best understood as wisdom genres, that is, as subgenres of wisdom. This conclusion is based on recent discussions about the inherent instability of the traditional constraints placed on certain examples of "Wisdom literature" in biblical and parabiblical texts. I leave it to specialists in the Hebrew Bible to continue the exploration of reading the genres of prophetic literature, psalms, and historical narratives as formative wisdom texts, but I point out in my appendix where that work has already begun.

---

17. So, for example, moral and spiritual formation are often treated as mutually exclusive activities because one deals with external moral action and the other deals with internal spiritual experiences. The explicitly Neo-Platonist spirituality of David G. Benner, *Spirituality and the Awakening Self: The Sacred Journey of Transformation* (Grand Rapids: Brazos, 2012), is a prime example. This bifurcation of moral and spiritual formation is dependent, in large measure, on the Cartesian chasm between *res cogitans* and *res extensa*.

PART 1

✦ ✦ ✦

TILLING THE SOIL

I

KNOWING AND READING

A hermeneutic of wisdom has to begin with the foundational questions that define hermeneutics itself. Hermeneutics refers to the self-reflective study of the various processes entailed in acts of communicative agency. As readers of the Bible we enter into a communicative process aimed at "understanding."[1] Hermeneutics attends to that process of understanding by observing it phenomenologically and by formulating guides to best practices and theories that undergird and serve those practices. It defines and promotes certain skills, dispositions, and contexts that foster the process of understanding.

This chapter aims to explore the connection between knowing and reading, or more precisely, epistemology and hermeneutics. Simply put, hermeneutics is a form of applied epistemology because it applies a theory of knowledge to a particular process of arriving at understanding.[2] Every theory of knowledge

1. See Sandra M. Schneiders, "The Gospels and the Reader," in *The Cambridge Companion to the Gospels*, ed. Stephen C. Barton (Cambridge: Cambridge University Press, 2006), 109, "Understanding, as both Ricoeur and Gadamer insisted, is not simply an epistemological process of arriving at new knowledge. Rather, in the ontological sense of the word understanding denotes the specifically human way of being-in-the-world. Understanding integrates us into reality. Consequently, to come to new understanding is to expand one's existential horizon (and thus to see not only more but also to see differently) and to deepen one's humanity. Gadamer talked about application and Ricoeur about appropriation, but essentially they both intended to designate the transformation of the subject that is effected by an enriched encounter with reality."

2. Some would say that all of philosophy, including epistemology, is only hermeneutics, or at the very least hermeneutically determined. See, for example, Merold Westphal, *Overcoming*

begins with a picture of the knower and the known—how a person engaged in knowing (the subject) is related to a field of study (the object).[3] In the same way, every hermeneutic assumes some picture of the relationship between the reader and the text. So in working toward a hermeneutic of wisdom our first foundational question will define the reader's stance or "comportment"[4] toward the text. To answer that question, though, we have to ask some basic questions about knowing.

Modern Knowing and Reading

The modern period gave us two pictures of knowing. The first is represented in Rodin's famous bronze *The Thinker*, in which all of reality is circumscribed in the individual's straining attempt to understand the meaning of human existence. This image is often associated with the philosophical movements of rationalism and subjectivism because it focuses on reason constituted in the subject as the path to understanding. The second modern picture, more prosaic and consequently not commemorated in bronze, is that of the scientist in the white lab coat. This image of empiricism embodies the

---

Onto-theology: Toward a Postmodern Christian Faith, Perspectives in Continental Philosophy (New York: Fordham University Press, 2001).

3. Traditionally this has been explored in the language of metaphysics. So, we could also say that standing behind every epistemology is a metaphysic (a picture reality) that renders it intelligible. Sometimes the metaphysic is explicit; sometimes it is simply assumed. Modern epistemology had a strong tendency to assume a metaphysic, which was later made explicit, deconstructed, and reformed in postmodernism. As Schneiders says, "Whether or not the interpreter attends to the fact, all particular approaches to interpretation, including those which focus on the reader, imply a philosophically based hermeneutics or global theory of what it means to understand, how the human subject achieves understanding, and what understanding effects. In other words, there is some ontological-epistemological theory operative, at least implicitly, in all interpretive processes" ("Gospels and the Reader," 104).

4. The basic concept of comportment is how one situates oneself toward or lives in relation to another person or thing. This usage of the word corresponds to that commonly found in English translations of the works of Heidegger (translating German *Verhältnis/verhalten*); see, for example, *Being and Time*, trans. Joan Stambaugh (Albany: State University of New York Press, 1996), 110–18 [117–26]). Cf. M. J. Inwood's observation that for Heidegger "*sich verhalten* suggests 'relating (oneself)' to someone or something." M. J. Inwood, *A Heidegger Dictionary*, The Blackwell Philosopher Dictionaries (Oxford: Blackwell, 1999), 135. Hubert L. Dreyfus, *Skillful Coping: Essays on the Phenomenology of Everyday Perception and Action*, ed. Mark A. Wrathall (Oxford: Oxford University Press, 2014), 87, says, "For Heidegger 'comportment' denotes not merely acts of consciousness, but human activity in general." He then goes on to quote Heidegger: "Comportments have the structure of directing-oneself-toward, of being-directed-toward." Martin Heidegger, *The Basic Problems of Phenomenology*, trans. Albert Hofstadter, Studies in Phenomenology and Existential Philosophy (Bloomington: Indiana University Press, 1982), 58.

virtues of objective observation and the submission of theories to evidentiary proofs. While these two images are hard to reconcile,[5] they share a similar stance toward reality—that of a subject that stands in a self-referential relationship to its object. The subject is in no way defined by its relation to the object; rather, the subject observes, interprets, and (from a distance) defines what of value is to be found in the object. As Mark Taylor describes it, the "sovereign subject relates only to what it constructs and is, therefore, unaffected by anything other than itself."[6] From this second picture arose a strong tendency in modern thought and practice for knowing to become an act of mastery and overcoming, which also gave rise to technologically driven hopes for social reform.

What has this meant for our reading of the Bible? Primarily, it has meant that the Bible is not something that determines our existence, but instead we as "sovereign subjects" determine the boundaries of its meaning and significance. The Bible is an object to be studied and subdued to fit within our understanding. Extreme, and therefore obvious, examples of this include Thomas Jefferson's cut-and-paste project of editing the Gospels[7] and the plebeian rationalism of Heinrich Paulus.[8] But we misunderstand modern interpretive practices if we only associate them with methods that "critically" question the content of the Bible. The real essence of modern comportment to the text is found in the act of objectifying it and determining what in it is valuable according to criteria congenial to modern prerogatives. The normative image for the modern exegete is the prospector, who sifts through the silt of the text for nuggets of gold. This prospecting stance equally describes "historical-critical" approaches as well as their (more conservative) "grammatical-historical" cousins. Whenever we read the Bible to extract nuggets, we are reading in a modern mode, relating to the text as "sovereign subjects." The three most

5. Kant attempted to reconcile subjectivism and empiricism in his *Critique of Pure Reason*. Cf. James Van Cleve, "Kant, Immanuel," in *A Companion to Epistemology*, ed. Jonathan Dancy and Ernest Sosa (Oxford: Blackwell, 1992), 230–34.

6. Mark C. Taylor, ed., *Deconstruction in Context: Literature and Philosophy* (Chicago: University of Chicago Press, 1986), 3. Here Taylor is talking specifically about Descartes in his role as the progenitor of the Enlightenment philosophical project. He adds, "In a move that remains decisive for all later thought, Descartes insists that the subject's relation to all otherness is mediated by and derived from its relationship to itself."

7. Sometimes now referred to as the *Jefferson Bible*, Jefferson published it under the title *The Life and Morals of Jesus of Nazareth*.

8. H. E. G. Paulus is famous today for finding creative naturalistic explanations for the miracle accounts in the Gospel narratives. So, Jesus didn't calm a storm at sea; the boat just sailed into calm waters protected by a coastal mountain. Nor did Jesus feed five thousand, but luckily a wealthy family with lots of sandwiches just happened to be passing by. Cf. William Baird, *History of New Testament Research* (Minneapolis: Fortress, 1992), 1:201–8.

common "prospecting" modes of reading are reading theologically, reading historically, and reading ethically.

In reading theologically we come to a text looking to extract theological nuggets.[9] Our questions are: What is the theology here? What does this text teach me about God? What does this text teach concerning the doctrine of _____ (fill in the blank: Christology, ecclesiology, etc.)? Similarly, reading historically sifts biblical texts for historical data. What does this tell me about when, where, and why someone did something? Where did this theological doctrine come from? Does this text give me data to help me in understanding the development of early Christianity or ancient Israelite religion? Likewise, reading ethically means sifting texts for ethical principles. What is the ethical principle taught, commanded, or implied in this text? How does this text supply foundations for the construction of a Christian ethic?

In the history of NT criticism this resulted in approaching texts as instrumental for unlocking a historical-theological puzzle. The chief questions of this puzzle concentrate on the origins of early Christianity, the genealogical relationships between texts, and the social contexts from which they came. So again the fundamental questions are: What is the doctrine here? Where did it come from? What historical data can be extracted from this text? The most obvious methodology to associate with this project is form criticism, which characterizes small pieces of tradition in terms of their value for historical reconstruction.

To be careful, labeling these modes of reading as modern does not strip them of their value in fostering close observation of the text and yielding fruitful understanding. What is important for our study is recognizing that *our questions are embodiments and expressions of our comportment toward the text.* These questions constitute an act of objectifying the text, treating it as an inert object from which data can be extracted. Some would gladly endorse this approach, while others might resist its implications. In the end, though, regardless of what doctrine of Scripture we might bring to the Bible, when we objectify and propositionalize[10] the text we are taking the stance

9. This differs significantly from the hermeneutical methods associated with the "theological interpretation of Scripture." For a good introduction see Daniel J. Treier, *Introducing Theological Interpretation of Scripture: Recovering a Christian Practice* (Grand Rapids: Baker Academic, 2008).

10. Cf. Kevin J. Vanhoozer, *The Drama of Doctrine: A Canonical-Linguistic Approach to Christian Theology* (Louisville: Westminster John Knox, 2005), 266–78. Here he describes how his dramatic canonical-linguistic approach to doctrine moves beyond a "propositionalist" framework for doing theology. Vanhoozer is not criticizing propositions per se, but theological formulations that embody a pseudo-objective outlook in reducing all theological reflection to propositional facts. By contrast, Carl Raschke rejects propositional language *itself* as the essence

of a prospector; the text becomes objectified and does not infringe on our sovereign selfhood.

So if we wanted to *apply* the text, this would require an *additional* task in our reading of the text. It is in no way tied by necessity to a reading of the text, nor is it demanded by the nature of the text. In fact, if we are committed to a modern approach, application is a violation of a "neutral" methodology because it creates a disturbance in the relationship between the text, as an inert object, and the reader, as a disinterested observer.

So while these modes of reading (theologically, historically, ethically) can bear important fruit, they embody a modern comportment to the text (that incidentally would have been unintelligible to anyone living prior to the eighteenth century). These hermeneutical practices view the text as a repository of knowledge, but one that takes some work to sift through to yield its treasure. As we will see later, this is the reason why, historically, as modern exegetes we have been very poor readers of narratives such as the Gospels and have been happier reading propositional theological material such as the letters of Paul. In Paul there are more nuggets lying on the surface, so it is easier (though not easy) work. Again, all of this is only intelligible in a context dominated by a modern picture of the world, where the attributes that define serious human reflection are objectivity and a reliance on reason as the arbiter of truth. Of course, if those sureties were to shift, our reading practices would necessarily have to shift as well.

Postmodern Knowing and Reading

And, of course, both have shifted. The move from modernism to postmodernism begins with the realization that the subject is not a neutral suprahuman observer but what Kierkegaard called an "existing person,"[11] a finite human person with desires, intentions, perspectives, and prejudices that

---

of logocentric theological method. "Language from the Creator's vantage point is not propositional at all. It is intersubjective." Carl A. Raschke, *The Next Reformation: Why Evangelicals Must Embrace Postmodernity* (Grand Rapids: Baker Academic, 2004), 71.

11. E.g., "Here it is not forgotten . . . that the subject is existing, and that existing is a becoming, and that truth as the identity of thought and being is therefore a chimera of abstraction and truly only a longing of creation, not because truth is not an identity, but because the knower is an *existing person*, and thus truth cannot be an identity for him as long as he exists." Søren Kierkegaard, *Concluding Unscientific Postscript to Philosophical Fragments*, trans. Howard V. Hong and Edna H. Hong, 2 vols., Kierkegaard's Writings 12 (Princeton: Princeton University Press, 1992), 196, italics added. He continues, "Modern speculative thought has mustered everything to enable the individual to transcend himself objectively, but this cannot be done. Existence exercises its constraint" (197).

shape their understanding. In the act of knowing the knower introduces herself and all her history into a relationship with the object of knowledge. The modern conceptions of knowledge as something objective, indubitable, and universal now strike our postmodern sensibilities as hopelessly naive and maybe even arrogant. Postmodernism recognizes that all knowing is conditioned by, and to some degree determined by, our history, gender, race, and nationality.

This also means that "knowledge" is most often seen as a construal of reality that reveals more about the subject's vantage point in knowing than it does the object of knowledge, and, therefore, knowledge is only interpretation. In this context all systems of thought come under suspicion as ideological constructs that serve to advance personal and political power. Also, because knowledge is shaped by sociological factors (such as race or gender), it becomes particular to a social class, formative for its own self-identity. Each social group has its own interpretation of reality that reinforces that group's cohesion and furthers its agendas.[12]

What does all this mean for reading the Bible? First, the old idea of the *wissenschaftlich*[13] observer reading the text neutrally is already a distant memory.[14] In contrast, it means that the reader is an active agent who comes to the text with intentions and expectations of what the text will say. From this many have emphasized the "openness" of the text and the reader's role in creating meaning (e.g., reader-response criticism).[15] In terms of our comportment to the text, this means that we are not neutral observers but bring our whole selves into the circle of the text and that the movement toward understanding involves a dialectic engagement with the text.

Postmodernism also provides us with a different account of what the text itself is. In the modern mode of interpretation the text was an inert object, a

12. Cf. the classic study by Peter L. Berger and Thomas Luckmann, *The Social Construction of Reality: A Treatise in the Sociology of Knowledge* (Garden City, NY: Anchor Books, 1967).

13. German adjective meaning something between "scientific" and "scholarly"; it carries a strong connotation of emphasizing objective scientific observation as the mark of scholarly activity.

14. Its demise has been long coming. More than a century ago (in 1909) Adolf Schlatter argued that "a historical sketch can only take shape in the mind of a historian, and . . . in this process the historian himself, with all his intellectual furniture, is involved. If this fact is lost sight of, then it is no longer science (*Wissenschaft*) in which we are involved, but crazy illusions." Adolf Schlatter, "The Theology of the New Testament and Dogmatics," in *The Nature of New Testament Theology: The Contribution of William Wrede and Adolf Schlatter*, ed. Robert Morgan, SBT (London: SCM, 1973), 125–26.

15. See Umberto Eco, *The Role of the Reader: Explorations in the Semiotics of Texts*, Advances in Semiotics (Bloomington: Indiana University Press, 1979).

repository of facts, to be mined for different types of information.[16] By contrast, in postmodern understanding the text is an active force that advances toward the reader with its own agendas. The biblical authors, in giving their interpretations of ideas and events, promote ideological structures that create a privileged space for the faithful. So the Bible itself projects interpretive schemes on reality that legitimate the social structures and political agendas of Israel and the NT church. So, in this context, the Bible's ideological construals need to be exposed (e.g., socio-rhetorical criticism)[17] and perhaps refashioned into something more palatable (e.g., feminist criticism).[18]

In the end we are left with a much more complex picture of agency on the part of both the reader and the text itself, where the two meet with their own agendas and preunderstandings, and hermeneutical understanding arising from a dialectic movement directed by the reader from a standpoint of suspicion. While this picture of comportment differs strongly from the lab-coat image of the modern paradigm, it still shares with it the conviction that the reader is the reference point for the dialectic process. The principle of the "sovereign subject," although sometimes tempered with the notion of "reading communities,"[19] has proven resilient in surviving the shift from modernism to postmodernism.

Sapiential Knowing and Reading

How then would a hermeneutic of wisdom relate to the hermeneutical traditions of modernism and postmodernism? In attempting to formulate a stance

16. Cf. Schneiders, "Gospels and the Reader," 97, "Texts were [treated as] free-standing semantic containers in which a single, stable meaning was intentionally embedded by the author. The meaning in the biblical texts was presumed to be primarily information about history. Thus, the task of the biblical scholar was primarily if not exclusively to extract from the text what it had to say about history."

17. Cf. Elisabeth Schüssler Fiorenza, *Rhetoric and Ethic: The Politics of Biblical Studies* (Minneapolis: Fortress, 1999), 51, "Kyriocentric language . . . constructs reality in a certain way and then mystifies its own constructions by naturalizing them. . . . Consequently, a hermeneutics of suspicion is best understood as a deconstructive practice of inquiry that denaturalizes and demystifies practices of domination."

18. See Schüssler Fiorenza, *Rhetoric and Ethic*, 52. She argues for a methodology that "seeks to displace the kyriocentric dynamic of the biblical text in its literary and historical contexts by *recontextualizing* the text in a sociopolitical-religious model of reconstruction that aims at making the subordinated and marginalized 'others' visible again. . . . Such a hermeneutics of remembrance utilizes *constructive methods of revisioning* insofar as it seeks not only for historical retrieval but also for a religious reconstitution of the world." Italics added.

19. E.g., Stanley Fish, *Is There a Text in This Class? The Authority of Interpretive Communities* (Cambridge, MA: Harvard University Press, 1980).

of engagement with the text, a wisdom hermeneutic would agree with the postmodern critique of "neutral" modern accounts as idealistic and inadequate explanations of the role of the reader in understanding the biblical text. It would likewise affirm postmodern appreciation for the agency of the text in the process of understanding (i.e., that the text is not an inert, neutral object of study). So it would likewise critique previous hermeneutical approaches that sift texts for propositions as not only indebted to modernist epistemology but as highly disruptive textual raids, often insensitive to the integrity and intentionality of the text.[20] At the same time, while modern approaches have tended to atomize the text, it must be admitted that postmodern approaches have not always had the best track record in preserving the voice of the text and can just as easily make the text a cipher for a host of agendas amenable to postmodern concerns.

The point of departure for a hermeneutic of wisdom from both of these traditions is found in Gadamer's critique of the Enlightenment's foundational "prejudice against prejudice."[21] The man in the white lab coat operates without prejudice, presuppositions, or preconceived notions shaped by either ideology or personal biography.[22] His knowledge is distinguished from mere opinion and belief by the ruthless exclusion of preconceptions and personal motivations. According to Gadamer, this comportment to reality defined the Enlightenment in all its pursuits, whether intellectual, artistic, religious, or political.[23]

What became clear in existentialist thinkers such as Heidegger is that knowledge without prejudice that is objective and indubitable is only possible for a supratemporal being who enjoys absolute knowledge (i.e., God). Human knowledge is historically conditioned. We each live in our own place and time with our own personal histories that shape our understanding. Postmodernism,

---

20. Cf. Hans-Georg Gadamer, *Truth and Method*, trans. Joel Weinsheimer and Donald G. Marshall, 2nd rev. ed. (New York: Continuum, 2004), 332, "Thus for the historian it is a basic principle that tradition is to be interpreted in a sense *different* than the texts, of themselves, call for. He will always go back behind them and the meaning they express to inquire in the reality they express *involuntarily*. . . . The historian's interpretation is concerned with something that is not expressed in the text itself and need have nothing to do with the intended meaning of the text." Italics added.

21. He famously argued that "the fundamental prejudice of the Enlightenment is the prejudice against prejudice itself." Gadamer, *Truth and Method*, 273.

22. No one has done a better job of exposing the positivist mythology of the scientific method than Michael Polanyi, *Personal Knowledge: Towards a Post-Critical Philosophy* (Chicago: University of Chicago Press, 1962).

23. These ideas were especially compelling in the context of the Enlightenment's project to forge a new basis for European societies to coexist in the aftermath of religious wars (such as the Thirty Years' War). Knowledge, worthy to become a basis for new societal structures, must be objective and indubitable—true for everyone, whether Protestant or Roman Catholic, French or German. Cf. John Locke, *A Letter Concerning Toleration* (Buffalo, NY: Prometheus, 1990).

as a child of existentialism, recognizes this reality and rightly concludes on this basis that there is no nonprejudicial knowledge, only our historically conditioned interpretations. What is curious at this point is that postmodernism did not question the definition of knowledge it inherited from modernism (i.e., knowing entails the absence of "prejudice" in the objective grasp of reality). In this respect postmodernism safeguarded its modern heritage. This is surprising, first, because of the disdain that postmodernism usually holds for anything smacking of modernist DNA. Second, it ignored the rich heritage in the Western tradition of definitions of knowledge that account for the finitude and historical embeddedness of human existence.

Believing and Reading

Alfred North Whitehead once quipped that all European philosophy is simply "a series of footnotes to Plato."[24] By this he didn't mean to belittle the work of subsequent philosophical reflections, including his own, but simply that Plato had laid out the chess board that all philosophers have played with since. In the area of epistemology the Western tradition inherited two models from Plato.[25] In *The Republic* Plato says that knowledge "is related to what is, and knows what is as it is."[26] Knowledge is the participatory apprehension of being. Plato argued that because true being is unchanging, so also true knowledge is unchanging and indubitable. From this he went on to distinguish knowledge from opinion (i.e., belief).[27] He defines opinion as something between ignorance and knowledge. Opinion is fallible; knowledge is unchanging and infallible. This definition of knowledge, and the corresponding contrast between belief and knowledge, became a staple for those after Plato and mother's milk for the Enlightenment definition of knowledge as an infallible, objective truth that is grasped indubitably.

But Plato gave a second, alternate picture of knowing that actually defines knowledge as a form of belief. In his *Theatetus* he describes knowledge as "true belief accompanied by a rational account [μετὰ λογού]."[28] Here, in contrast

24. Alfred North Whitehead, *Process and Reality: An Essay in Cosmology* (New York: Harper, 1960), 63.

25. See the excellent discussion of these two Platonic epistemologies in Dewey J. Hoitenga, *Faith and Reason from Plato to Plantinga: An Introduction to Reformed Epistemology* (Albany: State University of New York Press, 1991), 1–33.

26. Plato, *The Republic* §477b, trans. Desmond Lee (New York: Penguin, 1974), 271.

27. At §534 he describes belief (πίστις) as a form of opinion (δόξα).

28. Plato, *Theatetus* §201c–d, trans. Robin Waterfield (New York: Penguin, 1987), 115. Cf. Plato's *Meno* §§97–98.

to his statements in *The Republic*, Plato defines knowledge not in *contrast* to belief but as a *type* of belief. Knowledge is a true belief that can account for that belief reasonably, in terms of the content of the belief and a justification for it. Plato still distinguishes knowledge from opinion, but according to different criteria—the conditions of (1) *true* belief and (2) a "rational account" that accompanies that true belief. Admittedly, this account of knowledge gives rise to a host of difficult questions such as, "How do I know when a belief is a *true* belief?" and "What qualifies as a reasonable account?" But these questions are no more irksome than the questions that arise from *The Republic* account, such as, "How do I know when I have known 'what is as it is'?" In fact, they are just different formulations of the same questions about how to justify claims to know.

Both of these Platonic accounts of knowing may sound strange to our ears, but through our Enlightenment heritage the first will sound more natural than the second. Enlightenment philosophers rarely embraced Plato's metaphysics and thus made very different connections between being and knowing,[29] but at the same time, as we have seen, the dichotomy of knowledge and belief is well ingrained in our historical consciousness coming from the Enlightenment.

But in recent years there has been a shift among philosophers toward Plato's second account of knowledge. In the last few decades it has become a commonplace for analytic philosophers to define knowledge, in language reminiscent of Plato, as "justified true belief."[30] These philosophers, recognizing human finitude, have attempted to give shape to an epistemological understanding that recognizes the necessary element of belief in all knowledge. While much of the discussion among these philosophers has been concerned with what "justifies" belief,[31] what is important for our project is that we have a philosophical tradition going back to Plato that defines knowledge not in contrast to belief but as a form of belief. Therefore, we need not see belief as an *impediment* to true understanding but as a (potential) catalyst for it. This creates new possibilities for understanding the relationship between the "knower and the known"[32] and between the reader and the text.

A good example of this is the work of the chemist and philosopher Michael Polanyi. In articulating an understanding of scientific knowledge, Polanyi

29. E.g., the *cogito ergo sum* of Descartes in significant ways inverts the metaphysics of Plato by deriving being from knowledge instead of understanding knowledge as a participation in being.

30. See, for example, the classic work by Roderick M. Chisholm, *Perceiving: A Philosophical Study* (Ithaca, NY: Cornell University Press, 1957).

31. E.g., William P. Alston, *Epistemic Justification: Essays in the Theory of Knowledge* (Ithaca, NY: Cornell University Press, 1989).

32. See, for example, the monograph by that name, Marjorie G. Grene, *The Knower and the Known* (London: Faber & Faber, 1966).

rejects the traditional understanding of science as a strictly objective enterprise moving from observable data to theory. He demonstrates that scientific pursuits primarily entail the habituated skill of using tacit knowledge to judge the relevance of data in solving a question that first arose from a scientist's intuitive hypothesis. Polanyi describes scientific research as an act of "personal knowledge" in which the desires and convictions of the scientist (e.g., the beauty of order, and the desire to understand) play key roles in knowledge. He argues: "We must now recognize belief once more as the source of all knowledge. Tacit assent and intellectual passions, the sharing of an [intellectual] idiom and of cultural heritage, affiliation to a like-minded community: such are the impulses which shape our vision of the nature of things on which we rely for our mastery of things. No intelligence, however critical or original, can operate outside such a fiduciary framework."[33] Polanyi rejects the "white-lab-coat" picture of epistemology by deconstructing the white lab coat itself and providing an alternate account of scientific knowledge as dependent on intuition and personal commitments. He argues that a "fiduciary framework" is both *necessary* and *fruitful* in furthering scientific discovery.

From here it is not a huge leap to the ancient dictum of Augustine *credo ut intellegam* (I believe in order to understand).[34] For Augustine faith creates a fertile place for understanding to flourish. Augustine does not speak of belief as either a competitor with or component of knowledge.[35] Faith does not replace knowledge or fill in gaps in the field of knowledge. In his principle of *credo ut intellegam* Augustine is not chiefly concerned with giving belief a theoretical epistemological grounding, or even primacy, but rather in describing faith as a comportment to life that leads to deeper understanding. As James Peters puts it, faith for Augustine is "an act of trust enabling us slowly to gain in self-understanding and see through the veil of our limited comprehension."[36]

So in Plato, Augustine, and Polanyi we have examples, embedded in our intellectual tradition, of a fiduciary epistemology that acknowledges human finitude—where knowledge is defined as a species of belief and where belief can be a catalyst to understanding.[37] This is not an a priori argument for the

33. Polanyi, *Personal Knowledge*, 266.
34. A point that Polanyi himself acknowledges; see *Personal Knowledge*, 266.
35. Cf. Nicholas Wolterstorff, *Practices of Belief: Selected Essays*, ed. Terence Cuneo (Cambridge: Cambridge University Press, 2010), 2:334–49.
36. James R. Peters, *The Logic of the Heart: Augustine, Pascal, and the Rationality of Faith* (Grand Rapids: Baker Academic, 2009), 64.
37. There are many others who could be included in this tradition. See, for example, John Milbank, "Knowledge: The Theological Critique of Philosophy in Hamann and Jacobi," in *Radical Orthodoxy: A New Theology*, ed. John Milbank, Catherine Pickstock, and Graham Ward (New York: Routledge, 1999), where Milbank discusses, among others, J. G. Hamann

legitimacy of belief per se, where belief necessarily leads to true knowledge, but rather an argument against the a priori exclusion of belief as a possible component in knowledge.

So what does this mean for reading the Bible? If Augustine is right about belief being an instrumental agent in understanding, then it means that belief can play a positive role in reading well. Again, this is in contrast to modernism, which sees precommitments as something to be excluded, and postmodernism, which sees precommitments as wholly determinate in shaping understanding. But, as Gadamer argues, "If we want to do justice to man's finite, historical mode of being, it is necessary to fundamentally rehabilitate the concept of prejudice and acknowledge the fact that there are *legitimate* prejudices."[38] Gadamer's point is not that all prejudices are legitimate or beneficial. As we will see shortly, he recognizes that presuppositions can be deceptive and sabotage the process of understanding. At the same time, he recognizes that all our understanding as finite knowers is dependent on a web of preunderstandings and that sometimes these preunderstandings are "hermeneutically productive."[39]

Tradition and Difference

In referring to our "historical mode of being," Gadamer recognizes our lives and patterns of thought as conditioned by our environment and experiences. An important element in this is our historical connection to those that have shaped the environment of our intellectual landscape in the past (i.e., traditions). Our "prejudices" are deeply shaped by the traditions we participate in, whether we choose to consciously embrace those traditions or not. Gadamer sees tradition as an inescapable and (sometimes) fruitful catalyst to understanding. "Research in the human sciences cannot regard itself as in an absolute antithesis to the way in which we, as historical beings, relate to the past. At any rate, our usual relationship to the past is not characterized by distancing and freeing ourselves from tradition. Rather we are always situated within traditions, and this is no objectifying process—i.e., we do not conceive of what tradition says as something other, something alien. . . . To be situated within a tradition does not limit the freedom of knowledge but *makes it possible*."[40]

---

and F. H. Jacobi and their critiques of Enlightenment epistemology from the perspective of an Augustinian tradition.

38. Gadamer, *Truth and Method*, 278. Italics added.

39. Cf. Gadamer, *Truth and Method*, 284.

40. Gadamer, *Truth and Method*, 283, 354. Italics added. On the role of tradition in scientific research see Polanyi, *Personal Knowledge*, 53–54, 160–71.

Tradition is a given in shaping our hermeneutical stance toward the text. The picture of the reader as a tabula rasa, standing in isolation from any reality that may condition interpretation, fails to reckon with our nature as historically constituted persons. As Gadamer says, "Understanding is to be thought of less as a subjective act than as participating in an event of tradition."[41] All readings of texts take place within a space created by some tradition or set of traditions.[42]

Gadamer also recognizes that, when it comes to "traditionary" texts such as the Bible, the text itself is generative of tradition. The tradition is not identical with the text, but the tradition is informed by the "effects" the text has produced in previous generations.[43] A primary evidence of this is the set of questions with which we approach a text. The questions we bring to the text are an embodiment of an inherited stance to the text, a perfect example of "participating in an event of tradition."

At the same time, the true insight of Gadamer was to see that although we read from the standpoint of a tradition shaped by the text, real understanding only comes when we meet the text as a stranger, as something outside ourselves and our tradition. Recognizing that we read within a tradition does not mean that our reading *necessarily* becomes just a rehearsal of that tradition (although it can easily become that). Reading within a tradition simply means we recognize the historical conditionality of our knowledge and that traditions arise from a chain of historically conditioned communities. The text is not identical to this tradition but possesses its own voice, which has shaped the tradition but also continually questions it.[44] So true hermeneutical understanding comes as an exercise that moves *through* tradition to an

41. Gadamer, *Truth and Method*, 291. Whole sentence originally italicized.

42. Cf. Alasdair C. MacIntyre, *Whose Justice? Which Rationality?* (Notre Dame, IN: University of Notre Dame Press, 1988). MacIntyre argues, critiquing the doctrines of modern liberalism, that all rational inquiry is a "tradition-constituted" enterprise.

43. See Gadamer's discussion of *"Wirkungsgeschichte"* in *Truth and Method*, 299–305, and the work of his student Hans Robert Jauss, *Toward an Aesthetic of Reception*, trans. Timothy Bahti, Theory and History of Literature (Minneapolis: University of Minnesota Press, 1982). On the whole, biblical studies has filtered Gadamer through Jauss and understood *Wirkungsgeschichte* as a synonym for reception history, which is certainly not what it meant for Gadamer. Gadamer's primary point is that the history of effects is something every interpreter is conditioned by *in the act of interpreting.* Therefore, for him, *Wirkungsgeschichte* cannot become another object for historical research, as though the biblical interpreter could stand outside the history of effects. Cf. Mark Knight, *"Wirkungsgescichte,* Reception History, Reception Theory," *JSNT* 33, no. 2 (2010): 137–46. Also see Sandra M. Schneiders, *The Revelatory Text: Interpreting the New Testament as Sacred Scripture*, 2nd ed. (Collegeville, MN: Liturgical Press, 1999), 159–61.

44. The questioning of tradition from within the tradition is a sign of a tradition's continuing vitality. This is in contrast to a tradition that has become simply a repetition of the slogans of the past, which fails to recognize the historical conditionality of both the past and the present. It is

encounter with the text as something other.[45] Gadamer argues that the "true locus of hermeneutics" is found "in the play between the traditionary text's strangeness and familiarity to us, between being a historically intended, distanced object and belonging to a tradition."[46] He gives a description of the process of understanding that this creative tension produces:

> A person trying to understand something will not resign himself from the start to relying on his own accidental fore-meanings, ignoring as consistently and stubbornly as possible the actual meaning of the text. . . . [A] hermeneutically trained consciousness must be, from the start, sensitive to the text's alterity. But this kind of sensitivity involves neither "neutrality" with respect to content nor the extinction of one's self, but the foregrounding and appropriation of one's own fore-meanings and prejudices. The important thing is to be aware of one's own biases, so that the text can present itself in all its otherness and thus assert its own truth against one's own fore-meanings.[47]

No one reads the Bible apart from some tradition, whether those traditions come from Augustine, Luther, Spinoza, or Durkheim. Real hermeneutical insight, as described by Gadamer, comes through a dispositional openness to the voice of the text and a willingness to be guided by it. Tradition can aid us in developing our sensitivities to the text. Naturally, it will help us to see things that easily resonate with itself. At the same time, the light of tradition can easily blind us from things that do not resonate with it. In our comportment to the text, while we come with a fiduciary outlook, we come expecting to be met by something other than our own self-consciousness constituted in tradition; we come expecting an encounter that redirects and challenges us.

Miroslav Volf describes an analogous comportment in talking about the process of reconciliation beginning with "open arms" toward the other: "Open arms are a sign that I have *created space* in myself for the other to come in and that I have made a movement out of myself so as to enter the space created by the other."[48] Both reconciliation and sensitive readings require an act

---

also in contrast to the Enlightenment's naive repudiation of all tradition, itself now a tradition well rooted in our consciousness.

45. Cf. Schneiders, "Gospels and Reader," 110, "The text is not simply an object. The process of reading involves a co-construction of the text by the reader. But that construction is a response to an 'other' which places demands on the reader. In other words, the text is not a subject in the same sense that the reader is. The reader must come to terms with the reality of the text which is neither absolutely determined nor totally indeterminate."

46. Gadamer, *Truth and Method*, 295.

47. Gadamer, *Truth and Method*, 271–72.

48. Miroslav Volf, *Exclusion and Embrace: A Theological Exploration of Identity, Otherness, and Reconciliation* (Nashville: Abingdon, 1996), 141.

of making space for the other in the self, whether we define the "self" as the individual or the reading community. We do not meet the text as a complete self-sufficient whole with an impermeable boundary, but with a recognition and expectation that our identity will be reshaped in response to our encounter with the text. Fundamentally, this means that a wisdom comportment to the text recognizes it cannot predetermine the process of reorientation; one can create a space, but one cannot predetermine its shape.[49]

In this, again, we have to recognize the text as a material agency. In contrast to postmodern approaches, which still tend to embody the Enlightenment ideal of the "sovereign subject," a wisdom comportment recognizes the authority of the text, as wisdom, to remold the reader in the dialectic exercise of reading. This is not a collapsing of the reader into the text, but the reader's expectation of a life-giving voice from the text in what Gadamer calls "the ability to open ourselves to the superior claims the text makes."[50] As Richard Burnett explains, this comportment was central to Barth's hermeneutical approach:

> For Barth understanding the Bible or any other text has to do with bringing the right presuppositions to the task of interpretation, that is, presuppositions appropriate to the text's subject matter. It is dependent on a "living context

49. Paul J. Griffiths connects this expectation to a comportment toward all of life that he labels "living datively":
> Human existence, yours and mine and all of ours, is first lived datively, as people addressed, called, and gifted; and only secondarily nominatively, as subjects looking out over a world displayed for our delectation and consumption. . . . To live nominatively is to live as a grammatical and psychological subject, an "I" looking out at and manipulating the world. In this mode, the world is the field of your gaze: it assumes the status of something looked at, something spread passively before you for your delectation and manipulation. You, the looker, the gazing subject, as the active one, the one who initiates, undertakes, performs, and controls. By contrast, to live datively is to live confronted and addressed by a world that questions, forms, and challenges you, the one addressed. It is to live in a world prior to and independent of yourself, a given world, presented unasked, whose overwhelming presence presses you into a responsive mold whether you like it or not. (*Intellectual Appetite: A Theological Grammar* [Washington, DC: Catholic University of America Press, 2009], 31–32)

He continues,
> Agency, on this model, belongs as much to the given world as to the perceiving subject responding to it. And this is a more adequate and accurate way of describing the relation between world and person than an exclusive emphasis on the nominative life. You are constantly confronted and addressed by a world not of your making and largely beyond your comprehension and control. The sensory arrays that appear before you, the fabric of time that enmeshes you, the manifold of language in which you have your *habitus*, the social order in which your roles are given to you, the sea of faces of human others, constantly addressing you, calling you into being—all these make of you an indirect object and give you a dative, which is to say a called and donated life. (32)

50. Gadamer, *Truth and Method*, 310.

which . . . is *given* in the subject matter and in which one must *be*." Far from
any non-participatory distancing of oneself, interpretation requires the most
intense form of participation and personal engagement. . . . As Barth later said,
"Neutrality is really a decision of unbelief." This is what the dominant science
of biblical exegesis had failed in his view to understand.[51]

This comportment to the givenness of the text through sympathetic prejudices, what Richard Hays describes elsewhere as a "hermeneutic of trust,"[52]
is essential in recognizing the Bible as Scripture, as the canonical text that
has governed the life of the church for centuries. When we recognize the Bible
as the Word of God, then we come with an expectation of not simply reading a "traditionary" text but a text that God uses to realize the fruits of his
goodness in his people. This conviction was embodied in the Reformation
slogan "Christ rules His church through the teaching and preaching of the
Word."[53] We meet the Bible as something other because of its historically
conditioned nature but also because it is the saving self-revelation of God.
So in recognizing the agency of the text we also recognize the superintending
creative agency of God.

To read the Bible as Scripture, though, is not simply an approach that we
chose to superimpose on a "neutral" text, as a self-generated element we add
to it. Again that is to fall prey to the myth of the "sovereign subject" who
from the self determines the significance of the text.[54] Historically, these texts

51. Richard E. Burnett, *Karl Barth's Theological Exegesis: The Hermeneutical Principles
of the Römerbrief Period* (Grand Rapids: Eerdmans, 2004), 115–16. In his article "Atheistische
Methoden in der Theologie," *BFCT* 9 (1905): 229–50, Schlatter makes the same point about the
inherent unbelief embedded in the methodological "neutrality" of biblical studies. See Werner
Neuer, *Adolf Schlatter: A Biography of Germany's Premier Biblical Theologian*, trans. Robert
Yarbrough (Grand Rapids: Baker Books, 1996), 211–25. Cf. Stephen F. Dintaman, *Creative Grace:
Faith and History in the Theology of Adolf Schlatter*, American University Studies Series VII:
Theology and Religion 152 (New York: Peter Lang, 1993), 75–104.

52. Cf. Richard B. Hays, "A Hermeneutic of Trust," in *The Conversion of the Imagination:
Paul as Interpreter of Israel's Scripture* (Grand Rapids: Eerdmans, 2005), 190–201.

53. In the Reformation era the chief implication was that it was not the pope who ruled
the church but Jesus himself, through the agency of the Spirit in and through the preaching
of his Word.

54. Cf. Heidegger, *Problems*, 64, "Because the usual separation between a subject with its
imminent sphere and an object with its transcendent sphere—because, in general, the distinction between an inner and an outer is constructive and continually gives occasion for further
constructions, we shall in the future no longer speak of a subject, of a subjective sphere, but
shall understand the being to whom intentional comportments belong as *Dasein*, and indeed in
such a way that it is precisely with the aid of *intentional comportment*, properly understood,
that we attempt to characterize suitably the being Dasein." Here "Dasein" is understood as
the human person immersed in the world. As George Steiner puts it, "Dasein is 'to be there'
(*da-sein*), and 'there' is the world: the concrete, literal, actual, daily world. To be human is to

became canon and Scripture because the church recognized their *inherent* claims to authority.[55] To read these texts well means attending to their own claims to speak with a voice that calls forth and produces faith.[56] A fiduciary transformational comportment to the text is rooted in recognizing and accepting the inherent "illocutionary force"[57] of the biblical text and seeking to be shaped by this force.[58]

Reading and Seeking Wisdom

So a hermeneutic of wisdom begins with a certain stance toward the text that defines the relationship of the reader and the text in terms of a fiduciary engagement. But what sort of questions will a hermeneutic of wisdom ask of the text? We have seen how different approaches, embodying different epistemological outlooks, have asked different questions of the text. In a hermeneutic of wisdom we are seeking a certain kind of knowledge—one that fosters wisdom and leads us in a path of life. Wisdom is a practical knowledge lived out in concrete agency shaped by desire. Because wisdom seeks to shape human life, not just inform the intellect, the whole person is engaged in the hermeneutical process. When we enter the circle of the text looking for

---

be immersed, implanted, rooted in the earth, in the quotidian matter-of-factness of the world." George Steiner, *Martin Heidegger* (Chicago: University of Chicago Press, 1978), 83.

55. Cf. Bruce Manning Metzger, *The Canon of the New Testament: Its Origin, Development, and Significance* (Oxford: Clarendon, 1987), 282–88. Also see Herman N. Ridderbos, *Redemptive History and the New Testament Scriptures*, trans. H. De Jongste, Biblical and Theological Studies (Phillipsburg, NJ: P&R, 1988), 49–76.

56. Cf. Schlatter, "Theology of New Testament and Dogmatics," 122, "The word with which the New Testament confronts us intends to be believed, and so rules out once and for all any sort of neutral treatment. As soon as the historian sets aside or brackets the question of faith, he is making his concern with the New Testament and his presentation of it into a radical and total polemic against it."

57. Illocutionary force refers to the intentionality encoded in the text as a performative communicative act. Vanhoozer deftly defines illocutionary force: "Words do not simply label; sentences do not merely state. Rather, in using language we do any number of things: question, command, warn, request, curse, bless and so forth. A speech act has two aspects: propositional content and illocutionary force, the 'matter' and 'energy' of communicative action. The key notion is that of illocution, which has to do not simply with locuting or uttering words but with what we do in uttering words." Kevin J. Vanhoozer, *First Theology: God, Scripture & Hermeneutics* (Downers Grove, IL: InterVarsity, 2002), 118.

58. Cf. Nicholas Wolterstorff, *Divine Discourse: Philosophical Reflections on the Claim That God Speaks* (Cambridge: Cambridge University Press, 1995), 37–57. See J. Todd Billings, *The Word of God for the People of God: An Entryway to the Theological Interpretation of Scripture* (Grand Rapids: Eerdmans, 2010), 8, "The word of God in Scripture is something that encounters us again and again; it surprises, confuses, and enlightens us because through Scripture we encounter the triune God himself."

wisdom we bring our whole person: beliefs, convictions, devotions, hopes, and fears. Reading entails a knowledge of self ordered to the reality of God, the creation, and other people, because the fulfillment of our most significant human desires is inextricably linked to life in community.

The questions of wisdom are the questions of human flourishing: What should I pursue to experience fulfillment, and how should I pursue it? What is worth giving my life to, and what will I get in return? What realities determine what I should value in life? In contrast to modern philosophy, which focused its energies on the questions of knowledge (epistemology), ancient philosophy concerned itself chiefly with these basic questions of life and human flourishing. Aristotle, for example, in attempting to understand what human life ought to be directed at, reasoned that the most fundamental human desire is for εὐδαιμονία (happiness/contentment/joy). We seek after other things (e.g., wealth, family, and vocation) in order to be happy, but we don't seek happiness in order to get something else. From this Aristotle concluded that happiness must be the *chief* good that we desire. Augustine followed Aristotle in saying that the desire for happiness is a universal characteristic for human beings and an element in being constituted as God's image bearers.[59] Both Aristotle and Augustine recognized that there are innumerable (potential) paths to happiness just as there are innumerable obstacles to it. This is why both of them took discernment/wisdom (φρόνησις) to be the central virtue in the pursuit of contentment, because wisdom is needed to discern the right path in a journey through innumerable incommensurable goods.

Again, what might this mean for reading the Bible? We have talked already about how a hermeneutic of wisdom comes to the text with a comportment that expects an encounter that will form our consciousness and agency. We can add to that an expectation that the text will work in some way to recalibrate my understanding and loves, how I look at myself, God, and the world, and what I seek after as most valuable in the pursuit of happiness, as defined by some retuned criteria. The Bible, as a wisdom book, is written to communicate a vision of the world that not only names and values particulars but that contextualizes concrete moral actions and sustains moral integrity. In reading we expect to find a vision that reorients our lives, in how we see the world and how we live in it, in what we believe and what we love. To read for wisdom is to be attentive to how the Bible, as a voice from outside our own idolatrous construals of reality, challenges and retunes our understanding and desires,

---

59. See Augustine, *De Trinitate*, book 13. Cf. Luigi Gioia, *The Theological Epistemology of Augustine's De Trinitate*, Oxford Theological Monographs (Oxford: Oxford University Press, 2008), 41–43.

and to consciously open ourselves to that process.[60] The goal of that process is a deeper understanding that is further developed in and through concrete moral actions. Reading well and doing good are mutually sustaining actions in spiritual formation.

So hermeneutical understanding in the context of wisdom entails a holistic comportment, which brings the whole person, in all their historical conditionality, with all their conceptions, values, and affections, into the space created by the text. Wisdom eschews any claim to a self-sustaining field of reference but instead assumes a fiduciary transformational stance, expecting a reorientation of those same conceptions, values, and affections in a dialectic engagement with the text. This means that the whole person, in all their faculties, is involved in this dialectic movement toward understanding. The emotions, for example, as expressions of desire, play a hermeneutically productive role in their receptivity to the rhetorical dynamics of the text.[61] Likewise, they also enter into the process of reorientation by coming into direct contact with the world of the text and the desires that it endorses. Of course, desires, like other elements of preunderstanding, can hijack hermeneutical inquiry, but the answer to this problem is not to deny their necessary role in the hermeneutical process.[62] This would entail a flight from reality in failing to recognize all the elements that constitute our historical conditionality in approaching the text, because our desires are what bring us to the text in the first place. We come to the text in need of wisdom. We come seeking life.

A Test Case: Reading John 3

So what does all this look like in practice? It might be helpful at this point to turn to an example and see how different hermeneutical stances produce very different readings. We will take John 3 as a test case, giving in turn a modern

60. This assumes an Augustinian anthropology in which the process of reform is continually necessary.

61. I take emotions here, as distinct from feelings or moods, to be an unmediated human faculty operating in different modes (e.g., grief, joy, anger) to ascribe value to objects of possible devotion. Cf. Martha C. Nussbaum, *Upheavals of Thought: The Intelligence of Emotions* (Cambridge: Cambridge University Press, 2001), 19–88, where she speaks of emotions as "judgments of value." This means that emotions are primarily a moral faculty, instrumental in moral deliberation and the apprehension of the comparative value of competing goods. Therefore, the emotions are central to any project of moral and spiritual formation.

62. Cf. Jean Grondin, *Introduction to Philosophical Hermeneutics*, trans. Joel Weinsheimer, Yale Studies in Hermeneutics (New Haven: Yale University Press, 1994), 117, "The point is not to exclude the anticipations of meaning implicit in our questions but to foreground them so that the texts that we are trying to understand can answer them all the more clearly."

reading of the text, followed by a postmodern reading, and then a wisdom reading. In this way we will see how these different reading modalities ask different questions and get different answers from the text, and we will also get something of the flavor of these three hermeneutical approaches.

A Modern Reading

So what would a modern reading of John 3 look like? A modern comportment, again, seeks to sift texts for information that will aid in answering a set of questions regarding the historical origins of Christianity. Methodologically, this means that the text is treated as a repository of encrypted historical-theological data that must be deciphered and synthesized. The basic questions brought to the text focus on ideas and their genealogical relationships, and how the historical development of tradition became solidified in the form of the text.

So in John 3, where there are three distinct sections in the discourse (1–21, 22–30, and 31–36),[63] there is a long history of discussions about different traditions that stand behind the text and why these sections were stitched together in their present form. So, for example, Rudolf Bultmann argues that verses 31–36 originally came directly after verse 21 and that 22–30, which pertain to John the Baptist, were added later.[64] Similarly, Rudolf Schnackenburg argues that 31–36 belong to the kerygma of the evangelist and should follow the proper end of the Nicodemus dialogue in verse 12.[65]

The awkward intrusion of verses 22–30 has led most to consider this scene about John the Baptist as an independent piece of tradition introduced at this point to facilitate certain agendas of the evangelist.[66] Verse 22 has caused

---

63. See John Ashton, *Understanding the Fourth Gospel*, 2nd ed. (Oxford: Oxford University Press, 2007), 277–80. One could also take 16–21 as a separate discourse unit, since it is unclear how it relates to the previous verses. It is also common to include the end of chap. 2 (2:23–25) in this pericope (e.g., George R. Beasley-Murray, *John*, 2nd ed., WBC 36 [Nashville: Thomas Nelson, 1999], 45–46). It clearly functions as a transitional text between 2:13–22 and 3:1–15 and sets up the context from the Nicodemus discourse, but the transition of the introduction of a new character (Nicodemus) in 3:1 is enough to signal the opening of a new discourse unit. Cf. Andreas J. Köstenberger, *John*, BECNT (Grand Rapids: Baker Academic, 2004), 115.

64. Rudolf Bultmann, *The Gospel of John: A Commentary*, trans. George R. Beasley-Murray (Philadelphia: Westminster, 1971), 131–32. See the rebuttal of the coherence of this reconstruction in C. H. Dodd, *The Interpretation of the Fourth Gospel* (Cambridge: Cambridge University Press, 1953), 309.

65. Rudolf Schnackenburg, *The Gospel according to St. John*, trans. Cecily Hastings and Kevin Smyth (New York: Seabury, 1968–82), 1:380.

66. Brown proposes that these verses are displaced from their original context in 1:19–34. See Raymond E. Brown, *The Gospel according to John: Introduction, Translation, and Notes*, AB 29 (Garden City, NY: Doubleday, 1966–70), 1:154.

particular consternation because it portrays Jesus as having a ministry of baptism concurrent with John in Judea, which does not agree with the Synoptic portrayal of Jesus's ministry (sans baptism) beginning in Galilee *after* John's arrest (cf. Mark 1:14). The narrator's aside in 3:24 that these things happened *before* John's arrest likely underlines the Fourth Evangelist's awareness of this tension in the traditions. Naturally, many have brought into question the historical reliability of the Johannine witness at this point.

This skepticism is often paired with questions about the purpose of this passage in the context of its composition. Bultmann argues, "It ought not to be difficult to see that this scene . . . is a literary composition, reflecting the rivalry between the sects of the Baptist and Jesus, nor to see that the Baptist . . . is a figure from the Christian interpretation of history."[67] From this Bultmann concludes that this passage is a *"free composition* of the Evangelist"[68] with little, if any, historical tradition behind it. While there are some who would disagree with this assessment and argue for a more substantial element of historical tradition here,[69] what is important for our discussion is not who has made the best historical judgment (although this remains an important question). What we see here is different scholars giving different answers to the *same questions*. So while there are strong differences in answers that are given to questions such as these in John 3, all the exegetes share the questions and the methods of answering them, which are embodiments of a modern epistemological outlook. It does not then follow that these questions are bad or the information they produce is of little value. We are only trying to recognize that these are questions of a certain type that produce information of a certain kind.

Another chief concern of a modernist hermeneutic is tracing the genealogical origins of ideas. So, much talk is given to questions of the "new birth" ("born again" or "born from above"),[70] its place in early Christian thought, and the formative influences of various Hellenistic and Jewish ideas of rebirth or

---

67. Bultmann, *John*, 167.

68. Bultmann, *John*, 167. Italics original.

69. E.g., Beasley-Murray, *John*, 54, argues, "While at one time a number of scholars considered this a reflection back into the ministry of later rivalry between the Church and the followers of John, most now see this as a remnant of primitive tradition unknown to the synoptists." Cf. C. H. Dodd, *Historical Tradition in the Fourth Gospel* (Cambridge: Cambridge University Press, 1963), 279–87.

70. Various solutions have been given to the question of whether ἄνωθεν should be read as "again" (because Nicodemus takes it this way) or "from above" (because Jesus takes it this way). Most see the double meaning of the word in play in the typically Johannine misunderstanding on the part of Nicodemus, but there is still variation on which sense is "primary" and what historical tradition might stand behind it, especially since the wordplay is only operative in Greek. See Schnackenburg, *John*, 1:367–68.

metamorphosis.[71] Bultmann, for example, sees John transposing gnostic notions of rebirth into Christian language.[72] By contrast, George Beasley-Murray sees an idea derived from Jewish eschatology.[73] Along with the theme of new birth is a well-rehearsed controversy on what new birth "of water and the Spirit" (v. 5) might mean. John has already introduced the concept of divine agency in regeneration in the prologue (1:13), so tying new birth to the Spirit is not surprising. The controversy focuses on the significance of the water. Is this a reference to baptism, and if so, what kind of baptism? Or is "water and the Spirit" a hendiadys, where water adds a symbolic adornment to a reference to the Spirit? Good arguments have been adduced for both approaches;[74] Schnackenburg (a Roman Catholic) sees a clear reference to Christian baptism,[75] while Andreas Köstenberger (an evangelical Protestant) sees none.[76]

Again, the differences, though significant, are outweighed by the consensus on the methods of inquiry. What is of concern here is the explication of ideas present in the text and their genealogical connections to traditions both inside and outside the early church. The force that this text is meant to have on the faithful reader (or reading community) is not within the horizon of discovery. It is not a question on the table for modernist historical-theological inquiry. Such questions are out of the bounds of justifiable scholarly investigation, regardless of one's theological predilections, because they violate the "lab-coat" comportment to the text that is encoded in modern hermeneutical practices.

A Postmodern Reading

John's Gospel is commonly referred to as a "two-level drama."[77] On the first level the narrative is understood with primary reference to Jesus and the characters he has interactions with, and the drama of Jesus's confrontation with

71. For an excellent précis, see Craig S. Keener, *The Gospel of John: A Commentary* (Peabody, MA: Hendrickson, 2003), 1:539–44.

72. Bultmann, *John*, 135–36n4.

73. Beasley-Murray, *John*, 47–48.

74. Keener, *John*, 1:546–52, gives an excellent overview of the issue.

75. Schnackenburg, *John*, 1:369–71. See the (unsurprisingly) simpatico Brown, *John*, 1:141–44.

76. Köstenberger, *John*, 123–24. Cf. the good discussion in D. A. Carson, *The Gospel according to John*, PNTC (Grand Rapids: Eerdmans, 1991), 191–96. Also see Herman N. Ridderbos, *The Gospel according to John: A Theological Commentary*, trans. John Vriend (Grand Rapids: Eerdmans, 1997), 127–28, for a (Reformed) Protestant with real sympathies for a sacramental reading.

77. The phrase is most often associated with the groundbreaking work of J. Louis Martyn, *History and Theology in the Fourth Gospel*, 3rd ed., NTL (Louisville: Westminster John Knox, 2003).

Israel and his glorification in crucifixion. On the second level the narrative is understood with primary reference to the "Johannine community" and/or the Christian church at the time of the Gospel's composition. At this level Jesus's confrontation with "the Jews" becomes a narrative that projects a place for the church as a distinct persecuted community separate from Israel. This formulation of John operating at two levels has been an important presupposition for postmodern interpretation of this Gospel, which has tended to focus its energies on the second level of meaning. Postmodern readings tend to focus on how texts function to further the sociopolitical agendas of their authors/authorial communities. Texts serve to legitimate certain practices that define one community while delegitimizing the worldview and practices of competing communities.

In this context Jesus and Nicodemus emerge as actors playing out a drama scripted by the nascent Christian church to solidify its status in the face of conflicts with local synagogues and to embolden those who still reside in the indeterminate crossover territory between these two groups. The scene is transposed from interpersonal dialogue to intercommunal boundary definition. So when Jesus confounds Nicodemus when he speaks of being "born again/from above," according to Richard Rohrbaugh, this is not a simple example of Johannine misunderstanding or irony[78] but actually insider language meant to include Johannine Christians and exclude everyone else, whether they come from the synagogue or a rival Christian faction.[79] Social-scientific critics refer to this as a use of insider "antilanguage." The function of insider antilanguage is to define the boundaries between groups, clarifying who is in and who is out. Nicodemus, then, as an outsider, *should be* baffled by Jesus's mode of expression. He represents those who are deliberately alienated by the use of in-group language. At the same time, this language serves to unify those "in the know," because the antilanguage centers on key terminology of their shared worldview and privileges them as insiders who know the truth that those outside cannot understand.[80]

78. "While misunderstanding is in fact involved . . . to treat Johannine language as fundamentally ironic is . . . to obscure what is actually happening in the Nicodemus episode." Richard L. Rohrbaugh, *The New Testament in Cross-Cultural Perspective*, Matrix: The Bible in Mediterranean Context (Eugene, OR: Cascade, 2007), 176.

79. See Rohrbaugh, *Cross-Cultural Perspective*, 179, "The creativity and originality of the Gospel's language maintained boundaries not only between the Johannine anti-society and the dominant Judean world, but also between John's group and competing Christian groups."

80. Cf. Rohrbaugh, *Cross-Cultural Perspective*, 179, "Language is . . . what members of the Johannine group used to signal an identity and thereby gain solidarity and reassurance from each other." In addition, "This kind of antilanguage draws boundaries between an antisociety and the larger society from which it is alienated. So also does contrastive language about some people

The Nicodemus episode, following on from the cleansing of the temple in the previous chapter, gives a personal entry point into what will become Jesus's highly adversarial dealings with "the Jews," leading to his crucifixion. This polemic has been the focus of considerable scrutiny for its strong anti-Jewish outlook.[81] Again, if the Gospel is understood as chiefly speaking of the Johannine church's struggle with Judaism, experienced through the face of the local synagogues, then Jesus's polemic is simply a cipher for the anti-Jewish voice of the church, which demonizes Jews in order to draw stark boundary lines between the church and Judaism.[82] Understood sociologically, this is a characteristic move for a persecuted minority group that needs to justify and preserve its existence over against a persecuting majority.

In addition to its polemics with Judaism, John's Gospel also betrays conflicts with rival Christian communities, especially those with allegiances to John the Baptist.[83] (It may be that there is also some overlap of Christians who still are members of the local synagogue and also hold John the Baptist in reverence.) So it is interesting that John 3 also includes a passage focused on John the Baptist, which includes a polemic discussion about baptism (a social boundary ritual) and John confessing his inferiority to Jesus. Again, read at the second level of meaning, this passage validates the baptismal ministry of Jesus (i.e., the church[84]) vis-à-vis the baptismal ministry of John. It then goes on with John the Baptist himself responding to the concerns of his followers that Jesus is gaining a significant following at his expense. John allays their fears by reminding them that he is not the bridegroom but his attendant. If aimed at those who hold allegiance to John the Baptist alongside or over Jesus, it would be hard to construct a more powerful deconstruction of that allegiance than the confession of John that *"he must increase, but I must decrease"* (3:30).

So a postmodern stance to the text is sensitive to how the agendas of the Johannine community are bolstered and furthered by the narrative of John 3.

---

being exposed to the light in order to reveal their evil deeds while others love light, obviously because they do the truth. Boundary language drawn in such stark contrast (light-dark, good-evil) suggests sharp division and strong social conflict" (Bruce J. Malina and Richard L. Rohrbaugh, *Social-Science Commentary on the Gospel of John* [Minneapolis: Fortress, 1998], 86).

81. For an overview see James D. G. Dunn, "The Embarrassment of History: Reflections on the Problem of 'Anti-Judaism' in the Fourth Gospel," in *Anti-Judaism and the Fourth Gospel*, ed. R. Bieringer, D. Pollefeyt, and F. Vandecasteele-Vanneuville (Louisville: Westminster John Knox, 2001), 41–60.

82. But see Dunn, "Embarrassment of History." Dunn gives more weight to the first level of reference to the life of Jesus and consequently sees this as an expression of intra-Jewish conflict: criticism from within, not without.

83. See Raymond E. Brown, *An Introduction to the Gospel of John*, ABRL (New York: Doubleday, 2003), 153–57.

84. See 4:2, where the evangelist clarifies that it was the disciples and not Jesus who baptized.

The Nicodemus discourse betrays the careful use of in-group antilanguage that fosters the internal cohesiveness of the group but also legitimates its rejection by the local synagogue. The passage also serves to strengthen the place of the community over rival Christian communities with "deficient" christological understandings, especially adherents of John the Baptist.

These readings presuppose that the primary force that produced John's Gospel was communal self-preservation (i.e., that the text was born out of and exemplifies social conflict). This conflict then becomes the hermeneutical key to understanding the dynamics of the text. A postmodern reading, then, prizes attentiveness to the ideological moves of the text in projecting worlds that legitimate the life of the community over against competing institutions. Again, we have a methodology that asks certain questions of the text and reveals dynamics in the text in response to those questions. Here a postmodern approach exposes and objectifies the ideological moves of the text that derive their intelligibility from the social conflicts that shaped the Johannine community. In trying to understand those social dynamics, this methodology is useful. But in moving toward a wisdom reading of the text, it will play a limited role. Because it places the reader over the text and uses the text as a means to gain access to the social world behind it, this method still embodies a comportment of the sovereign subject and does not move us toward a fiduciary engagement with the text.

A Wisdom Reading

A wisdom reading begins by taking seriously John's own confession of his purpose as fostering faith in Jesus as the Christ (20:31). While there may be, and likely are, many subsidiary agendas encoded in this Gospel, its chief goal is to encourage growth in an active trusting comportment toward the person of Jesus. How John does this is complex, and a wisdom reading will look for narrative strategies employed by the author to promote faith in Jesus, but it will not simply be a process of communicating christological doctrines. Since faith is a complex phenomenon that touches the whole person and their deepest devotions, the ways faith is defined and promoted in John will be equally complex.[85]

85. Cf. Richard Bauckham, *Gospel of Glory: Major Themes in Johannine Theology* (Grand Rapids: Baker Academic, 2015), 16–17, "What the stories do is to draw the hearer or reader into imaginative empathy with each character encountering Jesus in his or her particular circumstances. The stories surely do draw hearers or readers into their own encounter with Jesus, but the idea that the hearer or reader must run through a range of characters and responses until finding one that fits for him or her is much too schematic and artificial. The characters are not

From the beginning John is a narrative defined by conflict (1:5). It is only in the midst of this conflict, where many reject Jesus and even seek to kill him, that some believe in him and have life in believing. This means that faith is not an automatic response to Jesus and that for those who do believe it is a dangerous commitment. So John is promoting a sober trust in Jesus. The idea that faith needs to be fostered assumes (1) a process of maturing faith, and (2) a process that is not automatic because there are many impediments to mature faith. So it is common in John's Gospel to meet characters who are examples of faith but all at different stages of faith or mixtures of faith and unbelief.[86] John, like the other Gospel writers, recognizes that faith is always partial and found in varying degrees, but is also characterized by teleological movement.

All of this is in play when we come to read John 3. Nicodemus comes to Jesus as a highly ambiguous character. The narrator deliberately gives us many ambiguous clues as to his motivations for coming to see Jesus.[87] Why does he come alone, and at night? He comes as a spokesman for some other group ("*we* know that you are a teacher come from God"). But who is this group, and why was *he* chosen to come? He honors Jesus by calling him a "Rabbi" who has "come from God." But is he just buttering Jesus up, or is this an expression of some kind of faith? Any sensitive reader of John's Gospel up to this point will recognize that calling Jesus a "teacher who comes from God" is close to the truth but also a deficient understanding. Jesus has "come from God," but Nicodemus probably simply means to say that Jesus is somehow approved by God, not that he shares in the Father's identity.[88] Nicodemus seems to show some genuine interest in Jesus, but he also understands him within categories that are comfortable to him and that would do little to shake up Nicodemus's understanding of himself, Israel, and God.

John provides us an interpretive key for this passage in his conclusion in 3:31–36,[89] often sidelined by reconstructions of the text's possible prehistory.

---

models of faith so much as illustrations of the wide variety of ways in which different people in different circumstances may encounter Jesus." This process serves to "encourage hearers or readers to expect Jesus to meet them and direct them in the particularity of their individual lives and circumstances."

86. See Colleen M. Conway, "Speaking through Ambiguity: Minor Characters in the Fourth Gospel," *BibInt* 10 (2002): 324–41.

87. See Raimo Hakola, "The Burden of Ambiguity: Nicodemus and the Social Identity of the Johannine Christians," *NTS* 55 (2009): 438–55.

88. On Jesus's sharing in the divine identity see Richard Bauckham, *Jesus and the God of Israel: God Crucified and Other Studies on the New Testament's Christology of Divine Identity* (Grand Rapids: Eerdmans, 2009), 1–59.

89. Cf. Dodd, *Interpretation*, 311, "It seems best therefore to regard iii. 31–6 as an explanatory appendix to the dialogue with Nicodemus and the discourse which grows out of it."

John 3:31, "He who comes from above is above all," describes who Jesus is revealed to be in this passage. He is the one sent by the Father to be his agent of judgment and salvation. He speaks as the voice of the Father, sharing in his identity and speaking with his authority (3:32–35).[90] He is revealed as a ruler and as a bringer of life, procured through self-sacrifice and offered through faith (3:14–16). Commentators who understand Jesus here as simply a "revealer of a mystery" or as "embodied Wisdom" fail to reckon with the absolute exaltation that Jesus assumes for himself in this passage.

"Truly, truly, I say to you, unless one is born again he cannot see the kingdom of God." Jesus's response to Nicodemus in 3:3 is a forceful rebuff that not only breaks with the standards of polite conversation but adopts the language of prophetic judgment.[91] Many commentators have tried to mollify the intensity of Jesus's response by speaking of the "implied question" of Nicodemus that Jesus "responds" to.[92] But Jesus refuses to be construed in any way that will fit into Nicodemus's understanding. Instead, he brings a message that threatens Nicodemus's whole understanding of God and Israel.[93] Jesus gives the conditions for participation in God's kingdom, and they do not include the categories of covenantal obedience that would have been central to Nicodemus's assumptions. Instead, participation in the kingdom is predicated on the free regenerating work of God, without regard to either ethnic heritage or works of righteousness. This is the meaning of Jesus's play on the double meaning of πνεῦμα, which can mean "spirit" or "wind," in verse 8; just as the wind "blows where it wishes," so also the Spirit, as the agent of new birth, operates in ways determined solely by divine prerogatives. This echoes the pronouncement in the prologue that the children of God are born "not of blood nor of the will of the flesh nor of the will of man, but of God" (1:13). As Schnackenburg says, "Prior to all human effort to attain the

90. Cf. Dunn, "Embarrassment of History," 48, "Probably the most consistent feature of John's Gospel is the emphasis on Jesus as the bearer of divine revelation. What he says has the stamp of divine authority, because as Son of God, sent by the Father, he speaks what he has seen and heard from the Father; as the Son of Man, he speaks with the authority of one who has descended from heaven; as one who is from above, his message outweighs in kind and quality anything said by one who is from below."

91. Cf. Hakola, "Ambiguity," 449–50. Hakola characterizes Jesus's response as "cruel" and "harsh."

92. E.g., Köstenberger, *John*, 121, "Nicodemus tacitly inquires as to what new doctrine Jesus is propagating." Cf. Bultmann, *John*, 134.

93. Cf. Ridderbos, *John*, 126, "Although in vs. 5 Jesus will explain his meaning further, his primary intent is obviously not to refute or correct Nicodemus's theological certainties by means of scribal terms or arguments, but to impress him at a much deeper level, where his entire existence before God is at stake."

kingdom of God, God himself must create the basis of a new being in man, which will also make a new way of life possible."[94]

Wisdom begins not in a self-sufficient act of the will but in reception of the eschatological new birth. Jesus's words point to the necessity of that new birth (because one cannot see or enter the kingdom apart from it) and indicate that the impetus for the new birth comes completely from the creative, fatherly act of God. Any synergistic formula is completely excluded. There can be no thought of a human catalyst in the regenerative act of God. This is the starting point of wisdom that seeks to shape life in Christian discipleship. It cannot begin with what I bring to God, but in what God has made of me and called me to be. It begins with humility and thanksgiving, and it moves into action forged in a heart of gratitude. The first act is faith in the one God has sent as his instrument of salvation, the one who is above all and reveals the will of God. This faith directed toward the Son as revealer, savior, king, and judge becomes the means of participating in eternal life[95] (John's term corresponding to the Synoptic "kingdom of God/heaven").[96]

One's comportment toward the Son is the determining factor in how one stands before God. "Whoever believes in him is not condemned, but whoever does not believe is condemned already, because he has not believed in the name of the only Son of God" (3:18). The coming of the Son brings salvation and condemnation, because in this story of conflict there are some who reject the Son. This rejection is an act that comes from and reveals the desires and character of the unbelieving. "And this is the judgment: the light has come into the world, and people loved the darkness rather than the light because their works were evil. For everyone who does wicked things hates the light and does not come to the light, lest his works should be exposed" (3:19–20). Guilt and shame for wicked deeds dominate the consciousness of those who fear the light and cling to the darkness. Because of this, they reject the Son, who reveals their deeds. By contrast, "whoever does what is true comes to the light" (3:21). Those of a good character, shaped by gratitude and faith instead of shame and guilt (although both are guilty of sin) do what is right through faith in the Son and a clean conscience.[97] This good character is not a self-

94. Schnackenburg, *John*, 1:368. Cf. Bultmann, *John*, 142.

95. "Eternal" is very likely here to be taken as another example of John's onto-ethical mode of expression. So it has less to do with duration in time than it does participation in what is pure, good, eternal, light, life, etc. In other words, this adjective has a chiefly moral content, pointing to a life that communicates the moral freedom and righteousness of the eschatological rule of God.

96. See Bultmann, *John*, 152n2.

97. Cf. Keener, *John*, 1:574, "In John, people demonstrate their character, either as part of the world or as those born anew from above, by their 'works.'"

reforming morality but a characteristic of the new birth, as John concludes, "so that it may be clearly seen that his works have been carried out in God" (3:21).[98] God's children recognize the Son for who he is and come under his rule in faith, trusting him for life and obeying his commands. So it is natural in 3:36 for *faith* in the Son to be equated to *obedience* to the Son. "Whoever *believes* in the Son has eternal life; whoever does not *obey* the Son shall not see life, but the wrath of God remains on him."

Nicodemus's response will become paradigmatic for Israel's rejection of Jesus, described by John as a worldly rejection of God himself (see John 19:15). John the Baptist, however, is a contrasting exemplar of faith, which is why this scene with John the Baptist is placed here in juxtaposition with the Nicodemus dialogue.[99] In John 3:26 John's followers bring a reasonable concern that too many people are leaving him to follow Jesus instead. John, embodying the virtue of gratitude, recognizes that his calling, ministry, and notoriety are all gifts, not things to be hoarded. "A person cannot receive even one thing unless it is given him from heaven" (3:27). Again wisdom begins with gratitude that embraces the gift of God as sufficient and moves in faithful action. John recognizes Jesus as the messianic bridegroom of Israel, the one who will bring about the consummation of God's kingdom. Recognizing Jesus's identity and orienting himself to it gives John the space to rejoice as the "best man" to the bridegroom. It also gives him the freedom to reverence and exalt the Christ above himself and to see himself as his servant who "must decrease" (3:30). John's actions embody countercultural values deriving from a faithful comportment to Jesus as the Son of God.[100]

The contrast between John the Baptist and Nicodemus, as embodied exemplars of the "two ways"[101] of true faith versus an ambivalent faith that is

98. Cf. Andrew T. Lincoln, *The Gospel according to Saint John*, BNTC (London: Continuum, 2005), 156, "The trial constituted by Jesus' mission exposes whether one's deeds are in conformity to its true judgment, and thus those who do the truth are revealed to be on the side of God rather than the world, which is opposed to the divine verdict."

99. Cf. Malina and Rohrbaugh, *John*, 90, "Nicodemus, the eminent Pharisee teacher, is thus contrasted with John, the prophet who baptized."

100. For a contextualization that reveals the audacity of John the Baptist's statement see Jerome H. Neyrey and Richard L. Rohrbaugh, "'He Must Increase, I Must Decrease' (John 3:30): A Cultural and Social Interpretation," CBQ 63 (2001): 464–83.

101. Wisdom literature often speaks of the "two ways," two paths that lead to two opposite ends—on one side happiness and fulfillment, on the other bitterness and desolation. John is fond of antithetical language (light/dark, above/below, flesh/spirit, etc.), and it is common for this language to be interpreted as evidence of "Johannine dualism." But it is important to see that John is speaking of ethical antithesis, not metaphysical dualisms. The Gospel nowhere betrays any kind of belief that ultimate reality is defined by the tension between two mutually subsisting opposing forces. Cf. Miroslav Volf, "Johannine Dualism and Contemporary Pluralism," in *The Gospel of John and Christian Theology*, ed. Richard Bauckham and Carl Mosser

equivalent to unbelief,[102] can be understood as two different understandings of the locus of control in their lives. John recognizes Jesus as the one "above all" and giver of life. John denies the premise of his disciples that his ministry belongs to him as a possession that is being stolen by Jesus because he understands his ministry as the gift of Jesus and his calling as the glorification of Jesus. So he can rejoice over his declining ministry because he has the joy of best man for the bridegroom. This faithful comportment of gratitude, joy, and service is in stark contrast to Nicodemus, who comes to Jesus from above and not from below. His position and status among the people of God are his possession, and Jesus may not displace those realities. The locus of control in his life is found within himself, not in the free gift of God but in the claim that he possesses God's promise. It is at this point that Jesus confronts him with the truth that the Spirit "blows where it wishes" and therefore Nicodemus can do nothing to facilitate or control the work of the Spirit. It is precisely at this point that John the Baptist finds joy and freedom in the wild and free gift of God, wherever it takes him. This life-giving comportment toward Jesus is what John promotes as the virtue of faith, which John the Baptist beautifully embodies.

Here we can see what is typical of Wisdom literature: a focus on fostering certain desires and dispositions. While this passage is theologically and narratively dense, that density creates a complex engagement with the reader in a process of identification and interrogation of their devotions. Here we meet Jesus as the king over all and the source of salvation. The impetus for salvation comes from his free gift and entails a life-giving submission to his person and will as the one who communicates the righteous presence and gracious will of God. And so faith in Jesus is synonymous with obedience to

---

(Grand Rapids: Eerdmans, 2008), 22–25. Also see Richard Bauckham, *The Testimony of the Beloved Disciple: Narrative, History, and Theology in the Gospel of John* (Grand Rapids: Baker Academic, 2007), 125–36, where Bauckham dismantles the oft-made identification of Johannine and Qumranic dualisms. John does not believe that human experience is normally defined by an absolute duality of good and evil, but more consistently in a state of moral ambivalence and confusion. Because devotional ambivalence is fundamental to human experience and decision making, two-ways language functions to clarify devotions by tying them to ultimate ends and desires (i.e., giving them a teleological grounding and motivation).

102. While Nicodemus has his own individual narrative of where this dialogue with Jesus will take him (and he will later show signs of faith in 7:50–52 and 19:38–40), at this point in the narrative he comes as a representative of the Jewish religious leadership and those who will come to be labeled as simply "the Jews." While this group often shows faith in Jesus, especially on the basis of signs, this initial faith results in unbelief, crystallized in their renunciation and condemnation of Jesus in the Passion Narrative. John wants to show that a certain kind of ambivalent faith can be dangerous because it can just as easily lead to unbelief, because it has the seed of unbelief—a deficient comportment to Jesus—at its core.

Jesus. This is a retraining of the affections that strikes at the heart of sinful self-reliance and finds the offer of life in obedient, reverent faith in Jesus as "the one above all."

Conclusion

From all this we can see that every hermeneutic strategy embodies a comportment to the text. For all the vast differences between modern and postmodern hermeneutics, both begin with the same comportment to the text as sovereign subjects that stand outside and above the text. Meaning and application are derived from the subject, sometimes imposed on the text and sometimes prompted by the text, but always filtered through the disposition of the subject as an arbiter of the appropriateness of application.

By contrast, a hermeneutic of wisdom seeks to position itself within and under the text. This entails an attentive engagement with the text, expecting both the text's familiarity and otherness, and through both a hermeneutic of wisdom opens itself to authoritative textual agency (as a superintending work of the Spirit). This is not a formula for the annihilation of the self, but the self's determination to attend to what Gadamer labeled "the superior claims of the text" on us in a fiduciary stance of epistemological humility.[103] This humility also extends to metaphysics and morality in readers' recognition of the limitations of their creatureliness and perpetual need of repentance and renewal. All of these acts of humility serve to free the self from delusions and enslaving fantasies that obscure the voice of the text and insulate us from its intentionality for us—to establish our communion with God in Christ and enable us to love.

---

103. As Schneiders has argued, this does not exclude critical engagement with the text, simply critical *distance from* the text. As she says, "The challenge today is to integrate appropriate critical strategies into an engagement of reader and text in such a way that the transformative participation of the reader is fostered while a relapse into a precritical naivety is forestalled" ("Gospels and the Reader," 103). Cf. Schneiders, *Revelatory Text*, 19–25.

2

THEOLOGY AND ETHICS

"Behold, a sower went out to sow." In the parable of the sower in Mark 4:1–20 Jesus uses the images of farmer, seed, and soils to illustrate what it means to receive the message of the gospel.[1] The focus of the parable is not actually the sower,[2] or the seed,[3] but the four soils,[4] distinguished by their varying receptions of the seed (identified in v. 14 as "the word"). This is a parable about reception, employing the language of "hearing," "receiving," and "accepting," and culminating in the command, "He who has ears to hear, let him hear." In this strange but familiar command Jesus provokes the central question posed by this parable, "What does it mean to *hear*?"

1. More precisely, in the context this parable is about the reception of the parabolic teaching of Jesus. This is a parable about the parables (cf. Morna D. Hooker, *The Gospel according to St. Mark*, BNTC [Peabody, MA: Hendrickson, 1991], 120, "Clearly Mark regards this introductory parable as the key to understanding the rest"), which comes as the first of the parables in all three Synoptics (Matt. 13:1–23; Luke 8:1–15). While this passage has certain things to say about the parables in particular (e.g., they are in some sense a communicative act of judgment on Israel [vv. 11–12]), there are also valid extrapolations to be made to the teachings of Jesus in general. Cf. Robert H. Stein, *Mark*, BECNT (Grand Rapids: Baker Academic, 2008), 216, "the absolute use of the term 'word' [identified with the seed of the sower in v. 14] serves as a Markan technical term for the gospel."

2. Robert A. Guelich, *Mark 1–8:26*, WBC 34A (Dallas: Word, 1989), 192, says, "Rather than central to the story, this figure simply sets the story in motion."

3. Contra Guelich, *Mark*, 196–97, "The focal point of the parable lies in the seed that has been sown."

4. So Stein, *Mark*, 201, "the focus of the parable lies with the four soils, not the seed."

In the course of the parable Jesus teaches that hearing is an act of the whole person, revealing the ultimate devotions of the hearer.[5] The one good soil, representative of ideal reception, is contrasted with three deficient models of reception, in which true hearing is short-circuited by hardness of heart, adversities, and competing devotions. The good soil represents "the ones who hear the word and accept it and bear fruit." The three actions that here denote authentic reception (hear, accept, and bear fruit) correspond negatively to the three types of defective soils. The first failed to hear at all. The second heard but did not "accept" the word in the midst of persecution, and the third soil proved "unfruitful" because of incoherent devotions. These negative examples help to clarify (by contrast) the significance of hearing, accepting, and bearing fruit by naming the impediments that threaten their realization.

Hearing is the first stage of reception and requires an openness to receive, a softness of heart that recognizes its need for the word. This is in contrast to the dusty, compacted footpath, where the seed finds no reception but lies on the surface ready to be consumed by the birds.[6] Accepting is the second stage of reception and implies something beyond simply an understanding of or openness to the word; it involves a reliant expectation, akin to the fiduciary comportment we outlined in the previous chapter. Accepting signifies a disposition of trust in the received word as the source of life, which can properly be prized above both acceptance by others and freedom from persecution. The rocky ground hears but fails to accept and so turns away from the word in times of persecution. The third stage of reception is bearing fruit—the performance of concrete moral actions that derive their motives and justifications from the word. The third soil fails in this regard because it is deceived by worries and desires that confuse primary devotion to the word as the mediation of the presence of the kingdom of God.

It is important to recognize that bearing fruit is not an action *in addition* to reception; it *completes* the act of reception. Bearing fruit shares in the same motivations and justifications that energize the actions of hearing and accepting. The parable does not allow us to see fruit bearing and understanding

5. Cf. Hooker, *Mark*, 120, "For Mark, the parables of Jesus both reveal and conceal: for those who have ears to hear they convey the good news of the Kingdom, to those who refuse to listen their message is obscure."

6. The identification of the birds with Satan is to emphasize that the word of Jesus goes out into a hostile spiritual environment, and each soil faces challenges. The emphasis of the parable is on the condition of the soil and its ability to receive. The path that has no reception at all is easy prey and, according to vv. 11–12, is also under God's judgment, because the parables are a barrier to exclude those who are hard hearted. Cf. Hooker, *Mark*, 120, "Those who do not respond are those whose hearts are hardened, whom Satan has in his power."

as incommensurable actions but as necessary complements in the singular act of reception. This understanding of bearing fruit as an essential element in receiving will likely feel unnatural to us. We are more comfortable with thinking of reception as an act of understanding that is distinct from moral actions based on that understanding. We can have an adequate understanding of something without acting on it. If we then choose to act on that understanding, that would be a discrete activity that may derive *coherence* from understanding but not *necessity*. The parable of the sower, however, resists this distinction. Reception of the word is constituted in action that is both coherent *and* necessary. Failure to bear fruit is a failure to hear, as in the example of the third soil, where the fruit is choked by weeds. In true reception the acts of understanding and fruit bearing are as inseparable as the acts of hearing and accepting. All three acts (hearing, accepting, and bearing fruit) are equally necessary elements in the act of reception.

This highlights a tension between our presuppositions and those of Jesus and the Gospel writers. We simply assume a separation of knowing and doing that would have been unintelligible to them. This separation, which traditionally discloses itself under several different dichotomies (e.g., being/doing, theology/ethics, and indicative/imperative), is deeply embedded in our Western philosophical outlook and constitutes a strong impediment to apprehending the Bible as wisdom because wisdom seeks to recognize how theology and ethics function *together* in shaping the convictions, affections, and actions of the people of God. So in fostering a hermeneutic of wisdom we will need to attend to this fundamental dichotomy of being and doing—to understand how deeply it affects our reading of the Bible but also how the Bible stubbornly resists this dichotomy.

Philosophical Roots

This tension between being and doing finds its roots in the origins of the Western tradition in ancient Athens. The first element in this tradition is the identification of being and knowing. Previously, we saw how Plato defined knowing as a participatory apprehension of being. While this definition may still sound alien to us, the main reason it sounds odd is that we do not share Plato's metaphysic. Every epistemology presupposes a metaphysic, which lends to that epistemology a framework of intelligibility. Plato saw a deep connection between metaphysics (being) and epistemology (knowing), and there are few since who have questioned some kind of essential link between the two. But Plato went further in describing this connection in terms of *identity*. While this might seem jarring at first, as soon as we recognize that Plato defined ultimate reality (being) as a form of rationality, then the identification becomes more obvious. What we have in Plato is the beginnings of the Hellenistic doctrine of the λόγος, an identification of being with reason, which proved foundational for all Hellenistic (and modern) thought to follow.

The second step, already nascent in Plato but more obviously articulated by Aristotle, is the identification of reason with the divine. As Martha Nussbaum says, "[Aristotle] gives an account of god as an immortal immaterial substance whose entire form is thinking."[7] Because this is thinking in its purest form, it cannot be a mode of thought that moves from unknowing to knowing, but only thinking that contemplates its own perfection.[8] Thus, in Aristotle's theology, god is a rationality engaged in the single action of contemplating itself. Its knowledge and actions are entirely self-referential to its own consciousness. For Aristotle, this rationality defines the good but at the same time never moves outside itself in either thought or action.[9]

This theological understanding engenders a sharp dichotomy between being on the one hand (along with knowing as the participatory apprehension of being) and action on the other. Because god is ultimate reality (being), he defines the good and is, therefore, the measure of human thought and action. Whatever does not correspond to god is either evil or (at best) neutral. Because god is a being whose only action is to reason, this legitimates the activity of human reason as a "communicable attribute."[10] But the converse is also true. Because god does not act outside contemplating his own reason, human moral action becomes something of an extra in the universe that finds no legitimization in the divine nature. Moral action then becomes a secondary noncommunicable attribute. From this emerges a divide between being and doing, where essence and knowing are prized above doing, and moral action

7. Martha C. Nussbaum, "Aristotle," in *A Companion to Metaphysics*, ed. Jaegwon Kim and Ernest Sosa, Blackwell Companion to Philosophy (Oxford: Blackwell, 1995), 27.

8. Cf. Diogenes Allen, *Philosophy for Understanding Theology* (Atlanta: John Knox, 1985), 128–29, "The First Unmoved Mover's activity is thought, but not discursive thought since that involves a move from not knowing to knowing and so a movement from potentiality to act. Its thought, then, is intuitive or perfect and its object can only be itself. . . . The First Mover in Aristotle, however, is not an object of worship. It does not know anything outside itself, and it is not a creator."

9. Cf. Alan Code, "Aristotle's Logic and Metaphysics," in *From Aristotle to Augustine*, ed. David Furley, Routledge History of Philosophy (London: Routledge, 1997), 68, "God's intelligence is not a thinking of us or of the universe but rather is a thinking of thinking or intelligence itself (1074b34). He [Aristotle] argues both that this activity is good, and that it is the source of the order and goodness of the universe."

10. I.e., an attribute shared by god and human beings.

is understood to emerge from an incommensurable sphere of human volition. The gulf between knowing and doing is quite literally infinite.[11]

Aristotle's theology becomes domesticated in the modern period through Descartes[12] in a process where the categories of divine reason are translated into the categories that describe human rationality.[13] Cartesian subjectivism begins with the human mind's contemplation of its own reasoning.[14] Descartes presupposes the ancient identification of being and thought[15] but turns it on its head by establishing being *from* reason in his famous *cogito*.[16] For Descartes, and those who would follow him, the highest human activity is self-consciousness, which mirrors Aristotelian theology, where god is defined solely in terms of his self-referential knowledge. Human moral agency, while commendable, is a secondary activity born of the will, which may find its *justification* in reason but is never bound to it of *necessity*.[17]

11. One way in which this works itself out can perhaps be seen in Augustine's description of the *summum bonum*. Still under the influence of Neo-Platonism, Augustine describes the highest action for the Christian as the contemplation of God. After all, according to Aristotle, that is the *summum bonum* for God himself. Contrast this with the teaching of Jesus on the "greatest commandment," where love of God and neighbor are given as the actions that define life in the kingdom of God.

12. I am not meaning to argue for nor imply a straight, unbroken line between Aristotle and Descartes; far from it. While Enlightenment philosophers were dismantling Aristotelian categories (especially his teleological understanding of being), their philosophical furniture is still Aristotelian. See Donald Rutherford, "Innovation and Orthodoxy in Early Modern Philosophy," in *The Cambridge Companion to Early Modern Philosophy*, ed. Donald Rutherford (Cambridge: Cambridge University Press, 2006), 11–36. Cf. Heiko Augustinus Oberman, *The Harvest of Medieval Theology: Gabriel Biel and Late Medieval Nominalism*, rev. ed. (Grand Rapids: Baker Academic, 2000).

13. Cf. Mark C. Taylor, ed., *Deconstruction in Context: Literature and Philosophy* (Chicago: University of Chicago Press, 1986), 3, "With the movement from Descartes, through the Enlightenment, idealism and romanticism, attributes traditionally predicated of the divine subject are gradually transferred to the human subject."

14. Although human consciousness is discursive in a way that divine reason never was in Aristotle.

15. It was the project of Heidegger to challenge this identification with the recognition of the distance between divine and human thought or, as he might say, the difference between Being and beings in the human experience of *Dasein*. See, for example, Martin Heidegger, "The Onto-Theo-Logical Constitution of Metaphysics," in *Identity and Difference*, trans. Joan Stambaugh (New York: Harper & Row, 1969), 42–74.

16. *Cogito ergo sum*: I think, therefore I am. In this statement Descartes derived the proof of his existence from the presence of his doubting consciousness. Descartes also magnified the separation of being and doing in creating an absolute metaphysical dichotomy between the mind and all external reality.

17. This corresponds closely to Descartes's voluntarist theology, in which he understands God as an indifferent absolute will whose agency cannot be constrained by moral, rational, or metaphysical necessity. See Steven Nadler, "Conceptions of God," in *Oxford Handbook of Philosophy in Early Modern Europe*, ed. Desmond M. Clarke and Catherine Wilson (Oxford: Oxford University Press, 2011), 529–34. Kant, among others, tried to solve this problem with

The Retrieval of Divine Agency

The first step in contending with this dichotomy of being and action is to return to the question of divine identity. An alternate picture of God in relation to knowing and doing would necessarily entail a correlate reformulation of the relationship of being and action. There are few in the twentieth century who saw this issue with more clarity than Karl Barth. At the center of Barth's work is a proclamation of the freedom of God in his acts of creation and redemption. For Barth, as John Webster says, "God is not a mute reality to be called into presence by language or practice, but the eternally creative and active word."[18] The Bible does not depict God as a rationality or as a projected therapeutic idea but as a personality with concrete agency constituted in thought, desire, will, and the creative power to effect that will. What Barth saw so clearly was that the Christian God cannot fit into an Aristotelian mold. They are, at core, competing understandings.

In the history of Western thought these two pictures have vied for prominence, and their struggle has (at times) produced fruitful theological reflection. But in the end, when we come to understanding the Bible and the God to whom it testifies, we are left with a true either/or. Either we possess a picture where God is an idea, or rationality itself (and subsequently any talk of God's agency is purely metaphorical), or we embrace the reality of God as "the eternally creative and active word."

If we do embrace the latter, ultimate reality becomes defined in terms of a being revealed in action, and we are no longer hampered by a dichotomy between being and doing at the heart of our metaphysic. We are free to see being and doing as distinct but inseparable because of their mutual coexistence (and essential unity) in the person of God. In the same way, our understanding of human agency can be remodeled to comprehend being and doing as mutually determined. This was a natural connection for Barth; as Eberhard Jüngel states, "Barth understands human being in the same way he understands divine being: as a 'being in action.'"[19]

---

the proposal of the "categorical imperative," wherein the recognition of the truth of a moral judgment necessarily entailed its complementary action. But even for Kant "pure reason" and "moral judgment" are two distinct spheres of intellectual endeavor to be critiqued separately, which reveals just how deeply embedded the Cartesian dualisms were in his thought. The necessity of action can only attach itself to moral judgments, not to pure reason.

18. John B. Webster, *Barth's Moral Theology: Human Action in Barth's Thought* (Edinburgh: T&T Clark, 1998), 125. See Karl Barth, *Church Dogmatics* II.1.6.1; §28, ed. Geoffrey William Bromiley and Thomas F. Torrance (London: T&T Clark, 2004).

19. Eberhard Jüngel, "Law and Gospel," in *Karl Barth: A Theological Legacy*, trans. Garrett E. Paul (Philadelphia: Westminster, 1986), 120. As quoted in Webster, *Barth's Moral Theology*, 202. Cf. Karl Barth, *Ethics*, ed. Dietrich Braun, trans. Geoffrey W. Bromiley (New York: Seabury,

So our metaphysical starting point will determine the possibilities for our conception of how being and doing are related. If we begin with identifying the divine with reason, we automatically create a fissure with being and thought on one side and moral action on the other. On the other hand, if we begin with a Christian understanding of the divine nature, then moral agency becomes a communicable attribute alongside rational thought. Being and action are equally legitimated as good, necessary, and interdependent in both theology and anthropology.[20]

Indicative and Imperative

In the history of biblical interpretation the dichotomy between being and action has most often expressed itself in questions about the relationship between theology and ethics, a discussion often pseudo-grammaticalized in the language of "indicative and imperative."[21] This is a dichotomy deeply embedded in the presuppositions and methodologies of biblical research. If our primary goal in approaching the NT is the unlocking of a historical-theological puzzle, or at least a small piece of that puzzle, then our primary aim will be to clarify the historical development of the formation and transmission of ideas (theology). This presupposes that the ethical teachings of the NT (1) can be easily detached from their theological contexts and (2) are materially inconsequential in formulating our understanding of the origins of early Christianity. This prejudice for theology over ethics has led to an often explicit condemnation of the ethics of the NT as a sub-Christian appropriation of bourgeois Hellenistic ethics.[22] (This includes an unwarranted assumption that someone like Paul included ethics in his epistles as an

1981), 50, "In ethics no less than in dogmatics God's Word is not a general truth which can be generally perceived from the safe harbor of theoretical contemplation. Nor is it a being from which an imperative may be comfortably deduced. God's Word gives itself to be known, and in so doing it is heard, man is made responsible, and his acts take place in that confrontation. The Word of God is the Word of God only in act."

20. There are, of course, other challenges in the discontinuity between knowing and doing, most obviously the moral failures of knowing what is right and still failing to do it. What we are speaking of here does not address or fix that moral problem; it simply addresses another way in which we have dissembled the call that the truth makes on our lives, by separating knowing and doing, or being and action.

21. The dichotomy between κήρυγμα (early church gospel proclamation) and διδαχή (the ethical instruction that developed later) is another formulation sharing the same presuppositional DNA. Cf. James I. H. McDonald, *Kerygma and Didache: The Articulation and Structure of the Earliest Christian Message*, SNTSMS 37 (Cambridge: Cambridge University Press, 1980).

22. E.g., Martin Dibelius, *A Fresh Approach to the New Testament and Early Christian Literature* (London: Nicholson & Watson, 1936), 217–37. See also C. H. Dodd, *Gospel and*

afterthought, feeling some compulsion to address the practical needs of the fledgling congregations he addressed, but that the "real" Paul is only evident in his theological argumentation.)

This kind of approach can help us answer certain very important questions about Christian origins but also produces a deeply distorted picture of the early church. The writers of the NT do not share our presupposition that knowing and doing are incommensurable spheres of human experience. When we impose this structure on these texts, we are anachronistically skewing our interpretation away from the self-understanding of the NT authors. So, NT scholars can write Pauline theologies and imagine that in describing the ideas of Paul they have described Paul himself and summarized his life and work, as though Paul could imagine the prospect of doing theology apart from the question of how belief in Christ shapes the life of the church community.

This is why Victor Furnish argues that Paul's "ethical concerns are not secondary but radically integral to his basic theological convictions."[23] Furnish represents the inhabitants of a tiny island of Pauline scholars who for decades have tirelessly undermined the "indicative and imperative" dichotomy as something wholly alien to Paul's thought.[24]

The first to chart this island in modern times was Rudolf Bultmann. In a famous article on Pauline ethics, he identified the relationship between indicative and imperative as the key to understanding Paul's ethics.[25] Where previous authors had seen deep, irreconcilable tensions,[26] Bultmann tried to reformulate the discussion in the direction of an integrated relationship between the two. Against those who too easily saw the separation of theology and ethics as structurally embedded in Paul's letters, Bultmann focused his attention on

---

Law: The Relation of Faith and Ethics in Early Christianity, Bampton Lectures in America (Cambridge: Cambridge University Press, 1951), 20.

23. Victor Paul Furnish, *Theology and Ethics in Paul*, NTL (Louisville: Westminster John Knox, 2009), xvii.

24. Cf. Richard B. Hays, *The Moral Vision of the New Testament: Community, Cross, New Creation, A Contemporary Introduction to New Testament Ethics* (San Francisco: HarperSan-Francisco, 1996), 18,

> The more closely we read Paul's letters, the more fragile these familiar dichotomies appear. In these texts, it is difficult to draw a sharp distinction between theology and ethics. They are packed together, under pressure: specific pastoral problems in Paul's churches elicit his theological reflection. Thus, we see theology in progress, unfolding. Paul is not simply repeating already formulated doctrines; rather, he is theologizing as he writes, and the constant aim of his theological reflection is to shape the behavior of his churches. Theology is for Paul never merely a speculative exercise; it is always a tool for constructing community.

25. Rudolf Bultmann, "Das Problem der Ethik bei Paulus," *ZNW* 23 (1924): 123–40.

26. E.g., Paul Wernle; cf. William D. Dennison, "Indicative and Imperative: The Basic Structure of Pauline Ethics," *CTJ* 14, no. 1 (1979): 57–59.

Paul's penchant for bolting indicative and imperative formulations of the same teaching directly to each other. His favorite example was Galatians 5:25, "If we live by the Spirit, let us also keep in step with the Spirit," where Paul speaks of corporate life in the Spirit in the language of both declaration and command. Bultmann saw this not as an isolated incident in Paul[27] but a habit of Paul's thought to conjoin declarations about the concrete reality of the new life with commands to embrace it through moral action. Bultmann summarized his understanding of this Pauline tension in the slogan "Be who you are."[28]

Furnish followed Bultmann in proposing an indissoluble union between indicative and imperative. Furnish's primary foil was the *kerygma* versus *didache* paradigm of C. H. Dodd. Dodd, and many of his contemporaries, understood the NT in terms of two main strata of tradition. The first was the *kerygma*, the gospel proclamation of the apostles and early church, understood as the message of salvation proclaimed to the church. Second, the *didache*, which came later, represented the moral teachings of the early church, necessitated by the ongoing maintenance of the young Christian communities. (Assumed here, against all historical evidence, is the idea of a "pure" gospel proclamation that included no moral instructions or commands, only a call to believe.) Furnish attacked this idea on two fronts. The first was to show that while Paul's letters have a surface structure of dividing theological reflections from practical advice, this paradigm only applies to some epistles (e.g., more true of Romans and Galatians than of 1 or 2 Corinthians) and fails to reckon with the diversity of modes of expression in Paul, even in his more structured epistles. His second angle of criticism demonstrated that Paul's own understanding of what it meant to proclaim the gospel included both theology and ethics, *kerygma* and *didache*. As Furnish says, "the good news Paul preaches finds expression now in theological statements, now in ethical exhortations."[29] He concluded that "the Pauline letters cannot be neatly divided into doctrinal and ethical sections at all, and that the distinction between *kerygma* and *didache* . . . is more misleading than it is helpful."[30]

27. Other Pauline examples include Gal. 5:1; Rom. 6:1–19; and 1 Cor. 5:17.

28. While this could easily sound like a moralism that leaves Christians up to their own devices to materialize the new life that has been declared by God, within his Lutheran-cum-existentialist approach Bultmann explicitly rejects this self-justifying, self-improvement approach by seeing the fulfillment of the command to be who you are not in moral reform but in the authentic moment of decision perpetually enacted. Cf. Rudolf Bultmann, *Theology of the New Testament*, trans. Kendrick Grobel (New York: Scribner, 1951–55), 1:332–33. At the same time, this is an inadequate solution in its reduction of Christian responsibility to a self-referential authenticating act of the will.

29. Furnish, *Theology and Ethics*, 110.

30. Furnish, *Theology and Ethics*, 69.

Furnish also has on his agenda the task of trying to clarify how we ought to describe the relationship between theology and ethics, once this dichotomy has been excluded. Furnish eschews the language of the imperative "being based upon" or "coming out of" the indicative, saying that "this suggests that the imperative is designed somehow to 'realize' or 'actualize' what God has given only as a 'possibility.'"[31] We could add that this formulation still embodies a fundamental dichotomy between being and action in that it posits no necessary connection between theology and ethics. In fact, it describes a one-way dependent relationship between indicative and imperative and in such a way that the indicative is sufficient in itself apart from the imperative.

Ultimately, Furnish recognizes failed attempts at defining the interdependency of indicative and imperative as a failure to understand the gospel as it is proclaimed in the NT. "For Paul, obedience is neither preliminary to the new life (as its condition) nor secondary to it (as its result and eventual fulfillment). Obedience is *constitutive* of the new life."[32] The gospel is equally gift and call, and so equally (and necessarily) expressed in the language of both indicative and imperative.

Further clarification came in the work of Allen Verhey, who, among others, pointed to the eschatological tenor of Paul's ethics, and particularly the eschatological tensions that defined the relationship between indicative and imperative. As he says, "The relationship of indicative and imperative . . . must be understood in terms of Paul's conviction that in the crucified and risen Christ God has acted and is acting eschatologically."[33] For Verhey the tension between indicative and imperative is an expression of the eschatological tension between the already and the not yet. This answers the question, posed by Bultmann, of how Paul can declare something to be already a state of being for the Christian and in the next breath call the same Christian to embody the reality that has been proclaimed about them. The already/not yet means that eschatological salvation is already present in reality but still awaits its fulfillment and that this tension provides a framework and impetus for the realization of salvation in present moral action. This explains how, for example, Paul's call for opposition to the present rule of sin in Romans 6:12–14 is sandwiched between two declarations that freedom from sin has already been accomplished (6:7, 17–18).

---

31. Furnish, *Theology and Ethics*, 225.

32. Furnish, *Theology and Ethics*, 226. Cf. Ernst Käsemann, *Commentary on Romans*, trans. Geoffrey W. Bromiley (Grand Rapids: Eerdmans, 1980), 175.

33. Allen Verhey, *The Great Reversal: Ethics and the New Testament* (Grand Rapids: Eerdmans, 1984), 104.

Finally, Wolfgang Schrage argued that the interdependence of theology and ethics in Paul is not only eschatological but also *christological*, because at the center of Paul's soteriology is the community's eschatological participation in the righteousness of Christ, which they experience as a gift that frees, empowers, and directs moral agency. Schrage, summarizing the work of Käsemann, argues: "Christians are so incorporated into the eschatological establishment of God's righteousness through Christ (Rom. 6:12ff.) that the very texture of their lives is determined by this salvific power, which permeates the world, so that they can now begin to bring forth 'fruits of righteousness' (Phil. 1:11; cf. also Rom. 8:10). This shows at the same time that the dialectic of indicative and imperative is not merely formal. It can be understood correctly only from the perspective of christology."[34] Union with Christ entails both a being and a becoming, not only ontologically but also morally. And so for Paul the community's connection to Jesus is always mediated through his death and resurrection, which the Reformers (especially Calvin) appropriated in the language of mortification and vivification. New life in Christ is not simply a declaration of forgiveness but a death to self and a new life in God that finds concrete realization in love toward God, community, and neighbor. And so the eschatological communion with Christ is at once both indicative and imperative, a reintegration of being and action, which were estranged by sin.

Discerning Speech Acts

The paradigm of indicative versus imperative, in addition to being problematic theologically, is also problematic in its presuppositions about language. The functional linguistic assumption here is that language is chiefly a medium of propositions, a communicative repository for data. The author puts propositions in, and the reader takes them out. This is a modernist "mailbox" picture of language. The postman puts my letters in the mailbox, and later I take them out. The mailbox is just there to hold the letters. In the same way language serves simply to hold propositions as they pass from the mind of the author to the mind of the reader or listener.

The first level at which this picture of language breaks down is in the basic recognition that not all communication is propositional. Imperatives, for example, are commands; they do not transfer information, but rather,

34. Wolfgang Schrage, *The Ethics of the New Testament*, trans. David E. Green (Philadelphia: Fortress, 1988), 171. Schrage has in mind Käsemann's comments on Rom. 6:1–14 in his *An die Römer*, as well as his essay, "Gottesgerechtigkeit bei Paulus," in *Exegetische Versuche und Besinnungen* (Göttingen: Vandenhoeck & Ruprecht, 1960), 2:181–93.

they demand action. Another example, among many, would be dialogue in a narrative, which can, but need not, communicate propositional information. The more it does so, usually, the worse it functions as narrative.[35] The mailbox view of language works well for scientific journal articles primarily because it is really the linguistic embodiment of a modern "lab-coat" epistemology.

The second level where this view of language fails is in understanding propositions themselves. Today linguists view propositions as primarily encoding intentionality, not information. Language is the medium that embodies the intentions of the author to convince, warn, cajole, entertain, inform, or entice. Human discourse, at all levels, is a means of producing effects in the world. This was first formally recognized in the development of speech-act theory,[36] in which discourse events are understood as pragmatic acts. As Kevin Vanhoozer says: "Words do not simply label; sentences do not merely state. Rather, in using language we do any number of things: question, command, warn, request, curse, bless and so forth. A speech act has two aspects: propositional content and illocutionary force, the 'matter' and 'energy' of communicative action. The key notion is that of illocution, which has to do not simply with locuting or uttering words but with what we do *in* uttering words."[37]

This insight into language helps us to move beyond an understanding of language as primarily a medium of knowledge and see it more as a medium of intentionality.[38] The classic example of a speech-act is the simple dinnertime statement "There is no salt on the table." No one says this to be appreciated for their keen gift of perception. It is a communicative act, whose obvious implicature is, "Can someone please bring the salt?" Here we have a statement in the indicative that functions as an imperative. What this exposes in the indicative/imperative model is that we cannot discern discourse function by simply labeling grammatical moods. We cannot assume that passages dominated by the indicative primarily serve to "inform" us or "teach us theology," or that imperatives simply "tell us how to live

35. Many different forms of storytelling have created characters whose primary function is exposition and/or interpretation. This is the role of the chorus in Greek tragedy and often the narrator in modern novels.

36. See J. L. Austin, *How to Do Things with Words* (Cambridge, MA: Harvard University Press, 1962), and J. R. Searle, *Speech Acts: An Essay in the Philosophy of Language* (Cambridge: Cambridge University Press, 1969).

37. Kevin J. Vanhoozer, *First Theology: God, Scripture & Hermeneutics* (Downers Grove, IL: InterVarsity, 2002), 118.

38. Cf. Jeannine K. Brown, *Scripture as Communication: Introducing Biblical Hermeneutics* (Grand Rapids: Baker Academic, 2007), 35, and her category of "perlocutionary intentions."

practically." Sensitive readings of texts will attend to the diverse illocution-ary forces encoded in texts.[39]

This insight also brings us, potentially, into a new understanding of the relationship between theology and ethics in the context of wisdom. Previously, common formulations have been based on insights such as "the imperative [command] is based on the indicative [information]." But if we no longer constrain the indicative to the act of information transference, then we can begin to see the relationship in new ways. If biblical texts are wisdom texts, then their chief intention will be to foster understanding and action deter-mined by love for God and neighbor, demonstrated in obedience to the will of God and practical sacrifice for others. When the Bible teaches theology, it promotes this kind of wisdom; when it gives practical moral instruction it is also promoting wisdom, just from a different angle.

Because all actions are measured according to the standards of Right ARM, it is important to see that wisdom seeks to shape its adherents in *all three areas*. In the NT we never find theology for the sake of theology; it is always a theology *pragmatically* shaped to contextualize moral action by informing and shaping right reasons and right desires. In this way "theology" promotes wisdom by projecting what Charles Taylor calls a "moral space," which he argues is "constitutive of human agency."[40] He describes this moral space as "a space in which questions arise about what is good or bad, what is worth doing and what is not, what has meaning and importance . . . and what is trivial and secondary."[41] A moral space is an evaluative space in which moral agents are given an interpretive grid to judge desires, actions, and attachments in light of a comprehensive vision of reality that ascribes relative values to possible objects of devotion.[42] In this way a moral space or "moral vision"[43] is a necessary ideational context that makes certain moral actions intelligible and attractive.

Applying this to Paul, for example, we can move past conceptions of Paul's "theology" as a free-floating development of ideas governed by his mystical experience of Jesus as the fulfillment of the story of Israel (or however we

---

39. For a better idea of what this sensitivity looks like in practice, see the excellent introduc-tion to discourse analysis in Jeffrey T. Reed, *A Discourse Analysis of Philippians: Method and Rhetoric in the Debate over Literary Integrity*, JSNTSup 136 (Sheffield: Sheffield Academic Press, 1997), 16–33. For a more in-depth treatment, see Gillian Brown and George Yule, *Discourse Analysis*, Cambridge Textbooks in Linguistics (Cambridge: Cambridge University Press, 1983).

40. Charles Taylor, *Sources of the Self: The Making of the Modern Identity* (Cambridge: Cambridge University Press, 1989), 27.

41. Taylor, *Sources of the Self*, 28.

42. Cf. Seneca, *Moral Epistles* 95.58–59.

43. Hays, *Moral Vision*, 4.

might want to summarize his theology) and instead embrace Paul as someone who saw the gospel constituted in the reality of the eschatological rule of Jesus manifested in mercy and righteousness in the Christian community. In this way we can be free of modes of interpretation that make it normative to see "ethics" as a bourgeois sideshow in Paul, easily detached from his "theology." In his theological discourses, Paul is situating Christian communities in a moral space governed by the Lord Jesus and given shape by his death and resurrection. In this way Paul's "theology" and "ethics" function together as wisdom, reshaping concurrently both identity and praxis.[44] This is fundamentally how theology and ethics relate to each other in Paul's writings.

Integrated Application

Another way in which our interpretations are limited by the separation of being and doing is in the separation of understanding and application. Theology and biblical studies as academic disciplines have historically been defined as descriptive, not prescriptive, undertakings.[45] They tell us what is or what was, but not what to do. Understanding and application are separated, conceived again as *possibly* but not *necessarily* connected. So it is the norm for a book in systematic theology to have no reference to application, a reality inconceivable for premoderns.[46] Likewise, scholarly biblical commentaries by definition exclude application from their purview because this is not a question accessible to historical investigation.[47]

There are two interconnected reasons for this reality, rooted in the identification of being and knowing and their mutual separation from doing. Epistemologically, at least since Descartes, knowledge has been defined as the product of a disinterested pursuit of truth. As we saw in the previous chapter,

44. Cf. Taylor, *Sources of the Self*, 28, where he testifies to the "essential link" between moral space and identity. "To know who you are is to be oriented in moral space."

45. This is a defining feature of the modern research university that arose in Germany in the early nineteenth century, beginning with the University of Berlin in 1810, as an implementation of the Enlightenment social and educational vision of Wilhelm von Humbolt, in honor of whom the university was later renamed. See Thomas A. Howard, *Protestant Theology and the Making of the Modern German University* (Oxford: Oxford University Press, 2006).

46. Cf. Ellen T. Charry, *By the Renewing of Your Minds: The Pastoral Function of Christian Doctrine* (Oxford: Oxford University Press, 1997), 5, "Sapiential theology waned with modernity. Theology came to be thought of as the intellectual justification of the faith, apart from the practice of the Christian life."

47. This was not always the case. Even a century ago scholarly commentaries regularly included application, usually in a section labeled "homiletical." The recent emergence of numerous "theological" commentary series signals a deep uneasiness, but not complete break, with this tradition.

the relationship between the knower and the known has been characterized as one of distance and indifference. Introducing questions of how truth is meant to direct the life of the knower, by definition, is an infringement on these fundamental convictions of modern epistemology. Such questions produce a disturbing dissonance in the relationship between the knower and the known. Behind this epistemological dissonance is a second metaphysical one, where questions of application violate the separation of being and doing whenever they seek to root action necessarily in the apprehension of being. Modern epistemology severs the connection between the knower and the known. Modern metaphysics severs the connection between knowledge and the will.[48]

In practice, this means that application, even when it is sought, is viewed as a secondary stage in the process of interpretation; after we establish the "meaning," then we can derive its "significance." Even for those who insist that this "significance" is a necessary element in biblical interpretation (i.e., those who believe that the Scriptures are not properly understood apart from some application), the *necessity* of application is something added to and extrinsic to exegetical understanding.[49] Application is something we can choose to do as an additional task in understanding a text. While some might find this disjunction of understanding and application disturbing, because it is a normative thought pattern for us, few will consider it a question of crucial significance for the discipline of biblical studies. It is perhaps surprising then that Gadamer labeled this question "the central problem of hermeneutics."[50]

Gadamer exposed the modern ideal of coming to the text as a tabula rasa as neither possible nor desirable. Especially for a "traditionary" text such as the Bible, Gadamer recognized that to read the text for what it is involves an openness to be determined by it, not as a final step in understanding but determinative from the beginning. As he says, "Application is neither a subsequent nor merely an occasional part of the phenomenon of understanding, but *codetermines it as a whole from the beginning.*"[51] For Gadamer this is simply a recognition of our historically conditioned access to the text. We come to the text within a tradition and with desires shaped by our history. We come to the text precisely *because* we desire an application that speaks to our historically conditioned existence. This does not mean that our desire

48. Again, this is different from the *moral* separation of knowing and doing in sinful actions. This metaphysical separation operates at another level, but of course these two forms are mutually reinforcing in their work to deconstruct the psychological and moral integrity of both persons and communities.

49. So we are accustomed to the sermonic form of interpretation followed by application.

50. Hans-Georg Gadamer, *Truth and Method*, trans. Joel Weinsheimer and Donald G. Marshall, 2nd rev. ed. (New York: Continuum, 2004), 306.

51. Gadamer, *Truth and Method*, 321. Italics added.

for application then determines the "meaning" of a text but simply that it is a fiction to imagine we can bracket ourselves off and come to the text as an ahistorical intelligence. Gadamer sees hermeneutical understanding in terms of a historically conditioned participation with the text:

> The interpreter dealing with a traditionary text tries to apply it to himself. But this does not mean that the text is given for him as something universal, that he first understands it per se and then afterward uses it for particular applications. Rather, the interpreter seeks no more than to understand the universal, the text—i.e., to understand what it says, what constitutes the text's meaning and significance. In order to understand that, he must not try to disregard himself and his particular hermeneutical situation. He must relate the text to this situation if he wants to understand at all. . . . All reading involves application, so that a person reading a text is himself part of the meaning he apprehends. He belongs to the text he is reading.[52]

Gadamer is describing application not as a secondary step in the interpretive process but as something determinative of understanding. This corresponds to our recognition of the Bible as a wisdom text, which invites a participatory engagement with a text that both assumes and proclaims the text's normative function for the church. Reading the Bible as wisdom is not a step of "application" that we can tack on after we have understood its "meaning." Rather, a hermeneutic of wisdom sees the text as a shaping force that the reader apprehends in an openness to its direction. In this way it is not the reader who derives application from a meaning he has discerned in a *neutral* text, but the application that arises from the reader's historically conditioned engagement with the *normative world* of the text. Application is not an extension that the "sovereign subject" of the reader creates ad hoc from the "meaning" and then appends to the text. Application, as Gadamer says, "codetermines" meaning "as a whole from the beginning" and is derived from the imaginative engagement of the reader, who recognizes the text as wisdom. In this way application is both inherent in the text and variously particularized in the historically conditioned life of the reader/reading community.

Historically Conditioned Application

Most often, especially in texts that do not give direct commands, the bridge between meaning and significance has been found in some "principlizing"

52. Gadamer, *Truth and Method*, 321, 335.

of the text.[53] In this common mode of interpretation a "universal principle" is derived from the "meaning" of the text and then used to formulate an application fitted to the circumstances of the reader.[54] The problems inherent in such an approach are legion.

First, it is built on an assumption that application is something that we have to generate as an appendage to a neutral text that is, for example, "just telling a story." Second, it makes the principle, which is usually not explicit in the text, the normative element in the process of application. This is all the more problematic in that this principle, while often anemic in its generality, just as often is expressive of ethical systems having little affinity with the Bible, whether derived from Kant, Hobbes, or National Public Radio. Third, these "universal" principles are creations of the culturally conditioned consciousness of the reader. The historically conditioned interpreter has no access to "timeless universal truths" apart from the cultural sensitivities that define her historical situation.[55] Fourth, it also assumes that the real truth of the Bible is found in its witness to a timeless universal ethic. But the Bible never aspires to embody such a rationalistic and ahistorical inhuman idea. This does not mean that the teachings of the Bible only speak to their own time but rather that they are embedded in their own time as cultural expressions of witness to the work and person of God in the context of historically situated human communities.[56] Fifth, there is little in the actual text that governs either the derivation of the principle or the connection between the principle and its application. Sixth, the actual application is likely to be a moralistic particularization of the principle, most likely deriving its motivational force from Kantian deontological presuppositions.[57] In this way neither the principle nor its application is likely to be reflective of either textual fidelity or a Christian ethic.

At the core of this principlizing approach is the notion of a "universal ethic." In the history of modern theology, the influence of German idealism

---

53. Cf. Brown, *Scripture as Communication*, 261–67.

54. As noted in the introduction, this scheme of application by means of a "universal" ethic is reflected in the influential work of J. P. Gabler, who sharply distinguished between biblical-historical research and the universal truths and principles implicit in the text, which were the means for dogmatic theology to apply the biblical text to contemporary life.

55. See Kevin J. Vanhoozer, *The Drama of Doctrine: A Canonical-Linguistic Approach to Christian Theology* (Louisville: Westminster John Knox, 2005), 316, "Those who principlize assume that what gets contextualized is a pristine, culture-free principle, when what actually gets imported is one's culturally conditioned understanding of a biblical principle."

56. Cf. Hays, *Moral Vision*, 299, "The effort to distinguish timeless truth in the New Testament from culturally conditioned elements is wrongheaded and impossible."

57. I.e., the primary motivation for adherence to the principle will be bound up with an idea of duty to an abstract ethical norm in contrast to, for example, gratitude toward God.

has always gravitated toward the "universal." In practice this meant seeking after a purified "universal religion" that at certain points the Bible attested to. (The determination of where in the Bible this happened was the raison d'être of the *Religionsgeschichteschule*.) The search for a universal religion necessarily entailed a process of dehistoricizing, where beliefs were excised from their historically conditioned origins.[58] This was also the principle at work in the search for a universal ethic, an idea inherent in the concept of universal religion. A universal religion or ethic was one that any reasonable person living at any place at any time would of necessity have to adhere to. While the search for these illusive "universal" conceptions has long since waned, in practice the idea of a universal ethic is still quite prominent as an assumed model for application.

Gadamer displayed little patience for this dehistoricized conception embedded in our ideas of application. "Application does not mean first understanding a given universal in itself and then afterward applying it to a concrete case."[59] He understood that application did not come from a move outside the circle of our historically conditioned consciousness or outside the historically conditioned text we seek to receive application from. Application comes through our historically conditioned resonance with the past. As Schlatter argues: "Our task is to attach our concrete, historically conditioned lives to God. We get the necessary assurances for this not by logical fictions and ideas, but through facts.[60] . . . [Not] from ideal man, but from men like ourselves, and

58. Cf. Wilhelm Dilthey,

All dogmas must be reduced to their universal value for every human life. They were formulated once under a historically conditioned restriction. . . . Hereafter the primary dogmas that are contained in the symbols of the Son of God, atonement, sacrifice, etc. are untenable in their restriction to the facts of Christian history, although in their universal meaning they refer to the most vital content of all history. But in this meaning these concepts lose their reference to the person of Jesus, which in its rigid exclusiveness transforms everything into a special facticity and expressly excludes all other references. (From Sigrid Schulenburg, ed., *Briefwechsel zwischen Wilhelm Dilthey und dem grafen Paul Yorck v. Wartenburg, 1877–1897* [Halle: M. Niemeyer, 1923], 154. Cited in Rudolf Bultmann, "New Testament and Mythology: The Problem of Demythologizing the New Testament Proclamation," in *New Testament and Mythology: And Other Basic Writings*, ed. Schubert M. Ogden [Philadelphia: Fortress, 1984], 22)

59. Gadamer, *Truth and Method*, 336.

60. The language of "facts" strikes us today as the lingo of naive realism. For Schlatter, "facts" (*Tatsachen*) are how the real presents itself to us. He, in contrast to the near-universal opinion of the German academy in his day, was a realist, but a critical realist. Before Heidegger, Bultmann, and Gadamer, Schlatter was keenly aware of the inescapable role of preconceptions in knowledge and that often these preunderstandings were detrimental to the process of coming to understand. In a move later echoed by Gadamer, Schlatter states that knowledge only comes through a process of surrender to the reality to be known. *Tatsachen*, in contrast to concepts, are truths rooted in our historically conditioned experience.

that means historically localized men who lived their lives with God as their source and their goal. . . . [Interpreters] do not need a general conception of faith and love. What they need is a definite perception of what is meant by good will and confidence in God in the concrete situations of a human life."[61]

This means that application *already exists* in the historical embeddedness of the text.[62] The Bible does not attest to a world of concepts but to the creative agency of God demonstrated in his redeeming work among and for his people—historically conditioned human communities. According to Schlatter, the material essential for application is not an abstract concept of love, but the Bible's attestation to the actual love that Jesus demonstrated, commands, and produces in his people. Application, then, is not something we add to a neutral text but something already embedded in the form of the text as a historical testimony to the redeeming activity of God among his people.

In this light application becomes a participatory act of what Hays labels "analogical imagination."[63] It is precisely the historically conditioned experiences attested to and communicated in the Bible that are the contact point for our analogical imagination, whereby we are able to identify with and enter into the world of the text while recognizing its historical and cultural otherness. It is precisely this cultural distance that puts into relief the points of human resonance that find analogous application in the present. This comes from a deep understanding of the historically conditioned shape of the text, of human experience historically located finding a resonance in the historically embedded experience of the reader. This process of imaginative identification is one where application is deeply tied to a close reading of the text and the illocutionary force of the text in shaping concrete moral action. At the same time, this method is also sensitive to the analogous translation of that same illocutionary force into the present historically conditioned world of the church.[64]

61. Adolf Schlatter, "The Theology of the New Testament and Dogmatics," in *The Nature of New Testament Theology: The Contribution of William Wrede and Adolf Schlatter*, ed. Robert Morgan, SBT (London: SCM, 1973), 134–35. He adds, "Abstractions cut loose from realities are just as useless in practice as they are vacuous in theory" (134).

62. Cf. Brevard S. Childs, *Biblical Theology of the Old and New Testaments: Theological Reflection on the Christian Bible* (Minneapolis: Fortress, 1993), 86, "The enterprise of Biblical Theology is theological because by faith seeking understanding in relation to the divine reality, the divine imperatives are no longer moored in the past, but continue to confront the hearer in the present as truth. Therefore it is constitutive of Biblical Theology that it be normative and not merely descriptive, and that it be responsive to the imperatives of the present and not just of the past."

63. Hays, *Moral Vision*, 298.

64. See Brown, *Scripture as Communication*, 248–55, where she outlines the criteria of "coherence" and "purpose" as marks of good "recontextualization."

Theology and Ethics Working Together

Ethical systems are chiefly distinguished from one another by their ideational and motivational structures. The distinctives in ethical prescriptions between different ethical approaches are real but dwarfed by the common ground of condemnations of lying, cowardice, injustice, child abuse, betrayal, murder, and theft.[65] This is why, for example, the Stoics were open about how they happily borrowed ethical instructions and proverbs from competing philosophical schools but at the same time were careful to incorporate them into their Stoic worldview.[66]

Where ethical systems diverge is in how they contextualize and motivate moral actions. So the real tensions between competing ethical understandings are in the questions of right reasons and right motivations. This means that wisdom, which by definition operates in the context of competing ethical systems, will emphasize its overriding worldview that gives a context to moral actions more than the actions themselves. A worldview provides a picture of reality in which certain affective motivations are tied to particularly characteristic virtues that, while usually common to other ethical systems, are given a particular prominence. So, for example, equanimity (ἀπάθεια), while already a virtue in the Hellenistic schools, in Stoicism became *the* defining virtue, because it crystallized a vision of life that prioritized reason over illusory material goods and rendered the Stoic impervious to the vicissitudes of life.[67]

So when we turn to the Bible, we will not be surprised to find (for the most part) common ethical standards given a unique contextualization in its theological outlook, governed by the ongoing revelation of the kingdom of God and its inauguration in the resurrection of Jesus. Law, love, and obedience are not uniquely Jewish or Christian notions. What gives the NT its particular significance as an ethical system is how it contextualizes and motivates virtues of love, fidelity, compassion, humility, and righteousness by grounding them in the life, death, and resurrection of Jesus. So it is not the least surprising to see Paul in Philippians 2:1–11 grounding his call to humility in the example of the humility and obedience of Jesus. Nor is it surprising that Peter also gives Jesus as an example of nonretaliatory faithfulness in his instructions

---

65. Cf. C. S. Lewis, *The Abolition of Man, or, Reflections on Education with Special Reference to the Teaching of English in the Upper Forms of Schools* (New York: Macmillan, 1955), especially the appendix.

66. See Seneca's *Moral Epistles* 2, 9, and 90.

67. See Martha C. Nussbaum, *The Therapy of Desire: Theory and Practice in Hellenistic Ethics*, Martin Classical Lectures (Princeton: Princeton University Press, 1994), 359–401.

to Christian communities suffering various injustices for their faith (1 Pet. 2:21–25).[68]

In these examples, early Christian authors not only ground works in faith, in the sense that genuine works are born from a disposition of faith, but also ground works in faith by establishing the internal logic of moral actions in fundamental Christian convictions. So NT texts, as wisdom, give "theology" to contextualize "ethics."[69] The NT's eschatological worldview[70] gives ideational context (right reasons) for moral actions grounded in a picture of reality in which just moral actions have significance in a world dominated by injustice but already showing signs of its final restitution (cf. 1 John 2:8). At the same time this worldview gives affective motivations (right motivation) rooted in Christian virtues of reverence and gratitude, responding to the benevolent rule of God revealed in Christ. This faith that recognizes the actions of divine rule cannot be trapped in its own dispositions but must find expression in concrete actions.[71] In these ways theological reflection renders certain moral virtues and actions intelligible and desirable.

New Testament authors are confronting competing ethical systems and therefore often speak in the language of contrasting theological understandings that give rise to competing systems of justifying moral action (e.g., justification by faith versus works of the law). So the understanding and motivations that underlie actions are a central concern for NT authors like Paul. To read

---

68. See J. de Waal Dryden, *Theology and Ethics in 1 Peter: Paraenetic Strategies for Christian Character Formation*, WUNT 2/209 (Tübingen: Mohr Siebeck, 2006), 163–91.

69. Cf. Hays, *Moral Vision*, 18, "Paul is not simply repeating already formulated doctrines; rather he is theologizing as he writes, and the constant aim of his theological reflection is to shape the behavior of his churches. Theology for Paul is never a speculative exercise; it is always a tool for constructing community."

70. On worldview see Walter T. Wilson, *The Hope of Glory: Education and Exhortation in the Epistle to the Colossians*, NovTSup 88 (Leiden: Brill, 1997), 100. He describes it as

> a person's comprehensive and pre-reflective understanding of reality, an integrating frame-work of fundamental considerations which gives context, direction, and meaning to life in light of one's ultimate commitments. This is a particular way of looking at the world, of integrating different provinces of knowledge and experience into a symbolic totality, a symbolic universe. Functionally, this universe serves as a map of fact and value for a person, legitimating all roles, priorities, and institutions by situating them in the context of the broadest horizon of reference conceivable, bestowing meaning on all domains of life. In adopting the elements of a worldview cognitively and normatively, individuals are able to "locate" themselves; all of history and the entire biography of the individual are seen as events occurring in this world.

71. Cf. Schrage, *Ethics of the New Testament*, 187, "As is the case of Jesus, there is no room here for a mere outward obedience or observance of the letter, nor is there any room, however, for a spiritualization that would make Paul the proponent of an ethics of pure subjectivity. Overemphasis on intention . . . at the expense of obedience in the real world and shaping the Christian life in its corporeal dimension would be for Paul a wrong-headed spiritualization."

these "theological" discourses independently of their ethical concerns is an examination under artificial conditions inconceivable to the original authors. This type of approach, in which theological understanding is a self-sustaining enterprise independent of its concrete expression in the life of the community, produces a deeply skewed picture of the convictions of early Christianity. This fits well within a modern romantic/existentialist framework in which religion is understood primarily in terms of internal psychological experience, but it does not correlate with either ancient Judaism or early Christianity, in which the primary language of religion was ethics. All of these tensions can be illustrated in the history of the interpretation of the Christ hymn in Philippians 2.

Philippians 2

Few texts in the NT have generated as much scholarly interest as Philippians 2:5–11. Markus Bockmuehl labels it "one of the most over-interpreted texts of the New Testament."[72] As one of the christological "hymns" in the NT, it is of critical importance for the historical study of the early church's theological understanding of Jesus;[73] and most Pauline interpreters would agree that it is the theological keystone for the book of Philippians. Michael Gorman goes so far as to call it "Paul's Master Story," the integrating narrative for *all* his theology.[74] This text is also, of course, one of the key instances of the *imitatio Christi* motif in the NT.[75] Unfortunately, the volume of study this text has garnered has not produced definitive answers regarding its meaning and purpose; in fact, just the opposite. But understanding this text as wisdom can alleviate many of its key exegetical challenges.

On the level of basic observation, the context for the hymn is sanctification. Paul's emphasis on "working out salvation" and his extolling the primary virtues of humility and obedience make that clear enough. Also, Jesus is given as an exemplar, in some sense, of these same virtues, as one who laid aside his rightful claims to authority and status in order to serve others in

---

72. Markus Bockmuehl, "'The Form of God' (Phil. 2:6): Variations on a Theme of Jewish Mysticism," *JTS* 48, no. 1 (1997): 1.

73. See Ralph P. Martin and Brian J. Dodd, eds., *Where Christology Began: Essays on Philippians 2* (Louisville: Westminster John Knox, 1998). Cf. Gregory P. Fewster, "The Philippians 'Christ Hymn': Trends in Critical Scholarship," *CurBR* 13, no. 2 (2015): 191–206.

74. See Michael J. Gorman, "'Although/Because He Was in the Form of God': The Theological Significance of Paul's Master Story (Phil 2:6–11)," *JTI* 1, no. 2 (2007): 150; and Michael J. Gorman, *Apostle of the Crucified Lord: A Theological Introduction to Paul and His Letters* (Grand Rapids: Eerdmans, 2004), 98–113.

75. In chap. 6 we will see that *imitatio Christi* texts are an example of a typical strategy associated with paraenetic epistles—the use of moral exemplars.

obedience to the will of God. The correspondence of the key term "humility" (ταπεινοφροσύνη), found both in the "hymn" and in Paul's commands to the Philippians in the verses just prior (see 2:3 and 2:8), makes all this clear. But no matter how clear this may seem, Paul's use of Jesus as an exemplar has been a contentious question in the modern interpretation of this text—the key figure in the history of this debate being Ernst Käsemann.[76]

Käsemann objected to the possibility of Jesus acting as an exemplar, chiefly on the grounds that this text points to actions that are particular to the person and vocation of Jesus himself. No Christian can be called to renounce his divinity, and certainly no Christian will be exalted "above all other names" as a reward for obedience.[77] These actions and honors belong to Jesus alone and therefore cannot serve as an ethical model for believers to emulate. As he argues, "The divine act at the enthronement of Christ shows that the action of him who was obedient on earth affects the whole world and is a salvation-event; it shows that this obedience was more than an ethical deed on the part of an individual, it was revelation."[78] But, we might ask, if the obedience of Jesus is "more than an ethical deed on the part of an individual," doesn't that mean that it was not less than an "ethical deed" that could be imitated at some level, even if it does not produce the same effects as the once-for-all obedience of Jesus? Isn't Käsemann throwing out the baby with the bathwater? To most contemporary interpreters Käsemann's rejection of imitation seems like an overcorrection.[79] While this is likely the case, for the interpretation of this text it is important to understand *how* he got to the place that he did.

There are two key theological considerations that lie behind Käsemann's exegesis. The first is his rejection of the Jesus of German Protestant liberalism, understood primarily as a moral teacher and exemplar who just happened to endorse the bourgeois ethics of German Protestant liberals.[80] This theological tradition understands Jesus through a bifurcated Nestorian Christology[81] where the human part of Jesus was the "historical" Jesus, an itinerant

76. In his famous article: "Kritische Analyse von Phil. 2, 5–11," *ZTK* 47 (1950): 313–60.

77. On the latter point Käsemann argues, "The statements concerning the exaltation have no paraenetic reference and are 'an unwarranted plus' in the present context. . . . If the conclusion lacks any paraenetic reference, then the passage as a whole can hardly be interpreted in terms of the ethical example." Ernst Käsemann, "A Critical Analysis of Philippians 2:5–11," *JTC* 5 (1968): 53.

78. Käsemann, "Analysis," 77.

79. E.g., Hays, *Moral Vision*, 30.

80. E.g., Ritschl and von Harnack. See Alister E. McGrath, *The Making of Modern German Christology: From the Enlightenment to Pannenberg*, 2nd ed. (Grand Rapids: Zondervan, 1994), 76–98.

81. Not simply, as it is often characterized, a low Christology, which denies the divinity of Jesus. It accepts the divinity of Jesus, but only as the Christ.

prophet who taught and exemplified a simple ethic of love for others.[82] At the same time, this tradition also worships Jesus as the divine Christ, although this Christ has little, if any, connection to the historical Jesus. So in his corrective against the liberal domestication of Jesus as an exemplar of humility, Käsemann is actually only rejecting one-half of this liberal Nestorianism and opting for the other side of this theological tradition, the divine Christ. This Christ is purely divine and not human, and so nothing of his life and actions is imitable on a human scale. This is what leads Käsemann to the conclusion that "No ethical model is posited."[83]

The other theological reason for Käsemann's rejection of the ethical imitation interpretation is his commitment to the paradigm of indicative and imperative, which he views as determinative for Paul's thought. As he says, "the typical Pauline scheme of paraenesis . . . deduces the imperative from the indicative, and thus Christian conduct from the act of salvation." We have met this paradigm above and seen its roots in the antithesis between being and doing dominant in Western thought forms. Because he understands the hymn as "a portrayal of the salvation-event," it belongs to the realm of the indicative and therefore "serves as the basis for the Christian's condition."[84] Because it is "indicative" it can only serve as a *foundation for* the imperative, not an imperative itself. Käsemann's problem with the ethical-imitation interpretation is that it takes the hymn as imperative. On this basis he concludes that "without doubt . . . Paul did not understand the hymn as though Christ were held up to the community as an ethical example."[85] As we saw above, there are serious reasons to question the model of indicative and imperative, especially as something either typical of or determinative for Paul's thought.

Käsemann's interpretation has not fared well over the years; few today would endorse his denial of *any* ethical imitation element in Paul's discourse here. But his questions are still important because, even though his interpretation has fallen out of favor, the fundamental tensions that he pointed to have never really been resolved; they have simply been ignored. The most obvious example of this is the number of interpreters who continue to deal with this passage as a piece of Christology (i.e., theologically) completely divorced from its paraenetic intentions, as though those intentions did not shape the content

82. While still a popular understanding in some circles, the scholarly demise of this "Jesus" began in the works of Johannes Weiss and Albert Schweitzer, both of whom recognized Jesus as an eschatological prophet of judgment, who understood the establishment of the kingdom of God as an apocalyptic event.

83. Käsemann, "Analysis," 88.

84. All quotes from Käsemann, "Analysis," 84.

85. Käsemann, "Analysis," 84.

of Paul's discourse, focusing on what Paul *said*, not what he was *doing*.[86] In this way the paradigm of indicative and imperative is still in effect, if only implicitly.[87] Even those who want to give a space to Paul's formative agenda struggle to know what in this passage is christological (theological indicative) and what is exemplary (ethical imperative). Sometimes this is solved by carving up the passage such that some verses go in the indicative basket and some go in the imperative basket. The other option is to read the text first christologically and then second ethically in two complementary but distinct iterations.

So what should our approach to this text look like? First, our expectation here, as elsewhere in Paul and the other NT epistles, is that theological discourse functions paraenetically to give reasons and motivations for moral action; that is to say, it functions as wisdom. This is not to deny the benefit or propriety of the careful theological study of rich christological texts such as this one and the others, including especially the hymn in Colossians 1:15–20. But we must recognize this as a second-order exercise, which helps us construct something not found explicitly in the Pauline corpus: a Pauline Christology.[88] This is in fact a vital and necessary theological exercise, but we must not mistake it for exegesis. Our construct of Paul's Christology tells us very little about the actual texts of Philippians or Colossians and what Paul is doing in writing to those congregations. To do exegesis our primary interest is in how Paul *uses* his Christology, to what end, not simply the questions of what that Christology is.[89]

So in Philippians 2 the first question we should ask about this text, and here Käsemann's instinct is correct, is, What exactly is Jesus an exemplar of? In this highly compressed outline of the incarnation, life, death, and resurrection/exaltation of Jesus that Paul narrates, what parts are for imitation? All of them, or only a few? How are we meant to decide? Käsemann's answer was that these events are the saving actions of Christ and belong only to him. Hays notes two fundamental problems with Käsemann's approach: First, it "fails to

86. This has been an unfortunate by-product of the presupposition of a pre-Pauline hymn that was appropriated by Paul. This has made it very easy to divorce the content of this "hymn" from both Paul and the context of the passage and to explore it as an independent piece of tradition.

87. The fine study by Gorman is a good example. It discusses the passage in detail and draws important theological implications from it about the "kenotic" nature of God. But it never draws any ethical implications from the text.

88. There can be little doubt that Paul has a Christology. The question is whether Paul ever sets out to give us what we could properly label a Christology—as a set of doctrinal affirmations isolated from any particular contextualization of those truths.

89. The latter question is one of the questions of central importance in the history of NT interpretation. The primary historical question in NT criticism is the form and genesis of NT Christology. Paul's writings, as the earliest witnesses to the early church's Christology, are the primary source for addressing those questions. Those questions remain vitally important, but they are not exegesis.

account for the function of the hymn in its context." Obviously Paul intends *some* correspondence between the humility he extols in the Philippians and the humility shown by Jesus in his incarnational vocation. Second, the model of imitation that Käsemann debunks assumes a "rigid notion of one-to-one correspondence between exemplar and imitator." Instead Hays argues for a "more supple notion of metaphorical correspondence," where "dissimilarities between Christ and his people are to be expected."[90] This approach is moving in the right direction but actually suffers from liabilities that are the mirror image of Käsemann's. While Käsemann found the saving actions of Christ inimitable because of their very nature, Hays makes them imitable by taking them as participatory metaphors, not saving events. As he says, "Paul offers a metaphorical reading of Christ's self-emptying and death."[91]

In reality the answer to the question of what is imitable is not as complex as it is often made out to be. When ancient writers utilize an individual as an exemplar of a particular virtue, they always specify what virtue they have in mind. In addition, and this is key, what is exemplary is always *dispositional*.[92] It is not actions that are exemplified; it is virtue—a dispositional character trait. All of this corresponds exactly to what Paul does here. He commands the Philippians not only to abstain from certain actions but to adopt a disposition toward one another, an attitude of humility (ταπεινοφροσύνη). This disposition is translatable into innumerable circumstances and can be realized in innumerable contextualized actions. Christ can display it in one realm, while the Philippian Christians can display it in another. So we can avoid Käsemann's dilemma about the nonrepeatability of Jesus's actions without having to take those actions in a "metaphorical" sense. Imitation happens at the level of dispositions/virtues. That is why Paul commands his readers to adopt a certain mode of thought (φρονεῖτε) "which was also in Christ Jesus" (2:5 KJV). So in terms of our Right ARM rubric, the right action prescribed here is humility (remembering that the category of right action can include virtues).

The hymn itself will supply the reasons and motivations to adopt this virtue of humility, which is so counterintuitive in a very Roman city such as Philippi.[93] To counteract this, Paul will point to Jesus himself as an example of humility, not simply as a blueprint to follow but in a way that makes the

90. Hays, *Moral Vision*, 30.

91. Hays, *Moral Vision*, 30. What exactly Hays means by "metaphorical" is not transparent but is likely connected to his excellent discussion on "moral judgement as metaphor-making" (298–304) as the central element in the art of application.

92. See Dryden, *Theology and Ethics*, 169–72.

93. The Christian virtue of humility was very nearly a vice in the Roman world, where personal honor and status were the key virtues for navigating Roman culture.

call to humility intelligible and attractive. As Webster argues: "Intrinsic to the Christological narrative is its function in forming Christian vision and identity, making him into a self with particular beliefs and dispositions which give direction to the moral life in choice and action."[94] So we are looking for what in the hymn shapes Christian "vision and identity" and how Paul imparts "particular beliefs and dispositions which give direction to the moral life."

First, Paul uses the example of Jesus to make the virtue of humility intelligible.[95] He does this by pointing to Jesus as the one with all authority, power, glory, and status, who laid that aside in order to become a servant. Paul makes humility a reasonable reality in pointing to Jesus as the God who chose to humble himself, "not count[ing] equality with God a thing to be grasped." This is the center of the narrative that projects a moral vision of the world governed by the actions of Jesus as the ruler of all and source of salvation. But his humbling action is not intelligible unless we have some insight into *why* he humbled himself. The answer comes in his putting aside "the form of God" and taking on "the form of a servant." There are two senses in which Jesus becomes a servant. The first sense is in his vocation to seek the welfare of his people in serving them. This is a theme more prominent in the Gospels than in Paul,[96] summarized in Mark 10:45, "For even the Son of Man came not to be served but to serve, and to give his life as a ransom for many." So Jesus became a servant of his people, but his deeper motivation in that service is that he is a servant of God. Whether or not Paul sees any relevant connection to the OT *ebed Yahweh*, he clearly connects the humility of Jesus with his obedience to God in 2:8: "And being found in human form, he *humbled* himself by becoming *obedient* to the point of death, even death on a cross." So the intelligibility for Jesus's self-humiliation derives from his desire to serve his people in a way that serves their good and in the desire to obey the will of God. This intelligibility is translatable to the Philippian Christians in a way that is formative for their service toward one another in obedience to God.

In addition, Paul also wants to depict humility in a way that is attractive as a way of life; he does this by supplying affective motivations for actions. The first is gratitude. The actions that Paul alludes to in the hymn are the same actions that procured their salvation. Jesus humiliated himself and took

94. John B. Webster, "Christology, Imitability and Ethics," *SJT* 39 (1986): 311. See chap. 6 below.
95. Cf. Stephen Fowl, "Some Uses of Story in Moral Discourse: Reflections on Paul's Moral Discourse and Our Own," *Modern Theology* 4, no. 4 (1988): 298, "Here we will see that Paul's specific demands receive their intelligibility from the story of Christ narrated in 2:6–11."
96. Those who deny the presence of this motif in the Christology of Paul fail to recognize that Paul's own service as a slave to Christ is the primary element in how he himself is an imitator of Christ and in this becomes worthy of imitation himself.

on the form of servant *for them*, and so their gratitude and love for Jesus is elicited as a driving motivation for humility. The reception of a great gift inspires acts guided by gratitude. The next motivation is admiration for the person of Jesus, which elicits emulation. The scope of the work of Jesus, the intensity of his self-resignation and humiliation combined with his steadfast pursuit of the will of God, engenders admiration, once again mixed with love and gratitude. Finally, the adoration of Jesus as Lord is a driving motivation for imitation and obedience. This is the main thrust of verses 9–11, which describe Jesus's exaltation over every other name or power. Käsemann is certainly correct that these verses are not part of what is imitable about Jesus, especially since the subject of the verbs changes from Jesus to God.[97] Paul inspires imitation by inspiring worship of Jesus as the exalted obedient one who is the source of salvation. In all these ways Paul seeks to overcome what would be a natural human distaste for humility, especially in Philippi. This retraining of affections is an essential element in how wisdom texts function in spiritual formation, not only prescribing changes in behavior but remolding the commitments and attachments that drive moral actions.

Conclusion

Application is something inherent in the nature of the Bible as wisdom and, therefore, equally inherent in the act of reading it. It is important to recognize that part of *our* historically conditioned reading of the text is determined by a long history of a theoretical division between being and action, and that this division translates into a tradition of exegetical practices that bifurcate theology and ethics, indicative and imperative, and understanding and application.

To read the Bible as wisdom for spiritual formation, it is necessary to begin to move outside these traditions and to recognize the illocutionary intentionality of the biblical text, which seeks to shape human communities in their historical concreteness, in obedient response to the grace of God. The separation of being and doing, with its roots in Athenian theology, fundamentally impedes the recognition and appropriation of the Bible as wisdom. As seen in the parable of the sower, Jesus teaches us that hearing the word is a singular act of hearing, accepting, and doing.

97. Some interpreters have tried to include these verses as in some way paradigmatic for the Philippians. Usually this maps the notion of vindication onto both Jesus and the community (e.g., Hays and Fowl). The major problem with this proposal is that vindication is not a theme present in the hymn. Vindication presupposes accusation or condemnation, neither of which is present in the text.

3

LAW AND GOSPEL

In our final chapter of "tilling the soil" for a wisdom hermeneutic we will need to attend to a common theological heritage that, to some extent, shapes all Protestant readers of the Bible. Our central question will be how to relate theological and biblical elements of law (especially the commandments that prescribe certain actions and duties for the people of God) to elements of gospel (the gracious promises of salvation for God's people). Are they antithetical or complementary, irreconcilable or intimately interconnected? There are many passages in the NT, particularly in Paul, that pit law and gospel against each other in absolute antithesis, and these passages have been critical to the Protestant (especially Lutheran) tradition.

But if we take law and gospel as irreconcilable, then we are left with the insurmountable question of how the NT actually shapes and directs human agency. In this way a strong dichotomy between law and gospel directly undercuts the function of the Bible as wisdom in its impetus to shape human agency in terms of devotions, convictions, and actions.

Faith versus Works

In Galatians 2:16 Paul states that "we know that a person is not justified by works of the law but through faith in Jesus Christ, so we also have believed in Christ Jesus, in order to be justified by faith in Christ and not by works of the law, because by works of the law no one will be justified." In this well-known statement, echoed elsewhere in his writings, Paul draws an antithesis between two means of justification—one by faith and the other by works of the law—and emphatically closes the door on the latter. Justification, understood as an eschatological acquittal from God, comes through faith, "apart from the law" (Rom. 3:21).[1]

The importance of this verse for Luther and the subsequent history of Protestantism is a well-rehearsed subject. The antithesis between works and faith became the bedrock for Luther's understanding of Paul's gospel, in which the sinner is freely justified before God not on the basis of good works but rather on the basis of the imputed righteousness of Christ received by faith. Luther formulated this antithesis of faith and works in the language of law and gospel.[2] In the context of justification, Luther saw law and gospel as two warring opponents, vying for dominion, one over the other. There is no place for collaboration between faith and works, no space for a synergistic compromise of faith proving itself in works. As Luther says: "The Law and the Gospel are two altogether contrary doctrines. . . . For the Law is a taskmaster; it demands that we work and we give. In short, it wants to have something from us. The Gospel, on the contrary, does not demand; it grants freely; it commands us to hold out our hands and to receive what is being offered. Now demanding and granting, receiving and offering, are exact opposites and cannot exist together."[3]

In Luther's reading of Paul, the fundamental touchstone for the doctrine for justification is the distinction between law and gospel, of faith and works as antithetical means for obtaining justification. For Luther, the loss of this distinction necessarily entails a misconstrual of salvation at its foundation. There can be no proper understanding of faith and works that sees them in any way as complementary. In the words of Luther, they are "exact opposites and cannot exist together." In his day, this naturally led to the accusation of antinomianism—of teaching a grace that provides no moral boundaries and makes no moral demands—and it is a charge that has haunted the history of Protestantism since.

---

1. Readers sensitive to discussions about the New Perspective on Paul will notice that I have treated "works of the law" and "law" somewhat indiscriminately. The first justification for this is that, in its context, "law" in Rom. 3:21a is a condensed shorthand reference to the "works of the law" in the previous verse (cf. Thomas R. Schreiner, *Romans*, BECNT [Grand Rapids: Baker Academic, 1998], 180). Second, Dunn has made it clear in his refinements of his arguments about "works of the law" that these works do not refer *exclusively* to the ceremonial boundary markers of Israel but through those markers reference the law in its entirety. See James D. G. Dunn, *The New Perspective on Paul*, rev. ed. (Grand Rapids: Eerdmans, 2005), 213–17.

2. Cf. Oswald Bayer, *Martin Luther's Theology: A Contemporary Interpretation*, trans. Thomas H. Trapp (Grand Rapids: Eerdmans, 2008), 58–62.

3. Martin Luther, *Lectures on Galatians 1535: Chapters 1–4*, trans. Jaroslav Pelikan, Luther's Works 26 (St. Louis: Concordia, 1963), 208.

Luther, while characteristically skewering his "papist" critics, vehemently denied this charge of antinomianism. He taught that good works were a necessary element in the life of the Christian, even going so far as to say, "faith without works . . . is a false faith and does not justify."[4] In the sphere of justification, works have no place. But when we begin to talk about what follows justification, namely sanctification, then good works become operative and in fact necessary. Again Luther:

> Therefore we conclude with Paul that we are justified solely by faith in Christ, without the Law and works. But after a man is justified by faith, now possesses Christ by faith, and knows that He is his righteousness and life, he will certainly not be idle but, like a sound tree, will bear good fruit (Matt. 7:17). For the believer has the Holy Spirit; and where He is, He does not permit a man to be idle but drives him to all the exercises of devotion, to the love of God, to patience in affliction, to prayer, to thanksgiving, and to the practice of love toward all men.[5]

So while Luther teaches that works play no part in justification, he escapes the charge of antinomianism by pointing to the presence of the Spirit producing sanctifying acts of charity and devotion. These works are unlike attempts to gain merit because they follow from the justifying declaration of God and are works actualized by the Holy Spirit.

But here we have to recognize a profound and irreconcilable tension in Luther's conceptions of justification and sanctification. In the context of justification, faith and works are absolutely *antithetical*, but when we move to sanctification faith and works are *complementary*, and faith is necessarily expressed in works. It seems that justification and sanctification operate on irreconcilable principles. Works are absolutely forbidden in one sphere but absolutely necessary in the other. This created in Luther's theology an unstable tension between justification and sanctification, which has led to deep ambivalence about the proper place of good works in subsequent Protestant theological development.[6]

---

4. Luther, *Lectures on Galatians*, 155. This statement is startling in its close correspondence to James 2:24, which Luther argued was the death knell for James's canonicity. See John Dillenberger, ed., *Martin Luther: Selections from His Writings* (Garden City, NY: Doubleday, 1961), 35, "In direct opposition to St. Paul and all the rest of the Bible, it [i.e., James] ascribes justification to works, and declares that Abraham was justified by his works when he offered up his son. . . . This defect proves that the epistle is not of apostolic provenance."

5. Luther, *Lectures on Galatians*, 154–55.

6. As O'Donovan says, "The Lutheran tradition, which of all theological traditions has most strongly cherished the Pauline dialectic of law and gospel, has usually found it difficult to accept that an ordered moral demand can be, in and of itself, evangelical." Oliver O'Donovan,

Because the cornerstone of Luther's reformational insight was justification, the weight of his theology, along with that of his theological progeny, habitually leans in the direction of the *antithesis* of faith and works as the most basic principle of the Christian gospel. This had the effect of undermining (without completely eliminating) a proper constructive relationship between faith and works in sanctification. Subsequent generations of Protestants inherited an ambiguous understanding of the connection between faith and works and an ambivalent relationship to both "works" and "law."[7] Protestants are habitually suspicious of works as dangerous—a legalistic Trojan horse in need of our vigilant circumspection—but only mildly suspicious of faith per se and its real potential to produce what Bonhoeffer rightly labeled "cheap grace," forgiveness without repentance.[8] This simply reveals that our more basic operating principle is a belief in a faith that excludes works (to which we have added a secondary principle that faith reveals itself in works). To understand exactly why, we have to look at the place of justification in our theological understanding, and this leads us into an old question in Pauline studies: What is at the center of Paul's theology?

The Center of Paul's Theology

This question of the center of Paul's theology was once a hotly debated topic, but in scholarly circles, especially since Heikki Räisänen,[9] this question has become something of a behemoth crushed under its own weight, and very few would dare to propose an answer to the question today for fear of accusations of scholarly hubris. At the same time, this question is, in reality, an unavoidable necessity in trying to understand Paul. Any reader of Paul has to make choices about what integrates his thought, and that choice is

---

Resurrection and Moral Order: An Outline for Evangelical Ethics (Grand Rapids: Eerdmans, 1986), 153.

7. One contemporary example of this ambivalence can be seen in the NIV's difficulty in translating the phrase ἔργον ἀγαθόν (good work). Consistently in 1 Timothy (2:10; 5:10, 25; 6:18) it uses the phrase "good deed." Less defensible is the translation of "doing what is good" in Titus 2:14; 3:1, 8, 14. This translation practice, clearly not simply a choice of stylistic variation, reveals a deep-seated discomfort with a positive connotation given to "works."

8. See Dietrich Bonhoeffer, *Discipleship*, trans. Barbara Green and Reinhard Krauss, Dietrich Bonhoeffer Works 4 (Minneapolis: Fortress, 2001), 43–56. In promoting an understanding of "costly grace," Bonhoeffer was exposing the dangers present in an institutionalized doctrine of "faith" that guarantees justification without any call to obedience.

9. See Heikki Räisänen, *Paul and the Law* (Philadelphia: Fortress, 1986). Whether one agrees with him or not, after Räisänen it became much more difficult to argue that Paul was a coherent theologian.

an answer to the question of the center of Paul's theology, whether we give it that label or not.[10]

Now, to be more precise, when we ask this question we are really asking: What is the center of Paul's *soteriology*? (The center of Paul's theology is God, the covenant God of Israel as revealed in the person of Jesus Christ.) The real problem with interpreting Paul comes in trying to integrate the multiple images that he uses in his discussions of salvation: justification, redemption, adoption, regeneration, glorification, sanctification, election, dying with Christ, and others. How are all these related? Are they different monikers for the same reality? Do they relate to each other temporally in an *ordo salutis* or some other scheme? And finally, the big question: Which one is most important in Paul's thought? While we might want to skip this question, in practice it is unavoidable. Every attempt to integrate Paul's soteriology automatically picks an integrating hub for his diverse descriptions of salvation. That doctrine, whether we want it to or not, functionally becomes our center for Paul's soteriology.

The modern history of Pauline scholarship, when it has addressed this question openly, has oscillated between two answers: (1) justification or (2) some kind of participatory union with Christ. (Interestingly, these were the same two options that the Reformers produced—for Luther justification, for Calvin union with Christ.) At this point, the question of which one is preferable is not our focus.[11] What is important to see is that *whatever we choose as the center of Paul's soteriology becomes an integrating concept that we will use to interpret all the other aspects of salvation.* So if we choose justification as Paul's central way of thinking of salvation, then we are not simply placing it at the head of a hierarchy but we are giving it an integrative function within our systematic reflection on soteriology. All our soteriology will be filtered through justification in some way. It would be the same if we chose another option such as election or union with Christ.

So, in the Protestant tradition, which has on the whole taken justification as the touchstone for understanding Paul, the defining characteristic of salvation has been the justification principle of faith versus works. This is the source of

10. E.g., Douglas A. Campbell, *The Deliverance of God: An Apocalyptic Rereading of Justification in Paul* (Grand Rapids: Eerdmans, 2009). Even though Campbell supplies a radical "rereading" of justification, he is still working from the premise that his apocalyptic participationist reading is the integrative key to understanding Paul correctly.

11. I will admit, however, that I think union with Christ is far preferable, both in terms of understanding Paul as well as the practical theological question being addressed in this chapter. See Grant Macaskill, *Union with Christ in the New Testament* (Oxford: Oxford University Press, 2013); and J. Todd Billings, *Union with Christ: Reframing Theology and Ministry for the Church* (Grand Rapids: Baker Academic, 2011).

the inherent tension between justification and sanctification in the Protestant tradition. It is not simply that justification and sanctification operate on different principles. The real problem is that sanctification has been interpreted *through* justification, and so the justification principle of the antithesis between faith and works is suppressing the necessity of the link between faith and works in sanctification and sustaining a suspicion of nascent legalism in all works. This tension is *inherent* in the prioritization of justification. No amount of corrective teaching on sanctification can eliminate it.[12]

In thinking about a hermeneutic of wisdom, this ambiguity about faith and works is a fundamental stumbling block to our understanding. If the Bible is wisdom, then it aims to inculcate both faith and action in a unified human agency. A framework that pits faith and works against each other at some fundamental level will automatically disrupt our apprehension of the Bible as wisdom. If our theology is perpetually deconstructing the legitimacy of human agency per se, then it is also undermining the function of the Bible as a wisdom text that is designed to inculcate certain devotions, actions, and virtues.

The Righteousness of God

The solution to this problem does not lie in some middle ground between legalism and antinomianism or in a "proper balance" of faith and works. The question of faith and works is a question about the gospel itself, not a question about what we can add to the gospel or how much holiness we can legitimately add to it before it becomes "legalistic." Such conceptions witness to a persistent assumption of the incommensurability of faith and works.

But for the writers of the NT the message of the gospel is at the same time both gift and call, because the nature of the gift connects the people of God to his saving righteousness.[13] For them the gospel reveals and establishes

12. This is an unforeseen but inevitable consequence of placing justification at the center of our understanding of Christian soteriology; it will always destabilize our understanding of sanctification, and especially the rightful place of good works, whether we want it to or not. It also defines justification and sanctification according to incommensurable principles, which severs the necessary linkage between them, and then promotes acts of obedience severed from gospel motivations.

13. As John Barclay has argued so persuasively, reciprocal responsibilities are inherent in the ancient understanding of the grace of God as gift. See John M. G. Barclay, *Paul and the Gift* (Grand Rapids: Eerdmans, 2015). While it seems almost criminal to find fault in a work that evidences so much insight, if there is a weakness in Barclay's overall argument it is an overreliance on a general anthropology of gift. For Paul it is the nature of the gift (not gifting per se) that defines the responsibilities and shape of redeemed human agency in Christ. Paul's

God's eschatological righteousness in his people. The gospel makes a path for righteousness to be realized in the new humanity created in God's image in Christ (see Eph. 4:24), to embody what Paul calls "the obedience of faith" (Rom. 1:5). Commenting on this phrase Adolf Schlatter argues:

> That which the message [of the gospel] is to produce, and does produce is the obedience of faith (*hypakoē pisteōs*), cf. 16:26. Faith is what the message expects from and generates in the hearer, since this message is declared in the name of God and shows the hearer who the Lord is, this faith denotes the surrender of the will to him and the readiness to act on his command. *Paul did not separate the acceptance of the message and the decision of obedience*; both belong to one and the same act of the will. . . . A gap between faith and obedience occurs only when the message of God is replaced with a doctrine of God.[14]

Schlatter rightly recognizes that the call of the gospel entails a response of faith in which the will of the believer is reoriented in obedient submission to God. This insight is based on the nature of faith itself and the nature of its object. First, faith is not a self-generative act of the will whereby it finds in itself a source of deliverance. Rather, faith is a response produced by the gospel as the message that reveals the rule of God present in judgment and salvation (Rom. 1:16–18). The threat and promise of the coming of the kingdom, focused in the person of Jesus, produce the free response of faith that embraces the salvific gift of the kingdom. Faith is a response produced by the presence of the call of God. Second, faith is defined by its object, the ruling glorified Jesus.[15] Faith attaches itself to the saving rule of God revealed in the person of Jesus and established in his resurrection. Intrinsic to this act is a comportment of reverence and worship with an expectation of commands to be followed. Both the disposition and expectation come from a recognition of the authority of God to rule and his righteousness that stands over against all evil, including that which infiltrates the life of the community and the individual believer. So, of necessity the gospel of God calls for repentance, both once and continually, because the gospel is the instrument of Christ's

---

understanding of the responsibilities entailed in the gracious election of God owes more to his Jewish covenantal theology than to the principles governing benefaction.

14. Adolf Schlatter, *Romans: The Righteousness of God*, trans. Siegfried S. Schatzmann (Peabody, MA: Hendrickson, 1995), 11. Italics added.

15. Cf. Wolfgang Schrage, *The Ethics of the New Testament*, trans. David E. Green (Philadelphia: Fortress, 1988), 172, "Jesus' liberating lordship is the beginning and the end of Christian life and Christian ethics. The sovereignty of Jesus Christ is nothing else than the sovereignty of God's saving righteousness, manifested in Jesus Christ 'so that in him we might become the righteousness of God' (2 Cor. 5:21; cf. 1 Cor. 1:30; Rom. 3:21ff.)."

rule whereby he expresses and establishes his righteousness before the world and in his people.

Schlatter first introduced to modern discussion the theocentric interpretation of Romans 1:16–17, in which the gospel is understood not simply as the revelation of an imputed righteousness *from* God but primarily as the revelation of the righteousness *of* God (i.e., his righteous rule that brings about the salvation and righteous ordering of his creation and his people in faithfulness to his covenantal promises).[16] The gospel turns out to be about God and his righteousness, where righteousness refers not simply to an abstract attribute of God but to his righteous actions, which manifest his righteousness in the new community, justified and empowered to embody the mercy and justice of God. Schlatter saw this reality obscured by the Reformation's sometimes myopic interest in personal justification. Commenting on Romans 1:16–17, he argues that

> *the distance between the interpretation of the Reformation and the text resulted from the exclusive desire to hear what the believer was to receive. . . .*
> The reader's need gave the impetus to what Paul was supposed to have said in fulfillment of his longing. By contrast, Paul expresses how God reveals himself to the individual as one who saves him. The interpreter began with his own self while Paul began with God; the interpreter's protasis was his own dilemma, whereas Paul's was that of the mission of Christ, his death, by means of which the indebtedness of humankind is removed, as well as his lordship that will render him the giver of life for them.[17]

While rejecting neither the truth nor importance of the sinner's need for justification, Schlatter demonstrates how this focus of the Reformers skewed

---

16. English translations translate δικαιοσύνη θεοῦ (Rom. 1:17; 3:21, 22) as either (1) "righteousness from God" or (2) "righteousness of God." The first option takes the genitival construction as a genitive of source, or possibly what Wallace terms a "genitive of production" (s.v., Daniel B. Wallace, *Greek Grammar beyond the Basics: An Exegetical Syntax of the New Testament* [Grand Rapids: Zondervan, 1996], 104–6), which denotes the righteousness that God gives (imputes) to the believer. The second option understands the construction as a subjective genitive, which stresses the verbal idea of God's power to manifest his righteousness through his eschatological works of judgment and redemption. The gospel not only reveals God's righteousness in the sense of revealing that he is righteous and just and faithful but it also denotes the righteous rule of God, which brings about the restoration (rightwising) of his creation. This includes the restoration of the people of God and so also includes something of the idea of the first option in that the one who believes is brought into a right standing with God (i.e., justified; cf. Peter Stuhlmacher, *Paul's Letter to the Romans: A Commentary*, trans. Scott J. Hafemann [Edinburgh: T&T Clark, 1994], 31–32.) The second line of interpretation, first proposed by Schlatter and subsequently stoked and refined in the fires of Tübingen by Michel, Käsemann, and Stuhlmacher, has gained increasing acceptance as an interpretive touchstone that integrates the various agendas of Paul in Romans (cf. Schreiner, *Romans*, 63–76).

17. Schlatter, *Righteousness of God*, 22. Italics added.

their reading of Paul and their understanding of his priorities. Paul's focus was bearing witness to the restorative righteousness of God demonstrated in the life, death, and resurrection of Christ. Schlatter goes on to describe the detrimental effects this produced in the church's understanding and practice:

> Since the sinner was assured forgiveness via the statement that the righteousness prepared for us by God is the saving power, he brought about the comfort needed by the one who is indebted. However, when Luther and Calvin express how the fellowship of God with humanity came to pass, *God's righteousness all but fades away and is replaced by God's mercy*. The assertion that it is God's mercy that grants fellowship with him expressed that it is our exigency which leads God to us. This assertion is still closely related to synergism, for God's relationship to us now arises from what the person is, . . . from his sin and his misery. For Paul God's work arises from God's work.[18]

Schlatter highlights two related consequences of this distorted emphasis. The first is the bifurcation of the righteousness and mercy of God, since it is only the mercy of God that is operative in salvation. The righteousness of God is that which condemns the sinner (law), while mercy accepts (gospel).[19] The result is that the sinner is brought into relationship with God's mercy but not his righteousness. This, again, results in an inherent implausibility to any instinct to manifest God's righteousness in moral action. Schlatter's argument is that for Paul the "saving righteousness" of God is what becomes manifest in the gospel proclamation. We are not saved *from* the righteousness of God but *by* the righteousness of God.

The second consequence Schlatter notes is the implicit "synergism" involved when God's work is said to arise from our need, while his righteousness is at best a passive force in the divine economy. By definition, mercy can only come alive in the context of need. Righteousness can be active in a world of perfect goodness and satisfaction, in acts that arise from the joy of righteousness itself. By defining God's salvific work as solely an act of his mercy, this interpretation placed the impetus for that act in the sinful condition of humanity. In contrast, Schlatter argues that Paul sees God's work of salvation as an act of his righteousness, born from his desire to reveal and communicate his righteousness to his creation.[20]

---

18. Schlatter, *Righteousness of God*, 22. Italics added.

19. This often translates (unconsciously or explicitly) into a heterodox location of divine righteousness in God the Father and divine mercy in the Son.

20. "Communicate" used here in a somewhat old-fashioned sense that denotes the transmission of a gift or substance as an act of relational communion.

What this means in the end is that the gospel communicates God's righteousness to his people and connects them to that same righteousness. The gospel reveals God's righteousness, which means his goodness that excludes evil intentions and actions as well as his faithfulness to his promises.[21] Thus to enter into fellowship with God through the promises of the gospel brings one into relationship with both his mercy and his righteousness. So faith is not only that which gains access through mercy but also that which answers the call of obedience that entails a self-denying attachment to righteousness.[22] The message of the kingdom of God is both a gift and a call, because God himself is at once gracious and just, merciful and righteous.

The Fulfillment of the Law

This means that the gospel proclamation promises not only forgiveness but the redemption of human agency. So both faith and works are properly constitutive of the gospel. What the gospel brings into being is a new path to the fulfillment of the law, an obedience made possible through the work of Christ to establish a free communion with God that revitalizes human agency. This is Paul's point in Romans 8:3–4: "For God has done what the law, weakened by the flesh, could not do. By sending his own Son in the likeness of sinful flesh and for sin, he condemned sin in the flesh, in order that the righteous requirement of the law might be fulfilled in us, who walk not according to the flesh but according to the Spirit." Paul, echoing Romans 7, finds fault not with the law itself but with the flesh corrupted by sin. He describes the walk of the believing community as both "the fulfillment of the law" and as a direct fruit of the work of Christ. Paul is clearly not speaking of the imputed righteousness of Christ, since he connects this fulfillment of the law with those who "walk according to the Spirit." Later, in Romans 13:8–10, Paul gives a concrete example of this fulfillment in the demonstrations of love in the Roman churches that overcome temptations of self-righteousness, arrogance, racial prejudice, and social exclusivity.[23] From this it is clear that

21. Cf. K. L. Onesti and M. T. Brauch, "Righteousness, Righteousness of God," in *DPL*, 827–37.

22. Cf. Nicholas Wolterstorff, *Justice in Love*, Emory University Studies in Law and Religion (Grand Rapids: Eerdmans, 2011), 276, "To have faith in God is to trust in God and seek to obey him, it is fully to acknowledge God as who God is. In the words of Peter, it is to fear God and do justice."

23. While the traditional tripartite division of the law into moral, ceremonial, and civil is something of a historical imposition on the OT conceptions of law, in the NT, especially in the teachings of Jesus and Paul, these divisions are already operative if not explicitly labeled as such, chiefly through an emphasis on the internal motivations that the law itself implies and

Paul sees the fruit of the gospel not simply in the forgiven sinner but in the redemption of human agency.

Jesus himself uses the same language of fulfilling the law, most famously in Matthew 5:17, "Do not think that I have come to abolish the Law or the Prophets; I have not come to abolish them but to fulfill them." This verse is often read in a way that signals the abrogation of the law in its fulfillment by Jesus himself.[24] Jesus is certainly speaking about his own obedience as the fulfillment of the law, but the connection he draws for his followers is not of the law's abrogation but rather its continuing importance as a standard for communal life.[25] "Therefore whoever relaxes one of the least of these commandments and teaches others to do the same will be called least in the kingdom of heaven, but whoever does them and teaches them will be called great in the kingdom of heaven. For I tell you, unless your righteousness exceeds that of the scribes and Pharisees, you will never enter the kingdom of heaven" (5:19–20). Jesus, in the context of the Sermon on the Mount, is clearly not talking about an alien, imputed righteousness but concrete moral actions in conformity with the law that mark this community's participation in the kingdom of heaven.[26]

But how does this fulfillment of the law avoid the pitfalls of legalism and moralism? When does the pursuit of righteousness become the pursuit of self-justification? The answer lies in the motivations that give rise to moral action. Again, the issue is right action, right reason, and right motivation. The ethical question for the NT authors is not whether the church should perform good works; the question is how those works can be authentically connected to faith.

---

prescribes. So Jesus can summarize the law as love of God and neighbor (Mark 12:28–34). (To the degree that Jesus's interlocutor in this passage reflects a common Jewish understanding, this summary of the law should not be considered an altogether novel theological development on the part of Jesus. This elevation of the moral law was a natural development within ancient Judaism under the conditions of exile and the Diaspora, where much of the civil and sacrificial law could not be practically realized.) Equally Paul can speak of acts of charity among Roman Christians as a fulfillment of the law, since this attends to the intentionality of the law. At the same time, Paul is free to eschew fulfillment of ceremonial aspects of the law, most obviously circumcision.

24. Cf. David L. Turner, *Matthew*, BECNT (Grand Rapids: Baker Academic, 2008), 157–59. This is especially true at a popular level, but much less so among Matthean scholars.

25. Cf. John Nolland, *The Gospel of Matthew: A Commentary on the Greek Text*, NIGTC (Grand Rapids: Eerdmans, 2005), 219, "The fulfillment language represents a claim that Jesus' programmatic commitment, far from undercutting the role of the Law and the Prophets, is to enable God's people to live out the Law more effectively."

26. Cf. Donald A. Hagner, *Matthew 1–13*, WBC 33A (Dallas: Word, 1993), 109, "Jesus expects . . . a new and higher kind of righteousness that rests upon the presence of the eschatological kingdom he brings and that finds its definition in and content in his definitive and authoritative exposition of the law."

Although Luther struggled to connect justification and sanctification, he had a powerful insight when he labeled faith as "the first, highest, and most precious of all good works."[27] He meant two things by this. First, Christian obedience begins with the act of faith, what Paul labels the "obedience of faith" (Rom. 1:5). This primacy of faith means all Christian self-understanding originates in the act of self-effacing acceptance of the gift of God (an idea present in the blessing of the "poor in spirit" in Matt. 5:3).[28] Second, Luther means that all other moral actions derive their integrity and intelligibility from this faith.[29] Internal disposition and motivation are the primary spheres for judging actions. This focus on internal dispositions, however, does not mean that good intentions are valid on their own apart from concrete acts of justice and charity. It is when gospel righteousness is wedded to gospel convictions that the law is fulfilled in the people of God.[30] This connection is easy on paper but hard to realize in practice, so it needs some further development.

Antinomianism and Authenticity

So what is the proper relationship between faith and works? If we observe some common ways in which this question is answered wrongly, this will give us a context to develop a healthy understanding. There are four common modes of misunderstanding: antinomianism, authenticity, legalism, and moralism. The first two are a pair of ideas that emphasizes freedom from the external constraints of the law, while the second pair emphasizes the importance of works but in ways that short-circuit basic gospel convictions. All four have compelling elements to them; if they didn't, no one would practice them. All four are reactions against their opposing pair: antinomianism over against legalism, authenticity over against moralism.

Antinomianism begins with Luther's conviction, with respect to justification, that faith operates in contradistinction to works, or more precisely to the law (i.e., anti*nomos*). The second step is to adopt this idea as the interpretive

27. Martin Luther, "Treatise on Good Works," in *The Christian in Society*, Luther's Works 44 (Philadelphia: Fortress, 1966), 23.

28. Cf. Turner, *Matthew*, 149, "To be 'poor in spirit' is to acknowledge one's total dependence on God for everything, for righteousness . . . as well as sustenance." Ancient interpreters favored understanding "poverty of spirit" as humility before God, which includes the idea of dependence but also connotes reverence (see Manlio Simonetti, ed., *Matthew 1–13*, ACCSNT [Downers Grove, IL: InterVarsity, 2001], 80–81). Cf. Ulrich Luz, *Matthew 1–7: A Commentary*, trans. James E. Crouch, rev. ed., Hermeneia (Minneapolis: Fortress, 2007), 192–93.

29. Cf. Luther, "Good Works," 23–39.

30. See J. de Waal Dryden, "Revisiting Romans 7: Law, Self, and Spirit," *JSPL* 5, no. 1 (2015): 142–51.

key for *all of soteriology*. There is always a dichotomy between grace and law, faith and works. The law is something both fulfilled and abrogated, having little if any utility in, or demand on, the life of the Christian. Christ has set us free from the demands of the law. What is most compelling about this approach is its self-authenticating opposition to legalism (after all, who is *for* legalism?), which certainly finds some justification in the teachings of Paul and Jesus. Antinomianism highlights a central biblical conviction that salvation comes through the electing grace of God,[31] not through keeping rules to earn favor with God. What then is the place for good works? It is clear that the gospel gives gifts *and* makes demands, but how do we incorporate both?[32] Again, if we begin with the principle that faith excludes works, then any proposed union of the two will be excluded or inherently unstable. Antinomian sensibilities will be highly suspicious of the incorporation of good works as a cloaked form of legalism, where good works quickly turn into self-justifying deeds that engender thoughts of superior status over others and before God. While exposing this very real danger of tacit legalism, antinomianism fails to provide a context to understand the proper place for good works, or a proper continuing function for the law.

Antinomian readings of the Bible will interpret the demands of the gospel as the demands of the law, revealing to us our gross inadequacy and the vicious entanglements of our sinful natures, which render us incapable of meeting the demands of God's righteousness. Such readings are designed to bring us first to a conviction of our own inadequacy, and second to a place of faith and gratitude that embraces the free gift of God in Christ. (As we saw in the previous chapter, all readings intrinsically involve application.) The application of an antinomian reading is to drive the hearer to a point of appropriating forgiveness. This often takes the form of a four-step process. First, a biblical text, because of its nature as a wisdom text, demands that life be shaped around Christian convictions. Second, this demand cannot be implemented perfectly, which is a sign to us of our moral inadequacy and is meant to bring us to a place of conviction and awareness of our need. Third,

31. Sanders is correct to identify this as a central conviction common to Second Temple Judaism. It is still a historical question as to whether the religious practices of Israel adequately embodied this conviction. Cf. Robert H. Gundry, "Grace, Works, and Staying Saved in Paul," *Bib* 66 (1985): 5, "As historians of religion we want to know what was (as a matter of fact), not what should have been (as a matter of logical consistency)."

32. While some are deeply committed to the principle of an absolute antithesis between law and gospel as constitutive of a Christian hermeneutic, it is still a difficult operation to read the Gospel accounts and produce a Jesus who makes no demands on his disciples as an essential element of communion with him. Any hermeneutic forced to interpret the majority of Jesus's teachings as law and not gospel is fatally flawed from the start.

Jesus in his life of perfect obedience fulfilled this demand in our stead, so that we do not fall under condemnation because we have failed to do what is right. But instead, fourth, we are called to believe that the righteousness of Jesus has been imputed to us, and so with gratitude we enter into God's presence as sons and daughters, accepted through the sacrifice of Jesus. While this kind of reading highlights certain deep gospel truths, it also inadvertently constructs a barrier between the commands of Jesus and the believing community. It is therefore an incomplete reading that is good at reaffirming the forgiven status of the sinner but does nothing to connect that sinner to the promises of her redeemed moral agency or the pleasures of the love of God and neighbor, which the gospel demands, promises, and enables.

Authenticity,[33] as an approach to the question of faith and works, is a close cousin of antinomianism. While it shares many of the same convictions *for* faith and *against* legalism, it is more defined by its opposition to *moralism*. Authenticity bristles at moralism's call to duty—a moral call divorced from true convictions. Duty is interpreted as the call "to do what you don't want to do" and subsequently an infringement on personal integrity and authenticity. To be authentic is to act from the heart in action marked by spontaneity and emotional commitment. By definition, the idea of duty is antithetical to authenticity. (Unless I desire to do what duty calls me to do, but if I already desire to do it, then I do not need the prod of duty to help me.)

This idea of authenticity is rooted in modern Western romanticism and its reaction against reason's claim to describe reality without remainder. Romanticism rescued the human realms of emotion and artistic expression and their important witnesses to realities that transcended the quantifiable and the "reasonable." We live in a time that highly values authenticity and consequently is very sensitive to manipulation and power plays that coerce people into inauthentic action. What marks authenticity is its commitment to "passion" as the mark of genuine human agency.[34]

So, authenticity is going to eschew rules, laws, and commands that prescribe duties as unlikely candidates for fostering Christian maturity. In fact, they are just the opposite. Faith, in this context understood as descriptive of an inner emotional state, will always be more important than rules or

33. The term "authenticity" is borrowed from the discussion about "authenticity" versus "keeping the rules" in N. T. Wright, *After You Believe: Why Christian Character Matters* (New York: HarperOne, 2010), 30.

34. So, for example, in the corporate world, while a previous generation might have praised hard work, commitment, and allegiance to the company (virtues that incorporate some sense of duty), today executives are successful to the degree that they are "passionate" about their business. See David Brooks, *Bobos in Paradise: The New Upper Class and How They Got There* (New York: Simon & Schuster, 2000), 103–39.

habits. Here we have the familiar dichotomy of faith and works, but in a different key. The gospel supplies a freedom from laws and constraints and self-delusions in which one can be authentic—to, in the words of Augustine, "Love, and do what you want."[35] Again, authenticity witnesses to something true in measuring actions by internal motivations as well as externals, and especially in valuing the integration of desires and actions as essential to Christian spiritual formation. In formulating a relationship between faith and works, authenticity becomes problematic in its foregrounding of "passion" as the essential mark of authentic action. Internal motivation is prioritized over concrete action to the extent that legitimate actions can be disregarded on the grounds of an inauthentic emotional state.[36]

Readings of Scripture guided by authenticity will, in a way analogous to antinomianism, skirt the commands of the gospel and interpret the biblical text as a means of self-actualization. Oftentimes these can be very powerful readings that allow the wisdom of the biblical text to expose the self-deceptions and idolatries of readers, but their goal is to bring the reader to a point of authenticity, not to a point of obedience. Ultimately this is a movement inward and toward the self, which undermines the Christian call to practice love that advantages our neighbors, even over our own sense of psychological integrity. This sort of reading, at its best, involves a reeducation of the passions, through the exposing of illegitimate devotions, and their redirection into proper devotion toward Christ. So in reacting against moralism, authenticity does an excellent job of seeing how biblical wisdom not only prescribes actions but redirects and reintegrates devotions. At the same time, it is also an incomplete reading in that its application is not directed at integrated action but at a psychological state of passionate authenticity as an end in itself.

Legalism and Moralism

On the other side of the fence are the (perhaps) more obvious evils of legalism and moralism, although these too have their kernels of truth to them. Legalism is often defined as "people trying to earn their way to heaven." A moment's reflection, however, will lead anyone to recognize that this is an absurd notion. Any god that I can place in my debt is clearly lesser than me

---

35. Augustine, *Homilies on the First Epistle of John* 7.8, ed. Boniface Ramsey, Daniel Edward Doyle, and Thomas Martin, trans. Boniface Ramsey, The Works of Saint Augustine: A Translation for the 21st Century (Hyde Park, NY: New City Press, 2008), 110.

36. This denies the truth, first articulated by Aristotle but long embraced in the moral theology of the church, that habit is an essential catalyst for virtue. Cf. Julia Annas, *The Morality of Happiness* (Oxford: Oxford University Press, 1993), 50–58.

and therefore not a god at all. Legalism is a practical, not a formal, belief. None of the great religions of the world have ever taught any kind of wholesale earning salvation through amassing good works. (This has never been the case for either Judaism or Roman Catholicism.)

At the same time, *appeasement* of the gods, trying to elicit the gracious favor of the gods, is a nearly universal feature of religion. Within the covenantal Abrahamic religions of Christianity, Islam, and Judaism, this desire for appeasement leads to some form of legalism. But it is important to recognize that legalism always *presupposes* grace. Legalism seeks to elicit gracious favor through law keeping. It begins with a picture of grace, but a reluctant grace that needs a catalyst, an act of obedience to release the gift. In this way the act of obedience is like a primer that ignites an explosion of grace. Legalism is defined by its *ambivalence* toward grace. Legalism accepts grace with one hand while attempting to control it with the other. At its heart legalism is an attempt to procure grace on its own terms, to place a hand on the tap of grace.

So legalism does not reject grace; it assumes it. But at the same time it is marked by its deficient understanding of that grace. This deficient understanding is often expressed in an effort to make the grace of God more "reasonable," less extravagant, and ultimately controllable (cf. Matt. 20:1–16). Good works done in the context of a deficient belief in grace, where there remains still some idea that we move into a better state of grace with God through doing something good, are legalistic. Whenever our works derive from a sense of "closing the distance" with God, we deny his presence already promised in the gospel. We act legalistically to address what we believe is God's ambivalence toward us. Good works that begin with the recognition of God's presence lose their legalistic tenor.

Oftentimes the correction to legalism is seen as a disparaging of rules and laws in the antinomian or authentic modes above, but the real issue is not rules per se; it is deficient motivations that give birth to action.[37] The solution to legalism then begins with a proper formative understanding of the grace of God as unmerited and unmeasured and continues with a proper formative understanding of gratitude and reverence as foundational for integral good works.

---

37. Cf. T. J. Deidun, *New Covenant Morality in Paul*, AnBib 89 (Rome: Biblical Institute Press, 1981), 208–9,

> This means that even when God's demand presents itself to man as *verbum externum*, it is never in any sense to be classed with the γράμμα that "kills," for in the christian economy the external word . . . always presupposes God's internal activity. . . . For Paul, christian liberty is first and foremost radical emancipation from the power of sin and release from the impotence of self [to keep the law]. This, of course, entails a break with (a "death to," cf, Rom. 7, 4.6; Gal. 2,19) the Law as γράμμα (mere demand); but it is not correct to suggest that Paul sees ἐλευθερία precisely as freedom from external law as such.

Legalistic readings of the Bible are those that typically fail to recognize the motivational structure that the Bible as a wisdom text gives to its commands. Instead, legalistic readings supply their own ready-made motivations as interpretive keys to understanding the text. Application involves action rooted in legalistic motivations. The most likely of these motivations is self-contemptuous guilt derived from past failures and the internal sense of inadequacy that derives from them. A self-understanding of worthlessness, in reality a strong shield against the gracious acceptance of God, stands behind most legalistic readings of Scripture. This produces initiatives that by definition command the impossible—gain acceptance through behavior—which inevitably deepen perceptions of inadequacy instead of alleviating them. In this way legalism promotes rigid obedience to external behavior that masks self-contempt, holding God at a distance, and condemning those who do not share the same mode of being.

Moralism is a close cousin to legalism, deriving many of its motivations from the same well, but with different emphases. Like legalism, moralism rightly recognizes that the gospel entails both a gift and a call and, like legalism, fails to connect call and gift in a meaningful way. It is that failure to contextualize moral action within convictions shaped by the gospel that is the distinguishing feature of moralism.

Moralism is often closely related to the practice of principlizing discussed above and the presupposition of a "universal ethic." Such an ethic is composed of precepts that are transparently obvious to all and therefore need no justification or motivation other than their witness to a self-evident "ought." The categorical imperative[38] is the modus operandi of moralism, usually taking the form of "Be _____" (e.g., Be good! Be nice! Be like David!). Again, the commands themselves are not bad. The cure to moralism is not to jettison the moral challenge of the gospel. Neither is it to prohibit goodness, niceness, or Davidic virtue. Moralism fails when it cuts biblical commands from the theological and affective contexts given to them by the biblical text.

Moralism, to a certain degree, presupposes the law/gospel dichotomy at the core of antinomianism. It is not comfortable with a reading whose only application is to believe but does not expect any substantive connection between

---

38. Immanuel Kant, who coined the term "categorical imperative," contrasted "hypothetical" and "categorical" imperatives. The former ties imperatives to ends or advantages for the agent, whereas the latter posits no justification for action beyond its conformity to universal principles of reason. Cf. Andrews Reath, "Categorical and Hypothetical Imperatives," in *Encyclopedia of Ethics*, ed. Lawrence C. Becker and Charlotte B. Becker (London: Routledge, 2001), 1:191, "A categorical imperative represents an action as necessary, without reference to any further end beyond the action, in which the agent has an interest."

faith and works. It feels the necessity of works but does not find that necessity in the gospel itself. So, it relies on the logic of modern deontological ethics[39] to formulate and justify its appropriation of the commands of the gospel. In this way, these commands are surgically excised from their gospel motivations. Often, this unintentional reliance on the concept of a "universal" ethic, which is really just a cipher for contemporary moral sensibilities, produces ethical priorities alien to the Bible. Contemporary bourgeois values such as being nice, respectable, healthy, and successful (not exactly priorities in the teaching of Jesus) tend to move to the front of moralistic consciousness. Smith and Denton catalog the virtues of contemporary Christian moralism as "being nice, kind, pleasant, respectful, responsible, at work on self-improvement, taking care of one's health, and doing one's best to be successful."[40] Moralism spiritualizes self-improvement with the language of salvation, but its sphere of concern is much more deeply rooted in social respectability than it is in the righteousness of the kingdom of God outlined by Jesus in the Sermon on the Mount. In this way, moralism domesticates the law into a moral code whose chief virtue is not love (understood as a disadvantaging of the self for the sake of the other) but politeness.

Finally, in practice these four modes of connecting faith and works can form some strange alliances. So, for example, while antinomianism justifies itself primarily in its rejection of legalism, it very often leads to a practical form of moralism when it feels the need to make some application of biblical truths to the moral life.

John 15

Thankfully, the fundamental questions of the proper connection between faith and works or grace and obedience are not only modern questions, but actually central questions for the biblical authors.[41] The nature of faithful obedience in

39. Deontological ethics describes ethical systems built around duties prescribed in "oughts." Kant's categorical imperative is characteristic of his deontological ethic. Freeman gives the example of moral precepts (such as "Keep your promises!") as typical of deontological moral reasoning. "Most ordinary moral rules are deontological in form, which is only to say that they are formulated as unqualified imperatives without reference to reasons or specific ends they may realize." Samuel Freeman, "Deontology," in *Encyclopedia of Ethics*, ed. Becker and Becker, 1:392.

40. Christian Smith and Melinda Lundquist Denton, *Soul Searching: The Religious and Spiritual Lives of American Teenagers* (New York: Oxford University Press, 2005), 163. They add that "Being moral . . . means being the kind of person that other people will like, fulfilling one's personal potential, and not being socially disruptive or interpersonally obnoxious."

41. The only possible exception to this is the strategy of "authenticity," which is a decidedly modern and postmodern phenomenon. But we will see that the biblical teaching on the question of faith and works has sufficient resources to answer this approach constructively.

response to the grace of God is a central topic of discussion throughout the Bible. So it is not surprising that both Paul and Jesus have to defend themselves in response to charges of antinomianism or that multiple authors in both the OT and NT invalidate various acts of covenantal obedience on the grounds of illegitimate motivations. One example of a NT text that consciously deals with these questions is John 15, where Jesus uses the illustration of a vine and branches to give a conceptual model for the understanding of good works (fruit) in the context of a gracious provision of salvation. "I am the true vine, and my Father is the vinedresser. Every branch in me that does not bear fruit he takes away, and every branch that does bear fruit he prunes [καθαίρει], that it may bear more fruit. Already you are clean [καθαροί] because of the word that I have spoken to you" (John 15:1–3). The image of the vine is, of course, not a generic agricultural metaphor but a Jewish metaphor for Israel as the vine planted by God.[42] Jesus's designation of himself as the "true" vine is a claim of his status as the true embodiment of Israel as well as a judgment on the false vine, within John's narrative identified as the "Jews" who reject Jesus.[43] Jesus names himself as the source of life that animates and defines the new community as the true people of God.

The role of the Father as the "vinedresser" is described as cutting away dead branches and "pruning" live branches. His work is in response to the fruit bearing of the branches. Those that produce none are removed, while those that do produce fruit are purified that they may become more fruitful. Fruit bearing is a transparent metaphor for righteous actions. Those that produce none are cut off.[44] Those that do produce fruit are sanctified to produce more. Jesus as the vine is not only an incorporate covenantal personality but also the source of salvation. "Already you are clean because of the word I have spoken to you."

From this it is clear that the focus of this extended metaphor is not on questions of Jesus's self-identification as Israel and what that might mean for the continuing validity of the Mosaic covenant, or any other such redemptive-historical question (no matter how fascinating and important those questions might be). The focus here is on the nature of fruit bearing in relation to Jesus as the messianic source of life and salvation.

42. See Craig S. Keener, *The Gospel of John: A Commentary* (Peabody, MA: Hendrickson, 2003), 2:988–93.

43. Cf. Rudolf Schnackenburg, *The Gospel according to St. John*, trans. Cecily Hastings and Kevin Smyth (New York: Seabury, 1968–82), 3:97, 106–7.

44. Within the logic of John's Gospel the primary referent is to the "Jews," who are characterized by their unbelieving rebellion. That said, this metaphor does not specify rejection of a class of people but judgment of individuals according to their actions.

Now that the picture has been drawn, the command comes. One would naturally expect the command to be directed at fruit bearing, possibly out of reverence for Jesus as the giver of life. What follows, however, is the command to abide: "Abide in me, and I in you" (15:4a). This compact command needs some unpacking. "Abide" is a barely adequate translation of the imperative μείνατε. Its biggest liability is, of course, that it scarcely qualifies as a word in current English usage. The primary contemporary alternative, "remain," is more useful in capturing John's sense here. Chiefly this is a metaphor about relational proximity and fidelity, defined and empowered by the life-giving love of Jesus.[45]

At one level the vine metaphor describes something completely natural—branches that are attached to a vine that nourishes them that the branches may produce fruit. But while this process is natural, it is not automatic; some branches will die, and some will not produce fruit. Translated into the moral sphere, Jesus locates this indeterminacy of fruit bearing in the "branches'" volition to abide, and so the command is located in the sphere of abiding, of maintaining a disposition of relational proximity and dependence. At the same time, the act of abiding is defined not as the act of the individual or community to *establish* a relational proximity but as remaining in an abiding relationship that is both an established gift and an ongoing promise. Along with Jesus's command to his disciples for them to "abide in me" is his promise "and I [will abide] in you." Again, the focus of this language is on relational communion and describes a mutual abiding dependent on the choices of two parties.[46]

In the verses that follow Jesus explains that abiding is not an end in itself but actually the entry point in the path of fruit bearing. "As the branch cannot bear fruit by itself, unless it abides in the vine, neither can you, unless you abide in me. I am the vine; you are the branches. Whoever abides in me and I in him, he it is that bears much fruit, for apart from me you can do nothing" (15:4b–5). Jesus returns to the logic of the metaphor—that branches bear no fruit apart from their connection to the vine—and again translates this as both a promise of fruit bearing, through the act of continued abiding, and a threat of fruitlessness for those who pursue fruit apart from the vine.

45. See Schnackenburg, *John*, 3:98–99.
46. This does not mean that the moral choices on both sides are exactly the same or have the same weight. The nature of Jesus's choice has already preemptively established the abiding relationship; its existence and continued life are determined by the acts of Jesus in a way that is not true of the disciples' choices to abide. This gives a necessary priority to the loving actions and disposition of Jesus, but one that creates and sustains the possibility and efficacy of the choices of his disciples.

Jesus gives a picture that explains the mechanism of Christian obedience in a way that makes moral actions intelligible. In all that Jesus has said up to this point there is an implicit command of bearing fruit, underlined with a threat of judgment for the branches that fail to do so. In this way fruit bearing has been described as both "organic" and necessary. But this returns us to our question above: How are we to pursue those moral actions entailed in the gospel message?[47] How are we meant to conceive of those actions? When are we doing them with integrity and when are we not? These are exactly the questions that Jesus answers here.

His answer begins at the place of abiding and the pursuit of abiding. Again, the command of Jesus is "abide in me." The priority of relational abiding gives a context for obedient fruit bearing. The disciple of Jesus cannot begin at the place of fruit bearing as a means of abiding. In placing abiding first, Jesus gives the life-giving relational union of mutual abiding as the context through which the disciples make sense of their actions. It also gives motivations that derive from the gift and the promise of the communion that Jesus has established and continues to sustain.

In this Jesus is confronting the temptations to legalism and moralism, both of which put fruit-bearing obedience first, as a means to appropriating abiding communion. Legalism, as we saw above, derives its impetus from a flawed appropriation of grace that requires the catalyst of works to release the reluctant grace of God. It is precisely this component that Jesus deconstructs in his teaching on the gift, the promise, and the priority of abiding. The abiding communion that Jesus has established with his disciples is already in effect. This is the point of Jesus's declaration: "Already you are clean because of the word that I have spoken to you." There is no catalyst required to release the grace of God.

Likewise, we saw that moralism finds its justification in a categorical imperative of duty—here the duty of fruit bearing. No reasons or motivations are necessary other than duty itself; it is by definition self-justifying. The teaching of Jesus here in John 15 is typical of biblical wisdom in rejecting this approach as both inhuman and ineffective (cf. Col. 2:20–23), and it therefore supplies reasons and motivations that sustain moral actions, especially since those actions often decenter the self in acts of love that prioritize the good of another. It is precisely in this context that Jesus emphasizes both the given reality of relational communion and its foundational relationship to all moral deliberation and action.

---

47. A moral agency given definitive shape in v. 12 of this passage: "This is my commandment, that you love one another as I have loved you."

But Jesus is not finished. In verse 9 he continues, "As the Father has loved me, so have I loved you. Abide in my love." He repeats the command to abide but here is more explicit that abiding entails a participation in and enjoyment of the love that Jesus has directed toward his disciples.[48] In addition, Jesus connects this same love to the intertrinitarian love that he shares with the Father. In a move that is typical of the second half of John's Gospel (chaps. 13–21), the relationship between the Father and the Son becomes paradigmatic for Jesus and his disciples.[49]

Jesus makes a startling shift in verse 10, explaining how one can fulfill his command to abide in his love: "If you keep my commandments, you will abide in my love." Given what Jesus has already said about the priority of abiding over obedience, this is a jarring and confounding statement. Jesus seems to be advocating something that, if we are right, he denounced above—namely, using obedience as a means of abiding. It is hard to see how he is saying otherwise. He clearly describes relational communion as a *product* of obedience to his commandments. Is Jesus really saying the opposite of what he said before? Half of the answer comes in the remainder of verse 10, where Jesus (again) uses his relationship with the Father as paradigmatic for that between Jesus and his disciples: "just as I have kept my Father's commandments and abide in his love."

Jesus's own active obedience becomes paradigmatic for Christian obedience in that it derives from his communion with the Father while at the same time also fosters that same communion. It is both a product of abiding as well as a catalyst for it. The only alternative is to conclude that the love of the Father is withheld from the Son, only to be given as recompense for obedience. Theologically this makes no sense, especially within the context of John, which stresses the love between Father and Son as a theological bedrock. But that truth creates another conundrum.

48. The repetition of the command forms an *inclusio* with v. 4 and sets off v. 10 as the beginning of a new section that ends in v. 17.

49. This moves beyond the love and relational union between the Father and Son to include the work the Father has appointed for the Son, which will also become paradigmatic for the disciples. One obvious example of this is that Jesus's primary identity in John is as "the one sent by the Father" (3:17, 34; 5:36, 38; 6:29, 57; 7:29; 8:42; 10:36; 11:42; 17:3, 8, 18, 21, 23, 25; 20:21). This is later transferred to the disciples as the ones sent by Jesus in John 20:21. "As the Father has sent me, even so I am sending you" (cf. 17:18). See Andreas J. Köstenberger, *The Missions of Jesus and the Disciples according to the Fourth Gospel: With Implications for the Fourth Gospel's Purpose and the Mission of the Contemporary Church* (Grand Rapids: Eerdmans, 1998). This is another example of how John creates an intelligibility structure to contextualize the Christian mission. The disciples stand in continuity with the mission of Jesus himself and gain insight and motivation from his obedience to the Father in fulfilling his mission. This connection is the reason for John emphasizing this aspect of Jesus's mission in language almost completely absent from the Synoptics.

If the communion between the Father and the Son is an eternal reality, how then can the obedience of the Son further it? Is there a deficiency in intertrinitarian love? Does it need periodic "topping up"? Those explanations make no sense either. What Jesus is speaking of here is the mutual enjoyment of the Father and the Son—the enjoyment of each other and their communion with each other is what Jesus claims is actualized in his obedience to the Father.

What this means for Christian obedience is that communion as a *reward* for obedience is excluded, because as we saw this is nonsensical to claim about the Father and the Son. Abiding is once again the starting point for Christian obedience. At the same time, the primary point of this verse is that abiding is in fact a *product* of obedience. Obedience is the *necessary* condition for abiding. There is of course a circular logic here: abiding produces obedience, and obedience produces abiding.[50] The first half of the vine discourse testifies to the first truth, while these verses testify to the second. What is important to see is that these two truths are *mutually defining and counterbalancing*. They are set against each other to correct possible misunderstanding of taking either one by itself. These verses, in speaking of the necessity of the Son's obedience to the Father for their continued communion, teach that Christian obedience is necessary to abide in Christ. There is no abiding apart from obedience. Obedience then cannot be a beneficial extra element of life; it is the lifeblood of communion with Christ.

Here some may object that we are confusing faith and obedience, overemphasizing the importance of the latter over the former. Don't we need to defend the priority of faith over obedience? We do need to define and defend their proper relationship, but one is hard pressed to find in the teaching of Jesus a priority of faith *over* obedience. What is preserved is the priority of faith, just as with abiding, as the starting point. But the other truth that is just as important is that faith and obedience are two sides of the same coin. So we shouldn't be surprised to find John using faith and obedience as synonyms in John 3:36: "Whoever *believes* in the Son has eternal life; whoever does not *obey* the Son shall not see life, but the wrath of God remains on him."

In returning to the vine discourse, the first part confronts the heart of legalism in proclaiming the priority of abiding, which embraces a communion that already exists between Jesus and his disciples. Likewise, the second part confronts the temptations to antinomianism and authenticity, which sever the necessary connection between faith and obedience. Antinomians see faith and obedience as two different species of human action, which in a strong law/gospel dichotomy are even enemies of one another. Here lies the importance

50. Cf. Bonhoeffer, *Discipleship*, 63, "only the believers obey, and only the obedient believe."

of Luther's teaching that faith is the "first act of obedience." First, because it breaches the divide that would define faith as an act of cognition and obedience as an act of volition (i.e., two different species of human action). Second, in recognizing faith as the *first* act of obedience Luther defines it not as the first in a series of actions but first in that all other acts of obedience derive their intelligibility from it. This is the same principle of saying that all fruit bearing begins with following the command to abide. Abiding is the first act of obedience.

As we have just seen, the solution to legalism is the priority of abiding, not the antinomian solution of removing the necessary connection between faith and obedience. Antinomians have a laudable motivation in seeking to shield people and communities from the psychological slavery of legalism, which necessarily perpetuates a self-understanding defined by shame and inadequacy. Unfortunately, the antinomian solution to this problem simply replaces these problems with others, primarily in severing the connections between the saving message of the gospel and human agency, since it ultimately describes all human agency as corrupt and futile. The only authentic Christian act is to feel forgiven.

The essential problem here is that human agency is simply part of everyday human life, in the choices we all make as friends, coworkers, family members, church members, teammates, and neighbors. For all of the myriad choices entailed in attending to these various relationships, an antinomian has no advice other than to feel forgiven, but that doesn't remove the necessity that choices have to be made. So people will make these choices on some other basis, since the gospel seems to say nothing directly to them, not because the Bible has nothing to say about them but because antinomianism deconstructs all human agency in the name of the gospel.

In a similar vein authenticity, while having a deep concern for the motivations for human actions, severs the tie between faith and obedience because it sees mended motivations as an end in themselves. The sphere in which authenticity operates is in the healing of the psyche. In this it is still a cousin of antinomianism, which also defines the fruits of the gospel in terms of an internal psychological state (i.e., feeling forgiven). It is a more nuanced cousin, but still a cousin, especially in cutting the necessary connection between concrete moral acts of obedience and faith. Authenticity is not necessarily as suspicious of obedience as antinomianism is; in fact, it may see Christian moral action as essentially good. The fault is that it also views these actions as a laudable extra, good but not *necessary*. The redemption of the soul is the priority and an end in itself and complete in itself. If moral actions follow, then all the better, but an absence of action does not detract from the redemption of the soul. As an antidote to moralism it is brilliant; as a summary of the gospel it severs the connection between internal psychological states and external moral acts that is typical of a modern (Cartesian) metaphysic and its postmodern (romantic) cousins.

Again, the gospel of Jesus and Paul proclaims the forgiveness of the individual within the context of eschatological presence of the kingdom of God that is re-creating all things so that they might find their freedom and fulfillment in the will of God. This means that forgiveness is not an end in itself. It also means that the redemption of human persons entails all of who they are: thoughts, desires, volition, and actions. None of these can be excluded, and none of these can be given essential priority over another. And so it is not surprising that the proclamation of the gospel necessarily entails both faith and obedience in the unity of human personhood and does not assign them to parts of a divided self or to disparate spheres of salvation. This is wisdom aimed at the redemption of God's people in their convictions, loves, and actions.

The New Perspective on Paul and the Law

Perhaps the utility of a wisdom approach can be seen in its assessment of the New Perspective on Paul. While still controversial in some circles, the basic teachings of the "new perspective" are largely considered uncontroversial and are in fact assumed in much Pauline scholarship today. The foundation for the "new perspective" came in E. P. Sanders's work *Paul and Palestinian Judaism*,[51] in which he convincingly debunked the common scholarly (and popular) assumption that Second Temple Judaism was a legalistic religion obsessed with the minutiae of law keeping in an effort to earn salvation through works of righteousness. Sanders proved that, based on its own self-understanding available through ancient texts, ancient Judaism was not a legalistic religion but one whose foundation was the electing grace of God. His description of ancient Judaism was summed up in the term "covenantal nomism," which gave a place to both the gracious promises of the covenant and the nomistic (law-keeping) demands of the covenant set within a system of liturgical and sacrificial practices that maintained the covenantal relationship through forgiveness.[52] From

---

51. E. P. Sanders, *Paul and Palestinian Judaism: A Comparison of Patterns of Religion* (Philadelphia: Fortress, 1977).

52. Sanders summarized covenantal nomism in the following eight convictions: "(1) God has chosen Israel and (2) given the law. The law implies both (3) God's promises to maintain election and (4) the requirement to obey. (5) God rewards obedience and punishes transgression. (6) The law provides for means of atonement, and atonement results in (7) maintenance

this Sanders concluded that pre-70 Judaism "kept grace and works in the right perspective"[53] and was not marked by "legalism."

If we define legalism as fundamentally an obsession with rules as a means of earning salvation by righteous merit, then Sanders is certainly correct in saying there is no historical evidence that such a doctrine had any formative influence in ancient Judaism. But as we have seen above, the heart of legalism is not "earning one's way to heaven" but the securing of divine favor through the mechanism of law keeping. Legalism, properly understood, presupposes gracious promises. So when Sanders argues that ancient Judaism could not be legalistic because it believed in the electing grace of God toward Israel, this is not so much wrong as it is simply a *non sequitur*.[54] Electing grace is not the *antidote* to legalism; it is actually the *necessary precondition* for legalism. Legalism can only exist where grace has been promised (i.e., in a covenantal context). But the other necessary precondition for legalism is a connection between that grace and a demand for obedience. This brings us back to our fundamental question of faith and works, grace and obedience, or in Sanders's terminology, covenant and nomism.

As we saw above, there are many different ways to conceive of the relationship between grace and obedience. We looked specifically at the deeply flawed conceptions of legalism, antinomianism, authenticity, and moralism. We also saw that this is an important question in biblical literature and how it functions as wisdom. The crucial flaw in Sanders's proposal is in his assumption that all forms of covenantal nomism are de facto legitimate because they have the element of electing grace to balance out the nomistic demands. This assumption is both historically and theologically unwarranted. The "balance" between covenant and nomism is far from automatic.[55] When biblical and extrabiblical authors condemn acts of covenantal obedience (e.g., "Your burnt offerings are not acceptable, nor your sacrifices pleasing to me" [Jer. 6:20b],

---

or re-establishment of the covenantal relationship. (8) All those who are maintained in the covenant by obedience, atonement and God's mercy belong to the group which will be saved" (*Paul and Palestinian Judaism*, 422).

53. Sanders, *Paul and Palestinian Judaism*, 426.

54. Sanders is not to be blamed for this misunderstanding of legalism himself, since he was using what was then and what is today a common definition of legalism, both in the church and in the academy.

55. In fact there is a whole tradition of Augustinian theology that argues that the "balance" between law and covenant is inherently unstable, because that balance is perpetually resisted by sinful human reason that is characterized by its ambivalence toward the grace of God and therefore in need of the corrective force of Scripture and the Holy Spirit to enjoy this balance. Whether one finds this narrative compelling, it calls into question that the balance between covenantal and nomistic elements is either theoretically or existentially automatic and therefore raises doubts that it can simply be assumed in the way that Sanders does without argumentation or proofs.

or "I desire steadfast love and not sacrifice, the knowledge of God rather than burnt offerings" [Hos. 6:6]), it reveals that there are ways to get covenantal nomism very wrong. Sanders's project has no way of distinguishing between legitimate and illegitimate forms of covenantal nomism (even if he were to admit that the latter category existed).

This is a curious oversight for Sanders as an expert on early Judaism since it ignores what is historically one of the most hotly contested questions in Second Temple Judaism: Whose covenantal nomism is the legitimate one? Competing groups within Judaism were not shy about denouncing the covenantal nomism of other groups and claiming their exclusive identity as the true embodiment of Israel, demonstrated in their particular brand of covenant-keeping obedience. Sanders is imposing a unity on a key question where, historically, there were competing, and often exclusive, forms of diversity.[56]

Sanders summarizes the dynamics of covenantal nomism in the language of "getting in" and "staying in." In Judaism "getting in" is a matter of membership in the chosen people of God and is therefore purely a matter of the divine grace of election, apart from acts of obedience. When the question turns to maintaining one's status in the covenant ("staying in"), then obedience is the operative element. Therefore, one "gets in" by grace and "stays in" by works of law keeping. Sanders offers the clarification that "obedience maintains one's position in the covenant, but it does not earn God's grace as such."[57] Given that it does not "earn God's grace as such," Sanders's definition here in no way excludes the idea that obedience can function as a catalyst for grace. Unfortunately for Sanders, the basic principle that he describes in the formula of "getting in" by grace and "staying in" by works corresponds closely to our definition of legalism. Worse still, it corresponds closely with the teaching that Paul denounces in Galatians 3:3, "Having begun by the Spirit, are you now being perfected by the flesh?"

Although we are used to connecting Paul's arguments in Galatians to the doctrine of justification, Paul's real question in Galatians is not about "getting

---

56. This is the primary criticism of Sanders in D. A. Carson, Peter Thomas O'Brien, and Mark A. Seifrid, eds., *Justification and Variegated Nomism*, vol. 1, *The Complexities of Second Temple Judaism* (Grand Rapids: Baker Academic, 2001). The editors of this volume argue that covenantal nomism is too expansive to describe the diversity of opinion and practice in Second Temple Judaism and that historically there were a plurality of covenantal nomisms operative. They argue, therefore, that the category itself is invalid. While I think it is true that covenantal nomism is something of a rubber nose that can be made to fit numerous ancient groups and their representative texts, my primary concern of Sanders is that he gives no conditions under which a given construal of covenantal nomism might be judged an invalid manifestation—all forms of covenantal nomism are definitionally valid.

57. Sanders, *Paul and Palestinian Judaism*, 420.

in" but about "staying in." What should gentile Christian obedience look like? Paul, like Jesus in John 15, is making an argument for a proper theological contextualization of Christian obedience over against a sinful contextualization of that same obedience. The question of gentile circumcision for Paul is not about "getting in" but "staying in." Paul argues that circumcision is a symbolic act that entails a wholesale embracing of a way of understanding Christian obedience that denies the work of Christ. As Paul says: "Look: I, Paul, say to you that if you accept circumcision, Christ will be of no advantage to you. I testify again to every man who accepts circumcision that he is obligated to keep the whole law. You are severed from Christ, you who would be justified by the law; you have fallen away from grace" (Gal. 5:2–4). Here Paul is speaking of an obedience to the law that functions instrumentally to secure divine favor ("justification"). In contrast to this, Paul argues for a different foundation for Christian obedience: communion with God, expressed in the language of union with Christ and adoption. "So then, the law was our guardian until Christ came, in order that we might be justified by faith. But now that faith has come, we are no longer under a guardian, for in Christ Jesus you are all sons of God, through faith. For as many of you as were baptized into Christ have put on Christ. . . . And because you are sons, God has sent the Spirit of his Son into our hearts, crying, 'Abba! Father!'" (Gal. 3:24–27; 4:6).

In a move analogous to the vine discourse in John 15, Paul focuses on a communion with God made possible through the work of Christ communicated by the presence of the Spirit. At the center of this picture is Christ as the locus of communion with God. As Paul states earlier in Galatians 2:20: "I have been crucified with Christ. It is no longer I who live, but Christ who lives in me. And the life I now live in the flesh I live by faith in the Son of God, who loved me and gave himself for me."

What is also clear for Paul is that this life in Christ is not simply an experience of communion with God, but a communion that produces moral action and has as its goal the redemption of human agency. "For in Christ Jesus neither circumcision nor uncircumcision counts for anything, but only faith working through love" (Gal. 5:6). Again in language reminiscent of John 15, communion with Christ apprehended by faith is expressed in obedience to Christ and love for one another within the community.[58] All this is summarized by Paul at the end of chapter 5:

58. I am not arguing for any conscious dependence of Paul on Jesus's teaching as presented in John's Gospel. My point is simply that the two give very similar constructs for how Christian obedience is meant to be understood and enacted.

For you were called to freedom, brothers. Only do not use your freedom as an opportunity for the flesh, but through love serve one another. For the whole law is fulfilled in one word: "You shall love your neighbor as yourself." But if you bite and devour one another, watch out that you are not consumed by one another. But I say, walk by the Spirit, and you will not gratify the desires of the flesh. For the desires of the flesh are against the Spirit, and the desires of the Spirit are against the flesh, for these are opposed to each other, to keep you from doing the things you want to do. But if you are led by the Spirit, you are not under the law. Now the works of the flesh are evident: sexual immorality, impurity, sensuality, idolatry, sorcery, enmity, strife, jealousy, fits of anger, rivalries, dissensions, divisions, envy, drunkenness, orgies, and things like these. I warn you, as I warned you before, that those who do such things will not inherit the kingdom of God. But the fruit of the Spirit is love, joy, peace, patience, kindness, goodness, faithfulness, gentleness, self-control; against such things there is no law. And those who belong to Christ Jesus have crucified the flesh with its passions and desires. If we live by the Spirit, let us also keep in step with the Spirit. Let us not become conceited, provoking one another, envying one another. (Gal. 5:13–26)

While there are many points to discuss in this passage, let's summarize some of the main ones. First, just as we saw above in Romans, Paul sees the message of the gospel as proclaiming a new path, through the agency of Spirit, for the fulfillment of the law. The chief sign of this fulfillment is seen in the reality of love within the Galatian churches. But Paul is a realist and not a dreamer; that reality is far from automatic. It will take the work of God in the fruit of the Spirit to transform the hearts of God's people, to instill certain virtues within them. At the same time, any time we find virtue and vice lists, together with the language of moral antithesis (i.e., the "two ways" of the flesh/Spirit) combined with commands and prohibitions, then we are clearly dealing with the direction and formation of moral choices and character. All this Paul sums up in the command "If we live by the Spirit, let us also keep in step with the Spirit."

Paul's final warning in this passage, "Let us not become conceited, provoking one another, envying one another," gives us a clue as to why Paul rejects justification by "works of the law" in favor of justification by faith. If Paul is in fact opposing something close to what we have defined as legalism, in which covenantal obedience becomes the mechanism of grace, then in Paul's understanding that obedience is a ground for what he elsewhere terms "boasting" (see 1 Cor. 1:29–31; Eph. 2:8–9).[59] Conceit, envy, provocations between

---

59. Cf. Simon J. Gathercole, *Where Is Boasting? Early Jewish Soteriology and Paul's Response in Romans 1–5* (Grand Rapids: Eerdmans, 2002).

individuals and groups are, for Paul, necessary products of this kind of boasting and therefore the natural fruits of seeking to be "justified by works of the law." Works that become instrumentalized in securing divine favor also serve in the same breath as a means of distinguishing individuals in a hierarchy and distinguishing groups as "in" and "out" of favor.

This is at heart the issue that Paul is addressing in Galatians 2:11–21, where he connects his Antioch confrontation with Peter over gentile table fellowship directly to justification by faith. (Two issues that the New Perspective is right to connect in Paul's thought.) The disruption in Peter's fellowship with gentiles is provoked by Jewish Christians who believe that they are in essence superior to gentile Christians, both by natural descent as children of Abraham and by religious observance. Paul understands that this is more than a breach of social conduct but a violation of a fundamental principle of the gospel. Justification by faith necessarily excludes the possibility of ascribing the impetus for God's favor to anything but the grace of God itself. And so, just as Jesus condemned the Pharisees for their conceit, so Paul sees the racial conceit of the circumcision party as an expression of a presumption of divine favor based on both ethnic heritage and religious observance, and he labels this presumption and conceit as being "justified by works of the law."

Conclusion

So we have seen that the traditional distinction between law and gospel is intended to preserve an essential truth of salvation—that it is the free creative act of God to save and that it comes to us as unworthy recipients. Unfortunately, though, when this dichotomy becomes a general soteriological principle it produces more distortions than clarifications; primarily it denies both the intent of the gospel to redeem human agency and the correlate demands that the gospel makes on human agency. This also results in, at best, a deep ambivalence to the proper place for good works as the goal of the gospel, not simply an ancillary bonus to the gospel (see Titus 2:11–14).

The solution to this comes in recognizing the importance the NT gives to the integration of right actions, right reasons, and right motivations, and that the same action can be judged differently according to the basis for its intelligibility or the internal motivations that gave rise to it. To clarify how ethical actions can be properly connected to reasons and motivation derived from the gospel we examined four misconstruals of this proper connection: Antinomianism, we saw, relies on a strong law/gospel dichotomy and thus rejects any necessary connection between gospel faith and gospel obedience, because it is the law that demands obedience. But this severs the church from the commands of Jesus himself, which are invariably understood as law, not gospel. The only genuine Christian activity is to feel forgiven. In a similar fashion, authenticity understands the gospel proclamation in terms of the realization of an internal psychological state of authentic integration. But in this it also denies the necessity of obedience to the commands of Christ. It views these commands as a means to internal self-actualization but not as real demands on our moral agency.

We contrasted antinomianism and authenticity with legalism and moralism; the latter both take the demands of the gospel seriously but fail to situate those demands within Christian reasons and motivations for obedience. Legalism begins with a deficient understanding of grace that views acts of righteousness as instrumental in actualizing grace, seeing them as a necessary catalyst for the gracious gift of God to be realized (what historically has been labeled "synergism"). But we also noted, contrary to wide opinion, that legalism does not seek to replace the necessity of grace—it actually depends on it—but rather it seeks to control it in some measure. Moralism also takes demands for Christian righteousness seriously but justifies those demands by connecting them to a "universal ethic" with deontological foundations.[60] In this way it severs Christian obedience from gospel truths and produces an ethic of achievable moral reform that focuses on social respectability.

These deviations drive us back to the truth that the moral demands of the gospel are not an appendage to the gospel proclamation but essential to its nature, and that the redemption of human agency is an essential expectation for both Jesus and Paul of what true acceptance of the gospel produces. Schlatter helped us to see that in Paul's understanding God's righteousness is revealed in both his judgment and salvation. And so in salvation we are not saved from the righteousness of God but by the righteousness of God. This means that the gospel proclaims our communion with God in both his righteousness and mercy and that his righteous mercy not only declares us forgiven but in the same breath condemns our corrupt natures and begins the transforming of our wills and affections.

---

60. In this sense moralism is a uniquely modern phenomenon, just as authenticity is a modern phenomenon in reaction to it.

PART 2

* * *

PLANTING THE SEEDS

4

READING GOSPELS FOR WISDOM
Theory

Having dealt with some of the impediments to our project, we now move to
building some positive models for reading the NT as wisdom. We will start
by looking at Gospel narratives. This theoretical chapter will be followed by
a practical one where the insights of this chapter are applied to a sample of
illustrative Gospel texts. Our task in this chapter is to understand how Gospel texts shape readers in wisdom, forming their convictions, devotions, and
actions. We will find that narratives are exceptionally well suited to realizing
formative agendas. But before we can get there, we will have to understand
what a Gospel is, so we will need to begin with a look at the genre of gospel.

The Gospel Genre

Prior to examining what defines the literary genre of gospel, we need to understand what genres *are* and what they do. First, genres are not primarily a set of
literary characteristics but rather a means of encoding communicative intentions in a literary form.[1] Because of this, genres create a field of interpretive

---

1. Cf. Jonathan Culler, "Towards a Theory of Non-Genre Literature," in *Surfiction: Fiction
Now and Tomorrow*, ed. Raymond Federman (Chicago: Swallow, 1981), 256, "To treat them
[genres] as taxonomic classes is to obscure their function as norms in the process of reading."

expectations for readers.[2] Genres give a form to acts of communication, and specific forms are suited to specific communicative intentions. Human beings are perpetually creating and revising genres to suit their communicative needs. Texting and Twitter, for example, are communicative genres that did not exist a generation ago, and, like all genres, are suited to particular kinds of communication (i.e., good for short bursts of personal communication but bad for quarterly reports). Genres package communication in forms that orient the expectations of the recipient. We automatically adjust our expectations when reading a textbook, a novel, a dictionary, a webpage, or a comic strip. We instinctively read them differently.[3] All of these literary forms perform different discourse functions, and their forms have developed over time according to their ability to realize specific communicative intentions.[4]

Genres, like cryptographic keys, are used for encoding and decoding communication. The point of this encryption is not to keep secrets but to allow for compact forms of communication. Because communicative intentions are, in large measure, encoded in the form, the author does not need to explain his intentions or delineate a set of possible expectations for the readers. All of this is already done by the genre encoding itself. Human communication, in most cases, strives for a balance between efficiency and precision and so favors systems of implicit communication backed up by some limited form of communicative redundancy. Because genres encode intentions, they are an efficient means of implicit communication that can facilitate complex communicative intentions without having to spell them out explicitly.

Genres can be identified by a recognition of both their communicative function and a corresponding set of literary characteristics. These literary characteristics include the type and length of discourse, the style of language, the physical formatting, and literary devices. Literary texts of the same genre share literary characteristics, although with a certain degree of flexibility (i.e., not all members of a genre necessarily share *all* the literary characteristics of that genre). Texts that share the same genre also share discourse function (what writers who employ a particular genre are typically trying to do). Genres shape literary characteristics around discourse function and are refined based on their effectiveness in realizing certain communicative intentions. Because

2. Cf. Charles Bazerman, "Genre as Social Action," in *The Routledge Handbook of Discourse Analysis*, ed. James Paul Gee and Michael Handford (Oxford: Routledge, 2012), 229, "Available and familiar patterns of utterances (that is, genres) provide interpretive clues that allow people to make sense of each other's utterances."

3. This "instinct" is acquired through a continual process of cultural socialization. So, in its particularities this instinct is a learned skill.

4. On this functional definition of genres see Alastair Fowler, *Kinds of Literature: An Introduction to the Theory of Genres and Modes* (Cambridge, MA: Harvard University Press, 1982).

of this, understanding the genre of a piece of literature gives us clues to the communicative intentions of authors and their expectations for their readers.

The question of genre becomes critically important when engaging with texts cross-culturally. Within a culture, genre recognition and the adjustment of communicative expectations is an automatic process. We do not have to think consciously when we switch from reading a novel to reading a blog, but our mode of reading shifts imperceptibly to a new set of expectations of literary characteristics and discourse function. But when we engage a text from outside our normal cultural bounds, the genre cues of that culture are often lost on us, and the task of decoding needs to become explicit instead of implicit. The shortcut to solving this cross-cultural dilemma is to employ a correlate genre in one's own culture, but this has inherent limitations and often leads to misunderstanding. Bridging this gap and doing it well means attempting to understand cross-cultural genres, as much as possible, on their own terms.

When thinking particularly about the genre of gospel, bridging this gap has produced an often-contentious debate,[5] including the fallback (surrender) position of taking the Gospels as a sui generis.[6] Despite this history of disagreements, over the last few decades a general consensus has emerged in line with the work of Richard Burridge, who has shown that the closest literary cousin to gospel in the Greco-Roman world was ancient biography (βίος).[7] Ancient biographies are similar to their modern counterparts, but with some important differences.[8]

What is especially interesting for our study is that ancient biographies were most often written explicitly as a form of wisdom, being more concerned with demonstrating how their subjects were exemplars of particular virtues than with giving a comprehensive personal history.[9] Plutarch, for example,

5. For a good survey see Jonathan T. Pennington, *Reading the Gospels Wisely: A Narrative and Theological Introduction* (Grand Rapids: Baker Academic, 2012), 18–35.

6. Sui generis means a genre unto itself, or its own genre unrelated to any others. Not only is this a lame answer; it is a socio-linguistic impossibility. If there were such a thing, no one would be able to understand it. Cf. Richard A. Burridge, *What Are the Gospels? A Comparison with Graeco-Roman Biography*, 2nd ed. (Grand Rapids: Eerdmans, 2004), 45, 247.

7. Burridge, *What Are the Gospels?* See especially 76–77, where he relates βίος and gospel and discusses the inherent flexibility of these (and all) genres.

8. Modern biographies are histories of an individual's life, usually rehearsing their life from birth or early childhood to their death (or present age if a contemporary). They adhere to strict chronological standards and attempt to avoid encomium. Ancient biographies are more episodic in that they feel no obligation to tell the whole story of the subject's life, just what episodes were viewed as being of particular importance. Chronological constraints, as with all forms of ancient history, were less strict, although by no means nonexistent.

9. Cf. David B. Capes, "*Imitatio Christi* and the Gospel Genre," *BBR* 13, no. 1 (2003): 1–19.

clearly distinguishes his purpose in writing his *Lives* (βίοι; biographies) from
that of a straight history:

> I do not tell of all the famous actions of these men, nor even speak exhaustively
> at all in each particular case, but in epitome for the most part. . . . For it is not
> Histories [ἱστορίαι] that I am writing, but Lives [βίοι]; and in the most illustrious
> deeds there is not always a manifestation of virtue or vice, nay, a slight thing
> [πρᾶγμα βραχύ] like a phrase or a jest often makes a greater revelation of character
> than battles where thousands fall, or the greatest armaments, or sieges of cities.
> Accordingly, just as painters get the likeness [ὁμοιότης] in their portraits from the
> face and the expression of the eyes, wherein the character [ἦθος] shows itself, but
> make very little account of the other parts of the body, so I must be permitted
> to devote myself rather to the signs of the soul in men, and by means of these to
> portray the life of each, leaving to others the description of the great contests.[10]

Plutarch's focus is on the virtuous character of his subjects. Because his
purpose in writing is to foster particular virtues embodied by his subjects,
he does not feel the need to be exhaustive in narrating an individual's life, or
even a necessity to narrate the major events. His real concern is with *events
that reveal moral character in a way that promotes key virtues.* This use of
moral exemplars to promote and teach moral virtue was ubiquitous in Greco-
Roman moral discourse.[11] Philo provides a typical example in his interpretation of the OT patriarchs: "These are such men as lived good and blameless
lives, whose virtues stand permanently recorded in the most holy scriptures,
not merely to sound their praises but for the instruction of the reader and as
an inducement to him to aspire to the same; for in these men we have laws
endowed with life and reason."[12]

Philo attests to the particular usefulness of exemplars by describing them
as "laws endowed with life and reason." Exemplars are real people, not ideas.
Although sometimes their depictions are idealized,[13] the benefit of these ex-

10. Plutarch, *Alexander* 1.1–3, in *Lives VII* trans. Bernadotte Perrin, LCL 99 (Cambridge,
MA: Harvard University Press, 1919), 225. When trying to understand cross-cultural genres on
their own terms, one of the best sources is someone from that culture reflecting on how they
perceive of and utilize that genre, even though their portrayal may be colored by their own
agendas and limited by the inherent implicit nature of genres as unarticulated assumptions.

11. See J. de Waal Dryden, *Theology and Ethics in 1 Peter: Paraenetic Strategies for Christian Character Formation*, WUNT 2/209 (Tübingen: Mohr Siebeck, 2006), 163–72. See also
Clifford A. Barbarick, "The Pattern and the Power: The Example of Christ in 1 Peter" (PhD
diss., Baylor University, 2011), 21–84.

12. Philo, *Abraham* 1.4–5, in *On Abraham, on Joseph, on Moses*, trans. F. H. Colson, LCL
289 (Cambridge, MA: Harvard University Press, 1935), 7.

13. For example, one would be hard pressed to describe the patriarchal accounts in Genesis
as depicting men who "lived good and blameless lives." The author of Genesis certainly wants

emplars is that they embody virtue by living it out in challenging concrete circumstances. Because of this, ancient moral philosophers preferred the use of historical exemplars over legendary ones.

Another major influence on the gospel genre is the historical narratives of the Hebrew Bible. Loveday Alexander, augmenting Burridge, has argued that OT narratives provide the best precedent for some features peculiar to the Gospels.[14] Again, of interest to our study are the recent works that have begun to explore the wisdom function of these OT narratives. A growing number of OT scholars (along with ethicists working outside biblical studies) have recognized the strong wisdom agendas incorporated in these narratives.[15] (This overlap of gospel and OT historical narrative also means that much of what we will uncover about how Gospels function as wisdom is applicable to OT narratives as well.)

Our expectations of the Gospels, as something of a combination of these genres of ancient biography and OT narrative, should be shaped around a narrative genre that is a subclass of Wisdom literature.[16] This means that we ought to expect gospel narratives to have a strong concern with fostering Christian convictions and virtues, using multiple narrative tools to achieve those ends. While there is not an absolute correspondence between the genres of βίος and gospel, we ought to expect, since genres provide expectations, that the life of the central character, Jesus, will in some way be given as paradigmatic in embodying certain virtues that are formative for Christian virtues.[17] This, of course, is exactly what we find. As one example, Mark 8:27–38 explicitly

---

his readers to reach a different conclusion—to see men in a sanctifying journey from idolatrous superstitions and manipulation to faithful dependence on the goodness of Yahweh, shaped over time by the persistent faithfulness of God.

14. As she says, "The evangelists' move from disjointed anecdotes and sayings to connected, theologically coherent narrative is most easily explained with reference to the narrative modes of the Hebrew Bible." Loveday Alexander, "What Is a Gospel?," in *The Cambridge Companion to the Gospels*, ed. Stephen C. Barton (Cambridge: Cambridge University Press, 2006), 28.

15. E.g., M. Daniel Carroll R. and Jacqueline E. Lapsley, eds., *Character Ethics and the Old Testament: Moral Dimensions of Scripture* (Louisville: Westminster John Knox, 2007). See also Richard G. Bowman, "The Complexity of Character and the Ethics of Complexity: The Case of King David," in *Character and Scripture: Moral Formation, Community, and Biblical Interpretation*, ed. William P. Brown (Grand Rapids: Eerdmans, 2002), 73–97. For ethicists see Leon Kass, *The Beginning of Wisdom: Reading Genesis* (New York: Free Press, 2003); and Eleonore Stump, *Wandering in Darkness: Narrative and the Problem of Suffering* (Oxford: Clarendon, 2010).

16. Wisdom literature here assumes a broader definition than those normally entertained by OT scholars in referring to a small collection of biblical books with explicit wisdom themes. Those concerned with this question are directed to the appendix on Wisdom literature.

17. Cf. Richard A. Burridge, *Imitating Jesus: An Inclusive Approach to New Testament Ethics* (Grand Rapids: Eerdmans, 2007), 62–79.

interprets Jesus's imminent death as defining both his kingship and the nature of discipleship.[18]

This also means that reading the Gospels as wisdom is part of recognizing their nature as wisdom texts, not simply an agenda we can fruitfully attach to the Gospels but recognition of and assent to the intentions of the Gospel authors signaled by both their content and form.[19] The Gospels were written for spiritual formation.

Currents in Gospel Criticism

Unfortunately, the history of gospel criticism has evidenced little concern for reading the Gospels as wisdom. The primary concern has been with historical and theological genealogy, in which the Gospels have been the primary source material scrutinized for clues to the set of vexing questions surrounding the birth of early Christianity. What did the earliest Christians believe? Who was the historical Jesus of Nazareth? How did the early church come to worship Jesus as God? What were the stages of theological development, and who was instrumental in the development of beliefs later embraced by the church as a whole? These kinds of questions fostered the development of historical-critical methodologies engineered to solve this complex historical-theological puzzle. These methodologies attempted to identify and strip away layers of the church's "mythological" beliefs about Jesus and gain access to the real "Jesus of history."[20] Once again, we develop reading strategies to answer certain questions. In this case, Gospel narratives were mined for data useful for the historical reconstruction of the origins of early Christianity. These questions are still vital, and still vexing; the results have been fruitful, but just as often incoherent.

18. See Hans F. Bayer, *A Theology of Mark: The Dynamic between Christology and Authentic Discipleship*, Explorations in Biblical Theology (Phillipsburg, NJ: P&R, 2012); and Suzanne Watts Henderson, *Christology and Discipleship in the Gospel of Mark*, SNTSMS 135 (Cambridge: Cambridge University Press, 2006).

19. Again, this is not to ignore the diversity and multiplicity of intentions embraced by each of the Gospels or to ignore each particular Gospel's way of implementing its own agendas. But, while recognizing this diversity as essential in reading the Gospels well on their own terms, another part of reading them on their own terms is recognizing their common goal of motivating and maturing Christian belief and practice.

20. Cf. William Wrede, *Paul*, trans. Edward Lummis (London: Philip Green, 1907), xi–xii, "Our testimonies to Jesus are only later accounts, which were not put together by eyewitnesses. The amount of true information which they unquestionably contain is overlaid with thick layers of legendary adornments and historical fancies, prompted by the faith of the later communities; it is only after a weary labour of discrimination, beset on all sides by many uncertainties, that we can hope to come near to the core."

What is most important for our study is to recognize the limited focus of readings produced by historical-critical methodologies. On the whole these methods, as we have seen before, embody a modern "lab-coat" epistemology that, while suited to their own ends, have limited viability in recognizing the Gospels as wisdom. The primary reason for this is that these methods view the form of the text as an *impediment* to understanding. In an effort to "get behind" it, the text is dismantled to surrender its historical-theological treasures. Instead of recognizing the text as narrating a normative vision to be embraced, it becomes a barrier to surmount in search of history. As Hans Frei argues: "The real history of the biblical narratives in which the historian is interested is not what is narrated or the fruit of its narrative shape; rather, it is that to which the story refers or the conditions that substitute for such reference. In short, he is interested not in the text as such but in some reconstructive context to which the text 'really' refers and which renders it intelligible."[21]

As historically conditioned texts, the Gospels cannot be read apart from meticulous attention given to their historical contexts: social, religious, political, and literary. So historical research and historical sensitivities are an essential element in any reading of the Gospels that seeks to understand them on their own terms. At the same time, reading them on their own terms also means recognizing the historically conditioned intentions encoded in the text, which historical-critical methodologies, of necessity, view as impediments to be overcome.

By contrast, the ideological criticisms of postmodernism are (hyper-) aware of motives and intentions of both biblical authors and interpreters. Social-scientific criticism's interest in historical reference only extends to giving a sociological context to the power plays of authors and interpreters, each seeking to give a privileged space to the interests of their clans. Gospel texts are decoded with reference to their attempts at bolstering the social identity and social position of the groups they represent at the expense of other "anti-groups" that serve as foils in the project of self-legitimization. Poststructural criticism exposes these ideological power moves with the purpose of either neutralizing them or redirecting them into an alternative avenue more amenable to the interest of the interpreter. Interpreters, in this context, are themselves (sometimes consciously) interpreting with hegemonic intentions, trying to establish the point of view of their class, race, gender, ecclesial body, academic guild, or academic subdiscipline over against the interest of competing

---

21. Hans W. Frei, *The Eclipse of Biblical Narrative: A Study in Eighteenth and Nineteenth Century Hermeneutics* (New Haven: Yale University Press, 1974), 134–35.

interpretive communities.[22] This type of approach will be of limited value in a wisdom reading of the Gospels because it admits to only a limited scope of textual intentionality (those with sociological repercussions), and it embodies a comportment of suspicion and not of assent, which, as we saw above, is essential in reading for wisdom.

Another strategy prominent in the history of Gospel studies that is more promising is narrative criticism.[23] Narrative criticism attends to the narrative dynamics of the Gospel texts—how they function as stories that incorporate the intersection of plot and characters and narrative techniques, such as characterization and point of view. Narrative criticism is highly sensitive to the intentions of a text encoded in the point of view of the "implied author" and how those intentions are directed toward an "implied reader" who is moved to engage with the text at multiple levels.[24] This attention to the integrity of the text and its intentions (i.e., not using the text primarily as a window into some other reality, either historical or sociological, behind the text) is a more appealing candidate in the project of trying to see the Gospel narratives as wisdom texts that are seeking to shape readers and reading communities in terms of their primary affections and understandings of God, self, and other. As we will see, the dynamic relationship between implied author and implied reader serves as a useful tool in recognizing and participating in the wisdom agendas of the Gospel writers.

Narrative criticism, at times in reaction to historical criticism, has often divorced itself from questions of historical reference in order to focus its energy on dynamics of the final form of the text. So there is a tendency for narrative criticism to suspend narratives in a self-referential space and ignore questions of history and, to a certain degree, theology as well. A hermeneutic

22. Cf. Robert P. Carroll, "Poststructuralist Approaches," in *Cambridge Companion to Biblical Interpretation*, ed. John Barton (Cambridge: Cambridge University Press, 1998), 50–51.

23. Historically, narrative criticism was something of a bridge between modern historical criticism and postmodern ideological criticism. Redaction criticism, the culmination of historical-critical methodologies, focused attention on the Gospel redactors as authors in themselves, with agendas revealed in their redactive moves. Subsequently, this interest has been seen as a catalyst for an interest in the narrative dynamics of the Gospel texts. At the same time, narrative criticism was a catalyst, at the right time, for the development of various forms of socio-rhetorical criticism, which is concerned with how the rhetorical dynamics of the text foster sociological agendas. See Robin Parry, "Narrative Criticism," in *Dictionary for Theological Interpretation of the Bible*, ed. Kevin J. Vanhoozer et al. (Grand Rapids: Baker Academic, 2005), 528–31.

24. Unlike historical authors and readers, implied authors and readers exist only in the world of the text. See Jeannine K. Brown, *Scripture as Communication: Introducing Biblical Hermeneutics* (Grand Rapids: Baker Academic, 2007), 40–42; cf. R. Alan Culpepper, *Anatomy of the Fourth Gospel: A Study in Literary Design*, FFNT (Philadelphia: Fortress, 1983), 6–8.

of wisdom will, therefore, need to augment these approaches because, as we will see, the historical conditionality of the Gospel texts is constitutive of how they function as wisdom.

Didactic and Narrative Dynamics

So, we have seen that gospel *as a genre* betrays wisdom agendas; but how do the Gospel writers implement those intentions? What literary forms do they utilize to impart wisdom? First, the most obvious vehicle for wisdom is found in the numerous teaching discourses in the Gospels (e.g., parables or extended discourses). But here we must be careful to recognize that the Gospel writers are not simply communicating ethical injunctions but a vision of life that highlights certain values, dispositions, and behaviors while at the same time challenging devotions to competing systems of understanding and values. The Sermon on the Mount (Matt. 5–7), for instance, does give instructions on the righteous demands of the kingdom in such areas as marriage, sexuality, worship, and forgiveness. But it would be a misconstrual to read this text as simply an example of casuistry.[25] The Beatitudes (Matt. 5:2–12), and the internal dispositions extolled in them, are the interpretive grid for the whole Sermon on the Mount, which explicates how to embrace one's spiritual poverty—seeking peace and righteousness while embodying counterintuitive, countercultural virtues of mercy, humility, and meekness. In addition, these values, dispositions, and actions are given grounding in the eschatological vision[26] of the revelation of the kingdom of God, inaugurated in the person of Jesus himself.[27] Hope, love, and righteousness are participatory signs of the establishment of God's rule. They particularize the righteousness of God as something established in and among his people.

---

25. See Jonathan T. Pennington, *The Sermon on the Mount and Human Flourishing: A Theological Commentary* (Grand Rapids: Baker Academic, 2017).

26. Cf. Richard B. Hays, *The Moral Vision of the New Testament: Community, Cross, New Creation, A Contemporary Introduction to New Testament Ethics* (San Francisco: HarperSanFrancisco, 1996), 104–10.

27. The blessings promised in the Beatitudes possess an unmistakably eschatological character, because their fulfillment will be brought about by God (hence the use of divine passives predominates; cf. Craig S. Keener, *A Commentary on the Gospel of Matthew* [Grand Rapids: Eerdmans, 1999], 167) in the eschatological fulfillment of his kingdom. David L. Turner, *Matthew*, BECNT (Grand Rapids: Baker Academic, 2008), 150, notes what is in view here is a "presently inaugurated kingdom that will be consummated in the future." Cf. William David Davies and Dale C. Allison, *A Critical and Exegetical Commentary on the Gospel according to Saint Matthew*, ICC (Edinburgh: T&T Clark, 1988), 1:439–40.

So these didactic portions of the Gospels demonstrate wisdom intentions in informing and reshaping right actions, right reasons, and right motivations (Right ARM). They prescribe certain actions and character traits as praiseworthy. They also contextualize those same actions and dispositions within an understanding of reality that renders those actions and dispositions intelligible and praiseworthy. Christian virtues and deeds are rooted in an understanding of God, self, and other that communicates a prioritization of values that orient the community within a moral landscape. The same picture also serves to reorient devotions—to desire ultimate goods over competing transient ones. In these ways the teaching portions of the Gospels function as wisdom, not simply communicating history, theology, or ethics, but engaging in confirming and inculcating Christian dispositions and actions, through various forms of instruction. This intention is clearly seen in Jesus's warning at the conclusion of the Sermon on the Mount (Matt. 7:24–27), where he contrasts wise and foolish builders (a classic wisdom motif). Those who hear and obey his words will find life, while those who choose to rely on other things embrace their own destruction.

At the same time, while the teachings of Jesus play a significant role in the Gospel narratives, the bulk of the Gospel material is not didactic but narrative.[28] The Gospels are narratives that contain teaching discourses, and while it is not difficult to see how the teaching elements can function as wisdom, it is much less obvious how narrative elements (both individual pericopae and the Gospel narratives as a whole) serve wisdom ends.

How then do the Gospels as narratives function as wisdom? Not simply in the sense that they *contain* wisdom or ethics, but how do they form character? Our real interest is to see how the Gospels *as narratives* function as wisdom texts and to discover how their narrative form is particularly well suited to certain modes of instilling wisdom in reshaping core devotions and dispositions. But to understand this, we first need to explore how narratives in general function as wisdom.

---

28. In reality the Gospel materials represent a continuum between "narrative" and "didactic" portions, with certain forms that combine elements of both. Parables, for example, are self-contained didactic narratives, often relatively independent of the narrative flow of the texts in which they appear (so Matthew and Luke can place them at different points within their narratives), although some parables are connected to contextual narrative tensions (e.g., Mark 4:1–20; Luke 15:11–32). Pronouncement stories, pericopae that conclude with some kind of pronouncement from Jesus (e.g., Mark 2:23–28, concluding with, "So the Son of Man is lord even of the Sabbath"), are a mixture of narrative and didactic text. Despite the presence of these "mixed" texts, defining the ends of the spectrum provides a helpful paradigm for understanding both the more clearly distinct cases and the intermediate ones.

The Ethics of Narrative

In recent decades the line separating the disciplines of literature and philosophy has significantly blurred. Many academics have traveled freely across what was once a tightly guarded border and returned to their home disciplines with fruits from the other side. Some reside in an academic Alsace-Lorraine:[29] equally part of both worlds, although technically part of one. These border crossings have produced some interesting results and opened new (and very old) questions about the relationship between philosophy and literature. One of the major fields of discussion has centered on questions of hermeneutics, since many believe that philosophy since Heidegger only exists within a hermeneutically determined space. From here, literary concerns for reading texts create a natural common field of interest for rich interaction, with the result that philosophical questions have become coordinate with certain literary ones.

One example of this is the exploration of how literature might be a tool to access philosophical questions in a way different from logical analysis. Martha Nussbaum, for example, argues that narratives are the ideal medium for engaging in certain kinds of moral discourse and are in fact better suited than abstract analysis because a narrative approach recognizes that neither moral deliberation nor moral education is purely an intellectual enterprise but must incorporate all of a moral agent's humanity. As it turns out, Nussbaum, by her own admission, is reviving an old concern that goes back to ancient Athens.[30]

In Athenian society the poets, who wrote tragedies, and the philosophers, who taught and debated philosophy, each had an important stake in trying to answer the same basic questions about human flourishing: How could a society be just and its people content and fulfilled? They came at these questions from different sides and with different tools. Both saw civic and individual contentment as dependent on both internal and external contingencies. Internally, the essential ingredient of flourishing was a moral character shaped by goodness/virtue. Externally, one needed beneficial circumstances of life, one of which was living in a society marked by justice and opportunity. But both admitted

29. Alsace, a province in northeastern France (and the boyhood home of Albert Schweitzer), sits on the Rhine, which separates it from neighboring Germany. The region has had a tumultuous history, at various times being under German and French rule, and even a brief stint as a sovereign nation (for eleven days in November 1918). Culturally, it is a mixture of German and French, although French governmental language policy has effectively suppressed local dialects (both French and German). Its unique history is reflected in its architecture, food, and certain legal statutes unheard of in the rest of France, including government subsidies for local synagogues and churches (Lutheran, Reformed, and Roman Catholic).

30. Martha C. Nussbaum, *Love's Knowledge: Essays on Philosophy and Literature* (Oxford: Oxford University Press, 1992), 15–23. Nussbaum's early work was as a philosopher and a classicist.

that the external circumstances of life are unpredictable and not governed by the internal virtue of the moral agent or the civic virtues of society. So while one had a certain degree of influence on one's internal moral life, controlling the external circumstances of life was much more elusive. What one needed to be happy was both virtue and good fortune.[31] Herein lies the central tension in Greek ethics and civic life: good fortune lies outside the locus of control of moral agency, while virtues lie within it.

Both philosophers and poets pondered this tension, but they addressed it in different ways that drove them in opposite directions. Philosophers tried to *solve* this tension, while the poets wanted to *explore* it, showing that the theoretical solutions of the philosophers were tenuous abstractions that failed to recognize the effect tragic turns of fate can have on the soul. External traumas have a profound ability to disrupt internal virtues. So the poets wrote tragedies, in which admirable, virtuous people were blindsided by horrific tragedies (such as the death or betrayal of a loved one), and their lives became consumed by grief, rage, and revenge. So, for example, Medea, in an effort to get back at her husband after he leaves her for an advantageous marriage to a younger woman, murders her own children in a vengeful rage. Medea begins as noble, admirable, and sympathetic but ends up corrupted by vengeance to the point that she abandons her natural maternal affections in favor of revenge. These tragic dramas were not only entertainment but a lesson in the illusive nature of happiness. Happiness, especially when tied to relationships, is inherently fragile and outside the control of the moral agent. So no matter how virtuous individuals are, they are susceptible to tragedy, and according to the poets, they will not survive with either their virtue or their happiness intact.

Plato's solution to this problem was to locate human flourishing in one's internal adherence to reason and to distance oneself from emotional attachments to external goods. Consequently, he trusted reason over emotions as a guide to happiness, which led him to denounce the poets, who prized emotional experiences over systematic constructions of reason. Plato's blueprint for Athenian society in *The Republic* almost completely excludes the poets.[32]

In contrast to Plato, Aristotle believed that emotions had an *essential* role to play in a virtuous life. He taught that a virtuous person is not simply someone who obeys reason and does virtuous things, but someone who takes pleasure in

31. See Martha C. Nussbaum, *The Fragility of Goodness: Luck and Ethics in Greek Tragedy and Philosophy* (Cambridge: Cambridge University Press, 1986).

32. See book 3 of *The Republic* for his censoring of the poets. Plato objects to narratives precisely because they elicit emotional responses and connections in the readers; see §398a–b.

doing what is right.[33] For him, the interdependent acts of loving what is good and hating what is evil are essential to formation in virtue. So Aristotle believed that progress in virtue was a process that functioned intellectually, practically, and psychologically.[34] Character formation involved habitual adherence to virtue but also a reeducation of values and devotions.[35] Reenter the poets. Nussbaum and other narrative ethicists believe that narrative literature is more suited to this kind of reeducation than theoretical discourses on virtue.[36]

So what is it about narratives that these philosophers and literary critics see as important for facilitating moral formation? Aren't stories just something we read for entertainment? The popularity of stories, whether in the form of novels, movies, TV shows, or comics, is the first element these critics would point to as signaling their formative importance. As Marshal Gregory says, "For human beings, the pull of stories is primal. What oxygen is to our body, stories are to our emotions and imagination."[37] Stories are a universal human phenomenon and an essential element in human experience; they provide models and categories to interpret our experience and form our identity.[38] Stories offer invitations to enter into another world and experience from inside the lives of their characters. Remarkably, we give our assent to this process dozens of times each day, in listening to the recounting of the events of someone's day (one of the most fundamental experiences of community), or reading a story at bedtime, or turning on the TV. Stories map on to our inner world in a way that is immediate and effortless. This fact is the starting point for reflections on how narratives can be formative for character.

Critics and philosophers who embrace such a notion freely admit that not all writers or storytellers intend to shape the moral character of their

33. See Nussbaum, *Love's Knowledge*, 78. Cf. Nancy Sherman, *The Fabric of Character: Aristotle's Theory of Virtue* (Oxford: Oxford University Press, 1989), 44–50.

34. See Aristotle, *Nicomachean Ethics* 6.2.1–6; §1139a–b.

35. Cf. Julia Annas, *The Morality of Happiness* (Oxford: Oxford University Press, 1993), 27–131.

36. Along with Nussbaum see Wayne C. Booth, *The Company We Keep: An Ethics of Fiction* (Berkeley: University of California Press, 1988); Stephen K. George, ed. *Ethics, Literature, and Theory: An Introductory Reader*, 2nd ed. (Lanham, MD: Rowman & Littlefield, 2005); Wayne C. Booth, *The Rhetoric of Fiction*, 2nd ed. (Chicago: University of Chicago Press, 1983); Peter Singer and Renata Singer, *The Moral of the Story: An Anthology of Ethics through Literature* (Oxford: Blackwell, 2005); Andrew Gibson, *Postmodernity, Ethics, and the Novel* (London: Routledge, 1999); David Parker, *Ethics, Theory, and the Novel* (Cambridge: Cambridge University Press, 1994).

37. Marshall Gregory, *Shaped by Stories: The Ethical Power of Narratives* (Notre Dame, IN: University of Notre Dame Press, 2009), 19.

38. See Stephen Crites, "The Narrative Quality of Experience," in *Why Narrative? Readings in Narrative Theology*, ed. Stanley Hauerwas and L. Gregory Jones (Grand Rapids: Eerdmans, 1989), 65–88.

audiences. Some want to inform, some want to entertain, some want to be famous. But even for those who do not have a particular wisdom intention in mind, the nature of stories themselves invites something of this process. As Gregory explains, "At the core of every story is a set of invitations to feel, to believe, and to judge as the story dictates."[39] Because narratives elicit these kinds of reactions in their readers, they project, whether intentionally or not, a normative field of interpretation that transcends the particular events of the story—a moral vision.

Stories do not exist in a self-referential morality of their own invention; they work because they share a moral space that exists outside the text. These normative pictures of the world may be rudimentary, but all stories possess them. Authors invite readers to share their interpretive lenses, to judge the world as they judge it. This is even true of complex narratives where the reader isn't meant to trust the judgments of the (often first-person) narrator and his or her interpretation of events.[40] But the reason the reader doesn't completely trust the narrator is that the author doesn't want the reader to—another case of the author (technically the implied author) gaining the reader's trust and inviting the reader to share his or her evaluations, beginning with their shared evaluation of a duplicitous narrator.[41]

Some stories are, of course, primarily written for entertainment value. But even these stories project a moral landscape by asking us to approve of certain characters and some, if not all, of their actions while disapproving of other characters. These stories tend to have likable, but not complex, main characters, whose internal worlds are relatively uncomplicated. The "action" of these stories is in the plot twists and difficult circumstances that the characters have to overcome.

Where narratives become especially interesting for our project is when the characters become more psychologically compelling in their complexity and we are asked to enter into their world of moral deliberations, inhabited by confusion, fears, and competing allegiances to family, God, nation, self-preservation, and acceptance by others. These narratives invite us to experience from the inside twists of fate and movements of the soul, and in so doing we initiate a parallel implicit process of self-examination in which we interrogate our own

39. Gregory, *Shaped by Stories*, 20. He adds, "The cueing, prompting and stimulating that we receive from stories to feel *this* way, to believe *this* way, and to judge *this* way bring our capacities for feeling, believing, and judging into active wakefulness."

40. Cf. Paul Ricoeur, *Time and Narrative*, trans. Kathleen Blamey and David Pellauer (Chicago: University of Chicago Press, 1984–88), 3:162–63.

41. One of the best examples of this can be found in C. S. Lewis, *Till We Have Faces: A Myth Retold* (London: G. Bles, 1956).

fears, hopes, and allegiances, with a potential for a reassessment and realignment of our own value structures. In this way, and others we will see below, stories possess the power to influence character. We can see that this mode of character shaping is something inherent to our experience of narratives. It is precisely for this reason that critics such as Nussbaum argue that narratives, by their nature, are ideal for certain types of moral discourse, especially those intending to shape the moral convictions of the readers in some measure.[42] As she says, "If philosophy is a search for wisdom about ourselves, philosophy needs to turn to literature."[43] To see why, we need to understand three things about the nature of wisdom and how narratives access wisdom.

How Do Narratives Access Wisdom?

Those who argue for the formative value of narratives do not believe that reading literature magically makes people better[44] or that readers are naturally inclined to ape the actions (positive or negative) of narrative characters.[45] Rather, narratives are formative because they inculcate wisdom. Aristotle defined wisdom (φρόνησις; variously translated as "practical reason," "discernment," or "wisdom") as the practical skill of perceiving the right action in a particular circumstance (cf. Rom. 12:2). This perception comprehends basic ethical principles alongside the situational particularities that make each moral deliberation unique. In Aristotle's system of virtue, aimed at the goal of human contentment (εὐδαιμονία), φρόνησις plays a central role as chief of the virtues but is also informed by all the others.[46] Like the other virtues, practical wisdom is a learned skill, developed through training and experience.

Nussbaum points to three central elements of Aristotle's account of practical reason that reveal how and why narratives are congenial to developing wisdom. First is the principle of incommensurable goods, where competing goods each have distinct attractions for us and cannot be arranged on some kind of evaluative number line. It is easy to see that $10 is worth more than $5, but how much is friendship worth (and not all friendships, or friendship as a concept)? Is *this* friendship always more

---

42. Nussbaum, *Love's Knowledge*, 5–7.

43. Nussbaum, *Love's Knowledge*, 290.

44. See Gregory, *Shaped by Stories*, 9, for a denial of this all-too-common altruistic assertion.

45. Even in the case of narratives that explicitly or implicitly employ characters as exemplars, exemplary actions are exemplary because they embody a certain virtue, disposition, or pattern of life, and the stress of imitation is on the embodied virtue, not on the specific action. See Dryden, *Theology and Ethics*, 169–72; cf. Phil. 2:1–11.

46. On the reciprocal dependence of wisdom and the other virtues, see Annas, *Happiness*, 74.

important than competing goods such as self-preservation or loyalty to family or country? Are there some cases where this friendship has to be sacrificed for the sake of a spouse but other circumstances where the opposite choice is warranted? If so, then we have to recognize that all goods do not exist together on an evaluative number line where each has a fixed value in relationship to all other goods. If all goods were commensurable, then moral deliberations would be as easy as choosing $10 over $5. This recognition necessitates a central role for discernment to judge among the claims of competing incommensurable goods.

Narratives swim in the tensions created by incommensurable goods. Much of the energy of narratives, especially those that incorporate real moral challenges for their characters, is derived from the tensions between competing goods or competing evaluations of the good life. What goods will Hamlet lay aside to avenge his father? Love for Ophelia, fidelity to friends, love for his mother? Or is there something of even greater value for which he might lay aside his desire to avenge and save his father? Narratives are an ideal medium for the sympathetic exploration of the competing pulls of incommensurable goods because they bring readers into the complex sphere of choice with attention to details that communicate psychological realism and the strengths of competing desires attached to competing goods, each promising an avenue to the good life particularly conceived.[47]

Another level of incommensurability that narratives are excellent at accessing is the distance between incommensurable *systems* of value. Moral tensions often arise not simply from our inability to discern the relative value of competing goods but from the tensions between competing systems for valuing goods that we inhabit and the different hierarchies those competing systems use to assign values to possible goods.[48] So instead of the question of whether $5 is worth more than $10, is $5 worth more than £5 or ¥10,000?[49] Narrative tensions often arise from characters who are stretched between two

47. This idea of incommensurable goods is not arguing for a relativism where the relative relationships between goods are seen as subjectively determined and therefore having no prescriptive force. It does not teach that goods cannot be recognized, nor does it assume that circumstances determine goods through some form of consequentialism. Rather, this principle argues that the perception of incommensurable goods in moral deliberation is dependent on the historical conditions of the situation. Practical wisdom is an act of perception deeply tied to particulars. The choices of Hamlet exist in a nexus of relationships. He does not contemplate vengeance in general, but vengeance for his father, betrayed by his uncle, who has stolen the king's throne and wife.

48. See Alasdair C. MacIntyre, *Whose Justice? Which Rationality?* (Notre Dame, IN: University of Notre Dame Press, 1988).

49. On the assumption there is no moral equivalent to international currency-exchange markets.

or more competing systems of value or moral spaces. If we think, for example, of the nineteenth-century British novel, the central tension oftentimes centers on a character trapped in the social constraints of Victorian social norms and habits who finds himself or herself drawn to a heartfelt pursuit (such as romantic love) that conflicts with these norms. This is a tension between incommensurable systems of value: one defined by Victorian bourgeois respectability and the other by the virtues of romanticism. Such narratives are setting whole systems of value at odds with each other and promoting an evaluative space that favors one over the other.

The narrative dynamics of the Gospels are often driven by analogous tensions between competing systems of value. One moral vision, which places Jesus and his kingship above all other devotions, comes into conflict with other moral hierarchies, often based on the religious traditions of Second Temple Judaism, but not exclusively so. Jesus's confrontations with the religious leadership of Israel are one manifestation of this. Likewise, Jesus confronts his disciples for their lack of faith when they evidence their continued devotion to a system of values that directs their devotions to personal glory and blinds them from recognizing the cross as the calling of Jesus and what describes their own vocation.

The second element in Aristotle's understanding of practical wisdom is his emphasis on particulars over general rules. Wisdom is the habituated skill of applying general principles to particular cases. No form of encyclopedic casuistry can produce an answer for every possible situation. Once we admit this, there are only two options to solve this problem of complexity. The first is to simplify particular situations down to common denominators that are covered in existing case law, which is the strategy that characterizes most modern approaches to ethics. The second is to recognize the necessity of the skill of discernment in applying general principles to specific situations and to use case law (as formative examples of discernment) as a tool in developing wisdom. The latter picture of how particulars relate to general principles (i.e., the priority of particulars over principles) also fits naturally with a belief in incommensurable goods.[50]

So Aristotle believes that discernment happens in the apprehension of the particulars, not so much in a reliance on an abstract system of logically related ethical norms. At the same time, he also recognizes the necessity and importance of such norms, because wisdom is an act of applying those norms to particular situations. He does not exclude ethical principles as such, but he subordinates them to practical wisdom, where rules assume an *instrumental*

---

50. Cf. Nussbaum, *Love's Knowledge*, 68.

role in perception.[51] While practical discernment is informed by principles, it is a skill (an intellectual virtue) fostered in particular acts of judgment deeply attentive to circumstances.

Narratives facilitate attentiveness to particulars in situationally specific deliberations. Narratives are typically reticent to offer explicit interpretations of persons or events, but they constantly elicit judgments and interpretations of actions based on descriptions of events, characters, and places. (That is to say, they primarily communicate judgments *implicitly*.) These descriptions can be sparse or verbose; either way, judgments are primarily communicated to the reader through narrative detail, through the particularities that define the boundaries of the moral deliberations characters engage in. As Nussbaum notes, narratives "direct us to attend to the concrete; they display before us a wealth of richly realized detail, presented as relevant for choice."[52] It is in their power to place us in a particularized world that narratives give a context for our understanding of characters and participation with them in the choices that confront them. In this way narratives foster the skill of discernment (φρόνησις) tied to the perception of particulars. Narratives do not speak in generalities or principles. They operate through particulars that are arranged in the shape of a plot that puts characters in places of conflict, longing, and deliberation. While we could reduce narratives down to their "morals," this would strip the narratives of their proper function, which is not simply to teach us "principles" but to foster wisdom.

Finally, the third element in Aristotle's description of practical reason is the essential place of the emotions in the act of perception. Again, for Aristotle the proper emotional attachment to various goods is a *necessary* element in virtue, not something that can be either excluded entirely or merely added on as an adornment to wisdom. Emotions such as anger, grief, and joy are unmediated value judgments because they correlate to the perceived value of objects.[53] So we experience joy in the context of a treasured relationship, grief when it is lost, and anger when it is betrayed. At the same time, if we come to understand the mitigating circumstances of that betrayal, then our anger might subside.[54] Because emotions are unmediated value judgments, they are useful and in fact *necessary* as acts of practical reason. As Nussbaum says, "The emotions are themselves modes of vision, or recognition. Their

51. Cf. Nussbaum, *Love's Knowledge*, 98, "Perception, we might say, is a process of loving conversation between rules and concrete responses, general conceptions and unique cases, in which the general articulates the particular and is in turn further articulated by it."

52. Nussbaum, *Love's Knowledge*, 95.

53. Emotions here are distinct from feelings or moods such as tired, cranky, or delirious.

54. Cf. Nussbaum, *Love's Knowledge*, 293.

responses are part of what knowing, that is truly recognizing or acknowledging, *consists in.*"[55]

Narratives engage readers emotionally in a story; in the development of attachments to particular characters, through some form of identification, readers are invited to enter into the space of their moral deliberations. Narratives are purposely built for this type of engagement where readers experience the confusion of the competing allegiances of characters from the "inside." This emotional identification facilitates the formation of wisdom by participating in a "virtual" act of discernment, rejoicing in good choices, or alternately grieving a choice the reader can see will lead to ruin. These are participatory acts of discernment that practice and foster wisdom.

These emotionally constituted acts of discernment develop wisdom by giving readers formative experiences of loving good and hating evil, where readers are drawn to admire honest, compassionate characters and to reject selfish, conniving ones. In reading we learn to evaluate characters, not necessarily as good or evil, but as attractive (because they embody some character trait we admire: curiosity, nobility, faithfulness, or humility) or repugnant (because they are manipulative, selfish, and arrogant). We learn values implicitly through these sorts of attachments. We want to "be near" certain characters and want to "distance ourselves" from others (while we wait expectantly for them to receive their comeuppance). This is learning to love good and hate evil, not as abstractions, but as realities that shape our devotions and moral agency.

So, discernment (φρόνησις) uses intellectual and affective perception of situational particulars to judge right actions among the claims of incommensurable goods. From this understanding of wisdom, we can begin to see how narratives naturally resonate with the project of fostering wisdom. In addition to instilling practical wisdom, narratives also take on an implicit formative role in promoting certain values.

Formative Narrative Dynamics

As noted above, while narratives do at times make explicit value judgments, their real power is in *implicitly* instilling certain perspectives and values in their readers. Narratives accomplish this through the shape of the plot itself and the reader's orientations toward the author and the characters. Through these devices, narratives take on a normative function, guiding the reader in

55. Nussbaum, *Love's Knowledge*, 79. Italics original. Cf. Martha C. Nussbaum, *Upheavals of Thought: The Intelligence of Emotions* (Cambridge: Cambridge University Press, 2001), 19–88.

forming judgments, convictions, and attachments that the author promotes.[56] The author describes a value-laden world, which ascribes values to characters and events, and provides an implicit but intricate evaluation of attachments to possible goods.

The first way that narratives communicate value systems is through the deeply embedded relationship between the implied author and the implied reader. Unlike the actual author and actual readers, the implied author and implied reader are defined by and only exist in the narrative dynamics of the text. The implied author is the sum total of the authorial moves embedded in the text. Likewise, the implied reader is the ideal reader who responds to the moves of the implied author. The real author creates the implied author, and the real readers relate to the story through the implied reader.[57]

The author uses literary devices to foster a certain kind of relationship between the implied author and implied readers. So for example, most narratives have an implied author who is omniscient and who can move freely between places and times.[58] This omniscient point of view elicits a certain degree of trust between the implied author and implied reader. The reader trusts the viewpoint of the implied author implicitly because the implied author is not limited in his or her vision or ability to judge the actions and motives of the characters in the story. These types of judgments are, again, sometimes explicit, but more likely implicit, asking the implied reader to form judgments by inference from the elements given in the narrative. At the same time such inferences are always *guided* inferences, led by the author.

As above, this is one of the ways that narratives invite readers to participate in formative acts of practical judgment. One example of a literary device of implied judgment is the use of irony. When characters in a story say or do something ironic unintentionally and unknowingly, and no other characters recognize it, then the irony of the scene is a shared experience between the author and the reader, and them only.[59] The irony arises from the dissonance between the apparent and actual (or surface and deeper) significance of an event or saying. Because the author and reader share some knowledge or

56. Cf. Brown, *Scripture as Communication*, 45.

57. The implied reader is a model that guides the real reader in the act of reception. As Ricoeur notes, in practice the distance between the implied reader and actual reader is less than that between the real and implied authors. See Ricoeur, *Time and Narrative*, 3:171.

58. This is even true of narratives with a narrator who is not omniscient and is fixed in a limited world of his or her experience and interpretation. The narrator is not identical with the implied author, although in some cases they are hard to distinguish.

59. Sometimes the technical terminology of *implied* author and *implied* reader can become cumbersome. In what follows I am simply going to use "author" and "reader" to refer to what are technically the implied author and the implied reader.

interpretation unknown to the characters in the narrative, they experience irony as a *shared secret*. This could be rather innocent knowledge of events or characters, especially in a comically ironic scene, but in a tragically ironic scene the author and reader stand together in their judgment of the moral significance of the scene.

The example of irony demonstrates how such devices form a bond between author and reader. The point of view of the author is normative for the reader, but this normativity is communicated in the context of relational trust and not as an act of coercion.[60] In using irony the author creates a shared space for the author and reader to inhabit together. They share a secret knowledge unknown to the characters who live at the story level.[61]

If we change the ironic scene slightly, we can see another way in which the author directs the responses, experiences, and judgments of the reader. We can add to our ironic scene a single character who shares the same knowledge as the author and reader, and then all three together understand the scene as ironic. This character understands events unfolding before her to have a different significance from all the other characters in the story, but in a way shared with the author and reader. What this establishes is a connection, created by the author, between the reader and this character. This connection involves an act of sympathetic identification. The reader shares the experience of this solitary knowledgeable character and identifies with her position vis-à-vis the other characters in the narrative who do not recognize the ironic significance of what has taken place. This is an example of *identification*, a complex but automatic mode in which readers engage with narratives.

The author directs the intensity and modes of identification readers engage in. Traditionally, the main character is the most prominent candidate for identification. This character embodies some character traits that the reader possesses or aspires to while at the same time being human enough (with psychological complexity, failings, and conflicting desires) for the reader to recognize something of themselves in them. Once this sympathetic portrayal is initiated, the reader is trained to get into the shoes of this character, imagining how they would react to the character's situation and choose in their circumstance.[62]

---

60. Booth, *Company We Keep*, speaks of the relationship between implied author and implied reader as a "literary friendship."

61. The "story level" is the narrative level at which the characters exist within a limited field of view defined by narrative place, plot, and time. The "discourse level" is the level at which the implied author and implied readers experience the narrative "from above," with more knowledge than those in the narrative.

62. Cf. Marshall Gregory, "Ethical Criticism: What It Is and Why It Matters," in *Ethics, Literature, and Theory: An Introductory Reader*, ed. Stephen K. George (Lanham, MD: Rowman & Littlefield, 2005), 56–57.

While the reader engages in the narrative by identifying with characters, it is important that the distance between reader and characters never collapses. For identification to function as a tool of self-reflection it is necessary to keep oneself and the character in the same moral field of vision but still distinct from each other. Identification is instrumental in the reader's exploration of incommensurable goods, when the reader enters into the deliberations of the character while at the same time reevaluating her own way of valuing incommensurable goods. This whole process is guided by the author, who directs the reader's evaluation of and identification with particular characters. The author creates both the identification with as well as the distance between the reader and the character, because both are necessary for an engaged process that results in self-awareness and realigning of the convictions and attachments of the reader.

Finally, narratives communicate normative values not only through particular characters and actions but simply through the shape of their plots. As Marshall Gregory says, "The arc of a particular plot is also the arc of a particular ethical trajectory."[63] Narratives take characters on a journey, and the particular shape of that journey, the kinds of challenges faced, and what their resolutions look like[64] all imply a normative view of ethical priorities, to the extent that certain values or dispositions played a necessary role in the resolution of narrative tensions. As Gregory explains, "The plot shows how people in stories became the persons they turn out to be, and our participation in that movement from point A to point B and beyond involves us in assuming beliefs, having feelings, and making judgments that, once we have made them, exert pressure on the ethical trajectory of our own lives."[65] The shape of the plot gives a normative context for our own moral choices and sense of self.

All narratives embody a certain teleology, because they are directed at some sort of conclusion. They do not wander aimlessly, and they do not simply end. The narrative is moving toward an end (a τέλος), the culmination of the circumstances and choices of the characters. The significance of those choices is seen most clearly in the form the end of the story takes. The conclusion is what gives a narrative its definitive shape, its teleological structure. What Gregory suggests is that the teleological trajectory of narratives informs readers' own understanding of what teleology is formative for their understanding of themselves and their choices.

63. Gregory, *Shaped by Stories*, 99.
64. The expectation of some kind of resolution is itself a very particular kind of "ethical trajectory" based on particular assumptions about the world and human life, and especially ideas about what redemption looks like.
65. Gregory, *Shaped by Stories*, 99.

We experience choices in life as primarily contingent; our ability to foresee the outcomes and implications of our actions is very limited. This is one of the aspects of choices that makes them difficult. In narratives, characters also experience story events as a series of contingencies, but the readers experience those same events teleologically, within a narrative unity supplied by the author. We see the characters' lives, at least the portion of their lives in the narrative, as an intelligible unity, shaped by their circumstances, desires, and choices. That intelligibility derives from the narrative arc (the shape of the plot), which readers can then use to inform some kind of narrative unity for their own contingent lives and choices, in the process of what Alasdair MacIntyre labels "seeing one's life as a whole." MacIntyre explains:

> We live out our lives, both individually and in our relationships with each other, in the light of certain conceptions of a possible shared future, a future in which certain possibilities beckon us forward and others repel us, some seem already foreclosed and others perhaps inevitable. There is no present that is not informed by some image of some future and an image of the future which always presents itself in the form of a *telos*—or of a variety of ends and goals—towards which we are either moving or failing to move in the present. Unpredictability and teleology therefore coexist as part of our lives; like characters in a fictional narrative we do not know what will happen next, but nonetheless our lives have a certain form which projects itself toward our future. Thus the narratives that we live out have both an unpredictable and partially teleological character.[66]

Narrative plots provide a normative shape to ethical deliberation, adding a degree of teleological narrative unity to the unpredictability of our experience of life. This renders actions intelligible, not only as isolated incidents but as connected events that give an ethical trajectory within which moral choices can be understood and evaluated. This gives a narrative context that not only measures individual actions according to principles of conformity to rules or laws but conformity to a characteristic shape of a life directed at a goal. In this way, narratives have a power to inform and contextualize both identity and considered moral action.[67]

66. Alasdair C. MacIntyre, *After Virtue: A Study in Moral Theory*, 2nd ed. (London: Duckworth, 1985), 215–16. For *the* seminal study on the connection between future vision and political life, see Frederik Lodewijk Polak, *The Image of the Future: Enlightening the Past, Orientating the Present, Forecasting the Future*, trans. Elise Boulding, 2 vols. (Leyden: A. W. Sythoff, 1961).

67. Cf. Paul Ricoeur, *Oneself as Another*, trans. Kathleen Blamey (Chicago: University of Chicago Press, 1992), 140–68.

Can We Apply This to the Gospels?

So what does all this mean for reading the Gospels? First, we will need to address two probable objections. Some will question whether these observations apply to the Gospels because, on the whole, the theories discussed above were developed specifically to deal with modern novels, and the Gospels are ancient historical testimony.[68] It is important to maintain the genre distinction between the Gospels (along with other ancient historical writings) and novels, whether ancient or modern. At the same time, as Ricoeur has shown, the boundary between these two genres is more permeable than widely admitted.[69] While we should certainly guard against collapsing the two genres or overlooking the importance of their differences, there is considerable overlap in their narrative dynamics and respective functions; where they chiefly differ is in their claims to a specific kind of referentiality (i.e., historical narratives make a claim to reference actual persons and events).

But we must also recognize that fictional narratives, while not referring to historical persons or events, do possess a type of referentiality to the world of historically conditioned human experience. To be interesting and effective, fictional narratives, as Aristotle saw with tragedies, have to possess an element of mimesis—the imitation of life.[70] This imitation is focused on the internal world where desires for significance and relationships compete with calls to righteousness, honor, and self-preservation. It is this internal world that creates the opportunity for identification between readers and characters, which only works to the degree that the characterizations are psychologically compelling. If characterization does not imitate life, then stories become uninteresting. It does not matter whether the character is a king, an orphan, or a hobbit; the connecting point of mimesis is located in the reality of the internal world of

68. The terminology of "historical testimony" is borrowed from Richard Bauckham, *Jesus and the Eyewitnesses: The Gospels as Eyewitness Testimony* (Grand Rapids: Eerdmans, 2006). Even if one does not consider the Gospels to have strong claims to historical reliability, the authors clearly adopted the modes of ancient historical biography, and they have to be read according to those standards.

69. See Ricoeur, *Time and Narrative*, 157–92.

70. As Ricoeur says, "Mimesis . . . marks the intersection between the world of the text and the world of the reader, the intersection, therefore, between the world configured by the poem and the world within which effective action is unfolded and itself unfolds its specific temporality." *Time and Narrative*, 159. See Erich Auerbach, *Mimesis: The Representation of Reality in Western Literature*, trans. Willard R. Trask (Princeton: Princeton University Press, 1953). In this famous study Auerbach catalogs different characteristics of how writers in the Western tradition (including the Bible) have engaged in mimetic representations of reality. While he is especially sensitive to the differences between these literary traditions, his work also assumes a common agenda among these traditions, namely to imitate life in a way that engages the reader and is psychologically compelling in its imitation of human experience.

hopes, fears, and choices. In fictional narratives this derives from the author's powers of human observation and imagination; in historical narratives it depends on the author's talent for historical reconstruction and characterization.

To this extent, the historian's job is easier in that the psychological reality of his characters derives from real persons and does not need to be invented. But the historian still needs to convey that reality in a compelling way, and for this he uses the same tools as the novelist, such as attention to details that create compelling characterizations. This is an example of how historical narratives adopt some of the tools common to all narratives.

Historians have an obligation to historical fidelity, to tie their accounts to historical events in a way that novelists do not, but they are also telling stories—utilizing characterization, point of view, irony, plot, and so on. Readers are responsible to recognize the historian's claims (implicit or explicit) to describe events that happened, but readers are also meant to engage with a narrative in the ways that it functions as a narrative, and those modes of engagement are substantially the same whether the narrative is historical or not.[71]

The second objection that some might have is that the Gospels are chiefly about Christology—that their purpose is to communicate theological truths about the person and work of Jesus—and so questions of wisdom and ethics are (at best) secondary considerations. While this objection has a very important kernel of truth (namely, the focus of the Gospels is on revealing the person of Jesus),[72] it understands this truth within a modernistic understanding of the Bible that views the text as a vehicle for transmitting information. While the Gospels as historical testimony communicate both historical and theological truths about the person and work of Jesus, their chief aim is to orient their readers' lives around those truths, not simply to teach Christology.[73] The Gospels, as communicative speech acts, utilize christological truths with an

71. Richard Bauckham's category of testimony is helpful in reorienting our understanding of historiography to recognize the nature of the Gospels as communicating historical reportage of events along with the significance given to those events by the apostles. This is the definition of apostolic witness. See Bauckham, *Jesus and the Eyewitnesses*, 472–508. Cf. also Herman N. Ridderbos, *Redemptive History and the New Testament Scriptures*, trans. H. De Jongste, Biblical and Theological Studies (Phillipsburg, NJ: P&R, 1988).

72. See Burridge, *What Are the Gospels?*, 248–51.

73. Cf. Culpepper, *Anatomy*, 4–5,

> The implicit purpose of the gospel narrative is to alter irrevocably the reader's perception of the real world. The narrative world of the gospel is neither a window on the ministry of Jesus nor a window on the Johannine community. Primarily at least, it is the literary creation of the evangelist, which is crafted with the purpose of leading readers to "see" the world as the evangelist sees it so that in reading the gospel they will be forced to test their perceptions and beliefs about the "real" world against the evangelist's perspective on the world they have encountered in the gospel.

eye to their illocutionary force; this incorporates, but goes beyond, intentions to communicate historical or christological truths.[74]

One example of how wisdom agendas shape Christology is the dichotomy at the center of Mark's Gospel between faith and fear. This dichotomy is an integrating motif in Mark's depiction of how the disciples and other characters relate to Jesus (see Mark 4:41; 5:33, 36; 6:50; 9:32; 10:32; 11:18; 16:8). If Mark's aim was to produce a certain state of knowledge in his readers (i.e., to teach Christology), then the dichotomy would be between faith and *doubt* or faith and *ignorance*. But for Mark faith in Jesus means a trusting dependence on his benevolent kingship, and the opposite of this is to live in fear (which can attach itself to innumerable objects).[75] Faith in Mark is not assent to a certain set of christological truths; it is a practical disposition of personal trust. Mark's aim is to form that kind of faith in his readers by engaging them in a participatory process where their convictions and beliefs come under deep scrutiny and are remolded around the person of Jesus.[76]

Still, the idea persists that biblical narratives such as the Gospels are meant to be read "theologically," with an eye to what they can "teach us about God."[77] Such a hermeneutical approach, while having the appearance of wisdom, is relatively useless in reading biblical narratives. Vast portions of biblical narratives teach us next to nothing explicitly about God. (This is especially true of OT historical narratives.) This kind of understanding is a modern cousin to historical-critical approaches that seek to harvest texts for certain kinds of information (historical or theological). It is based on the same epistemological assumptions and views the narrative integrity of the text as an impediment to be overcome in favor of a real truth "behind the text." But biblical narratives function as Scripture as narratives, not in their supposed witness to some "universal" truths or principles hidden within or behind the text.

---

74. This intention of the Gospel writers is the chief reason why attempts at neutral readings of the Gospels as "history" have yielded mostly indeterminate results. This does not then mean that the project itself is misguided but that often the *nature* of the Gospels themselves, as communicate acts with illocutionary force, has been ignored or misconstrued, as through these illocutionary intentions were easily identifiable and could be neutrally stripped away, when in reality the illocutionary forces present in the text cannot simply be identified with the "theology" or "faith elements" in the text.

75. For example, fear of a storm, fear of loss, fear of being "last," or fear of death.

76. See Bayer, *Theology of Mark*, 41–124.

77. E.g., Brown, *Scripture as Communication*, 162, where she contrasts coming to narratives with the "God question" with ethical approaches that extol imitation of biblical characters. This simplistic dichotomy again is a rehearsal of the separation of theology and ethics where we are asked which one comes first or has priority. Recognizing biblical narratives as wisdom texts averts such hermeneutical constraints. Brown's failure here is especially surprising in an excellent book that shows real sensitivity to communicative intentions.

So, while these modern approaches can yield helpful results for historical reconstruction or theological construction, they display a marked insensitivity to the illocutionary moves typical of biblical narratives. The Gospels were written for spiritual formation. Biblical narratives seek to form the people of God, with lives centered on key convictions about God's holiness and mercy and how those realities are embraced and embodied in the communal life of his people.

Gospels as Wisdom

How then do the Gospels, as historical testimony, function as wisdom? Like other narratives, the Gospels teach practical wisdom by instilling in readers a personal allegiance to a particular value-laden picture of the world. Through narrative engagement, readers have their cultural and instinctive systems of values questioned, realigned, and reinforced. This happens through the relationships the implied author directs between himself and the reader and the reader's identification with particular characters. In addition, as we should expect, the shape of the narrative itself imprints a normative ethical vision on its readers.

The characters in the Gospel narratives can, first of all, be broken down into two groups: those who run through the whole story (Jesus, the disciples, the Pharisees and other religious leaders, and "the crowd"[78]), and those who appear in one-off encounters with Jesus (the woman at the well, the rich young ruler, the Capernaum paralytic). These onetime encounters are laid out by the author to prompt responses from the reader. Characters who come to Jesus in need and openly (as opposed to those who come sure of themselves or come trying to trick, trap, or manipulate Jesus) are targets for identification. Readers sympathize with their needs and so, guided by the author's characterization, identify with the character as a vehicle for their own needs and begin to learn how Jesus would meet them in these needs. In addition, the author often signals how readers are meant to engage with characters through Jesus's responses to those characters. When Jesus pushes back on them, we know we are supposed to push back as well. When he accepts them, we enter in and learn from their encounter with Jesus. In this way the Gospel narratives instill in their readers certain dispositions, such as embracing their own "spiritual poverty," learning that Jesus accepts and blesses those who come to him in such a state. These encounters serve to humanize concepts such as

---

78. In John's Gospel the line between the religious leadership and the crowds at times disappears under the general designation "the Jews."

faith and doubt, because each of these characters lives in the space *between* these two realities and embodies the movement toward one and away from the other. So, certain priorities become clarified, refined, and implanted in the reader as they engage with these one-off characters.

The reader's relationship with constant characters, such as the disciples,[79] involves a more complex dynamic because the author has time to develop that relationship over the course of the whole narrative and to introduce challenges, diversions, and resolutions that could not be played out in a short pericope. So, for example, as has been well documented elsewhere,[80] in Mark the implied reader is meant to identify with the disciples at first, but the cracks in their understanding of Jesus begin to show in chapter 4, and by the middle of the narrative they are denounced by Jesus for their hard-heartedness (8:17–18).[81] This initiates a deep self-examination in the reader, who has been led to identify with these characters whose understandings and convictions have been thrown into confusion by the trenchant criticisms of Jesus himself. Through this process, readers are formed in wisdom, in a reorientation of beliefs, attachments, and actions. In a process of entering into the Markan narratives through an identification with the disciples, they arrive at an understanding of what faith in the Messiah entails, what fundamental convictions and commitments are paramount and which competing understandings are brought into question.[82] Most importantly, this is experiential wisdom, a participatory

79. Of the constant characters the Pharisees are the least dynamic; their collective character and role of opposition are fixed. The crowd is also relatively fixed; although it can praise Jesus and condemn in the next breath, this is not a shift in its character role but representative of its deep ambivalence and indecisiveness. Jesus's character, while fixed in some regards, is dynamic in that its complexity is revealed as the narrative unfolds, especially in the Passion Narratives. He undergoes struggles and is vindicated, but it would be hard to characterize this as a major shift in his character, but more of a revelation of his character. Finally, the disciples undergo the strongest buffeting and are the most dynamic and the most obvious candidates for identification, but how readers are invited to engage with them is something particular to each Gospel. While Mark wants us to identify, reject, and replace the disciples, Matthew wants us to maintain more of a straight identification with them. In terms of the constant characters, the disciples are the main identification point for readers and so their main entry point into the narrative.

80. See Robert Tannehill, "The Disciples in Mark: The Function of a Narrative Role," in *The Interpretation of Mark*, ed. William Telford, Studies in New Testament Interpretation (Edinburgh: T&T Clark, 1995), 169–95.

81. Echoing the judgment that falls on those outside the kingdom who "have ears but cannot hear" in Mark 4:11–12.

82. Cf. Wolfgang Iser, *The Implied Reader: Patterns of Communication in Prose Fiction from Bunyan to Beckett* (Baltimore: Johns Hopkins University Press, 1974), 290,

> The efficacy of the literary text is brought about by the apparent evocation and subsequent negation of the familiar. What are first seemed to be an affirmation of our assumptions leads to our own rejection of them, thus tending to prepare us for a re-orientation. And it is only when we have outstripped our preconceptions and left the shelter of the

form of application that comes from attending to the historically conditioned particularities of the narrative.

Another aspect of how the Gospels promote wisdom can be seen in how the narrative constructs the relationship between the author and reader in such a way that the implied author takes on a discipling role of a trusted instructor, whose understandings and convictions assume a normative influence on the reader. Alan Culpepper has shown how John's Gospel creates an implicit line of communication between the author and reader, where the normative bond between the two is established in the prologue and nurtured throughout the Gospel.[83] Culpepper notes the Johannine use of misunderstanding and irony as key components in what he calls the "silent communication" between author and reader.[84]

Both misunderstanding and irony in the narrative of John create what some have referred to as a "two-story" experience of the narrative.[85] At the story level, characters often misunderstand Jesus, for example, taking a metaphorical saying literally (2:19–21; 3:3–4; 4:10–11; 6:50–52) or misunderstanding his origins/identity (7:27–28; 8:14; 9:29–30; 19:9). Likewise, characters often make deeply ironic statements that have double meanings they are unaware of (3:2; 11:48) or enact symbolically ironic actions (12:6; 19:19). These misunderstandings and ironies are hidden from the characters, who operate at the story level of the narrative, but are transparent to the reader, who shares an interpretive box seat with the author. The irony exists because of the distance between the limited perspectives of the characters and the knowledge that the implied reader shares with the author.

The central tragic irony of John's Gospel, which also involves the theme of misunderstanding, is introduced in 1:11: "He came to his own, and his own people did not receive him." This irony of the rejection of Jesus by those he came to rule and redeem overshadows the whole narrative and culminates in the crowds calling for Jesus's crucifixion (19:15). The scene in chapter 19 underscores the irony of the event by adding a Jewish confession of allegiance to Caesar in the same breath with the call to crucify Jesus. "They cried out, 'Away with him, away with him, crucify him!' Pilate said to them,

---

familiar that we are in a position to gather new experiences. As the literary text involves the reader in the formation of illusion and the simultaneous formation of the means by which the illusion is punctured, reading reflects the process by which we gain experience.

83. See Culpepper, *Anatomy*, 151–227.

84. The Synoptic Gospels also employ the same literary devices (misunderstanding and irony), with similar design and effect, but each has a particular nuance to how they are utilized that corresponds to the distinctive narrative strategies particular to each Gospel.

85. See Culpepper, *Anatomy*, 167; Wayne C. Booth, *A Rhetoric of Irony* (Chicago: University of Chicago Press, 1974), 36–39.

'Shall I crucify your King?' The chief priests answered, 'We have no king but Caesar.'" How is the reader meant to interpret these events? The reader was handed an interpreting grid back in 1:11, and that text gives these events their tragically ironic significance.[86]

In this way the author confirms his role as the interpretive guide for the reader, offering the reader an insider's perspective on the significance of events as they unfold. This insider's perspective is formative for the life and convictions of the reader. To recognize the irony of the chief priests proclaiming their sole allegiance to Caesar, the reader knows that their true allegiance ought to be to Yahweh and his Son, whom he sent. But this recognition happens at an emotional level, because the tragic irony here invites a sense of anger and outrage at the depth of irrational rebellion and sin. Regardless of what they believe (or misunderstand) about Jesus, it is an abomination for the chief priests to declare their sole allegiance to Caesar, over and above God. So the normative stance of the author is deeply imprinted on the implied reader in the visceral recognition of injustice and rebellion in the act of rejecting Jesus and engineering his death. At the same time this also deeply imprints a "backdoor" affirmation of the person of Jesus as the rightful recipient of faith and allegiance, because it is only in relation to a proper response that this negative assessment can take place. In this way, through the use of irony, John is forming his readers in line with the stated intentions of the Gospel, establishing a disposition of faith, by creating an antipathy toward the rejection of Jesus. All of this happens implicitly, and primarily at an emotional level, as readers learn to love good (light) and hate evil (darkness).

Finally, the shape of the Gospel narrative itself is formative for wisdom. While each Gospel could be subjected to a fruitful detailed exposition of how it develops its plots, each of these narratives shares a basic underlying plotline in which (1) Jesus comes as the messianic agent to establish God's rule, resulting in (2) his rejection by religious authorities (3) and his establishing a new Israel in the calling of twelve disciples, who possess sputtering faith in him, all culminating in (4) the crucifixion of Jesus and (5) his subsequent resurrection. Again, while we could certainly greatly expand and nuance these for each Gospel, the basic form itself is enough to draw some normative themes.

The establishment of God's rule necessarily produces personal and institutional conflict in which some "receive" and some "reject." This realization creates a field of expectations of what is normative for Christian experience

---

86. It also serves to intimate the influence of a sinister force standing behind the outrageous, irrational hatred the Jewish leadership has toward Jesus.

and excludes assumptions that tend toward "triumphalism" and/or "overrealized eschatology."[87] At the same time, it also fosters an evaluative recognition that sets allegiance to the rule of God over competing incommensurable goods such as freedom from suffering or a life of ease and prosperity. Jesus himself places allegiance to the kingdom above allegiances to family and friends (Luke 14:26), but does so in a way (i.e., describing greater rewards) that excludes Stoic detachment from external goods. Sacrificial choices between incommensurable goods become normalized by the nature of the conflicts that arise from the presence of God's rule, which establishes itself in the correlative acts of judgment and salvation.

This self-sacrificial mode is given shape most clearly in the life of Jesus himself, whose messianic calling is expressed in acts of establishing God's rule in a life that literally culminates in sacrifice and evaluates all claims to self-sufficiency, self-preservation, and self-promotion in light of the cross of Jesus. The Gospels explicitly connect the form of Jesus's life, the kernel element that defines the plot of all four Gospels, as paradigmatic for the church, most famously in Mark 8:31–38. There the nature of discipleship is defined in terms of the cross and death to self. "For whoever would save his life will lose it, but whoever loses his life for my sake and the gospel's will save it" (Mark 8:35). In this way the plot of the story becomes explicitly normative for discipleship. The words of Jesus speak of deep self-sacrifice for the sake of greater realities: communion with Jesus ("for my sake")[88] and the furthering of God's rule ("for the gospel's sake"), with the result that these greater goods communicate a greater life than what was sacrificed ("the one who loses his life . . . will save it"). In the plot of the Gospel this also intimates an experience of eschatological salvation inaugurated in the resurrection of Jesus, which adds the final keystone of hope to the gospel vision and provides motivating force and ideational context to acts of gospel service.

The resurrection signals the teleological lens through which both the death of Jesus and discipleship are interpreted. The resurrection, as the focal manifestation of the revelation of God's rule, grounds the narrative of self-sacrifice in hope. The narrative arc of the Gospels inseparably binds together in eschatological tension the *theologia crucis* and the *theologia gloriae*. This teleological arc projects a moral landscape with a direction, which provides affective and intellectual contexts for considered moral action set within an eschatological vision of God's kingdom.

87. Cf. Hays, *Moral Vision*, 88–91.
88. The previous verse connects communion with Jesus, the invitation to follow him, with self-denial.

We can easily see, even in such a brief sketch, how the shape of the Gospel narrative gives evaluative markers that define the form and motivations that describe Christian discipleship. Once again, this is a narrative feature that functions both explicitly and implicitly. Explicitly it ascribes special significance to particular beliefs and dispositions and promotes them as normative for Christian belief and action. Implicitly the shape of the narrative imprints values by directly tying them to the person and work of Jesus. It is the life of Jesus himself, not a set of principles or values, that gives shape to the convictions and affections of the Christian disciple. This locates the core of motivation for a sacrificial gospel life in devotion to the person of Jesus and recognition of his benevolent rule. Imitation of Christ is not then an act of self-will that seeks to determine one's relationship with God through imitating some pattern of life. Rather, imitation begins with affection and admiration directed at Jesus in recognizing his own determination to honor God with his life in the face of betrayal and radical injustice. In this way the shape of the Gospels implicitly appeals to our gratitude, love, and allegiance as key dispositions that determine and animate concrete acts of discipleship. It also places these movements within an eschatological, teleological understanding of the manifestation of God's rule that grounds those same acts in motivations of hope and worship.

Conclusion

From all this we can see that narratives are tools of formation and that they do much more than communicate ideas or morals. Narratives invite a participatory engagement where readers enter into a story, sympathetically identifying with characters and their travails, longing for a favorable resolution to their struggles. Through this process the readers' own affective judgments are invoked and reaffirmed but also opened to questioning and reformation.

All of these participatory acts of engagement are essential to the nature of narratives themselves. This is why Nussbaum and others have argued that narratives are an ideal medium for moral formation, and in fact much better suited to formative enterprises than analytic and deliberative forms of discourse.

Where Nussbaum is most helpful for our discussion of Gospel narratives is that she is consciously retrieving for moderns what was an obvious truth for the ancients—that narratives enact a formative engagement with readers.[89] So,

89. Cf. Plato, *Republic* §§377a–398c.

again, engaging the Gospels as formative narratives is not simply a beneficial mode we can choose to apply to a neutral historical text, but it is actually a recognition of their intentionality encoded in their generic form. This means we can take seriously that the Gospels were written for spiritual formation.[90]

90. Cf. Sandra M. Schneiders, "The Gospels and the Reader," in *The Cambridge Companion to the Gospels*, ed. Stephen C. Barton (Cambridge: Cambridge University Press, 2006), 116.

5

READING GOSPELS FOR WISDOM
Practice

In this chapter we want to explore how Gospel narratives function as wisdom in practice by working through some illustrative texts. Our focus will be on acclimating ourselves to how narrative dynamics form wisdom in readers. In many ways this is simply learning a new set of questions with which to interrogate texts, but it is also about developing sensitivities to the formative agendas inherent in the gospel form itself. These narratives were written to shape our faithful comportment to the person of Jesus and the kingdom he came to establish. From the previous chapter, we should expect that process of shaping to be complex and multifaceted, to address our deepest devotions and convictions, and to call for a practical response of allegiance and obedience.

Mark 5: Jairus and the Bleeding Woman

In Mark 5:21–43 we have a classic example of a character who has a "one-off" encounter with Jesus. In verse 21 the scene is set to a new locale: "And when Jesus had crossed again in the boat to the other side, a great crowd gathered about him, and he was beside the sea." Then we are introduced to a new character: "Then came one of the rulers of the synagogue, Jairus by name, and seeing him, he fell at his feet and implored him earnestly, saying, 'My little daughter is at the point of death. Come and lay your hands on her, so that she may be made well and live.'" Whenever we are introduced to a new character in the Gospels, or in any narrative, the first question we are meant to ask is: Do we trust them, or are we suspicious of them? This is a value judgment, but not a simple "is this a good person or a bad person" judgment. We are deciding how to *relate* to this character, not how to turn them into an idea.[1] All narrators, whether historical or fictional, set us up to relate to characters in particular ways. Mark tells us things about Jairus, primarily through his actions and words, which immediately lead us to form an opinion about him. We might be suspicious of him because he is a "ruler of the synagogue," but he does not come trying to trick Jesus, the way that many of the religious authorities of Israel do. More importantly he is a man in desperate need: his daughter is dying, and he believes that Jesus can help. He shows real faith in Jesus; he falls at Jesus's feet and believes he can heal his daughter. Exactly what he knows and believes about Jesus is unclear and, at this point, unimportant. He comes in need with some kind of real faith.

All this leads us to trust Jairus. But it is important to note we trust him because Mark wants us to. Mark did not give us a neutral portrait of Jairus from which we formed our own opinion of him. Mark is leading us to trust him. (Learning to read narratives well is learning to be led by their authors, because authors are always trying to take us somewhere.) Mark has laid out the basic narrative problem that will move the plot along: a dying girl needs to be healed. More importantly, he has put us in a position to trust Jairus. This trust is important because it facilitates our identification with Jairus. Trusted characters are our entry points into narratives and how we participate directly in them. At this point we begin to walk in Jairus's shoes, as those who also come to Jesus in need with some kind of faith in him. Through this we will learn something of how Jesus relates to us in our faith.[2]

Verse 24 continues the narrative, telling us that Jesus "went with him." This is (actually) important, because one of the ways in which the Gospels signal how we are to relate to characters is in watching how Jesus relates to them. When Jesus "goes with them" in some sense, then we know we are supposed to "go with" those characters—to participate in their encounter with Jesus. When Jesus pushes back on characters, such as the rich young ruler (Luke

---

1. Only in the past few decades have NT scholars begun to repent of treating Gospel characters as "flat" and uncomplicated. See Cornelis Bennema, *A Theory of Character in New Testament Narrative* (Minneapolis: Fortress, 2014). Sifting Gospels for theology, NT critics have historically treated characters like ideas with beards and not looked for how they actually function as narrative characters that facilitate the process of identification, which is a crucial element in how the Gospels promote spiritual formation.

2. Cf. M. Eugene Boring, *Mark: A Commentary*, NTL (Louisville: Westminster John Knox, 2006), 160, "Here as elsewhere the narrative functions at two levels, and the there-and-then account modulates into the here-and-now experience of the readers."

18:18–25), we know there is something suspicious about them; they are a negative example of something we are meant to be wary of.

Mark continues the narrative by telling us that "a great crowd followed him and thronged about him." Then Mark does something startling: he introduces another character into the scene. This is an example of Mark's tendency to "sandwich" one story inside another, where the two stories interpret each other by juxtaposition while also building narrative tension.[3] So the Jairus narrative gets put on hold momentarily. Mark tells us, "There was a woman who had had a discharge of blood for twelve years, and who had suffered much under many physicians, and had spent all that she had, and was no better but rather grew worse. She had heard the reports about Jesus and came up behind him in the crowd and touched his garment. For she said, 'If I touch even his garments, I will be made well.'"

Do we trust her? We feel compassion for this nameless woman who has suffered with illness for twelve years and wasted all her money on doctors who couldn't help her.[4] She also has a disease that makes her perpetually unclean in Jewish society, which underscores her isolation in her suffering.[5] Compassion is the first step in our beginning to trust and identify with this

3. As Boring, *Mark*, 157, notes, "This dramatic combination of two stories represents a distinctive Markan literary technique, variously called intercalation, insertion, dove-tailing, sandwich, interweaving, interlocking, framing one story with another, interlude of one story within another, or, in the jargon of narratology, 'heterodiegetic analepsis.'" Boring references the monograph study by Tom Shepherd, *Markan Sandwich Stories: Narration, Definition, and Function*, Andrews University Seminary Studies Dissertation Series 18 (Berrien Springs, MI: Andrews University Press, 1993), as well as Shepherd's article-length summary in "The Narrative Function of Markan Intercalation," *NTS* 41 (1995): 522–40. See also James R. Edwards, "Markan Sandwiches: The Significance of Interpolations in the Markan Narratives," *NovT* 31 (1989): 193–216.

4. See R. T. France, *The Gospel of Mark: A Commentary on the Greek Text*, NIGTC (Grand Rapids: Eerdmans, 2002), 236, "The second suppliant, whose social standing is in marked contrast to that of Jairus, is introduced in a sentence which piles seven participial clauses on one another before reaching the main verb (ἥψατο) in v. 27. This interesting departure from Mark's more usual paratactic style allows the reader (or hearer) to build up a sympathetic mental portrait of the woman's situation before her story begins, and predisposes us in her favour, despite the unappealing nature of her complaint, especially in light of Jewish Purity laws."

5. As Boring, *Mark*, 159–60, describes her, she is "physically sick and weak, ritually unclean and unable to participate in synagogue and community life, and impoverished (though once a person of means). Mark does not mention husband or children. Since vaginal bleeding prohibited marriage and was grounds for divorce, in the understanding of her culture which she shared, the woman cannot fulfill her function as a woman, to bring new life into being as a mother." Cf. James R. Edwards, *The Gospel according to Mark*, PNTC (Grand Rapids: Eerdmans, 2002), 163, "Josephus's testimony that 'the temple was closed to women during their menstruation' (*War* 5.227) indicates that this particular Torah ruling was carefully observed in Jesus' day. Accordingly, a menstruating woman—and whoever touched her—was banished from the community until purification."

woman. She displays real faith in Jesus, a strong faith that his power is so great that she only needs to touch his garment to be healed.[6] So we have another character to identify with, a new entry point into the narrative. She touches Jesus; what will happen next? "And immediately the flow of blood dried up, and she felt in her body that she was healed of her disease." Twelve years of suffering ends in an instant. She can simply wait for the crowd to pass, return home, and begin rebuilding her life. But Jesus doesn't do anonymous healings.

"Jesus, perceiving in himself that power had gone out from him, immediately turned about in the crowd and said, 'Who touched my garments?'" There are two very odd things in this verse. The first is the description of Jesus perceiving "that power had gone out from him." What we are used to in the Gospels is Jesus using his healing powers intentionally, commanding the blind to see or the lame to walk, or even the dead to rise. In this case Jesus seems completely passive. Healing power gets sucked out of him. It's odd.

The other strange element here is Jesus's question addressed to the assembled crowd, "Who touched my garments?" The awkwardness of the question is underlined in the disciples' confused reply, "You see the crowd pressing around you, and yet you say, 'Who touched me?'" But Jesus's question is not for the disciples or the crowd; it is for one person. Do we believe that Jesus does not know who touched him? So why does he ask? It is an invitation, but for this woman it feels like a threat.

Finally, she comes forward "in fear and trembling," and she "fell down before him and told him the whole truth." Here the most important question we have to answer is "Why is she afraid of Jesus?" One of the key characteristics of biblical narratives is that they are highly compressed.[7] They do very little explaining, but this is an intentional characteristic of their style. Compact narratives leave gaps to be filled by the reader. The author gives just enough detail to instigate interpretive surmises—guided inferences—but the reader still has work to do. This type of narrative demands the participation of the reader in a way that stories that explain everything do not. Readers can glide over narratives where there is no ambiguity or holes to fill. But here, readers need to be active, especially in discerning why characters do what they do, because it is in the internal motivations that the reader can find a reflection of their own internal world.[8]

6. Cf. Boring, *Mark*, 160, "Her faith has caused her to violate conventional social constraints by appearing in public and especially by touching the revered holy man."

7. Cf. V. Philips Long, "Scenic, Succinct, Subtle: An Introduction to the Literary Artistry of 1 & 2 Samuel," *Presb* 19, no. 1 (1993): 32–47.

8. The gaps we are meant to fill are determined by the text, much like missing pieces in a jigsaw puzzle. Mark is not leading us to wonder what this woman or Jairus had for breakfast. The focus

So why is this woman afraid? What does she have to fear from Jesus? The answer is that she operates from her deepest self-understanding of uncleanliness and a belief that she is unworthy of Jesus's attention. First of all, she has broken the laws of her culture and brought her uncleanness into a crowd of people without announcing it. Not only this, she has *touched* Jesus, thereby, in Jewish law, making him unclean. We can also infer from her action of coming to Jesus to steal a healing from him, instead of asking the way Jairus did, that she does not believe that Jesus would have stopped for her. More than a decade of illness, suffering, and isolation have confirmed her self-understanding as unclean and worthless. So what she expects from Jesus is condemnation and public humiliation. This is why she comes in fear and trembling.[9] It is this fear, and the self-understanding of worthlessness behind it, that Jesus stops to take away.

Jesus's response transcends her expectations. He begins with a note of tender consolation: "Daughter." This one word communicates Jesus's acceptance and affection for this woman and silences her fears. He continues with a startling affirmation: "Your faith has made you well; go in peace, and be healed of your disease." Jesus not only praises her faith but locates the origin of her miraculous healing in her faith, not in his power.[10] Jesus

---

of inference is on the internal motivations of a character. Why did they do what they did or say what they said? The advice of Robert H. Stein, *Mark*, BECNT (Grand Rapids: Baker Academic, 2008), 268, that "we should concentrate on what the text tells us rather than speculate on the hypothetical mental states of the woman," shows a deep insensitivity to narrative dynamics, rooted in a modernist presupposition that narratives transmit information.

9. Some commentators mistakenly take the woman's "fear and trembling" as a proper expression of faith. So Stein, *Mark*, 270, "The response of 'fear' toward Jesus and his mighty power has already been referred to in 4:41 and 5:15. Here, unlike 5:15 (cf. also 16:8), it refers to a positive response and appropriate awe in experiencing the mighty healing power of the Son of God. See 4:40–41. 'Fear and trembling' is described in Phil. 2:12 as the appropriate manner in which Christians should 'work' out their salvation." Stein imports Paul's positive use of this phrase into Mark, where the dichotomy between fear and faith is absolute, as is obvious in Jesus's words to Jairus just a few verses later in this narrative, "Do not fear, only believe." Stein assumes that the fear of the disciples in 4:41 is positive, but their response to Jesus's calming of the storm, "Who then is this, that even the wind and the sea obey him?" hardly sounds like a reverent confession.

10. There are two errors that can be derived from this text. The first takes Jesus's word here as establishing a principle in the connection between faith and miracles, where faith is the instrument to unlock a divine storehouse of blessing. The second error, reacting to the first, reminds us that it is actually the power of Jesus that heals the woman, not her faith as such, and that faith is itself a gift of God. Both approaches mistakenly approach Gospel narratives with the intent of extracting a "principle." It is not simply that both answers are wrong; it is that both asked the wrong question to begin with. This is a wisdom text, but it does not teach wisdom by encapsulating some "timeless principle." Mark is not trying to answer questions of divine and human agency; he is showing us how Jesus dealt with this particular individual, and through that shaping our understanding of and experience of faith.

affirms her faith as extraordinary, good, and powerful. This focus on her faith was already set up in the unusual description of miraculous power "going out from" Jesus, as though it were drawn out. Nowhere else in the Gospels do we have a healing miracle like this. Jesus's point is not to say that she has superpowers but to affirm something good in this woman that led her to touch him and that she needs to know it, and so does everyone else in the dumbfounded crowd. Why? Because, although her faith is strong, it is still incomplete. As with everyone who expresses faith in the Gospels, her faith is only partial. No one is ever finished; faith always has a place to grow deeper.

In Mark's Gospel two things characterize faith. The first is that faith is an active trust in the person of Jesus as the King who has all authority and who uses that authority to bring life to his people.[11] What that means is faith that Jesus is powerful and seeking my good. The other characteristic of faith in Mark is that its antithesis is fear. Those who lack faith are afraid because they do not believe that Jesus is both good and powerful. So in Mark 4:35–41, when a storm on the Sea of Galilee threatens to kill all the disciples, along with the napping Jesus, the disciples are afraid. After calming the storm with a word, Jesus reprimands his disciples for their lack of faith. They do not yet understand Jesus's power or his faithfulness.

When this woman comes to Jesus "in fear and trembling," her faith is lacking a crucial element. She believes that Jesus is powerful, but she does not believe Jesus has any real concern for her, nor would he have if she stopped him to ask for healing. This is why she came in secret to begin with and why she expects rejection and public humiliation from him. She does not believe in his goodness *toward her*. And so Jesus stops and draws her out to affirm her faith and in so doing to affirm that she is worthy of his time. This is what enables her to "go in peace." He also tells her "be healed of your disease," with the implication that although her physical disease has been healed, there are many levels at which she still needs to be healed.

As soon as Jesus finishes speaking, the narrative whips back to Jairus. Messengers come from his house to inform him that "your daughter is dead." Mark leaves us to imagine what Jairus might be thinking now. He might be angry at Jesus for wasting time with an unclean woman.[12] Whatever hope he might have had for his daughter has now been extinguished. There is nothing more to be done. This is why the messengers ask, "Why trouble the Teacher

11. As France, *Mark*, 238, explains, "Such πίστις consists more of a practical conviction of Jesus' ἐξουσία than a theologically developed understanding of who he is."

12. The drastic separation in social status between Jairus, the synagogue ruler, and this unclean woman is highlighted by her never being named.

any further?"[13] But overhearing this, Jesus turns to Jairus and says, "Do not fear, only believe."

While Jesus is speaking compassionately, it is hard to imagine him saying anything more demanding to Jairus. Again we see that the fundamental dichotomy is either faith or fear. Whatever faith Jairus came with, Jesus commands it to grow exponentially. What is Jairus thinking now? Mark will be ruthlessly silent on this point, even though this is exactly the question he wants us to ponder as we once again enter into Jairus's story. What makes Jesus's words to Jairus especially hard is what he does not say. There are no promises connected to his command. He demands faith, trust, and allegiance as goods in themselves, not instrumental goods. There is no promise to Jairus about his daughter. No "if/then" statements, just "trust me and don't be afraid." Jairus is stretched thin between the call of Jesus and the "realism" of his servants, "Why trouble the Teacher any further?"[14]

The narrative quickly moves to Jairus's home, awash with mourners and their loud cries of grief. Jesus interdicts himself into the scene: "Why are you making a commotion and weeping? The child is not dead but sleeping." They all laugh at him. What is Jairus supposed to think now? Jesus turns them all out, except for Jairus, the mother, and his inner circle of James, John, and Peter. Taking the girl by the hand, Jesus simply speaks to her, Mark tells us in Aramaic, "Little girl, . . . arise." And she wakes as from sleep and is restored to her mother and father. And all those in the room are "overcome with amazement" (5:42).

So what is Mark's point in sandwiching these two stories together? What is he wanting us to understand about Jesus, and how is he trying to form our faith? Again, we short-circuit Mark's agenda if we simply substitute a christological question here. Mark has asked us to identify with these two characters: both come to Jesus in desperate need, and both come with some kind of faith in Jesus.[15] His goal is to shape our comportment to Jesus through an experience of how Jesus meets us in our need and in our faith.

13. This is another case of guided inference. Mark wants us to wonder how Jairus is coping, but he doesn't tell us directly. He does, however, hint at it in the rhetorical question posed to him by his servants.

14. Cf. Stein, *Mark*, 271,

> Having described the hopelessness of the disciples in the storm (4:38), of the demoniac (5:3–5), and of the hemorrhaging woman (5:25–26), Mark now describes the utter hopelessness of Jairus's situation. His daughter is no longer sick and at the point of death. She has died! It is now too late. At this point not even the "teacher" can help. The readers of Mark, however, unlike the messengers from the house of Jairus, have learned in the preceding chapters of the Gospel that no situation is hopeless for Jesus, the Son of God, for he, like God, possesses mastery over nature, demons, and illness.

15. As Edwards says, "Jairus and the woman have only one thing in common: both are victims of desperate circumstances who have no hope apart from Jesus" (*Mark*, 168).

Just like these characters, our faith is a product of our need as well as faltering, imperfect, and weak. Mark wants us to learn two things about our faith. The first is that Jesus celebrates it: even though it is frail, it is also real and strong. This is the message to the woman who had faith in Jesus's power but doubted that he would use that power for her. Jesus affirms the strength of her faith, despite her fears of Jesus's reprimand, and also affirms her worth as a recipient of his grace. Despite her commitments to her own worthlessness, she pushed her way through the crowd and touched him. Something good inside her knew he could heal her. This is why both Jesus, in his affirmation of her faith, and Mark, in his description of "power going out" from Jesus, put the focus of the event on her faith. Mustard-seed faith can move mountains, and Jesus celebrates it.

At the same time, it needs to grow. Again, faith in the Gospels is always partial and always in motion, either growing or putrefying. The challenge to Jairus, and to us, is that whatever faith we came with, it needs to grow exponentially. Faith repeatedly faces the challenge of the impossible. The same Jesus who is tenderly affirming of faith is also ruthlessly demanding of the same faith.

These two messages sound contradictory and can make Jesus seem schizophrenic. In reality these twin affirmations are defining faith, our comportment to Jesus, from two opposite sides and countering two opposite misunderstandings. On one side is the threat of perfectionism as related to faith—that our faith will be acceptable when it is absolute. This is another form of idolatrous legalism, where faith becomes the mechanism to release the recalcitrant grace of Jesus. Jesus's affirmation and celebration of the woman's faith is the antidote to this idolatrous construal of faith. The second challenge to true faith is moral and spiritual complacency, what moral theologians historically labeled the vice of "sloth." The affirmation that "mustard seed faith is good enough" is meant to produce gratitude and freedom, but it is just as likely to produce a complacent disposition that defuses Jesus's perpetual challenge to decenter the self and find life in dependence on him alone.

The gospel brings life by first deconstructing all human pride, whether that pride is expressed in self-sufficient complacency or self-deprecating worthlessness. Faith is the virtue that stands as the antidote to these diseases of the soul. Mark uses this short pericope to shape our understanding of faith and to allow us to appropriate faith, not simply as an idea but as a comportment to Jesus that frees us from our corrupted construals of faith that still find room for the malignancy of self-determination. This is Mark's primary purpose in this narrative: not to furnish us with theology or history but to form us in our faith in Jesus.

In terms of our Right ARM rubric, narratives embody and foster an intimate connection between actions, reasons, and motivations. If we divorce the action of faith from its context and turn it into "the moral" of this story we destroy how this text functions as wisdom. Our engagement with this narrative gives us a deeper sense of what faith is (what action is called for) and also shapes our reasons and motivations of why we would pursue faith in Jesus as someone who can give us life but will also take us beyond ourselves and our ability to control life.

John 11: Mary and Martha

The story of the raising of Lazarus (found only in John's Gospel) falls in the narrative transition zone of John 11–12, in which themes from the "Book of Signs" (John 1:19–10:42) are brought to a conclusion while at the same time intermingled with the themes of the "Book of Glory" (John 13:1–20:31). Many commentators see the raising of Lazarus as John's seventh and culminative "sign."[16] As with most of the miraculous signs, there is an accompanying "I am" saying: "I am the resurrection and the life" (11:25). The bulk of the narrative is taken up with Jesus's dialogues with Martha and then Mary, prior to the climactic raising of Lazarus.

While there is ample christological material in the passage, John's intention, as he states it in 20:31, is to inculcate faith as a certain dispositional comportment to those christological truths. The dialogues with Mary and Martha will serve as our focus for discovering how John wants to shape our faith as readers. But before we get to these dialogues, John sets the scene at the beginning of the chapter. John introduces Mary, Martha, and their brother Lazarus and tells us that the sisters have sent word to Jesus that their brother Lazarus is dying: "Lord, he whom you love is ill." The sisters want Jesus to come and heal their brother, but Jesus's response in verse 4 is aloof and confounding. "This illness does not lead to death. It is for the glory of God, so that the Son of God may be glorified through it." But this illness *does* lead to death. Does Jesus believe that the death of Lazarus is immaterial as long as it provides a stage for his glory? Are we really supposed to believe that?

John is not going to help us here; in fact, he intends to make things worse. Jesus is about to move from confounding to inscrutable. "Now Jesus loved

---

16. As Andrew T. Lincoln, *The Gospel according to Saint John*, BNTC (London: Continuum, 2005), 315, notes, "The seventh and climactic sign is given far more attention and space in the narrative than any other." Cf. Rudolf Schnackenburg, *The Gospel according to St. John*, trans. Cecily Hastings and Kevin Smyth (New York: Seabury, 1968–82), 2:316.

Martha and her sister and Lazarus. So [οὖν], when he heard that Lazarus was ill, he stayed two days longer in the place where he was." John does us the favor of reminding us that Jesus does in fact love this trio. (The statement is all the more profound for its rarity. Gospel writers routinely *show* Jesus displaying love in words and deeds, but it is extremely rare for them to say explicitly that Jesus loves someone.) Unfortunately, here it only makes matters worse, since John tells us that Jesus waited for Lazarus to die *because* he loved them.

This is the tension that animates the whole narrative that follows. John goes out of his way to tell us that Jesus genuinely loves Martha, Mary, and Lazarus. Then we watch Jesus do something that certainly doesn't *seem* loving; in fact, Jesus looks callous and uncaring. Many commentators have tried to defuse this tension by saying that Jesus's actions are governed by God's timetable or by simply saying we cannot know why Jesus did what he did.[17] But this kind of premature theological closure defuses the narrative and shuts down its power as a formative wisdom text. John forces us into an uncomfortable position where Jesus is said to be loving but doesn't look loving. He does this to interrogate and form our faith at this very point.

This might seem like a counterintuitive and even bizarre strategy for spiritual formation, but Henri Nouwen reminds us that "spiritual formation begins with the gradual and often painful discovery of God's incomprehensibility in the face of life's great mysteries and limitations."[18] John is facilitating exactly this kind of formative engagement by forcing us to sit with the inscrutable will of Jesus in the midst of confusion and grief. This is (perhaps surprisingly) not an uncommon strategy to find in the Gospel narratives. But if we imagine spiritual formation primarily in terms of amassing knowledge about God, then texts like these become completely opaque to us. Nouwen's spiritual

17. E.g., Schnackenburg, *John*, 2:324, "Anyone who still has the last remark about Jesus' love for the family in Bethany in his mind must be brought up sharp by the announcement that Jesus stayed a further two days where he was, the baptismal site east of the Jordan (10:40). Perhaps the evangelist intends this effect, to make clear that Jesus' behavior is determined by another will. His reactions, which, humanly speaking, are so strange (cf. v. 15 'I am glad'), can only be understood in terms of the Father's commission. No reason for his delay is given."

Cf. Wendy E. S. North, "'Lord If You Had Been Here . . .' (John 11:21): The Absense of Jesus and Strategies of Consolation in the Fourth Gospel," *JSNT* 36 (2013): 40. Elsewhere she remarks: "It is noticeable that John supplies no explanation for this curious delay; no objection by Jesus, for example about his 'hour' or his 'time' not yet having come, that we find in other instances of negative response earlier in the Gospel (2.4; 7.6; cf. 4.48). Instead, we have an assurance in the previous verse of Jesus' love not only for Lazarus, but for the entire Bethany family, an aside that looks designed to ward off any impression on the reader's part that Jesus' inaction was out of indifference." Wendy E. S. North, *The Lazarus Story within the Johannine Tradition*, JSNTSup 212 (Sheffield: Sheffield Academic Press, 2001), 137.

18. Henri Nouwen, *Spiritual Formation: Following the Movements of the Spirit* (New York: HarperOne, 2010), 3.

insight is critical for understanding how John intends to shape us—by driving us deeper into "God's incomprehensibility."[19]

Lazarus has been entombed for four days by the time Jesus finally arrives in the outskirts of Bethany, where he is confronted by Martha. "Lord, if you had been here, my brother would not have died" (11:21). Martha, speaking from her grief but not wanting to offend Jesus, offers a somewhat polite version of complaint. Behind her words is the question: Why didn't you come sooner? This question stings more for us as readers since we know what Martha doesn't—Jesus chose to wait—and now Lazarus is dead. But Martha still has faith that Jesus can in fact do something. "But even now I know that whatever you ask from God, God will give you" (11:22). What does she want Jesus to do? Obviously, raise Lazarus. But if that is what she wants, why doesn't she ask for it?[20] She is ambivalent. Jesus didn't show up when she needed him to. (And *we* know he did it deliberately.) She believes, but she is also unsure. Why didn't Jesus come in the first place? So Martha gives Jesus a test. If he raises her brother, knowing that is what she wants, then he cares. Martha is also hedging her bets by not asking explicitly for Jesus to raise her brother. She wants it too much to bear the disappointment and shame if Jesus chooses not to do it. Faith in the Gospels is only partial—real, but marked by ambivalence. This is what we see in Martha. Real faith that God will give Jesus whatever he asks; but will he ask? He is powerful, but is he good?

Jesus names exactly what Martha wants: "Your brother will rise again." But he does so in a way that is deliberately ambiguous and that hits the ball back into Martha's court. Jesus might be saying exactly what Martha wants to hear, that he is going to raise Lazarus from the dead, or he might be saying that Lazarus will rise on the last day in the resurrection of the righteous.

---

19. Affirming God's incomprehensibility is not a denial that true knowledge of God is possible or beneficial, but an affirmation that Christian wisdom recognizes God is never circumscribed by our knowledge of him and that the fear of the Lord (our comportment toward him) is the beginning of wisdom, especially when our understanding runs dry. Biblical wisdom puts definite limits on foundationalist constructions of knowledge, especially in the ways that foundationalist epistemologies preempt and short-circuit spiritual maturity. Many of our contemporary models for spiritual formation err at this point in two opposite directions. The modernist/Stoic model identifies theological understanding and ethical principles as the engine of spiritual formation. The existentialist/postmodern model understands authentic emotional experience as the engine of formation. Neither reshapes the heart in its deepest desires, devotions, and commitments to serve God for the sake of his glory.

20. Commentators routinely drop the ball here, arguing that Martha does not explicitly ask for Jesus to raise Lazarus but only makes a general statement about his miraculous power. What other options are there for Lazarus at this point? Does Martha want Jesus to provide more food for the mourners? She wants one thing. That she cannot name it is significant in the narrative space between her and Jesus, but it does not mean she does not want it.

The ambiguous form of Jesus's statement speaks directly to her ambivalence about Jesus's real power and real care for her and her brother and sister. She chooses to play it safe. "I know that he will rise again in the resurrection on the last day."

Jesus's response in verses 25–26 is simultaneously personal and prophetic: "I am the resurrection and the life. Whoever believes in me, though he die, yet shall he live, and everyone who lives and believes in me shall never die. Do you believe this?" If we are not careful, we will see Jesus speaking right past Martha with a theological pronouncement, but Jesus's appeal at the end ("Do you believe this?") tells us that his focus is still on her and that his words speak directly to her ambivalence. The real question is, how? Jesus does not accept her response about the future hope of resurrection in the end. Instead he invites her to look to him. The resurrection is not simply a hope or a future event; it is standing in front of her. He is the fulfillment and embodiment of all the hopes of Israel. He is life itself (cf. 1:4; 5:21–29), and the one who believes in him will never die. What is Jesus's point? Martha is in a fragile place. Her faith in Jesus has been shaken by his failure to come when called, and she is left grieving the death of her brother, for which Jesus shares some responsibility. She believes but is struggling to trust in Jesus's benevolence toward her. She wants her brother back, but she is stuck between the intensity of that need and her fear that Jesus is ambivalent toward *her*. His final appeal to Martha is not to hide in theological platitudes, but to trust him. He is the resurrection. Raising her brother will be effortless for him.[21] At the same time, Jesus does not make shortcuts for faith. He still needs her to trust him.

Martha's response to Jesus's question in verse 27 perfectly embodies her ambivalent faith. "Yes, Lord; I believe that you are the Christ, the Son of God, who is coming into the world." In John's Gospel this is a perfect christological confession.[22] Martha genuinely believes, and her faith certainly surpasses that of Jesus's disciples at this point. And yet, it is not satisfying.[23] She does

21. See Jesus's prayer at the tomb, John 11:41–42.

22. Schnackenburg, *John*, 2:332, "Martha's confession, like Peter's, is a Messianic confession in the full Christian sense. She declares her firm faith (πεπίστευκα), in the identical words which the evangelist uses at the end of his book to sum up what he understands by Christian faith (20:31)."

23. As Lincoln, *John*, 325, says, "It is strking, however, that, complete as Martha's Christological confession is, it makes no explicit reference to what Jesus has said about resurrection and life." Cf. Raymond E. Brown, *The Gospel according to John: Introduction, Translation, and Notes*, AB 29 (Garden City, NY: Doubleday, 1966–70), 1:433, "Throughout the incident involving Martha we see that she believes in Jesus but inadequately. In vs. 27 she addresses him with lofty titles, probably the same titles used in early Christian professions of faith; yet 39 shows that she does not as yet believe in his power to give life. She regards Jesus as an intermediary who is heard by God (22), but she does not understand that he is life itself (25)."

not actually answer Jesus's question. She affirms what she can believe in the moment, but she is unable to step into the place where Jesus has invited her. Despite this, there is no rebuke from Jesus. She might have made a better choice, but she did not make a bad one. As we will see, Mary will make a better choice, but the contrast between them is not between good and bad but between good and better.[24] Both sisters respond in faith.

Now Mary goes out to meet Jesus, followed by a group of mourners. As verse 32 tells us: "Now when Mary came to where Jesus was and saw him, she fell at his feet, saying to him, 'Lord, if you had been here, my brother would not have died.'" Mary's words to Jesus are exactly the same as her sister's, but they come off as completely different. She bears the same grief as Martha, but her words do not carry the accusation aimed at Jesus's apparent indifference, and she does not demand that Jesus "fix" the situation. She simply comes to him openly and reverently and shares her grief in the belief that Jesus will understand, accept, and enter into her grief with her. Her grief is an invitation, not a complaint or a demand.[25] This is because her grief is an expression of her unwavering faith in Jesus's care for her. She has the same question as Martha, but her faith is not governed by her ability to understand why Jesus does what he does. It begins with the benevolence of Christ. But for her this belief is not a tool to suppress her griefs and doubts, but drives her to bring those griefs and doubts to Jesus himself.

And Jesus accepts the invitation of Mary's grief. "When Jesus saw her weeping, and the Jews who had come with her also weeping, he was deeply moved [ἐνεβριμήσατο] in his spirit and greatly troubled [ἐτάραξεν ἑαυτὸν]." The typical translation of "deeply moved in his spirit and greatly troubled" is an artifact of a modernist Apollinarian Jesus, whose displays of emotion are limited to some polite forms of stoical internal discomfort.[26] Schnackenburg rightly says, "The word ἐμβριμᾶσθαι (basically to sniff or snort with anger)

---

24. There is, almost inexplicably, a significant scholarly history of seeing Martha as having the better response to Jesus. The primary reason for this, once again characteristic of a historical-theological reading, views Mary's faith as inferior because it seems less theologically developed than Martha's. These interpreters fail to see that Martha's theological knowledge is actually her defense mechanism and that she ultimately chooses it as the only safe way for her to relate to Jesus. So, it has to be admitted that Martha is the better theological robot, which apparently these interpreters believe represents faith in Jesus. This is another example of interpreters reading narratives looking for theology and treating characters like walking theological placards instead of as narrative characters.

25. Contra Schnackenburg, *John*, 2:333, "Mary thus gives the impression of being nothing but a complaining woman, an impression strengthened by the context (v. 33)."

26. See Charles H. Talbert, *Reading John: A Literary and Theological Commentary on the Fourth Gospel and the Johannine Epistles*, Reading the New Testament Series (New York: Crossroad, 1992), 174–75.

indicates an outburst of anger, and any attempt to reinterpret it in terms of an internal emotional upset caused by grief, pain or sympathy is illegitimate."[27] This term, repeated in verse 38 when Jesus stands before the tomb of Lazarus, is an expression whose sense is closer to "rage" than "deeply moved." It, along with the companion term ταράσσω, depicts Jesus as overwhelmed by indignation and anguish, not as one who experiences tragedy from a cool distance. *It is these emotions that drive him to the tomb*, not his sense of destiny or the inevitability of an action to be fulfilled. In his anger Jesus demands to know, "Where have you laid him?"[28] As the crowd leads him to the tomb, Jesus begins to sob, recorded by John as simply, "Jesus wept." Jesus is taken up by and participates in the community of mourning.[29]

Seeing his grief, the crowd (taking up the role of a Greek chorus) says, in verse 36, "See how he loved him!" But then John tells us that some of them questioned, "Could not he who opened the eyes of the blind man [in chapter 10] also have kept this man from dying?" Yes, he could have, but he chose not to. Just before Jesus raises Lazarus, John wants to remind us of the tension that hangs over this whole narrative. Jesus loves Lazarus, but he waited. It underscores John's purpose that this comment comes before Lazarus is raised and reunited with his sisters. The formative lesson for faith does not come in the raising of Lazarus. (Many will believe on the basis of this miraculous sign, but, as elsewhere in John, this kind of faith is fleeting.) The formative lesson for faith can be seen in the faith of Mary. It was her faithful grieving that moved Jesus into his own grief, expressed in anger and tears. And it is this that convinces both the crowd and us as readers that Jesus does truly love Lazarus and his sisters, even if we still don't understand why he waited.

John began by putting us in a place to identify with Martha. Jesus looks distant and inscrutable, and his love for this family looks implausible. But now we can see that Jesus is not distant but identifies with and participates in the sufferings of his friends—a group that includes not just these three but all believers. If we return to the beginning of the story, to which the crowd points us, when John told us that Jesus loved these three and that therefore

27. Schnackenburg, *John*, 335.

28. Anger can be a clarifying emotion that drives one to action. It is when anger is frustrated and/or suppressed that it produces confusion and resentment.

29. Cf. Lincoln, *John*, 326, "Intriguingly, it is in this public setting that Jesus reveals his deepest personal emotions. The change in the characterization of Jesus is striking. The one who from the beginning of the episode has displayed detachment from the death of his friend, Lazarus, so that God's glory could be revealed, the one who has exhibited supernatural knowledge, the one who has proclaimed his sovereignty over death and his embodiment of life, is now by contrast described as profoundly human in his response."

he didn't go to heal Lazarus, we are still left with a conundrum. The problem remains unsolved. But what has changed is that now we actually believe that Jesus does love them. His action is still inscrutable; there is an inherent element of mystery to it that John does not intend to resolve. But Mary has taught us something about how to reconcile ourselves to that mystery, or at least modeled how to comport ourselves to Jesus in the midst of it. She relates to Jesus from the knowledge that he will join her in her grief, anger, and bewilderment. She doesn't understand why Jesus did what he did, but she trusts that he loves her. That is not an "answer" to her grief or her doubts, but it is a counterweight that gives a new context to those griefs and doubts. This is the kind of faith that John wants us to see, admire, and move toward. It is not free from ambiguities but rather clings to Jesus in the midst of life's turmoil, griefs, and confusion.

All of this saves the raising of Lazarus, when it comes in the next few verses, from having a triumphalist overtone as the climactic sign of Jesus's ministry. It is a climactic miracle, but John's message is not that belief in Jesus solves all our ills. There are countless brothers who have not been brought back to life. John makes clear that this climactic sign has a tragic side to it. In the verses that follow (11:45–54), it is actually the raising of Lazarus that leads the Sanhedrin to decide to kill Jesus. As Lincoln argues, "Jesus' movement towards Lazarus' tomb to give life to Lazarus is at the same time Jesus' movement towards his own death."[30] The darkness wants to kill the light.[31]

All of this provides a context to shape our understanding of Right ARM, where faith in Jesus (right action) is given a context that provides reason and motivations to surmount the challenges of bitter tragedy, confusion, and betrayal, chiefly found in the bitter tears of Jesus who joins us in our suffering.

Matthew 5:3–12: The Beatitudes

Of course one of the most obvious ways in which the Gospels teach wisdom is in their transmission of the teachings of Jesus, which invariably reflect the wisdom intention of shaping followers in their deepest convictions and desires. The most famous collection of Jesus's public discourses is found in the Sermon on the Mount in Matthew 5–7. A treatment of the whole Sermon

30. Lincoln, *John*, 335.

31. This principle is fundamental to the moral vision of John's Gospel, which projects a field of expectations for life and moral guideposts for individual and communal life. See Richard B. Hays, *The Moral Vision of the New Testament: Community, Cross, New Creation, A Contemporary Introduction to New Testament Ethics* (San Francisco: HarperSanFrancisco, 1996), 153–56.

is beyond the scope of this work;[32] a look at the Beatitudes, which introduce the Sermon, will have to suffice.

Like so many areas of biblical research, the large volume of work written about the Beatitudes and the Sermon on the Mount has, unfortunately, not furnished us with a consensus interpretation but only deepened controversies. The chief interpretive controversies for the Beatitudes are symptoms of the dichotomies of law/gospel and indicative/imperative, which we dealt with in chapters 2 and 3. As David Turner explains: "There are two contrasting views on the meanings of the Beatitudes. One sees them as indicative pronouncements of gracious kingdom blessings. The other sees them as ethical exhortations about entrance requirements (Guelich 1976). If the latter view is correct, human effort must produce the characteristics mentioned here so that one might earn God's approval. If the former view is correct, one can only thankfully acknowledge these characteristics as evidence of God's gracious working in one's life and cultivate them as one lives as a disciple of Christ."[33] Here we have a classic law/gospel paradigm: the Beatitudes (and the rest of the Sermon) have to be understood as *either* promise *or* demand. Either they are obeyed to earn favor with God, or they are gifts to be received with thanksgiving.[34] As Turner goes on to say, "The Beatitudes reveal key character traits that God approves in his people. These character traits are gracious gifts indicating God's approval, not requirements or works that merit God's approval."[35]

The problem with this approach is how quickly it turns into nonsense in the Sermon. In 5:20 when Jesus says, "For I tell you, unless your righteousness exceeds that of the scribes and Pharisees, you will never enter the kingdom of heaven," he means exactly what he says. The righteousness he speaks of is not imputed but one realized in the lives of his disciples.[36] The question of

---

32. See Jonathan T. Pennington, *The Sermon on the Mount and Human Flourishing: A Theological Commentary* (Grand Rapids: Baker Academic, 2017).

33. David L. Turner, *Matthew*, BECNT (Grand Rapids: Baker Academic, 2008), 146–47.

34. Turner seems to be hedging his bets with his admission that the Beatitudes identify traits that should be cultivated "as one lives as a disciple of Christ." But this "cultivation" is Matthew's real priority, not the question of justification apart from works.

35. Turner, *Matthew*, 147.

36. See Rudolf Schnackenburg, *God's Rule and Kingdom*, trans. John Murray (New York: Herder and Herder, 1963), 108–9,

> The otherworldly, uncompromising commandments of the Sermon on the Mount . . . refer to conduct in the world of here and now, they are directed to the heirs of the future kingdom, and summon them to high purity of mind and determined action. . . . The intention of Jesus is not to release his disciples from the world and their surroundings but from a worldly way of thought and life (Mark 10:42–44 par.). For the heir to the kingdom God's holy will, without distortion or abridgement, is the one and only guiding

whether righteousness is the free gift of God *or* the demand of God is foreign to Jesus's logic in the Sermon. The righteousness Jesus demands is something inherent to the proclamation of the eschatological gift of the kingdom of heaven in which the rule of God is made manifest. The law/gospel dichotomy, while it has a use in certain contexts, only occludes our vision when we come to the Beatitudes and the Sermon on the Mount.[37] As Ulrich Luz rightly says: "The obvious question for Protestants is whether there is not then a 'legalistic interpretation . . . which makes the gifts of the kingdom of God dependent on the person's moral capacity.' *Matthew obviously did not have this concern.* He lets Jesus pronounce people happy whose inner attitude and outer practice correspond to the kingdom of heaven that Jesus promises them. He binds the promises of salvation to a Christian life lived in its entirety. . . . For him the divine promise of salvation and human practice are inseparable."[38]

Equally unhelpful is the related question of whether the Beatitudes are to be understood as "indicative" or "imperative." Here the question is not about whether the Beatitudes teach salvation by works, but whether they are to be understood as imperatives (implicitly in vv. 3–10) prescribing a moral code or are simply indicative declarations that offer hope and consolation in the promise of salvation. As William Davies and Dale Allison argue: "It would be foolish to deny the imperatives implicit in 5.3–12; there is no going around this. . . . But the question is whether the primary function of the Matthean beatitudes is moral, and whether a moral dimension excludes a promissory or conciliatory dimension. The answer in both cases is negative. 5.3–12 serves firstly to bless the faithful as they are now."[39]

---

star. Jesus is not asking how it may be realized practically in the circumstances of the world. But both Jesus and the early Church were convinced that it should be, and with God's assistance could be, so realized.

37. It is actually not only a problem for the Sermon but the interpretation of Matthew as a whole. Matthean scholarship has for a long time been burdened with a dichotomy between Matthew's focus on lived righteousness and the fictive "law-free" gospel of Paul.

38. Ulrich Luz, *Matthew 1–7: A Commentary*, trans. James E. Crouch, rev. ed., Hermeneia (Minneapolis: Fortress, 2007), 200. Italics added. Luz quotes from Hans Weder, *Die "Rede der Reden": Eine Auslegung der Bergpredigt heute*, 2nd ed. (Zürich: Theologischer Verlag, 1987), 83. Luz rightly adds that "the active, toiling Christians who are sustained by God's grace and to whom Matthew, horror of horrors, promises a 'reward' (5:12) are precisely not the people who want to be justified by their own works" (202).

39. William David Davies and Dale C. Allison, *A Critical and Exegetical Commentary on the Gospel according to Saint Matthew*, ICC (Edinburgh: T&T Clark, 1988), 1:440. They add, "When Jesus speaks, the drudgery and difficulties of day-to-day life fade away and the bliss of the life to come proleptically appears." It is hard to see how Jesus's words about the inevitability of suffering and persecution along with the necessity of hungering and thirsting for righteousness are to be understood as a message that takes one out of "the drudgery and

Once again, this question does not arise from the text itself but from the indicative/imperative paradigm that undergirds so much biblical research. Davies and Allison recognize the tension between the text and their question by asking which is *primary* instead of asking a simple either/or between the two, but in the end a little yeast works through the whole dough. There is no safe, "decaffeinated" version of this paradigm. The whole category of indicative/imperative creates a dissonance with the text and forces alien questions into the interpretive discussion.

Instead, we should recognize the Beatitudes as wisdom—as a text that extols a series of virtues that are formative for Christian spirituality.[40] The notion of "implicit imperatives" is an unhelpful intrusion of deontological categories that turn enticements to embrace certain moral dispositions into moral duties. Stating that these moral duties are *secondary* does not solve the problem. The solution is to recognize the Sermon as a wisdom discourse whose primary purpose has to do with the formation of devotions and moral agency. As Talbert argues, "The Sermon on the Mount functions primarily as a catalyst for the formation of character."[41] While this observation might seem obvious (or inconsequential), it actually removes all the difficulties of approaches that are still tied to the dichotomies of law/gospel and indicative/imperative.

A wisdom approach to the Sermon will quickly recognize the Beatitudes as extolling a set of virtues that are constitutive of the righteousness of the kingdom of heaven. The Beatitudes list dispositions of the heart—how one directs one's love and agency toward God, self, and other. These are not commands but character traits that define desires and dispositions, what in the ancient world were called virtues. Wisdom discourses not only *define* virtues but, more importantly, *promote* virtues (and denigrate vices). This is why the Beatitudes are not simply a list of virtues but a benediction on those who possess certain virtues. The repeated term for this is μακάριος, which is usually translated as "blessed."

This adjective is notoriously difficult to translate and combines the ideas of eschatological blessing with "contentment/happiness."[42] If we keep in mind

---

difficulties of day-to-day life" to be transported to the "bliss" of eschatological hope. Thankfully Jesus does not embrace the same escapist sentimentality as our interpreters do here.

40. The repetition of the benediction μακάριος, almost assuredly drawn from Ps. 1:1 (a wisdom psalm), is proof enough that we are dealing with a wisdom discourse.

41. Charles H. Talbert, *Reading the Sermon on the Mount: Character Formation and Decision Making in Matthew 5–7* (Columbia: University of South Carolina Press, 2004), 29. Talbert adds, "This study flies in the face of a long and venerable tradition of interpretation of the Sermon that sees the function of Matthew 5–7 exclusively as providing norms for ethical decision making."

42. Cf. Pennington, *Sermon*, 41–67.

that the Bible understands joy as a gift of God, then "joyful" would be a good translation. However we translate it, the point of these benedictions, connected to certain virtues, is to make those virtues desirable.

Connecting these virtues to promises of future eschatological blessings is another way of accomplishing the same thing. Those who embody these virtues are those who will enjoy countless blessings in the eschatological rule of God's kingdom, both now and in the future. This is vital, because all of these virtues are counterintuitive and countercultural. We do not need enticements to be selfish. Vices are easy. What we need are virtuous desires more powerful than our cravings for self-indulgence and self-promotion. We immediately misunderstand the Beatitudes when we make them into a list of moral imperatives. The form of the Beatitudes reveals their intentionality as spiritual formation; they are designed to shape devotions—to interrogate and reeducate them.

Jesus's first benediction that "blessed are the poor in spirit, for theirs is the kingdom of heaven" (Matt. 5:3) is typical of this process. "Poverty of spirit" describes a disposition, a virtue that is connected to blessing and promise. It is also a benediction that is shocking in its counterintuitive and countercultural force. Membership in the kingdom of heaven and God's blessing are supposed to belong to the spiritually wealthy, the spiritually together, the righteous, the rich, and the beautiful. Here the blessings of God are promised to the spiritually poor, the wretched, the wayward, those who come to Jesus in perpetual need because they are empty and they know it.

Every virtue can be defined in relation to its antithetical vice (its opposite) and its counterfeit vice (which tries to emulate virtue).[43] So spiritual poverty stands over against spiritual wealth in the perpetual embrace of spiritual need; we are, in the imagery of the prophets, broken cisterns in need of perpetual filling by God. The opposite is the presumption of spiritual wealth that finds a source of life in the self, under its own locus of control, which the Bible makes clear is a form of self-deception. But the *counterfeit* to spiritual poverty is spiritual worthlessness, a pseudo-humility that hides the self in shame and refuses to accept the life-giving spring of God's grace. In the end, spiritual worthlessness, as a counterfeit to spiritual poverty, is just as idolatrous as the prideful presumption of spiritual wealth—both are shields against the grace of God, and both ground the locus of control in the self. The embrace of our spiritual poverty brings liberation from self-delusion and the need for

43. This is something of a reformulation of Aristotle's understanding of virtue as defined by a mean between two vices. The liability with the Aristotelian "golden mean" is that virtue is defined as the midpoint between two negations, leading to the formative notion that one can be courageous by simply not being foolhardy or cowardly.

the projection of a self that is worthy of accolade based on merits of good works, or good looks, or good diet, or good zip code, or good wardrobe, and frees us into a life-giving communion with God. That is why the poor in spirit are blessed and are the true participants in God's kingdom.

The next benediction comes to those who grieve: "Blessed are those who mourn, for they shall be comforted" (Matt. 5:4). In an allusion to Isaiah 61:2, Jesus proclaims blessing and comfort for those who grieve.[44] But what do they grieve? In the original context of Isaiah they grieve the bitterness of exile. It also includes a mourning of the conditions that produced the exile—the disobedience of Israel.[45] So in Jesus's proclamation there is a note of fulfillment of Isaiah 61 and the resolution of exile in his own person and ministry. At the same time, exile here is transformed and extended through the already/not yet eschatological arrival of the kingdom of heaven. The exile is not simply resolved but transformed into an image that describes the church's sojourn in its awaiting the consummation of the kingdom (cf. 1 Pet. 1:1; 2:11). In this way mourning itself is transformed into a virtue, not just grieving hardship but embracing a hopeful expectation. Grief certainly includes sorrow for sin and adversities, but in its connection to a hopeful longing for the fullness of the righteousness of God to be revealed it grieves everything in the world, in the community, and in the self that does not incorporate and embody the shalom of God. It is a grief with an eye on the eschatological horizon that produces hope, but a hope that provides a context for grief. Here the space for grief and hope are the same, and they each create space for the other.[46]

44. Isaiah 61:1–3:
>   The Spirit of the Lord GOD is upon me,
>   because the LORD has anointed me
>   to bring good news to the poor;
>   he has sent me to bind up the brokenhearted,
>   to proclaim liberty to the captives,
>   and the opening of the prison to those who are bound;
>   to proclaim the year of the LORD's favor,
>   and the day of vengeance of our God;
>   to comfort all who mourn;
>   to grant to those who mourn in Zion—
>   to give them a beautiful headdress instead of ashes,
>   the oil of gladness instead of mourning,
>   the garment of praise instead of a faint spirit;
>   that they may be called oaks of righteousness,
>   the planting of the LORD, that he may be glorified.

45. This can be seen in Isaiah's identification of the poor and the mourners with the righteous who become priests for the world.

46. Cf. Walter Brueggemann, *Reality, Grief, Hope: Three Urgent Prophetic Tasks* (Grand Rapids: Eerdmans, 2014), 57–128.

As a virtue, mourning means a disposition that opens itself to grieve unrighteousness, human depravity, and brokenness wherever they reveal themselves. It is a grief informed and sustained by eschatological hope in longing for not simply the end of grief but the flourishing of righteousness. Again, this is a deeply counterintuitive and countercultural virtue; the natural assumption is that God has forsaken the grieving and blesses those who are happy and secure. (This was no less true in the first century than it is today.) Bonhoeffer understood how this beatitude undercut this worldly conviction: "Those who mourn are those who are prepared to renounce and live without everything the world calls happiness and peace. They are those who cannot be brought into accord with the world, who cannot conform to the world. They mourn over the world, its guilt, its fate, and its happiness."[47]

Alongside this, the counterfeit to mourning is a grief divorced from hope, in a despair that is consumed by itself and unable to see the eschatological horizon. This kind of despair is a vice because it ultimately has no vision outside the locus of the self and its suffering. Since it can see no means within the self to solve the horrors of the world, it retreats into the solace and the familiarity of despair. But in this way it fails to connect itself to the work of God that calls for repentance from self-reliance, whether in the self-satisfied vision of a divinely blessed, romanticized happiness or self-protective, cynical despair. The virtue of mourning stands against the vices of self-indulgent pursuit of happiness on the one hand and despairing self-pity on the other by combining a proper grief that recognizes all human pursuits are cursed with a longing hope for the heart's proper joy in righteousness and shalom.

"Blessed are the meek, for they shall inherit the earth" (Matt. 5:5).[48] This benediction will likely sound the strangest to our ears. This is in large measure a result of the negative connotations contemporary English attaches to "meekness" as a spineless disposition of relinquishing one's agency to dominant circumstances or authorities. This kind of fearful resignation is a good description of the counterfeit vice associated with meekness. But true meekness requires strength of character and courage. It is a radical trust in the practical provision of God as giver.[49] Meekness stands in contrast to the

---

47. Dietrich Bonhoeffer, *Discipleship*, trans. Barbara Green and Reinhard Krauss, Dietrich Bonhoeffer Works 4 (Minneapolis: Fortress, 2001), 103.

48. Here again we have an echo of Isa. 61, specifically the LXX of Isa. 61:7: "Thus shall they inherit the land [κληρονομήσουσιν τὴν γῆν] a second time, and everlasting joy shall be upon their head." Lancelot Charles Lee Brenton, *The Septuagint Version of the Old Testament* (London: Bagster, 1844).

49. Contra Davies and Allison, *Matthew*, 1:449, "The πραεῖς are not so much actively seeking to avoid hubris (an attitude) as they are, as a matter of fact, powerless in the eyes of the world (a condition)." While it is correct to guard against an overspiritualized interpretation that dislocates

heroic individual's power to be, or radical self-reliance, as someone determined to make life work on their own terms. This kind of heroism was extolled in the ancient (especially Roman) world, just as it is today. Meekness does not mean passivity. It can find expression in many forms of agency. Meekness speaks chiefly to the devotions that shape agency. In contrast to ambitious self-reliance, which is rooted in fear of want, meekness acts in strength but without the demand that our agency produce admiration or security.

But admiration and security are not evils; they are good things, and so worthy of desire. True meekness seeks the admiration and security that come as gifts of God. Ambition seeks to secure them by any means necessary. False meekness denies that they are goods to be sought. This is why the one who waits on the Lord with meekness is the person who is (counterintuitively) the most secure in herself. It is counterintuitive because it rebels against our sinful nature that seeks life first in the self and the created order instead of God.

The next beatitude speaks explicitly in the language of desire: "Blessed are those who hunger and thirst for righteousness, for they shall be satisfied" (Matt. 5:6). In the context of the Sermon on the Mount, "righteousness" does not primarily refer to the imputed righteousness of Christ but to (1) the revelation of the righteousness of God's rule and (2) moral agency shaped by God's righteousness in form and possibility. Righteousness in this context is not simply moral rectitude but refers to the boundaries that protect life and facilitate communal shalom.[50] So the one who hungers and thirsts for righteousness desires for the will of God to be manifest in the world. This includes, but is not limited to, personal righteousness, because individual moral integrity finds its τέλος in the revelation of God's righteousness in all the created order, including all human institutions and communities. This can be seen in the eschatological promise that "they shall be satisfied" in the full revelation of the glory of God. In many ways this benediction is a positive version of the benediction for those who mourn. Both have a disposition to desire righteousness.

The antithesis of this virtue is the vice of moral complacency. This complacency can refer, most obviously, to a moral laziness that is satisfied with moral turpitude as a condition of life. But moral complacency need not include passive resignation. It can just as easily include a scrupulous moral self-satisfaction. Moralism always creates stringent but obtainable goals that can be realized and used to justify oneself and judge others. This is just as far

---

the text from the dismal economic conditions of ancient Palestine, it is unlikely that Matthew or Jesus intends to teach that salvation (the inheritance of the land) comes as a result of one's economic deprivations. Such a conclusion hardly makes sense in the context of the Sermon.

50. Cf. Pennington, *Sermon*, 87–91.

from the pursuit of righteousness as moral sloth, and a more dangerous vice because it is the counterfeit to the true pursuit of righteousness. Moralism is deceptive because it pretends to pursue righteousness but does so in a way that does not act with reference to the righteousness of God, and in this it fails to submit itself to the reign of God. By contrast, the hunger for righteousness decenters the self in the love of God and his righteousness and pursues the realization of God's will "on earth" as it is done "in heaven."

Jesus's next benediction for "the merciful," that "they shall receive mercy" (Matt. 5:7), is very likely paired with the previous beatitude about the pursuit of righteousness. Just as we struggle to hold together the holiness and grace of God conceptually, in practice the pursuit of righteousness is too rarely marked by compassion for others and the practices of asking for and granting forgiveness (whether individually or corporately). Later in the Sermon it will become clear that this mercy involves a radical love for neighbor defined by one of Jesus's most challenging commands: "Love your enemies and pray for those who persecute you" (Matt. 5:44). To show mercy goes beyond bearing persecution and forgiving, but actively seeking the good of one's enemy. But, as Nicholas Wolterstorff says, "Forgiveness as a mode of caring about the other is hard to bring off. It does not come naturally. What comes naturally is nursing one's anger and lusting for revenge."[51] The disruptive counterintuitive force of the virtue of mercy is often defused by means of its counterfeit vice of niceness/tolerance. The audacious challenge to love one's enemies is easier to swallow when it is translated into a call to act politely to all. This counterfeit vice is a form of self-protection that shows contempt for the other because it fails to seek their good, while holding them at a safe distance.

The antithesis to mercy is, of course, judgment. In the sphere of virtues and vices, the antithetic vice of mercy is the judgmental disposition that arises from self-righteousness. This is at the heart of Jesus's criticisms of the Pharisees. While they certainly believe in the electing grace of God, they live as though they are spiritually wealthy and not spiritually poor, and therefore not in need of the mercy of God. They enjoy God's favor because of their obedience. The leading edge of Jesus's criticisms is most often directed toward their contempt for "sinners" as a practical expression of their belief that they themselves are not in need of radical mercy from God.[52] Self-righteousness and contempt for others are comorbid twins. The most likely reason for Jesus's focus on the latter is that contempt for others can be seen expressed in action, whereas

---

51. Nicholas Wolterstorff, *Justice in Love*, Emory University Studies in Law and Religion (Grand Rapids: Eerdmans, 2011), 190.

52. See Hays, *Moral Vision*, 99–101, on what he refers to as Matthew's "hermeneutic of mercy."

self-righteousness is an internal disposition. Even though self-righteousness is ultimately an idolatrous pride (i.e., a theological vice), Jesus focuses on the (external and visible) ethical manifestation of this theological error. Again we see that theology and ethics are two sides of the same coin. The moral failing of the Pharisees is also their failure to submit to God. Mercy finds its impulse in the reception of divine forgiveness. Love for neighbor and especially love for enemy find their impulses in God's love for his enemies (Matt. 5:45–46).

The next blessing is for the "pure in heart," who will "see God" (Matt. 5:8). Purity of heart seems like a straightforward concept, but our tendency is to understand purity negatively, as the absence of impurity. This negation simply leaves a vacuous heart, not one marked by purity. In a post-Kantian world we might also imagine a pure heart to be one free of passions and desires. The counterfeit to purity of heart is Stoic apathy, which sees freedom from desire itself as a virtue. But real purity of heart is a heart determined by appropriate desires, where the heart hungers and thirsts for righteousness, where the affections are at the same time insatiable and appropriate to their objects. This is not the same as the contemporary romantic notion where having "passion" for something legitimates that pursuit as authentic.[53] Instead, it is passion liberated by its submission to the will of God.

The antithesis to purity of heart is a heart torn asunder by incoherent and idolatrous devotions. It seeks to find life apart from God's gracious rule, through what is given in creation, without gratitude (cf. Rom. 1:21–25). Without the worship of God as an integrating teleological devotion, all these devotions necessarily become fractious and incoherent. So purity of heart—a heart ruled by coherent desires—is a product of a heart that first enjoys and glorifies God, or in Jesus's own words, "Seeks first the kingdom of God." So it is natural that the promise made to the pure in heart is that they would have their chief desire fulfilled and "see God."

---

53. This is a contemporary manifestation of the existentialist principle that "happiness is to will one thing." While a singularity of vision and longing can provide a certain coherence to life, this principle renders all possible objects of devotion as having equal value because it is founded on a nihilistic metaphysic that despairs of the reality of goods outside the consciousness's will to assert itself. Interestingly, this is a secular version of Kierkegaard's principle that "Purity of heart is to will one thing," in his discourse "On the Occasion of a Confession." See Søren Kierkegaard, *Upbuilding Discourses in Various Spirits*, trans. Howard Vincent Hong and Edna Hatlestad Hong, Kierkegaard's Writings 15 (Princeton: Princeton University Press, 1993), 7–154. But for Kierkegaard it was the object of a singular will, not the singularity of will that was the source of contentment. "Because only the pure in heart are able to see God and consequently keep near to him and preserve his purity through his keeping near to him; and the person who in truth wills only one thing *can will only the good*, and the person who wills only one thing when he wills the good can *will only the good in truth*." Kierkegaard, *Upbuilding Discourses*, 24. Italics original.

The final virtue to receive a benediction is for the "peacemakers," for "they shall be called sons of God" (Matt. 5:9). While "peacemaking" is often associated with conflict resolution, the meaning here is much broader, particularly if we take "peace" in the sense of shalom—the peace that enjoys and protects the flourishing of life within the freedom of God's created order.[54] So peacemakers are those who facilitate the conditions of social shalom through their moral integrity in personal relationships and institutional engagement. Like those who hunger and thirst for righteousness, they long to see the righteousness of God made manifest in his life-giving rule in the world.

The antithesis of the peacemaker is the ambitious self-promoter who demands recognition for their agency and sows dissension against the agency of others, whom the self-promoter views as competitors. Today we would label such a person a narcissist. They can be very accomplished and are often found in positions of leadership, because they can get things done. But they tend to treat other people as tools for their agendas and are paralyzed by their vanity, viewing all disagreements as personal attacks. In this way they do not create a space for others and difference and therefore do not facilitate communal shalom.

The counterfeit to the peacemaker is the people pleaser who desires for everyone to be happy but in so doing fails to draw boundaries in the community to protect the vulnerable. People pleasers value politeness and view conflict as essentially sinful and not as a natural (if uncomfortable) by-product of life in community. They tend to practice counterfeit mercy and are usually caring people, but they fail to bring real communal peace because their aim is not the righteousness of God but freedom from conflict and uncomfortable emotions. By contrast, peacemakers use their agency to promote communal integrity and life by providing a safe place for difference and mutual edification in the context of mutual forgiveness.

The Beatitudes conclude with a double blessing on the persecuted—those who are "persecuted for righteousness' sake" (Matt. 5:10) and those who are persecuted "on my [Jesus's] account" (Matt. 5:11). This benediction for the persecuted is not extolling a virtue (of being persecuted) but defining a moral vision that corresponds to all the previous virtues of the Beatitudes. That moral vision includes the natural, irrational hostility that will arise if and when Jesus's disciples take these virtues to heart. Jesus himself is the model for not only all these virtues but also the consequences of practicing them. So these final beatitudes remind disciples of the cost of virtue. They

54. On "created order" see Oliver O'Donovan, *Resurrection and Moral Order: An Outline for Evangelical Ethics* (Grand Rapids: Eerdmans, 1986), 31–52.

will be blessed by God for them but often cursed by others for them. This is a mark of the countercultural depth of the Beatitudes. This does not mean that *everyone* will hate them, but some will violently hate them. So Jesus prepares his disciples for this inevitability, but he also pronounces a benediction on the persecuted. He does not tell them to seek persecution, but he does ennoble it with blessing. In this he also removes the temptation to see persecution as a sign of God's abandonment.

So what we find in the Beatitudes is a moral/spiritual vision of discipleship in the kingdom of heaven. The focus of the Beatitudes is on extolling a set of deeply counterintuitive and countercultural virtues and giving those virtues contextualizing reasons and motivations (especially in tying them to eschatological blessings, both present and future) that make those virtues intelligible and desirable. In this way the Beatitudes engage in what has traditionally been called moral theology, or what we today call spiritual formation, especially when we understand the beatific virtues in the context of their counterfeit and opposing vices.

Mark: Narrative Moral Vision

One of the most important, and underappreciated, aspects of Hays's *Moral Vision of the New Testament* can be found in his descriptions of the specific moral visions projected by particular NT texts. His insightful analysis describes the moral vision particular to each Gospel, the Pauline corpus, and the book of Revelation.[55] Hays aims to describe these works in terms of the moral world that they project, not simply in terms of what morality they explicitly teach but what virtues and vices become intelligible in them through theological and narrative description. Looking at his treatment of Mark will prove illustrative of his technique and insight.

Hays summarizes the narrative moral vision of Mark in six propositions. (1) "The world according to Mark is *a world torn open by God*."[56] As Hays says, "This is a story of God's powerful incursion into the created order."[57] What this means is an establishment of God's rule, not as a gradual process

---

55. Luke and Acts are treated, correctly, as a unity, and he treats the Johannine Epistles along with the Gospel of John. The other General Epistles, unfortunately, get no treatment, but this is hardly a slight particular to Hays.

56. Hays, *Moral Vision*, 88. Italics original. This is a deliberate allusion to Mark 1:10: "And when he came up out of the water, immediately he saw the heavens being *torn open* [εἶδεν σχιζομένους τοὺς οὐρανοὺς] and the Spirit descending on him like a dove," and Isa. 64:1a, "Oh that you would *rend the heavens* and come down."

57. Hays, *Moral Vision*, 88.

but in an apocalyptic event. "The appearing of the kingdom of God in Jesus ruptures the status quo, just as new wine bursts old wineskins. Illusions of stability and authority—both the authority of Roman rule (12:13–17) and the authority of the Jewish religious establishment (11:27–12:12)—are stripped away."[58] What this means for the moral vision of Mark is an expectation of reversals of power where hope attaches itself to the salvific righteousness of God. Allegiances to human institutions, whether civil, religious, or economic, are immediately relativized.

One of Mark's favorite words is the adverb "immediately" (εὐθύς).[59] But as Hays says, "This is not just a clumsy device to link separate pericopes; rather, it describes the breathless pace with which God's apocalyptic campaign is unfolding." This means that (2) "Because the cosmic conflict is underway, *time becomes compressed.*"[60] This temporal compression gives a moral urgency and moral seriousness to Mark's Gospel. No one in Mark's Gospel forms a study committee to address a social issue. In Mark's narrative world, direct action is required. The intervention of the rule of God opens up new possibilities in Jesus's shocking attack on the religious institutions and mores of his day. But it also demands immediate and unquestioning allegiance. In Mark's Gospel Jesus calls disciples to leave all that they know and possess, and they all do so *immediately* (see 1:18, 20). Of course, these disciples will become as dumb as rocks by the end of Mark's Gospel, but at the beginning they exemplify true discipleship. Jesus commands, and they follow.

(3) "God's apocalyptic invasion of the world has also wrought an inversion: *God has reversed the positions of insiders and outsiders.*"[61] This is where Mark's Gospel pits two incommensurable systems of value against each other. One is defined by allegiance to Jesus and the apocalyptic reign of God he is inaugurating. The other is defined by ambition for self-aggrandizement and self-sufficiency. This is why the disciples do not come off any better in Mark's Gospel than the Jewish religious authorities who condemn Jesus to death. In the end the disciples are blinded to Jesus's person and mission by their ambition (see 10:32–52). So the favored "insiders" in Mark's Gospel are not the religious authorities or the disciples but, as Hays points out, "The lepers, the demon-possessed, the woman with the hemorrhage (5:25–34), the Syrophoenician

---

58. Hays, *Moral Vision*, 89.

59. It appears forty-one times in Mark, as opposed to six in Matthew, six in Luke, four in Acts, and zero times in John.

60. Both quotations from Hays, *Moral Vision*, 89. Italics original. Hays adds, "This gospel plunges us into the midst of a cosmic conflict careening forward; if we want to follow the story we need to pick up the pace."

61. Hays, *Moral Vision*, 89. Italics original.

woman (7:24–30), the little children (10:13–16), blind Bartimaeus (10:46–52), the nameless woman who anoints Jesus at Bethany 'for burial' (14:3–9), the Gentile centurion at the cross (15:39)—these are the examples put forward by Mark of faithful response to Jesus."[62] What this means is that Mark's moral vision is governed by the principle that "Many who are first will be last, and the last first" (10:31). This is Mark's formulation of the principle "Whoever exalts himself will be humbled, and whoever humbles himself will be exalted" (Matt. 23:12; cf. Luke 14:11). This apocalyptic reversal is the judgment of God on all human self-importance.

(4) The same apocalyptic reversal can also be seen in how "Mark's Gospel *redefines the nature of power and the value of suffering*."[63] This is the primary moral significance that Mark sees in the cross.[64] And so Jesus defines his messianic calling in terms of the cross in the same breath that he also defines discipleship in terms of the same cross (Mark 8:27–38). This theme is repeated as Mark's narrative moves toward Jesus's demise in Jerusalem. Twice more he will predict his imminent betrayal and immediately apply the cross to his disciples as they fight about "who was the greatest" (Mark 9:34), most famously in Mark 10:42–45: "And Jesus called them to him and said to them, 'You know that those who are considered rulers of the Gentiles lord it over them, and their great ones exercise authority over them. But it shall not be so among you. But whoever would be great among you must be your servant, and whoever would be first among you must be slave of all. For even the Son of Man came not to be served but to serve, and to give his life as a ransom for many.'" The cross is the touchstone of Mark's moral vision. In Mark's world all human agency is interrogated by the cross: all hubris is shattered, but all humble charity is simultaneously validated.

This is essential to what narratives do—they project a moral vision that makes certain actions and dispositions intelligible and desirable. Self-renunciation, taking up the cross, is a deeply counterintuitive and countercultural disposition. This virtue is not going to be easily fostered in the hearts of God's people, neither individually nor corporately. It will need a very strong counternarrative that consciously sets two incommensurable systems of moral evaluation against each other. In Mark the centrality of

62. Hays, *Moral Vision*, 90.

63. Hays, *Moral Vision*, 90. Italics original.

64. Mark certainly has a theological understanding of the atoning significance of Jesus's death, most obviously in Mark 10:45 and the institution of the Last Supper, but we should not make the mistake of separating the atoning significance from the moral significance of the cross, despite the centuries of theological discourse that lead us to pick one over the other. Mark, like all the other NT authors, sees the cross in terms of both gift and demand. Human sin is judged in the cross to provide not only forgiveness for sin but also freedom from sin.

Jesus's cross is that counternarrative, which judges all competing apprehensions of value that are unwilling to submit to suffering the death of self. Jesus's own obedience to the call of God, to suffer and serve, becomes the inspiration for (and means of) the renunciation of self-reliance and self-promotion. The way of the cross only becomes easy when we domesticate it into a call to "be nice to others." Mark's narrative not only excludes this option but also grounds the way of the cross in love and gratitude toward Christ. Jesus's call to the cross is connected to his invitation to be with him (Mark 8:34). This is Mark's way of using a narrative to inculcate and encourage a disposition of faith in the person of Jesus, with devotions and actions shaped by that faith.

(5) Hays describes this counterintuitive vision as "profoundly *ironic*."[65] What he means by this is more than simply recognizing irony as a prominent literary feature in Mark. He means that Mark relies heavily on irony as an instrument of spiritual formation. Jesus is surrounded by irony in Mark's Gospel. Everyone who comes to Jesus with a firm conviction of who Jesus is and what he will do is destined to crash on the shoals of irony. This is especially true of the disciples. In one of Mark's most dramatic twists of irony, Jesus chides his disciples after his second miraculous feeding because they are worried about their meager provision of one loaf of bread (Mark 8:1–21). The scene is both comically and tragically ironic as Jesus interrogates them: "Why are you discussing the fact that you have no bread? Do you not yet perceive or understand? Are your hearts hardened? Having eyes do you not see, and having ears do you not hear?" (Mark 8:17–18a). This last phrase, an echo of Isaiah 6:9, was previously used by Jesus in Mark 4:11–12, in his explanation of the parable of the sower, as a message of judgment on "outsiders." The disciples themselves are now the outsiders, not simply because they are dimwitted but because "their hearts were hardened" (Mark 6:51–52).

Mark's plan for the spiritual formation of his readers, most clearly seen in the way he treats the disciples as the primary focus of our identification as readers,[66] begins with deconstruction. Our preconceived notions of who Jesus is and what he can do for us are, through the disciples, put through the shredder as idolatrous maneuvers to contain Jesus. We are left to identify with the disciples in the boat with Jesus after the calming of the storm, bewildered

65. Hays, *Moral Vision*, 90, "Mark's vision of the moral life is profoundly *ironic*." Italics original. Cf. Jerry Camery-Hoggatt, *Irony in Mark's Gospel: Text and Subtext*, SNTSMS 72 (Cambridge: Cambridge University Press, 1992).

66. Cf. Robert Tannehill, "The Disciples in Mark: The Function of a Narrative Role," in *The Interpretation of Mark*, ed. William Telford, Studies in New Testament Interpretation (Edinburgh: T&T Clark, 1995), 169–95.

and terrified (cf. Mark 4:41, ἐφοβήθησαν φόβον μέγαν).[67] They have no more categories to contain him, but they continue to follow.

Later in Mark's Gospel, in the crucifixion narrative, after the disciples have abandoned Jesus, the rhetoric of tragic irony reaches its peak:

> And the inscription of the charge against him read, "The King of the Jews." And with him they crucified two robbers, one on his right and one on his left. And those who passed by derided him, wagging their heads and saying, "Aha! You who would destroy the temple and rebuild it in three days, save yourself, and come down from the cross!" So also the chief priests with the scribes mocked him to one another, saying, "He saved others; he cannot save himself. Let the Christ, the King of Israel, come down now from the cross that we may see and believe." (Mark 15:26–32a)

Mark's purpose in this description goes beyond historical reportage. Using tragic irony, he intends to clarify our devotions through inciting our outrage and anger. While revenge is always a corrupting emotion, anger can be a clarifying one. Here Mark's purpose is not to incite vengeful desires on the perpetrators of these injustices but to recognize the irony of the truth of their words. They mean to mock Jesus by calling him "the Christ, the King of Israel," but we recognize that the cross is what proves Jesus to be the King of Israel. The cross is the sign of Jesus's messianic rule, not the negation of it. Our indignation seals this truth in us at a very deep level. This is how Mark uses irony as a powerful tool of spiritual formation, shaping our comportment to Jesus at the level of our devotions and convictions.

Finally, Hays argues that (6) "this Gospel's lack of closure calls for *active response* from the reader."[68] By "lack of closure," Hays is referring to the abrupt ending of Mark 16:8, "And they went out and fled from the tomb, for trembling and astonishment had seized them, and they said nothing to anyone, for they were afraid."[69] Despite the fact that they were told in the empty tomb to "tell his disciples and Peter that he is going before you to Galilee. There you

---

67. This is not, as so many commentators declare, a proper awe and reverence for Jesus. The question of the disciples in the boat, "Who then is this, that even the wind and the sea obey him?" is hardly a confession of faith in Jesus but reveals their confusion and fear that they are trapped in a boat with such a person.

68. Hays, *Moral Vision*, 90. Italics original. He adds, "It is a Gospel of uninterpreted gestures and suggestive silences. Precisely for that reason, it summons readers to supply the ending by taking up the cross and completing the interpretation in their own lives of discipleship" (91).

69. While the early church supplied two alternate endings to augment Mark, the "shorter" and "longer" endings, and some contemporary scholars argue for an original ending mysteriously lost in a manuscript mishap, the ending at 16:8 fits perfectly in Mark's overall arc for the spiritual formation of the reader, even if it leaves the historian wanting.

will see him, just as he told you," Mark makes a point of telling us, "They said nothing to anyone, for they were *afraid*." So Mark's Gospel ends with the question, "So who is going to tell them that Jesus is alive?" Hays is right that this is an invitation, very nearly a command, for the reader to fulfill. But Mark set up this response far earlier in his Gospel.

Back in the turning point in Mark's Gospel (Mark 8:27–38), where Jesus reveals his identity and mission and has to rebuke Peter for his worldly (satanic?) rejection of Jesus's mission, it is important that Jesus calls "the crowd to him with his disciples" before he defines discipleship in terms of fellowship with Christ through his cross. This is the point where Mark begins to make space for the reader to assume the role of the faithful disciple, a thirteenth disciple who gets it. This is another use Mark makes of irony as the narrative proceeds toward Jerusalem and the cross, where a savagely ironic distance opens up between Jesus and his disciples. Despite his patient leading, they continue to obsess about who is, or will be, the greatest among them, as Jesus is determined to accept his fate as the servant of God. Mark creates the space for the reader to question what it would be like if just one disciple actually understood what was happening. When Jesus is in his darkest hour at Gethsemane (in a tragic ironic reversal of the scene where Jesus is asleep in the stern of a boat full of screaming disciples), all the disciples are asleep. Couldn't one have stayed awake? Couldn't one disciple have been at the cross with Jesus, instead of having a Roman centurion be the only one at the scene who understands (Mark 15:39)? In all these ways Mark is setting up the reader to assume the role of a true disciple to replace those who do not see, and do not hear, and do not understand.

In this way the narrative form of Mark is best understood in how it supplies Right ARM—all of these narrative features construct a normative moral vision where certain types of convictions and actions become intelligible and virtuous.

Conclusion

We can see from these exemplary texts that the Gospel narratives function as wisdom at many levels and use a host of literary strategies that engage the reader in various dialectic processes. These narrative strategies are utilized by the Gospel writers to expose, assess, reform, and reinforce the convictions and affections of their readers. We saw how Gospel narratives use identification with characters as a means of forming convictions of what faith looks and feels like in the context of an encounter with Jesus, often in the face of tragedy. Through this process the readers' faith, understood as their trusting comportment to the person and rule of Jesus, is both affirmed and challenged. We also saw how Gospel authors use literary tools such as irony and other forms of indirect commentary to form the convictions of readers through the relational trust built between implied author and implied readers.

In addition, the shape of the Gospel narratives, their narrative arcs and modes of description, projects a moral vision that contextualizes moral actions, making certain pursuits intelligible and desirable. Hays supplies an account of Mark's moral vision and explains how that vision creates a moral landscape that produces expectations for the shape of one's life as a disciple of Jesus. At the center of that moral vision is Jesus's life, as the servant of all, who shows compassion for sinners, the disadvantaged, and the possessed, and sacrifices himself as a means of redemption. The shape of Jesus's life sets the mold for the life of discipleship. This is most clearly seen in Mark 8:28–35, where Jesus links his own death on the cross with the pattern of discipleship. Thus, the narrative as a whole gives a value-laden picture of the world that guides disciples in the most fundamental wisdom questions: "Who am I, and is there anything worth spending my life to pursue?"

We also saw that the Beatitudes give direct teaching on the nature of discipleship, and in particular the essential virtues that define human agency, determined by the presence of the eschatological kingdom of heaven. The recognition of spiritual poverty, the openness to grief, and the hunger for righteousness are all virtues ordered toward the revelation of the glory of God and his righteousness, in both their eschatological fullness and in their realization in the world, in the church, and in the heart as evidence of the reign of God realized in and through the life, death, and resurrection of Jesus.

In all these ways, and innumerable others, we can see that Gospel narratives were written for spiritual formation. In this context it becomes clear that reading strategies that sift these narratives for theological ideas or historical information simply ignore the nature of the Gospels themselves and the intentions that are encoded in both their form and content. The Gospels as narratives are purposely built for the formative process. As Nussbaum argues, this is what narratives are best suited for, because of the ways in which narratives invite our engagement as whole persons—in all our hopes, fears, longings, self-doubt, shame, and pride. In all this the Gospels bring us into a deeper reality of faith in Jesus as righteous Lord and compassionate Savior, and in this way they free us from idolatries and enjoin us to experience love and joy.

From these examples it becomes clear that the Gospels are designed to function as formative wisdom texts and that reading them for christological truths and historical information are modes of reading that necessarily ignore both the form and content of the Gospel narratives. While the Gospels can be utilized to answer questions about the origins of Christian beliefs or constructions of a historical Jesus or a Christian theology, all these exercises are secondary engagements with the text that extract information only through a process of ignoring their form as narratives and their formative intentionality. The Gospels were written for spiritual formation, and if we seek to understand them on their own terms, then we need to adopt reading methodologies that are shaped around and honor their wisdom agendas. As Schneiders argues: "Biblical interpretation reaches its ultimate goal when it actually promotes and nourishes the transformation of the reader (whether the individual or the community) in relation to God, self, world and society. In other words, spirituality as the lived experience of the faith is the ultimate goal and final fruit of the engagement of the reader with the gospel message which is mediated in the gospel texts."[70]

Once again, it is important to recognize that this is not simply a beneficial agenda that we can use to engage a neutral text for our spiritual benefit. This is an act of allowing the nature of the text as wisdom to shape our hermeneutical comportment to the intentionality of the text, signaled in both its form and content. The formative nature of the text is not something created by our needs as readers but inherent in the Gospel narratives as wisdom texts.

70. Sandra M. Schneiders, "The Gospels and the Reader," in *The Cambridge Companion to the Gospels*, ed. Stephen C. Barton (Cambridge: Cambridge University Press, 2006), 116.

6

READING EPISTLES FOR WISDOM
Theory

In this chapter we turn to look at the other predominant genre in the NT to understand how epistles function as wisdom. We will see that epistles, like gospels, are an ancient wisdom genre.[1] Their form tells us something about their intentionality to mold recipients in their affections, convictions, and actions. How epistles do this is markedly different from gospels, so we will have to pay particular attention to the tools used by epistolary writers and how those tools serve formative ends. Along the way we will critique the history of how epistles have been interpreted, especially in light of the unhelpful category of indicative/imperative.

The Genre of Epistle

As with gospels, genre is our first question in reading epistles.[2] Again, genres are not simply a list of literary features shared by a group of texts. Genres are chiefly a means of encoding intentionality and prefiguring the expectations of readers. Genres develop over time according to their usefulness in achieving

1. See John G. Gammie, "Paraenetic Literature: Toward the Morphology of a Secondary Genre," *Semeia* 50 (1990): 41–77.
2. As Fowler reminds us, "The processes of generic recognition are in fact fundamental to the reading process." Alastair Fowler, *Kinds of Literature: An Introduction to the Theory of Genres and Modes* (Cambridge, MA: Harvard University Press, 1982), 259.

particular communicative (illocutionary) ends. Therefore, identifying the genre of a particular literary object is essential in discerning its illocutionary force. This is not simply what an author means to communicate (i.e., a set of ideas) but what the author wants the recipient to do. This intention is discoverable in the communicative form and content—the genre and words. But the interpretation of the content is dependent on the identification of the genre, which supplies the intentional grid through which the content can be understood.[3]

As we saw above, the scholarly debate surrounding the genre of gospel has been contentious but has, for the most part, resolved itself around the consensus that the best correlate to gospel is the ancient genre of βίος (biography). The story for epistolary genre research is quite different. While a scholarly consensus has emerged over the last few decades and remains uncontested, it has simply been ignored. This consensus view contends that the ancient epistolary genre of paraenetic epistle is the closest correlate genre for the epistolary literature of the NT.[4]

Ignoring this research consensus, NT scholars still commonly define the genre of epistle as simply a document containing a greeting, body, and closing.[5] This definition is as useless as it is anemic, because it fails to speak substantively about either the literary characteristics or the communicative intentions associated with the genre.[6] This truncated definition overlooks the genre distinctions that ancient letter writers consciously made between different

---

3. Cf. Fowler, *Kinds*, 22, "At any rate there is no doubt that genre primarily has to do with communication. It is an instrument not of classification or prescription, but of meaning."

4. See Abraham J. Malherbe, "Hellenistic Moralists and the New Testament," *ANRW* II.26.1:278–333; and Troels Engberg-Pedersen and James M. Starr, eds., *Early Christian Paraenesis in Context*, BZNW 125 (Berlin: de Gruyter, 2004).

5. E.g., Jeffrey A. D. Weima, *Paul the Ancient Letter Writer: An Introduction to Epistolary Analysis* (Grand Rapids: Baker Academic, 2016). Cf. James D. G. Dunn, "The Pauline Letters," in *The Cambridge Companion to Biblical Interpretation*, ed. John Barton (Cambridge: Cambridge University Press, 1998), 278–79.

6. Cf. Stanley Kent Stowers, *Letter Writing in Greco-Roman Antiquity*, LEC 5 (Philadelphia: Westminster, 1986), 22,

> According to some scholars, the salutation and thanksgiving are followed by two other sections in the Pauline letter, the body and the paraenetic section—a text that strings together moral exhortations. Problems with these two divisions of the Pauline letter illustrate the limitations of the prevailing approach to earliest Christian letters. When Greek and Roman writers reflect on letter writing, they either discuss the "body" or consider the letter as a functioning whole. Modern epistolary research has found very little to say about the body of the letter. This major lacuna has occurred because scholars studying "epistolary" style have limited their analysis to elements thought to be unique to letters. Defined in that way, what is "epistolary" about letters shows up only at the beginnings and conclusions. Thus the beginnings and endings of letters contain true epistolary features, and what comes between seems to be merely the information or message to be conveyed.

types of letters (all of which had a greeting, body, and closing). Professional letter writers, who were used for everything from Roman proclamations to the simplest domestic correspondence, were trained in epistolary rhetorical techniques and aided by handbooks with lists of exemplary letters.[7] These handbooks attest to many ancient epistolary "types," each one designed for a particular purpose. As Stanley Stowers notes: "Epistolary types provided the ancient writer with a taxonomy of letters according to typical actions performed in corresponding social contexts and occasions. The types in the handbooks give a sample, in barest outline, of form and language that is appropriate to the logic of the social code in a particular instance. The author, then, could elaborate, combine, and adapt this ideal according to the occasion in view, his purpose and his literary abilities. Rhetorical training provided the letter writer with techniques for the endless elaboration and development of the basic ideal captured in the handbook descriptions."[8]

One of the more complex letter types that developed over time was the paraenetic epistle. Its origins date back to letters of Plato and Aristotle[9] and major developments occurred within the Hellenistic philosophical schools, although it was not a genre exclusive to the schools.[10] In the Hellenistic period, as Greek ideas spread along with Greek governance and culture, letter writing became an important means of maintaining relationships between teachers and pupils, often separated by long distances. The letter became as important to philosophers as formal treatises and dialogues. One type of philosophical letter was the paraenetic epistle.[11] The purpose of these epistles was to

7. The epistolary handbooks are not to be confused with the "rhetorical handbooks" of those such as Cicero. Cf. David Aune, "The two most important treatments of epistolary theory are *On Style* 4.223–235 (ca. first century B.C.), incorrectly ascribed to Demetrius of Phalerum, and *Epistolary Styles* (fourth to sixth centuries A.D.), erroneously ascribed to Proclus or Libanius. Cicero's familiarity with Greek epistolary theory indicates that handbooks on epistolography were circulating during the first century B.C. Also important is Pseudo-Demetrius' *Epistolary Types* (first century B.C. or later), and an appendix 'On Letter Writing' in the *Rhetorical Arts* of Julius Victor (fourth century A.D.)" (Aune, *The New Testament in its Literary Environment*, LEC 8 [Philadelphia: Westminster, 1987], 160–61).

8. Stowers, *Letter Writing*, 56.

9. As Stowers notes, "Going back to Aristotle's famous *Protrepticus* there was a long tradition of putting exhortations to the philosophical life into the form of letters. Conversion literature in the Greco-Roman world came from philosophy and not the Greek and Roman religious cults, which offered myths and rituals but not an articulated worldview and a way of life" (*Letter Writing*, 37).

10. Cf. Walter T. Wilson, *The Hope of Glory: Education and Exhortation in the Epistle to the Colossians*, NovTSup 88 (Leiden: Brill, 1997), 12, "Ancient paraenesis was not exclusively or even distinctively a philosophical type of discourse."

11. There is a well-established scholarly tradition of loosely distinguishing between paraenetic and protreptic letters, where the latter was chiefly apologetic and the former for young converts (e.g., Leo G. Perdue, "The Social Character of Paraenesis and Paraenetic Literature," *Semeia*

sustain the relationship between teacher and pupil and to encourage progress in the philosophic life. This was not the arena for developing complex formal arguments but typically reminded students of the basic teachings of the school and encouraged the formation of character in conformity with those basic teachings.[12]

So paraenesis[13] is typically a form of exhortation concerned with promoting discernible progress (προκοπή) toward maturity, where maturity is understood as a substantial and deepening union of beliefs and praxis, which leads to contentment/happiness (εὐδαιμονία).[14] Paraenetic literature uses a host of literary-rhetorical tools to foster this kind of maturity, recognizing that the road to progress is arduous and its obstacles numerous and multifaceted. The focus of paraenesis is on character formation.

---

50 [1990]: 5–39). But Swancutt has shown the distinction is actually based on the social class of the intended audience and has nothing to do with whether the reader is already a convert to philosophy. See Diana M. Swancutt, "Paraenesis in Light of Protrepsis: Troubling the Typical Dichotomy," in *Early Christian Paraenesis in Context*, ed. James Starr and Troels Engberg-Pedersen, BZNW 125 (Berlin: de Gruyter, 2005), 113–53.

12. Again, Stowers, *Letter Writing*, 38, "The philosopher's purpose was not to inform. Even when information about philosophical dogmas is given, *a moral purpose is usually in view*. We possess a few truly didactic letters, such as Epicurus' letters to Pythocles and Herodotus, but numerous hortatory letters from philosophers. The primary purpose of the philosophical hortatory letter is to affect the habits and dispositions of the reader(s) according to a certain model of what it means to be human." Italics added.

13. In biblical studies "paraenesis" is used to refer to two different literary phenomena. The first is a genre classification to designate literary works. The second is a subgenre classification, used in form criticism, to designate certain literary elements, and the traditions they represent, as paraenetic. For clarity's sake, I will only use "paraenesis" in the first sense, as referring to a genre. Cf. Stowers, *Letter Writing*, 23, "Paraenesis has been understood too narrowly in New Testament studies. It is not just the stringing together of traditional precepts and exhortations. A whole paraenetic or hortatory tradition of rhetoric developed in antiquity. Paraenesis includes not only precepts but also such things as advice, supporting argumentation, various modes of encouragement and dissuasion, the use of examples, models of conduct, and so on." In his allegiance to form-critical categories Popkes argues that "there are no 'paraenetic texts' as such." Wiard Popkes, "Paraenesis in the New Testament," in *Early Christian Paraenesis in Context*, ed. James Starr and Troels Engberg-Pedersen, BZNW 125 (Berlin: de Gruyter, 2005), 15. He bases this on a lack of sufficient evidence that ancient authors labeled their work as such. But this is an insufficient cause to deny that we can recognize a group of texts with shared purposes and literary characteristics as a genre and give to it a label that some ancient authors themselves gave to that literary enterprise (such as Seneca and Isocrates). After denying the existence of paraenetic texts per se, Popkes goes on to admit that we have many texts that "serve paraenetic *purposes*" (15, italics original). Why this should not be a sufficient basis to label them as paraenetic is unclear and seems to depend on a theory of genre that excludes both common intentionality and common literary characteristics; what it might include is hard to guess.

14. "But by far the most prominent concern of a philosophical program would be evident in efforts to realize doctrinal assumptions concretely by putting them into practice through appropriate personal conduct." Wilson, *Hope*, 9.

As Julia Annas notes, "Ancient ethical theories are concerned with the agent's life as a whole, and with his character. Concern with character and choice, with practical reasoning and the role of the emotions, is central rather than marginal."[15] Authors of paraenesis were practitioners in the ancient art of "psychagogy,"[16] which understood that psychological barriers to virtue were more deeply entrenched than intellectual ones. To counter these obstacles to progress, authors used a collection of literary strategies that included commands, admonitions, lists of virtues and vices, moral exemplars, household instructions (*Haustafeln*), diatribe, and rehearsals of philosophical teaching. In different ways each of these literary-rhetorical tools functioned to foster both the love for and the practice of virtue and, conversely, to break the enticements of vices. Philosophical paraenesis is a complex, manifold approach chiefly concerned with the formation of the character of the moral agent,[17] which focused on promoting (1) virtuous habits, (2) the development of "practical wisdom" or "discernment" (φρόνησις), and (3) a reeducation of devotions.[18]

Virtue: Habits, Affections, and Discernment

In Hellenistic ethics, virtuous habits are a principal means of character formation (ἠθοποΐα).[19] Aristotle, and the Hellenistic traditions that followed him,

15. Julia Annas, *The Morality of Happiness* (Oxford: Oxford University Press, 1993), 4.

16. Abraham J. Malherbe, *Moral Exhortation: A Greco-Roman Sourcebook*, LEC 4 (Philadelphia: Westminster, 1986), 48, "The moral philosophers gave considerable attention to developing methods by which to cultivate moral growth. These methods, which were perpetuated and further developed in later Christian monastic orders, included what we would call psychotherapy, psychological and pastoral counseling, spiritual direction or soul care, and the most general exhortation. The term used to describe this entire range of activity is 'psychagogy.'"

17. Walter Wilson defines paraenesis as

a teacher's commendation, through moral exhortation, instruction, and correction, of a prescribed way of life to individuals who are at a novice or liminal stage of development within their philosophical group. This manner of address is delivered within the framework of a previously-shaped and comprehensive understanding of reality that derives from the movement's particular teachings. . . . Because the recipients of paraenesis find themselves at a cross-roads, both in life and in terms of their training within the school, the formulation of paraenesis will take into account facets of prior competing worldviews, which possess their own agendas for human thriving. Since it is oriented towards the personal formation and palpable moral progress of students, paraenesis exhibits a clear persuasive interest, as it seeks to shape the concrete behavior and decision-making process of neophytes so that every aspect of their lives corresponds with and verifies that teachings to which they subscribe. (*Hope*, 12)

18. Cf. Annas, *Happiness*, 48–49.

19. As Aristotle says, "Virtue of character [ἦθος] results from habit [ἔθος]." *Nicomachean Ethics* §1103a, 2nd ed., trans. Terence Irwin (Indianapolis: Hackett, 1999), 18.

understood moral choices as interconnected, not discrete. Moral character was primarily envisioned as the cumulative product of previous choices.[20] This introduced character questions into moral deliberation such as, What kind of person is this choice making me? and, What kind of person do I want to become? If good choices and illicit choices are equally formative for character, then it is vital to develop a set of virtuous habits that promote virtuous choices, even when the moral agent is not inclined toward the good.[21] Virtuous habits, though, are not an end in themselves but an essential tool in the formation of a virtuous character. (Assumed here is the basic principle that virtues are not given at birth but must be learned through practice.)

Virtuous habits are necessary not only to promote good practices but also to engender good desires. As noted above, Aristotle believed the virtuous person is not simply the one who does what is right but the one who *loves* the good and takes *pleasure* in doing what is right.[22] So the path to maturity involves a reeducation of devotions, breaking ties to illegitimate devotions and imparting proper devotions attached to worthy objects.[23] As Alisdair MacIntyre says: "Virtues are dispositions not only to act in particular ways, but also to feel in particular ways. To act virtuously is not, as Kant was later to think, to act against inclination; it is to act from inclination formed by the cultivation of the virtues. Moral education is an 'éducation sentimentale.'"[24] MacIntyre reminds us that for the ancients emotions were central to an understanding of the virtues.[25] Therefore the process of maturity is not simply learning to do what is right instead of wrong, but learning to love and admire what is good and learning to hate and

---

20. Biblical authors frequently express the same concept negatively in the language of "slavery to sin," where sinful actions dull the conscience and are formative of negative dispositions to pursue sinful actions with increasing frequency and severity. Cf. Rom. 7:13–25; 1 Sam. 24:13.

21. An anathema to modern and postmodern romantic ethics, which ascribes an absolute value to unconstrained, univocal motivations.

22. Cf. Aristotle, *Nicomachean Ethics* 2.6.10–13; §1106b.

23. Cf. Seneca, *Moral Epistles* 95.37, "Certain things sink into us, rendering us sluggish in some ways, and hasty in others. These two qualities, the one of recklessness and the other of sloth, cannot be respectively checked or roused unless we remove their causes, which are mistaken admiration and mistaken fear [*falsa admiration et falsa formido*]." Seneca, *Moral Epistles*, trans. Richard M. Gummere, LCL 75–77 (Cambridge, MA: Harvard University Press, 1925), 3:83.

24. Alasdair C. MacIntyre, *After Virtue: A Study in Moral Theory*, 2nd ed. (London: Duckworth, 1985), 149. MacIntyre's allusion is to Gustave Flaubert's novel *Sentimental Education*.

25. As opposed to modern deontological understandings, where the rationality of an action is the only necessary moral justification. This assumes a much less complex (and exceedingly optimistic) anthropology, where any person who knows the right action will perform that action. The only job of ethics is to prescribe duties, and actions will follow as a matter of course. Less abstract anthropologies are more likely to recognize that the central human moral struggle is to *do* what one knows to be right.

disparage what is evil.[26] This is only possible through a continual process where ultimate devotions are exposed, examined, reshaped, and reinforced.

The Hellenistic schools see growing in the skill of discernment/wisdom (φρόνησις) as essential to growth in maturity. Wisdom is the ability to "see" the right moral action required by a given situation through a combination of understanding basic ethical principles and a sympathetic attending to circumstantial particulars.[27] Like all the virtues, discernment is learned by practice. If the virtuous person is to love and perform virtuous actions, then they have to know what those actions are. Wisdom is the skill of discerning those actions in particular cases. Unlike modern ethical systems, which seek to reduce ethics down to some kind of moral Euclidian geometry with fixed answers for given coordinates, ancient systems saw each moral deliberation as irreducibly complex. First, because they included the moral agent and their history within the circle of deliberation, and second because they assumed that all potential goods were, as Nussbaum argued above, incommensurable goods. In such a context the practical skill of discernment necessarily takes on an integrating role among the other virtues. For this reason all ancient programs of moral formation emphasized the development of wisdom.

Paraenetic Strategies

Recognizing the centrality of these three elements—habits, devotions, and wisdom—authors of paraenetic literature developed strategies for (1) promoting virtuous habits, (2) critiquing and reforming core devotions, and (3) fostering a mature moral discernment. It is important to realize that when paraenetic authors give moral advice they are not simply populating an "ethic" but have these three goals in mind.

Commands

Perhaps the most obvious tool of paraenesis is the incorporation of moral advice in the form of commands and prohibitions. Paraenetic letters are well

---

26. As Plutarch says, "The translating of our judgments into deeds, and not allowing our words to remain mere words, but to make them into actions, is, above all else, a specific mark of progress [προκοπή]. An indication of this is, in the first place, the desire to emulate what we commend, eagerness to do what we admire, and, on the other hand, unwillingness to do, or even to tolerate, what we censure." Plutarch, *How a Man May Become Aware of His Progress in Virtue* §84B, in *Moralia I*, trans. Frank Cole Babbitt, LCL 197 (Cambridge, MA: Harvard University Press, 1927), 447, 449.

27. Cf. Annas, *Happiness*, 73.

known for giving direct ethical commands in various forms (e.g., exhortations, admonitions, house codes [*Haustafeln*], and maxims). These are not explorations of ethical theory or ideas to be contemplated. They are commands to be obeyed. Their function is to produce action, leading to the development of virtuous habits. Their content is, by design, incontrovertible and incontestable, and rarely touches on controversial claims.[28] Modern deontological ethical constructs have often misled us to believe that the purpose of commands is simply to supply a list of duties. In reality their purpose is to promote *both* moral actions *and* moral formation.

Commands apply foundational principles to concrete situations. The first function of such commands is to promote virtuous actions and their incorporation as habits. In this they also serve to reshape affections, because the virtuous actions are a mode of reeducating devotions. The more we do what is right, the more we learn to enjoy the fruits of righteousness, even if we have to struggle to do it. In addition, ethical commands are often accompanied by motivational statements. "Do X, that it may go well with you."[29] These motivational warrants elicit affective desires, not simply to incite action but to promote the connection between those affections and virtuous actions.

Ethical commands also serve to facilitate the acquisition of wisdom/discernment, first because they themselves are examples of general principles applied in concrete moral actions. Those who are learning discernment learn by imitation.[30] At the same time, advice to, for example, "admire and imitate

28. As Wilson notes, "The author of a paraenetic text conveys predominately material that is already familiar to the recipients, material expressing patterns of conduct commonly accepted within the movement, as opposed to concentrating on novel, debatable, or speculative concepts that require special proof or further study. Thus from the readers' perspective what is said in a paraenetic text appears self-evident and uncontroversial, and so lengthy arguments are rendered unnecessary. Indeed, the moral norms articulated by paraenetic discourse are regularly predicated upon widely accepted ideas as to what constitutes proper conduct" (*Hope*, 92).

Cf. Stowers, *Letter Writing*, 95. This has often caused confusion for biblical scholars trained to look for genealogical relationships between texts and to draw certain inferences from textual borrowing. Such approaches assume (1) the text quoting another derived its knowledge from the original text and (2) it accepts the worldview of that text wholesale. Neither is logically or historically necessary, and neither is representative of ancient attitudes toward such textual borrowing.

29. For example, Isocrates, *Demonicus* §21, in *Discourses I*, trans. George Norlin, LCL 209 (Cambridge, MA: Harvard University Press, 1928) 17, "Train yourself in self-imposed toils, that you may be able to endure those which others impose upon you."

30. So Seneca, *Moral Epistles* 94.50–52,

Wisdom by her own agency may perhaps show herself this path without the help of admonition [i.e., commands]; for she has brought the soul to a stage where it can be impelled only in the right direction. Weaker characters, however, need someone to precede them, to say: "Avoid this," or "Do that." Moreover, if one waits the time when one can know of oneself what the best line of action is, one will sometimes go astray and by going

virtuous men, and flee from self-important ones," while specific advice, still requires acts of discernment to determine how to turn that admiration into action. Such commands take the novice halfway down the road of discernment by prescribing a disposition in a particular circumstance, but the final act of discernment, while guided by such advice, is still a matter for the practitioner.

In addition, ethical commands are often accompanied by philosophical warrants that ground the command in some principle. This serves to make the connection between a specific command and the general principle explicit, thereby aiding the recipient in the process of acquiring the skill of discernment. Isocrates, for example, exhorts Demonicus to "guard more faithfully the secret which is confided to you than the money which is entrusted to your care"; and then follows up with the general principle, "for good men ought to show that they hold their honor more trustworthy than an oath."[31] In making the connections between principle and praxis, Isocrates aids his student in developing wisdom.

Virtue and Vice Lists

Another common literary feature of paraenetic epistles is contrasting lists of virtues and vices. These virtue and vice lists are another marriage of form and function, of a literary form (*Gattung*) designed to promote progress in moral maturity and practical wisdom. Such lists are an example of the ubiquitous ancient wisdom theme of the "two ways": a path of life, blessing, and honor set against a path of death, destruction, and humiliation.[32] The point of such lists is not to enumerate new virtues or new vices; their content is, once again, uncontroversial. Their true utility is in clarifying devotions to courage, relational fidelity, personal integrity, self-control, industry, and the like while at the same time disparaging sloth, cowardice, self-indulgence,

---

astray will be hindered from arriving at the point where it is possible to be content with oneself. The soul should accordingly be guided at the very moment when it is becoming able to guide itself. Boys study according to direction [*ad praescriptum*]. Their fingers are held and guided by others so that they may follow the outlines of the letters; next, they are ordered to imitate a copy and base thereon a style of penmanship. Similarly, the mind is helped if it is taught according to direction [*ad praescriptum*]. Such facts as these prove that this department of philosophy [moral instruction through commands] is not superfluous. (Gummere, LCL, 3:43, 45)

31. Isocrates, *Demonicus* §22 (Norlin, LCL, 1:17).

32. See Aune, *Literary Environment*, 194–97. Gammie, "Paraenetic Literature," 56–57, labels this literary form "sygkrisis." An OT example is the "choose life or death" discourse in Deut. 30:11–20, along with the blessings and curses dramatically enacted in Deut. 27–28. The dichotomies between "the righteous"/"the wicked" or "the wise"/"the fool" that run throughout the Wisdom literature proper are also examples of *sygkrisis*.

avarice, and self-importance. Learning to love good and hate evil—to admire the good and to be disgusted with evil. But here general ideas of the good are replaced with specific character traits such as courage. What is the point of all this? Well, it is easy to be a coward, and hard to be courageous (that is why we call it courageous).

Hellenistic moralists understood that simply telling people to be courageous had limited value because the self-protective pull of vices such as cowardice and sloth is very strong. Extricating such deep-seated vices requires powerful rhetorical tools. Before the coward can learn to be courageous, he must first learn to despise his cowardice, not simply agree that it is wrong but be disgusted by it. How do virtue and vice lists do this? First by pairing cowardice, which still has some pull for the hearer, with a list of atrocious vices that in its cumulative effect no one can endorse without shame. So he may be a coward, but he still believes that homicide and treason are abhorrent. At the same time, the list of virtues, including courage, is a list that all can and should aspire to. No matter what one's moral failings, who does not aspire to fidelity, bravery, and integrity? They are aspirational because they are hard to practice, but the point of the list is to ignite such aspiration.

Secondarily, such lists aid in the formation of virtuous habits and practical wisdom. The virtue and vice lists function implicitly as lists of commands and prohibitions. Implicitly they prescribe certain actions in keeping the virtue while simultaneously proscribing actions associated with vice. They also promote habitual actions, because virtues are not simply ideas to be contemplated but character dispositions formed through concrete moral actions. Likewise, the lists also promote discernment, first by defining virtues in antithetical relationships to their vices. Both cowardice and a foolhardy lack of self-preservation give substance to our understanding of courage by supplying contrasts.[33]

Another way in which virtue and vice lists shape wisdom is in the particular virtues listed and in the special prominence given to particular virtues. As we said, the general content of virtue and vice lists is usually unremarkable and incontestable. Novelty in such lists would have been viewed with suspicion and is rare. At the same time, different schools did emphasize the prominence of particular virtues in their teaching.[34] So, for example, ἀπάθεια (detachment from external goods), while not unique to Stoicism, was elevated to central importance in Stoic thought and practice. Likewise, the early Christians

---

33. Cf. Aristotle, *Nicomachean Ethics* 3.6–7; §§1115a–1116a.

34. Cf. Malherbe, *Moral Exhortation*, 4, 138, "In their content they tended to represent generally held views; nevertheless the presence or absence of certain items reflected the values of their authors. It is noteworthy, for example, that as common a pagan virtue as 'humane' (*philanthropos*) appears so rarely in early Christian writings."

gave φιλαδελφία (brotherly love), although not unique among ancient lists of virtues, a prominence with no contemporary correlate. This fronting of particular virtues is part of the framework that shapes practical wisdom and aids in moral deliberations concerning competing incommensurate goods. Stoic wisdom, for example, while not despising external good, would always choose an internal good (of the soul) over an external good (tied to something or someone external to the self).

Conversion and Antithesis

Another paraenetic tool, which operates with a similar antithetical "two ways" logic, focuses on the act of conversion as a paradigmatic and definitive life-altering event. The language of conversion was common in the Hellenistic schools, which inhabited varying distances from wider cultural norms.[35] While the voluntary connection to a school of philosophy could in some cases be seen as an aristocratic move, particularly in Roman Stoicism, such an association usually meant adopting the social status of an outsider and always involved a serious commitment to moral reform. For these reasons philosophers adopted the practice of interpreting the act of conversion to philosophy in the language of antithesis, with a special emphasis on the duality of life before and life after conversion. So, for example, Epictetus derides his students for not making a clean break with the past: "You go back to the same things again; you have exactly the same desires as before, the same aversions, in the same way you make your choices, your designs, and your purposes, you pray for the same things and are interested in the same things."[36] He censures his students, "Flee from your former habits . . . if you want to begin to become somebody."[37] This is typical of paraenetic discourse, clarifying devotions by connecting them to a value-laden interpretive narrative. Epictetus shames his students for not making a significant break with their pasts but also describes their past lives in terms of vice and emptiness.

---

35. See J. de Waal Dryden, *Theology and Ethics in 1 Peter: Paraenetic Strategies for Christian Character Formation*, WUNT 2/209 (Tübingen: Mohr Siebeck, 2006), 91–98. Cf. James Starr, "Was Paraenesis for Beginners?," in *Early Christian Paraenesis in Context*, ed. James Starr and Troels Engberg-Pedersen, BZNW 125 (Berlin: Walter de Gruyter, 2005), 73–111.

36. Epictetus, *Discourses* 2.17.36–37, trans. W. A. Oldfather, LCL 131–32 (Cambridge, MA: Harvard University Press, 1961), 1:347, 349.

37. Epictetus, *Discourses* 3.16.16 (Oldfather, LCL, 2:109). Cf. 3.22.13, "First, in all that pertains to yourself directly you must change completely from your present practices, and must cease to blame God or man; you must utterly wipe out desire, and must turn your aversion toward the things which lie within the province of moral purpose, and these only; you must feel no anger, no rage, no envy, no pity; no wench must look fine to you, no petty reputation, no boy-favourite, no little sweet cake" (Oldfather, LCL, 2:135).

We see the same strategy in NT epistles, where life before conversion is compared, most unfavorably, with life in Christ. This is usually done in a marriage of both ontological and moral antithesis, that is, a moral antithesis based in a substantive change of person and identity—often in the language of old self versus new self. So, for example, Colossians 3:1–10:

> If then you have been raised with Christ, seek the things that are above, where Christ is, seated at the right hand of God. Set your minds on things that are above, not on things that are on earth. For you have died, and your life is hidden with Christ in God. When Christ who is your life appears, then you also will appear with him in glory. Put to death therefore what is earthly in you: sexual immorality, impurity, passion, evil desire, and covetousness, which is idolatry. On account of these the wrath of God is coming. In these you too once walked, when you were living in them. But now you must put them all away: anger, wrath, malice, slander, and obscene talk from your mouth. Do not lie to one another, seeing that you have put off the old self with its practices and have put on the new self, which is being renewed in knowledge after the image of its creator.

Here we have all the hallmarks of NT conversion paraenesis: new self/old self, the old life associated with vice, and new life resulting from the salvific agency of God in Christ. As with other antithetical rhetorical strategies, the purpose of this emphasis on conversion is to foster attachments to virtues and deconstruct the appeal of vices. In the already/not yet eschatology typical of the NT, the narrative of salvation includes a definitive eschatological break, which understands the new life in Christ as a participation in the new creation.

At the same time, this narrative also includes elements of process and expectation, in recognition that the new creation still awaits its unveiling. In this context, the theme of conversion is a means for NT authors to teach their readers to navigate the distance between the already and the not yet. Christians on the path of salvation do not experience life in terms of a simple, definitive break where all their thoughts, affections, and actions are completely transformed. Instead, they experience a life "in between," where their devotions and agency are a mixture of virtue and vice. The purpose of conversional antitheses is not to create perfectionist expectations of a simple life but to provide guideposts in the midst of moral confusion and to rehabituate the affections to love and embrace new life in Christ, while deconstructing well-rehearsed vices. In the passage above Paul rightly labels these vices as a deadly form of idolatry, not because this is news to the Colossian churches but as a moral wedge to loosen attachments to vice. In the same vein he connects them to virtue and the pure heavenly realm, where Christ rules now: "For you have died, and your life is hidden with Christ in God."

Moral Exemplars

A fourth example of a staple literary feature of paraenetic epistles is the use of exemplars to be imitated.[38] Once again, this is a literary/rhetorical device purposely built for the interrelated agendas of reshaping fundamental affections, fostering wisdom, and promoting virtuous action. Exemplars accomplish this, first of all, by putting a human face on virtue; they translate ideals into realized personal biography. Exemplars create a human connection between virtue and those seeking the path of virtue through a process of identification and admiration.[39] The moral challenges exemplars face are universal, even if their particular circumstances are unique. But the response of the exemplar to those challenges is a bold realization of certain virtuous ideals, and so the exemplar is also an object for admiration and affection.[40] The effectiveness of exemplars trades on these two elements. Imitators recognize something of their own experience in the exemplar, but they are also led to admire his or her virtue as something desirable and worthy of admiration. This creates a personal emotional connection between the exemplar and the imitator, characterized by admiration and affection, and at the same time instills a desire for the virtue embodied by the exemplar (as well as a desire for the fruits of that virtue enjoyed by the exemplar). This is another means of reeducating the affections.

Exemplars are admirable because they put ideals into practice in concrete, historically conditioned circumstances. They embody a mature wisdom that applies principles to particular situations and act accordingly. In this way exemplars function to teach discernment by demonstrating it as expert practitioners. As exemplars demonstrate how virtues are lived out, they provide guideposts for the moral landscapes of those who are learning the path of wisdom. Exemplars also *inspire* virtuous actions. They are exemplars not because they contemplate virtue but because they live it out in especially challenging circumstances. To imitate an exemplar is to admire their virtue and to copy it in considered moral action—to understand why a particular action is good and admirable and then to do it. One of the functions of exemplars is to show that the virtuous life, while hard, is possible.[41] In these ways they incite virtuous desires and deeds, which promote the formation of virtuous habits.

---

38. See Plutarch, *Progress in Virtue* §§84b–85c, and Dryden, *Theology and Ethics*, 163–72.

39. See Plutarch, *Pericles* 1.3–4; 2.2–4.

40. Cf. Plutarch, *Progress in Virtue* §84e, "Indeed a peculiar symptom of true progress is found in this feeling [καὶ γὰρ τοῦτο προκοπῆς ἀλεθοῦς ἴδιόν ἐστι πάθος] of love and affection for the disposition [διάθεσις] shown by those whose deeds we try to emulate, and in the fact that our efforts to make ourselves like them are always attended by a goodwill which accords to them a fair meed of honour." Plutarch, *Moralia* 1:450–51.

41. See Seneca, *Moral Epistles* 104.22–34.

Through these diverse literary tools, paraenetic authors seek to habituate virtuous actions, not only as a means to changing behavior but also a means to reeducating the affections and fostering the skill of discernment (φρόνησις). These are not simply free-floating bits of tradition taken from the ancient soup of ethical traditions; they are evidence of a coherent intentionality to shape character.

New Testament Paraenetic Epistles?

But can we apply the genre of paraenetic epistle to the epistolary literature of early Christianity, and especially the NT? As with our previous discussion regarding the application of the genre of βίος to the Gospels, we have to remember some basic principles about how genres function. First, literary communication only exists within established genres.[42] Those genres are flexible and can evolve over time into new genres, but only through a process of morphing an existing genre.[43] Second, genres are identified by both form and function: what performative intentions they serve and what literary devices they typically utilize in realizing those intentions. The use of genre forms is flexible in that literary devices are not a mandatory list but rather a pool of typical features that authors can work from as they see fit in realizing their purposes. Third, as with βίος, while the utilization of a genre implies a common intentionality, it has no implications for the philosophical content or outlook contained therein or relationship to the philosophical background that gave birth to the genre. So, authors from competing Hellenistic schools used the genres of βίος and paraenetic epistle to achieve similar ends, promoting progress in the philosophical life, even though they had competing definitions of what characterized that life and especially the path to it. Authors of paraenetic letters nowhere assume that such letters have a particular philosophical outlook built into them that needs to be either recognized or countered. Biblical scholars have often mistakenly assumed that any Christian appropriation of the genre of paraenetic epistles is either an endorsement of

42. As Derrida says, "Every text participates in one or more genres, there is no genreless text." Jacques Derrida, "The Law of Genre," *Critical Inquiry* 7 (1980): 65.

43. Cf. Fowler, *Kinds*, 24, "Some think that genre theory is irrelevant, in that it fails to correspond to actual literary works. This opinion rests often on a misapprehension about genres. It assumes that they exist simply and immutably, that they are permanently established once and for all, so that they apply equally to all literature, before and after, past, present, and to come. Hence, that all genre theory has the same (lowish) value. But, as we have seen, genres are actually in a continual state of transmutation. It is by their modification, primarily, that individual works convey literary meaning."

or a correction to a philosophical outlook built into the genre and the history of its use, but such an assumption is neither necessary nor supported by any ancient evidence.

It has long been recognized that paraenetic literary devices (e.g., commands, admonitions, virtue and vice lists, *Haustafeln*, and exemplars) are extensively appropriated in the epistles of the NT. We will note below some other paraenetic literary features common to the NT as well, but these alone make the designation of these epistles as paraenetic highly likely. But can we describe the purpose of these epistles as paraenetic? Insofar as they betray intentions of fostering progress in the Christian life and define that progress in terms of realized gains in conforming praxis to beliefs, then yes. Here, perhaps, the genre of paraenetic epistles can free us from conceiving of NT epistles simply in terms of either correcting theological heresy or maintaining social cohesion.[44] There is little doubt that they do both; but the real question is whether either is their *primary* intention. A theological or communal crisis may be the *occasion* for the epistle, but we have no examples of NT epistles that address these questions in isolation from the challenges they present to long-term spiritual formation. Paul's Epistle to the Galatians, for example, betrays deeper agendas than simply settling the question of gentile circumcision.

Paul and other NT writers do not accidentally utilize a few paraenetic literary devices. These epistles regularly engage in exhortations that promote moral progress as an essential and necessary sign of life in Christ. As many scholars have demonstrated over the last several decades, this correlation of form and intentionality is sufficient to describe these epistles as a Christian appropriation of the genre of paraenetic epistle.[45]

Still, there will be some who object that this type of epistle was something exclusive to the philosophical schools and unknown or unused outside those environs. This objection fails to recognize Jewish precedents to the NT appropriation of this genre[46] and cannot reckon with the presence of paraenetic

---

44. Cf. Stowers, *Letter Writing*, 16, "The study of early Christian letters has suffered because the letters have too often been forced into an interpretive mold formed by two questions: What theology does it contain, and what was the author trying to defend or attack?"

45. Abraham J. Malherbe, *The Letters to the Thessalonians: A New Translation with Introduction and Commentary*, AB 32B (New York: Doubleday, 2000). On Colossians, Wilson, *Hope*; and Andrew T. Lincoln, "The Spiritual Wisdom of Colossians in the Context of Graeco-Roman Spiritualities," in *The Bible and Spirituality: Exploratory Essays in Reading Scripture Spiritually*, ed. Andrew T. Lincoln, J. Gordon McConville, and Lloyd K. Pietersen (Eugene, OR: Cascade, 2013), 212–32. On 1 Peter, Dryden, *Theology and Ethics*.

46. E.g., *Testament of the Twelve Patriarchs*. See Johannes Thomas, "The Paraenesis of the *Testament of the Twelve Patriarchs*," in *Early Christian Paraenesis in Context*, ed. James M. Starr and Troels Engberg-Pedersen, BZNW 125 (Berlin: de Gruyter, 2004), 157–89.

epistles among the trash heaps of Oxyrhynchus.[47] But the most significant problem for denying the NT's appropriation of paraenetic traditions is simply how then to account for the obvious presence in these epistles of literary devices such as the household codes, virtue and vice lists, moral exemplars, and various moral directives—all literary types without precedents in either the OT or Jewish apocalyptic literature.

The question that still needs clarification is the level of continuity and discontinuity between Christian and philosophical traditions and how much continuity should be inferred from the use of paraenetic forms. It should be noted that in the Greco-Roman context Judaism and Christianity had more in common with the philosophic schools than they did with their contemporary religious counterparts. As Loveday Alexander notes, "To the casual pagan observer the activities of the average synagogue or church would look more like the activities of a [philosophical] school than anything else. Teaching or preaching, moral exhortation, and the exegesis of canonical texts are activities associated in the ancient world with philosophy, not religion."[48] This made the adoption of philosophical argumentation a natural move for both Judaism and early Christianity. Philo is an obvious example, but Josephus is just as illustrative. Early Christian apologists, such as Justin Martyr, also attest to this natural affinity. This is not to say that Judaism and Christianity were philosophical schools or were heavily indebted to the schools for any of their basic teachings or doctrines. (Although they did all hold certain beliefs in common: most importantly a moral order rooted in monotheism, a belief largely absent in Greco-Roman religions.) Christian and Jewish apologists felt free to pick up Hellenistic forms and language and fill them with new content, but this was consistent with established Hellenistic philosophic practices.

47. E.g., Papyrus 3069. Cf. G. H. R. Horsley, ed. *New Documents Illustrating Early Christianity*, vol. 4, *A Review of the Greek Inscriptions and Papyri Published in 1979* (North Ryde, NSW: The Ancient History Documentary Research Centre Macquarie University, 1987), 67–70.

48. Loveday Alexander, "Paul and the Hellenistic Schools: The Evidence of Galen," in *Paul in His Hellenistic Context*, ed. Troels Engberg-Pedersen, Studies in the New Testament and Its World (Minneapolis: Fortress, 1995), 60. Along similar lines, see the influential essay by E. A. Judge, "The Early Christians as a Scholastic Community," *JRH* 1 (1960–61): 4–15; 125–37. Cf. Wilson, *Hope*, 86,

> Surprisingly perhaps, in antiquity the enterprise of describing and facilitating a personal transformation of this sort did not belong especially to the domain of what we would call "religion," where a more casual, less drastic degree of allegiance was the norm, but was the concern of the philosophic schools, a fact that reveals some important features regarding their function in Greco-Roman society. Insofar as both Judaism and Christianity expected of their followers a wholesale relocation and an abiding commitment of the type summarized above, their evaluation of the human condition would have approximated that of the schools more than that of most pagan cults.

It is important to remember the continuities and discontinuities that existed among the schools themselves. They held many fundamental, especially metaphysical, beliefs in common, and all held to a common conception of the virtues. Although some emphasized particular virtues, none invented a unique system or set of virtues in distinction from the other schools. So, none are *for* cowardice, self-indulgence, or a lack of regard for personal integrity and honor. Where the schools differ in practice is in how they contextualize and advocate for the *same* virtues. It is in the philosophical grounding of the virtues that one finds the most significant diversity among the schools. So what we find is that the schools are happy to borrow from one another in their moral maxims and commands,[49] but in the philosophical grounding and motivations for moral actions they diverge and do not usually borrow from one another.

This is exactly what we find in NT paraenetic epistles. In their ethical teaching, as many have noted, there is a close appropriation of Hellenistic form and content, the most obvious example being the household codes. Biblical scholars, focused on intertextual genealogies, have tended to mistake this for either an indiscriminate adoption of a "bourgeois" ethic or a naive endorsement of Hellenistic systems of thought. This fails to recognize that all ethical systems are working from a common pool of ethical norms and that ancient cultures saw this as incontrovertible. Where we expect to find divergence is in the philosophical/theological groundings and motivations that contextualize ethics. In NT paraenesis this is what we find—a Jewish eschatological outlook dressed in Hellenistic clothes.[50] Some who have stressed the correspondence between philosophical and NT paraenetic epistles have sometimes overinterpreted this continuity and produced a very Hellenistic picture of Paul.[51] (Suspicion of this conclusion may partially account for why research into paraenetic epistles has remained a scholarly backwater.)

So what we find in NT epistles is the adoption of the form of the paraenetic epistle and the adoption of its typical literary devices aimed at fostering progress toward maturity. The definitions of "progress" and "maturity"

---

49. The extent to which certain maxims are repeated by different schools was seen as a confirmation of the veracity and utility of those maxims.

50. Cf. Malherbe, *Moral Exhortation*, 4, 30, "While Jews and Christians put to their own use much of what they found in philosophic practice and teaching, they nevertheless grounded their morality in their religion." Cf. Markus Bockmuehl, *Jewish Law in Gentile Churches: Halakhah and the Beginning of Christian Public Ethics* (Edinburgh: T&T Clark, 2000).

51. See especially Troels Engberg-Pedersen, *Paul and the Stoics* (Edinburgh: T&T Clark, 2000). For a brilliant critique see C. Kavin Rowe, *One True Life: The Stoics and Early Christians as Rival Traditions* (New Haven: Yale University Press, 2016), especially 175–205.

are analogues to, but not copies of, Hellenistic understandings. As we have said, paraenetic literature aims at a movement of beliefs being realized in moral action, and the same is also true for Christian paraenesis. Left behind, though, are Hellenistic notions of virtue rooted in self-reliance. At the center of Christian belief is the worship of the Son of God, and progress in Christian practice is seen not only in moral integrity but in a reverent dependence on Christ as the giver of life. So we have an ethical system given its own distinct theological grounding.

Indicative and Imperative

The recognition of these epistles as paraenetic has important implications for the question of "indicative and imperative" in NT epistles. As we discussed previously, this paradigm, which typically bisects epistles into theological and ethical sections, tells us more about the mental furniture of modern interpreters than it does about the epistles themselves. This paradigm has proved resilient despite the pleading of many Pauline scholars and NT ethicists that it be laid to rest as an inherently distorting heuristic.

A typical example of this would be a common approach to Romans of labeling the first eleven chapters as theological discourse and labeling chapters 12–16 (or 12–15) as ethical or practical. There is obviously some prima facie justification for such a schematic. The first eleven chapters are theological and incorporate some of Paul's most forceful examples of diatribe, whereas much of 12–15 is concerned with the practical question of interracial table fellowship. *Where this paradigm introduces distortion is in the assumption that the theological and ethical parts of the epistle are aimed at achieving different ends.* The purpose of the theological discourse is didactic; it aims to inform and correct the intellectual understanding of the hearers so that they may have a proper understanding of the gospel as "the revelation of the righteousness of God." The purpose of the ethical discourse is to exhort and command—to reshape and reinforce behaviors that, at least in Paul's understanding, reflect the norms of Christian communal life. So we have a theological discourse that is directed at addressing theological misunderstandings and an ethical discourse that addresses practical community concerns. Figure 6.1 provides a representation of this approach.

With regard to Romans, a detailed exegesis will show repeatedly how such a paradigm produces more difficulties than it alleviates. Given this, very few exegetes still openly endorse such a paradigm as formative for their analysis of Romans. And yet, it often remains formative at the most important

Figure 6.1

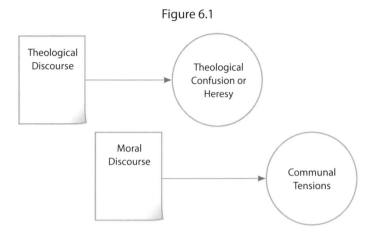

level—in the assumption that theological and ethical discourses are serving different purposes, one to inform and the other to command; one deals with ideas, whereas the other deals with actions. It is precisely at this point that an understanding of paraenetic epistles can be most helpful.

In his letters to his student Lucilius, Seneca gives us a prime example of the genre of paraenetic epistles in the hands of a moderate Stoic from the first century.[52] He also gives us something very rare: an ancient author reflecting on his own practice. In epistles 94 and 95 Seneca discusses how paraenetic epistles function to promote moral progress. Specifically, Seneca argues for the *mutual interdependence* of philosophical reflection and moral exhortation in the paraenetic aim of character formation. In epistle 94 he argues against those who believe that a philosophical understanding of the good is sufficient to bring about progress. Seneca begins by arguing that "Virtue is divided into two parts—into contemplation of truth, and conduct. [Philosophical] training teaches contemplation, and admonition teaches conduct."[53] Virtue involves virtuous actions, not simply contemplation of virtue. Admonition (i.e., moral exhortation) promotes virtuous actions and habits and is therefore necessary. Seneca continues: "Virtue depends partly upon [philosophical] training and partly upon practice; you must learn first, and then strengthen your learning by action. If this be true, not only do the doctrines of wisdom help us, but the precepts [commands] also, which

52. Lucius Annaeus Seneca (4 BC–AD 65) was a Spanish philosopher, playwright, and statesman, most famously the tutor of Nero and later one of his political advisers. He was a contemporary of Paul; his older brother Junius Gallio (born Lucius Annaeus Novatus) was the proconsul Paul met in Corinth during his second missionary journey (see Acts 18:12–17).

53. Seneca, *Moral Epistles* 94.45 (Gummere, LCL, 3:41).

check and banish our emotions by a sort of official decree."[54] Here Seneca seems to be repeating that action is helpful in instilling virtue, but he adds another element. Precepts (i.e., moral exhortations) not only prescribe moral duties, but they facilitate those actions by cutting through disordered emotions and eliciting the hearer's love for virtue.[55] In addition, Seneca argues that moral exhortations promote the development of practical wisdom. As he says, "We are hindered from accomplishing praiseworthy deeds not only by our emotions, but also by want of practice in discovering the demands of a particular situation. Our minds are often under good control, and yet at the same time are inactive and untrained in finding the path of duty—and advice makes this clear."[56] So, according to Seneca, moral exhortations are *necessary* because they promote virtuous actions, reshape emotional attachments, and teach practical wisdom.

In his 95th epistle Seneca argues for the complementary truth that moral precepts are insufficient on their own and need grounding in a philosophical worldview in order to be effective in bringing about real change in character. As he says, "Precepts by themselves are weak and, so to speak, rootless if they be assigned to the parts and not to the whole. It is the doctrines which will strengthen and support us in peace and calm, which will include simultaneously the whole of life and the universe in its completeness."[57] Seneca here argues that the practical work of character formation needs a marriage of a philosophical worldview with practical advice. For Seneca, this philosophical understanding is a "map of fact and value"[58] that not only describes reality but provides a value-laden orientation toward that reality. He argues that

> if you would always desire the same things, you must desire the truth. But one cannot attain the truth without doctrines; for doctrines embrace the whole of life. Things good and evil, honourable and disgraceful, just and unjust, dutiful and undutiful, the virtues and their practice, the possession of comforts, worth and respect, health, strength, beauty, keenness of the senses—all these

54. Seneca, *Moral Epistles* 94.47 (Gummere, LCL, 3:41).

55. Cf. Seneca, *Moral Epistles* 94.29, "Such maxims need no special pleader; they go straight to our emotions, and help us simply because Nature is exercising her proper function. The soul carries within itself the seed of everything that is honourable, and this seed is stirred to growth by advice, as a spark that is fanned by a gentle breeze develops its natural fire. Virtue is aroused by a touch, a shock" (Gummere, LCL, 3:29).

56. Seneca, *Moral Epistles* 94.32 (Gummere, LCL, 3:33).

57. Seneca, *Moral Epistles* 95.12 (Gummere, LCL, 3:65). Cf. 95.34, "In order to root out a deep-seated belief in wrong ideas, conduct must be regulated by doctrines. It is only when we add precepts, consolation, and encouragement to these, that they can prevail; by themselves they are ineffective" (Gummere, LCL, 3:79).

58. Wilson, *Hope*, 100.

qualities call for one who is able to appraise them. One should be allowed to know at what values every object is to be rated on the list; for sometimes you are deceived and believe that certain things are worth more than their real value; in fact, so badly are you deceived that you will find you value at a mere penny-worth those things which we men regard as worth most of all—for example, riches, influence, and power.[59]

Such an understanding, then, gives a means of properly orienting desires according to real valuations. Again, practical wisdom is integrated with the reorientation of desires, which gives both ideational and affective motivations for moral action. So, for Seneca, philosophy serves to confirm and correct theoretical understanding and affective attachments. At the same time, it performs these duties in service to the primary goal of character formation. Establishing a coherent philosophical outlook or a corresponding set of coherent devotions is not an end in itself; these are elements in the formative pursuit of the philosophic life.

Formative Wisdom Texts

If we return to NT epistles we can begin to see how theological and ethical sections of epistles together serve a common end—the spiritual formation of God's people as those called by his righteousness. As in philosophical paraenesis, theological discourse corrects misguided beliefs and confirms true ones. But it also projects a moral vision of reality that ascribes values to certain objects. In doing this it serves the Christian paraenetic end of spiritual formation. Its purposes are more than didactic. Likewise, ethical materials serve to promote actions consistent with gospel convictions and to promote a practical wisdom guided by both theological understanding and reverential devotions.

Therefore, both theological and ethical discourse in NT epistles serve to further spiritual formation. Neither competes with the other, nor is either subsumed by the other. They function together from opposite sides, serving the same goal. The two work together in a complex wisdom text to foster growth in Christian affections and praxis. Instead of moving along parallel lines, each with its own particular concerns and agendas, theology and ethics represent interdependent modes of discourse aimed at addressing a common challenge with a complex, integrated agenda, as illustrated in figure 6.2.

59. Seneca, *Moral Epistles* 95.58–59 (Gummere, LCL, 3:95).

Figure 6.2

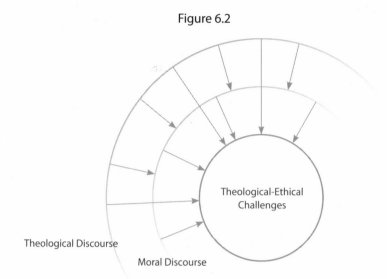

In this model theological and ethical challenges are treated as an organic unity, not as two separate problems. This is more in keeping with presuppositions of the ancient authors, who understood communal tensions through their theological roots, and theological heresies in terms of the moral and social chaos they unleashed. For NT authors theology and ethics are two sides of the same coin—distinguishable but inseparable. (Our inclination to separate them is another manifestation of the modernist dichotomy of being and action.) This is why we find no example in the NT that deals with theological or ethical issues in isolation from each other. It is always both because each is rooted in the other. Theological aberrations lead to moral turpitude, but moral corruption just as often leads to theological confusion.

In response to this theological-ethical challenge, both theological reflections and ethical instructions are shaped to respond to a *single* complex challenge. This inevitably means that theological reflections are guided more by pragmatic concerns than systematic ones. Paraenetic letters are not treatises; they do not normally aim at systematic or theoretical doctrinal development. Typically, paraenetic discourse offers reminders of a few key doctrines selected on the basis of their relevance to a presenting theological-ethical challenge.[60] This

---

60. Cf. Wilson, *Hope*, 134–35,

    None of the paraenetic texts that we have been examining could be confused with a treatise on systematic theology. In keeping with the style of this literature, a paraenetic author will simply remind the readers of specific elements of the belief-system that they have already accepted as members of their movement, selecting those that are most pertinent

does not deny the presence of logical argumentation or elaborations of doctrine but simply asserts that formative goals determine rhetorical strategies. Discourse coherence relies on pragmatics before systematics.[61] Unfortunately, we have a habit of reading Paul as though he were Plutarch. We want him to be more systematic than he really is.

"Theological" sections of paraenetic epistles, then, do more than simply teach doctrine as a system of thought to be accepted. To be sure, one of the roles of theological discourse is to confirm some beliefs and correct others. As we saw with Seneca, this is a necessary element in effective paraenesis. So we should expect to find theological argumentation in NT epistles. But these *theologically driven discourses serve paraenetic ends*. So they do more than simply teach or instruct. These sections, for example, serve to reeducate and realign devotions. They give a picture of God, self, and world that is not simply given for assent but teaches what realities are to be loved, pursued, worshiped, and honored, and conversely which ones are to be rejected, disdained, purged, and held in contempt. They often do this in highly rhetorical ways that invite us to love what is good and hate what is evil by making good beautiful and admirable, and evil repulsive and shameful.[62]

Another primary purpose of theological reflection in paraenetic letters is to project a moral vision that renders certain ethical actions intelligible and praiseworthy. Theological discourse grounds calls to self-sacrificial love for the other in the fundamental truths of the gospel story of a God who embraced humiliation and self-sacrifice for the benefit of his people. The gospel's demands only make sense and serve their proper function when they are attached to the gospel proclamation. This proclamation of the love of God in Christ supplies reasons and motivations for love that serves others before self. It makes those commands intelligible by placing the nature of the rule of God at the center of all reality. It also supplies motivations of worship, love, gratitude, and reward, which serve to supplant affective commitments to self-sufficiency and self-preservation. Hays gives a prime example of how Paul's theology operates as a moral vision: "According to Paul the death and

---

to the problem at hand. . . . The goal of this sort of theological anamnesis and dialogue is to construct a morally-guided and situation-specific appeal for the readers to act in a manner that is consistent with their beliefs, to mature spiritually.

61. As Wilson notes, "the pragmatic dimensions of such communication are by no means incidental to their character." Wilson, *Hope*, 92–93.

62. Cf. again Wilson, *Hope*, 93, "In any attempt to transform belief into action for a particular individual or group of individuals, close attention must be paid to the persuasive aspects of the appeal, to the manner in which the listener will be moved to respond. The paraenetic approach, then, is both therapeutic and rhetorical, as the spiritual guide aims for a presentation that is striking and inspiring, an aid to the process of interiorizing teachings so as to amend one's life."

resurrection of Jesus was an apocalyptic event that signaled the end of the old age and portended the beginning of the new. Paul's moral vision is intelligible only when his apocalyptic perspective is kept clearly in mind: the church is to find its identity and vocation by recognizing its role within the cosmic drama of God's reconciliation of the world to himself."[63]

Hays argues that Paul's theological reflections are not first and foremost a construction designed to confront heretical understanding but rather primarily serve the purpose of defining a moral space in which Christian love and obedience become intelligible and desirable. For Paul, theological discourse reshapes convictions, desires, and moral responsibilities. The eschatological story of the revelation of God's righteousness is not properly understood as simply propositions that frame a Christian ontology but at the same time is a teleological frame that gives form and substance to Christian devotion and obedience.

The Imitation of Christ

An instructive example of theology operating in a paraenetic mode can be seen in how NT epistles utilize Christ as an exemplar to be imitated. As we saw above, the use of exemplars is a staple literary device in paraenetic epistles, and so it is no surprise to find it employed by various NT authors. But the use of Christ as an exemplar has historically elicited unease and controversy among exegetes. For many the use of Christ as an exemplar threatens convictions about his divinity, moral perfection, and unique vocation in the economy of salvation. Imitation texts are also controversial because they violate the revered distinction between indicative and imperative. These texts incorporate some of the most compact and rich christological affirmations in the NT, but those affirmations are brought to bear on moral challenges facing the community. Somewhat predictably, this has led many to argue that such texts have to be taken *either* theologically *or* ethically.[64]

Such exegetical gymnastics becomes unnecessary if we recognize, with Hays, that the primary function of these and other theological discourses is to project a moral vision that gives shape to the convictions, hopes, and actions of the Christian community. The story of the life of Jesus, variously alluded to in imitation texts, then takes on a normative function in the moral imagination of his followers. As John Webster put it:

63. Richard B. Hays, *The Moral Vision of the New Testament: Community, Cross, New Creation, A Contemporary Introduction to New Testament Ethics* (San Francisco: HarperSanFrancisco, 1996), 19.
64. As we saw above in our look at Phil. 2:5–11 at the end of chap. 2.

Intrinsic to the Christological narrative is its function in forming Christian vision and identity, making him into a self with particular beliefs and dispositions
which give direction to the moral life in choice and action. The Christological
narrative is thus a story of both a gift and a call, at once indicative and imperative. To rehearse that story is to be recalled to both the source of salvation and
the source of obligation. Moreover, because the story elicits "imitation," its
relation to the moral life is not only that of a *source* of obligation; it also serves
to specify the shape of human life in response to obligation. It thus provides
not simply initial impetus to Christian morality but also a perceptible form or
contour for its growth.[65]

Webster rightly claims this is the *intrinsic* function of the christological narrative. This is not something we add to that narrative or that we can choose
to do with a neutral narrative, but this is its inherent function. As we saw
in our discussion of the Gospels, the form of the christological narrative in
itself provides a normative shape for Christian experience, devotions, and
actions. *Imitatio Christi* passages simply give abbreviated allusions to the
larger gospel narrative that is assumed to be shared knowledge, as is typical
of paraenesis.

What guides the extent and content of those allusions are the paraenetic
needs of the author. Such passages access the story of the Christ at a particular
point, ordinarily localized within the Passion Narrative, which demonstrates
a particular virtue, relevant to the specific challenges being addressed by the
author. So, for example, in Philippians 2:1–11 Paul is extolling the communal
virtue of humility to confront theological-ethical divisiveness in the Philippian
church. Likewise, 1 Peter 2:21–25 highlights Christ's moral integrity, seen in
nonretaliation in the midst of unjust suffering, as an example to be followed
by those who are unjustly persecuted for their faith and life.[66]

This is consistent with Hellenistic paraenetic practices where the biography
of an exemplar is alluded to in highlighting a particular virtue they embody.
Paraenetic authors do not recount whole biographies. They are useful as examples at the particular moments in which they concretely embody a specific
virtue. Authors engaged in paraenesis utilize exemplars to extol a particular
virtue that is relevant to the needs or deficiencies of their readers.[67] Sometimes
they can use the same exemplar in different contexts to demonstrate different
virtues, but in their use of exemplars they specify what virtue those exemplars
embody and consequently the readers are supposed to admire and imitate.

65. John B. Webster, "Christology, Imitability and Ethics," *SJT* 39 (1986): 311.
66. See Dryden, *Theology and Ethics*, 174–91; cf. Jason B. Hood, *Imitating God in Christ:
Recapturing a Biblical Pattern* (Downers Grove, IL: InterVarsity, 2013).
67. See Dryden, *Theology and Ethics*, 169–72.

So when Jesus is given as an exemplar by NT epistolary writers, they specify what about his life is exemplary. This saves us from all the strange conundrums of how the divinity of Christ or his moral perfection might be exemplary; they are not. His moral integrity, as a demonstration of real moral volition, is exemplary, but not the saving significance of his death. So the life of Jesus in its totality is not accessed as an example but only particular communicable virtues and dispositions.

Again, this is a prime example of how theology in NT epistles functions paraenetically, not simply to communicate Christology but to form the followers of Christ in his image. Paul and others confront the theological-ethical barriers to that formation by using Christ as an example. This serves not only to give a realized form to particular virtues but to connect those virtues to the focal narrative of their existence in Christ.[68] In this way the christological narratives give shape and impetus to Christian devotion and obedience, making certain actions intelligible and desirable. In addition, it provides a strong affective motivation through the believer's connection to Christ as not simply exemplar but also Lord, redeemer, and brother. In this way moral actions are infused with motivations of love, reverence, and gratitude.[69] This is an example of how paraenesis fosters virtuous actions and habits, reeducates ultimate devotions, and reorients practical wisdom through a narrative moral vision.

Conclusion

What this means practically for reading epistles for wisdom is being sensitive to how theological and ethical discourses function *together* in an epistle to bring about formative goals. Such an approach will attend to how theological discourse defines a moral space that elicits desires and makes certain actions intelligible and praiseworthy. In recognizing that epistles are directed at particular theological-ethical challenges, we will seek to identify that challenge in terms of the connection between its theological and ethical aspects—not as two separate issues but one issue with two faces. This kind of approach will also understand ethical injunctions not simply as a pattern of morality that delineates duties but also as another means of fostering maturity and wisdom and shaping affective attachments.

68. As Webster says, "To rehearse that story is to draw attention to the origins of the Christian's status and character beyond himself; his moral choosing is neither arbitrary nor self-directed, but determined at all points by the acts of Christ." Webster, "Christology, Imitability and Ethics," 310–11.

69. This is analogous to the use of exemplars in Hellenistic epistolary traditions we discussed above.

7

READING EPISTLES FOR WISDOM

Practice

In reading NT epistles as wisdom we have to remain cognizant we are reading texts that are representative of a particular form of ancient moral discourse—paraenetic epistles—and this genre *itself* communicates a set of intentions that are deliberately formative. This is why these NT authors chose this form of discourse over others. Properly attending to the embedded intentionality of this literary form will give us a set of sensitivities to the dynamics of the text, and especially how these texts function as wisdom to shape the convictions, hopes, and actions of the individuals and communities they address.

Practically, we will focus on how theological and ethical modes of discourse function *together*. As we noted above, when moral commands and actions are taken independently of gospel convictions the results are legalism, antinomianism, moralism, and authenticity. So when NT epistles are divided up using dichotomies of theology/ethics, indicative/imperative, or kerygma/paraenesis, the result is a neutering of textual intentionality and a reduction of the content of the epistle to a set of ideas and a set of moral proclamations with no particular connection between the two.

Our focus in this chapter will be on the vital link between theological and ethical modes of discourse, recognizing that theological discourse promotes a moral vision, which provides a context for moral actions, making those actions intelligible and desirable. As Oliver O'Donovan has said, "A belief in Christian ethics is a belief that certain ethical and moral judgments belong to the gospel itself."[1] This connection is the engine of spiritual formation, as it reorients affections and understandings, and promotes the rehabituation of new devotions in moral actions understood as acts of service and worship. This effective marriage of moral actions with ordered affections is the key element in the development of wisdom (φρόνησις), as a moral and spiritual intuition, which Paul describes in Romans 12:2 as the capacity to "discern what is good and acceptable and perfect."

Ephesians as a Test Case

To see this at work, we will start with shorter texts and work our way up to larger ones. One illustrative place to begin is Ephesians 4:32: "Be kind to one another, tenderhearted, forgiving one another, as God in Christ forgave you." Here we have a series of moral imperatives commanding kindness expressed in tenderhearted forgiveness. Paul roots these injunctions not in social contract theory or the categorical imperatives of reason but in the character and actions of God mediated through his Son. This is typical of NT paraenesis; it uses theology to give reasons and motivations that contextualize calls to specific moral actions and virtues. Being tenderhearted and forgiving toward others might sound simple, especially when read in terms of modern social contract theory as "Be nice to others and they will be nice to you." But Paul is speaking about something deeply counterintuitive and countercultural. Real kindness, tenderheartedness, and forgiveness is dangerous and costly. Why would someone take the risk of forgiving those who have hurt them (and will likely continue to do so)? Why show kindness to one's enemies? Paul turns to a moral vision in which God himself is tenderhearted, kind, and forgiving. In this way Paul gives a theological grounding for moral actions. He roots his counterintuitive call to kindness and forgiveness in the fundamental truths of the gospel; in Christ there is forgiveness with God. If this connection is cut, while keeping the call to tenderhearted forgiveness, then we will be left with a moralistic ethic that tells us to be nice to others.

This example of the connection between moral demands and theological grounding is hardly an isolated case. *In fact, it is always the case that NT epistles ground moral advice in some way to the essentials of the gospel as a contextualizing moral vision.* We simply do not find NT authors giving

1. Oliver O'Donovan, *Resurrection and Moral Order: An Outline for Evangelical Ethics* (Grand Rapids: Eerdmans, 1986), 12.

commands that stand in isolation from a theological grounding.[2] (The common belief that Paul gives moral advice that is not integrated with his gospel is projecting a set of anachronous dichotomies onto his writings that he would have found unintelligible.)[3]

Once again, our Right ARM rubric will prove helpful in identifying how epistles function as wisdom. Specifically, right actions will correlate to commands, both explicit and implicit, contained in the ethical discourses of the epistles. Right reasons and right motivations will be provided by what we normally label the "theology" of the epistles. Let's look at another example from the verses just prior to the one we just read:

> Therefore, having put away falsehood, let each one of you speak the truth with his neighbor, for we are members one of another. Be angry and do not sin; do not let the sun go down on your anger, and give no opportunity to the devil. Let the thief no longer steal, but rather let him labor, doing honest work with his own hands, so that he may have something to share with anyone in need. Let no corrupting talk come out of your mouths, but only such as is good for building up, as fits the occasion, that it may give grace to those who hear. And do not grieve the Holy Spirit of God, by whom you were sealed for the day of redemption. Let all bitterness and wrath and

2. The most obvious counterexample to this claim is the Letter of James, especially given Dibelius's famous complaint that "the entire document lacks continuity in thought." Martin Dibelius, *James: A Commentary on the Epistle of James*, trans. Michael A. Williams, Hermeneia (Philadelphia: Fortress, 1976), 2. However, Todd C. Penner, *The Epistle of James and Eschatology: Re-reading an Ancient Christian Letter*, JSNTSup 121 (Sheffield: Sheffield Academic Press, 1996), 133–213, makes an extended argument that "the opening and closing sections of the main body of James frame and control the reading of the central portion of the letter" (133). In addition, Bauckham recognizes that this question has been exacerbated by expectation of what theological development should look like, and that James has to be interpreted not as a sub-Pauline epistle but as a wisdom text.

> James is not a sequential argument, to be read in a linear manner, as recent attempts to demonstrate unity and coherence of the work have tended to suggest, but nor is it a haphazard collection of heterogeneous paraenetic traditions, as Dibelius' approach suggested. It is a compendium of James' wisdom, arranged, after an introductory epitome, in a series of discrete sections on various topics. Linear progression of thought is largely confined to each section. Coherence must be sought at a deeper level. The form and structure of the work are well suited to its purpose, which is to provide a resource for acquiring the wisdom that is expressed in obedience to God in everyday life. (Richard Bauckham, *James: Wisdom of James, Disciple of Jesus the Sage*, New Testament Readings [London: Routledge, 1999], 108)

3. For example, the long heritage of NT criticism that understands Paul's true gospel as experiential and not incorporating ethical demands is a fiction. Equally popular is the belief that Paul, or a later follower of Paul, simply pasted Greco-Roman ethics into his letters. Both of these proposals privilege the thought of Paul as the true expression of his gospel, but this divorces Paul from his ancient context and strips him of his Jewishness.

anger and clamor and slander be put away from you, along with all malice.
(Eph. 4:25–31)

Here we have a string of commands and practical moral advice, almost
all of which could be labeled as prescribing right actions. Such moral advice,
if taken on its own, out of context, leads to moralism. But in the previous
verses we find the reasons and motivations Paul gives to contextualize these
commands.

> Now this I say and testify in the Lord, that you must no longer walk as the Gen-
> tiles do, in the futility of their minds. They are darkened in their understanding,
> alienated from the life of God because of the ignorance that is in them, due to
> their hardness of heart. They have become callous and have given themselves
> up to sensuality, greedy to practice every kind of impurity. But that is not the
> way you learned Christ!—assuming that you have heard about him and were
> taught in him, as the truth is in Jesus, to put off your old self, which belongs to
> your former manner of life and is corrupt through deceitful desires, and to be
> renewed in the spirit of your minds, and to put on the new self, created after
> the likeness of God in true righteousness and holiness. (Eph. 4:17–24)

Paul grounds moral commands in the renewal of the heart and the new
self in Christ. As we saw above, paraenetic writers often utilize the theme
of conversion in drawing sharp antitheses between life before and after the
experience of conversion. Here Paul contrasts the old and new self, where
the old self is associated with "corrupt . . . deceitful desires" that characterize the "alienation" and "futility" of gentile existence apart from God. The
majority of the Ephesian church likely came from this gentile background.[4] So
when Paul denigrates gentile "hardness of heart," his target is not outsiders
but the moral dispositions that formerly described these Christians. His goal
is not to foster enmity toward outsiders but a disdain for the vices that still
cling to these gentile converts. At the same time their new self is identified
with a heart renewed "after the likeness of God," reflecting his holiness and
righteousness. The antithesis between these two modes of existence could not
be more stark. Antithetical imagery provides a context for moral judgment,
providing reasons and motivations where certain actions become reasonable
and admirable.

4. Cf. Ernest Best, *A Critical and Exegetical Commentary on Ephesians*, ICC (Edinburgh:
T&T Clark, 1998), 4, "Since a large portion of the argument of the letter relates to acceptance
of Gentiles as believers and since the readers are addressed in the second plural as Gentiles who
have forsaken pagan ways (2.1f; 3.1; 4.17), the majority of them must have been Gentiles." So
also Andrew T. Lincoln, *Ephesians*, WBC 42 (Dallas: Word, 1990), lxxvi.

This antithesis makes the commands of verses 25–31 intelligible by giving a moral vision of the new self created by God to reflect his righteousness. Calls to abandon anger, malice, selfishness, and sloth and to demonstrate mercy, kindness, and respect become intelligible in the context of this moral vision. But Paul also aims at a reeducation of devotions. He is doing more than saying that certain actions are good and others are bad. His aim is to foster *disdain* for vices and *desire* for virtues. This is why Paul utilizes the rhetoric of antithesis. Former "Gentile" existence is associated with vice, ignorance, and alienation. New Christian existence is characterized by fellowship with God and fellow believers. The rhetorical impact of this is the affective endorsement of the new life and a desire for it to become a stronger element of normative experience. It means a reinterpretation of the self and its desires in terms of the loving righteousness of God as both a recipient of and participant in that righteousness. By contrast, it also means a deconstruction of the old self and its strategies to define the self and control it.

Paul also recognizes that Christian experience is not a simple dichotomy between an old and a new self. The old self is still present (if it were not, Paul would not need to give prohibitions to vice). In Paul's already/not yet eschatology the old and new selves are both present, where the new self is the present manifestation of the eschatological destiny of the Christian. Paul routinely moves back and forth between absolute ontological antitheses and muddled existential tensions.[5] The purpose of antitheses is to provide moral clarity in the midst of existential confusion, not simply by labeling some actions good and others bad but in retraining the affections to disassociate the self from vices as aberrations of character while also promoting identification with virtue through the enjoyment of righteousness. All this provides the context for considered moral actions that marry actions, reasons, and motivations. Spiritual formation is a product of the reorientation of the heart realized in acts that reflect the loving righteousness of God.

This formative intent marks all of Paul's letters throughout. As Hays says, "Theology is for Paul never merely a speculative exercise; it is always a tool for constructing community."[6] When Paul is "doing theology," his purpose is never simply didactic—to teach, to inform, or to fight heresies. Obviously,

---

5. See James D. G. Dunn, *The Theology of Paul the Apostle* (Grand Rapids: Eerdmans, 1998), 473–82. Cf. J. de Waal Dryden, "Revisiting Romans 7: Law, Self, and Spirit," *JSPL* 5, no. 1 (2015): 135–38.

6. Richard B. Hays, *The Moral Vision of the New Testament: Community, Cross, New Creation, A Contemporary Introduction to New Testament Ethics* (San Francisco: HarperSanFrancisco, 1996), 18. Hays argues Paul is doing communal spiritual formation, not that this is something we can choose to do with Paul's letters if we like, as though this were something extrinsic to Paul's writing that we can add as a beneficial extra.

he does all of these things, but Paul has more significant agendas than producing orthodox thoughts; he is training orthodox devotions, along with deconstructing heterodox ones.

From this we can see that Paul's theology is primarily shaped around discourse pragmatics, not systematic concerns. Therefore, our primary question in reading Paul's theology needs to be, What is he doing? Too often we have stopped with the question, What is he saying? Put differently, our real goal is to surmise how Paul intends to shape his hearers *through* what he is saying.[7] Perhaps a look at another Pauline text can demonstrate the importance of this.

Romans 6:1–14

"What shall we say then? Are we to continue in sin that grace may abound? By no means! How can we who died to sin still live in it? Do you not know that all of us who have been baptized into Christ Jesus were baptized into his death? We were buried therefore with him by baptism into death, in order that, just as Christ was raised from the dead by the glory of the Father, we too might walk in newness of life" (Rom. 6:1–4). From the start let us admit that Paul is leading us into deep theological waters (from which he will not come shallow until chapter 12). Paul's response to the charge of antinomianism, whether real or rhetorical, is theologically dense, and more is assumed in Paul's argument than is actually stated (especially regarding baptism). Unsurprisingly, then, this has been a highly contested text in the history of interpretation. As Douglas Moo explains, "What makes for the controversy are the related questions of the meaning and importance of baptism (vv. 3–4) and the relationship between baptism and the 'with Christ' language that is so characteristic of the paragraph."[8]

More specifically we might ask: Why does Paul introduce the theme of baptism at all in this context? What does it mean to be baptized into the death of Christ? What about that baptism/death nullifies the reign of sin? What does Paul mean by the "form" (ὁμοίωμα) of Christ's death? Are we baptized into Jesus's resurrection as well as his death? What does it mean to be united to Christ? What is the connection between the death of Christ and the life of the one who believes in him? Are the death and resurrection of Jesus simply metaphors for saying no to sin and yes to righteousness? These are just some of the difficult questions posed by this text.

---

7. What Brown calls "perlocutionary intentions." See Jeannine K. Brown, *Scripture as Communication: Introducing Biblical Hermeneutics* (Grand Rapids: Baker Academic, 2007), 111–14.
8. Douglas J. Moo, *The Epistle to the Romans*, NICNT (Grand Rapids: Eerdmans, 1996), 355.

While Paul speaks powerfully about the *significance* of baptism, he says virtually nothing about baptism per se (neither the mode of its implementation nor its connection to faith). Historically, this void has created a playground for speculation among NT historians as to the origin of Paul's baptismal theology among the ancient mystery religions, along with the implications those origins necessitate for our understanding of Paul's soteriology.[9] Despite all the ink spilled in this endeavor, today these studies are increasingly viewed as a dead end with very few substantial exegetical payoffs.[10]

The more important questions pertain to what is signified in baptism—our "coburial" with Christ in his death. What on earth does that mean? Both assumed and explicit here is Paul's doctrine of union with Christ, by means of which Christians participate in the death and resurrection of Jesus, but what exactly Paul means by this is still a matter of considerable debate.[11] In what sense do Christians die with Christ? Clearly in some metaphorical sense, but that does not get us very far. Unfortunately this is not a question we can solve by simply repeating what Paul says; nor is it a question we can ignore or evade, since it is at the heart of Paul's argument.

The complexity of these questions and the theological profundity of Paul have very often left interpreters lost in the trees and unable to see the forest—once again, failing to ask what Paul is *doing*. This is why the majority of interpreters seem to simply forget that Paul's question here is actually a moral one, not a theological one. Why is it that the believer in Jesus should refrain from sin? Granted, Paul's answer to this question is profoundly theological, but this should not lead us to forget that Paul is engaged in moral discourse, or more precisely a *wisdom* discourse.[12]

Paul dismisses his initial question, "Are we to continue in sin that grace may abound?" with his characteristic μὴ γένοιτο. But this is still a question he plans to take very seriously for the next several chapters. After the apocalyptic narrative of 5:12–21 of the defeat of sin by the righteousness

---

9. Cf. Ernst Käsemann, *Commentary on Romans*, trans. Geoffrey W. Bromiley (Grand Rapids: Eerdmans, 1980), 160, "From the very beginning historical study has been inflamed by Paul's sacramental teaching as well as his eschatology."

10. See the excellent survey of A. J. M. Wedderburn, "The Soteriology of the Mysteries and Pauline Baptismal Theology," *NovT* 29, no. 1 (1987): 53–72.

11. Cf. Moo's excursus in "Paul's 'with Christ' Conception," in *Romans*, 391–95. See Grant Macaskill, *Union with Christ in the New Testament* (Oxford: Oxford University Press, 2013), 17–41.

12. "Wisdom discourse" is a term that breaches the division of didactic versus hortatory modes of discourse, recognizing these distinctions as dependent on a metaphysic that separates being and doing, which is alien to the Bible. Elsewhere I have used the terminology of "onto-ethical" discourse to address the same issue. See J. de Waal Dryden, "Immortality in Romans 2:6–11," *JTI* 7, no. 2 (2013): 295–310.

of God, Paul needs to show how this defeat is realized in the Christian community. But what is most intriguing is Paul's strategy for applying this truth to the moral life of the Christian. In answering the question of "continuing in sin," Paul does not begin with the language of obligation (one would be hard pressed to imagine a less Kantian response), or law, or consequentialism.[13] Rather, Paul's starting point is baptism as the sign of union with Christ and his primary motif of "sanctification"—dying and rising with Christ.

As is customary for him, *before* Paul responds directly with commands to resist sin and embrace righteousness in verses 12–13, he answers the question of why those who are in Christ should want to do that. Using Right ARM, before he prescribes right actions ("Let not sin therefore reign in your mortal body, to make you obey its passions. Do not present your members to sin as instruments for unrighteousness, but present yourselves to God as those who have been brought from death to life, and your members to God as instruments for righteousness"), he gives reasons and motivations that make those commands not only intelligible but effective. Understood outside this wisdom context Paul is just "doing theology," and the interpreter's role is simply to explain that theology.[14] No matter how well this is done, this theological reading distances us from Paul.

Once again, conversion (here under the sign of baptism) arises as a tool for a "two ways" rhetoric. The purpose of this kind of rhetoric is to ground moral deliberations, where virtues and vices often *feel* indistinguishable, in a metaphysical moral antithesis where the distance between them is absolute. The goal is a retraining of convictions and affections—to desire righteousness and despise vice.

So it can be no surprise, then, that Paul's discourse in 6:1–11 is dominated by moral and ontological antitheses and that these antitheses are grounded

13. This only underlines the distance between Paul and ourselves, since all our contemporary answers to this question revolve around deontological or consequentialist ethics.

14. Many interpreters separate vv. 1–11 and 12–14 as distinct sections, primarily on the grammatical move from indicative to imperative. So, for example, Joseph A. Fitzmyer, *Romans: A New Translation with Introduction and Commentary*, AB 33 (New York: Doubleday, 1993), 444, argues that vv. 12–23 "are not well integrated into the letter and seem to be a résumé of a baptismal exhortation that Paul may at times have preached." But as Tannehill says, "A basic division of the chapter at vss. 11 or 12 must be rejected. . . . This exhortation is present as the inference which is to be drawn from the argument in the preceding part of the chapter (vs. 11-οὕτως; vs. 12- οὖν)." He continues, "For Paul the imperatives which begin in vs. 11 can no more be separated from the indicatives which precede than conclusion can be separated from premise, and so the chapter cannot be divided at vss. 11 or 12 without playing havoc with Paul's argument." Robert C. Tannehill, *Dying and Rising with Christ: A Study in Pauline Theology*, BZNW 32 (Berlin: Töpelmann, 1967), 8–9.

in baptism as the Christian initiation rite.[15] Paul chooses baptism as the sign of conversion (instead of faith) because he wants to focus on what has been accomplished in and for the believer in their union with Christ. As he summarizes in verse 4: "We were buried therefore with him by baptism into death, in order that, just as Christ was raised from the dead by the glory of the Father, we too might walk in newness of life." Paul's death/life and buried/raised antitheses put aside all theories of moral formation that envision a gradual process based on the knowledge of first principles (or Torah) and the strength of one's moral convictions. (In other words, all the theories that dominated both the Greco-Roman and Jewish worlds as well as their modern deontological cousins.)

Paul's starting point is more radical and is rooted in the Christian's participation in the apocalyptic determinative events of the death and resurrection of Jesus. It is these eschatological events that give Christians a new existence and orientation to life, a new understanding of the self as interpreted through the christological narrative of death and resurrection.[16] Along with these comes a new orientation for the affections: desirous of "newness of life" brought about by the glory of the Father and suspicious of those desires that lead to death. As Paul says, "We know that our old self was crucified with him in order that the body of sin might be brought to nothing, so that we would no longer be enslaved to sin." Sin, operative in the "old self," brings slavery through the weaknesses of the "body of sin." But it is this old self that was crucified with Jesus and buried with him through baptism. This eschatological antithesis of before/after is the foundation of an ethical either/or.[17]

There are two exegetical challenges in this passage that have long confounded interpreters. The first is the meaning of the "form" or "likeness" (ὁμοίωμα) of Jesus's death in verse 5.[18] The second is what Paul means when he says that "one who has died has been set free [δεδικαίωται] from sin" in verse 7; the meaning of this verse is complicated by Paul's use of δικαιόω in a way that seems free of juridical connotations. *Both* of these issues are important for our understanding of the passage, and both remain resistant to repeated attempts to solve them. But it may be that coming at these verses

15. See James D. G. Dunn, *Romans*, WBC 38A (Dallas: Word, 1988), 1:308–14.

16. Cf. Stephen Fowl, "Some Uses of Story in Moral Discourse: Reflections on Paul's Moral Discourse and Our Own," *Modern Theology* 4, no. 4 (1988): 298; and Michael J. Gorman, *Cruciformity: Paul's Narrative Spirituality of the Cross* (Grand Rapids: Eerdmans, 2001).

17. In the language of speech-act theory: the discourse locution is the antithesis of before/after death communicated through participation in the death of Christ. The illocutionary force of this utterance is the call to the ethical either/or of righteousness over sin.

18. See Florence A. Morgan, "Romans 6, 5a: United to a Death Like Christ's," *ETL* 59, no. 4 (1983): 267–302, for a full treatment of the history of interpretation and the possible options.

from a wisdom perspective can help us see them in a new light and understand how they are connected.

First, 6:5: "For if we have been united [σύμφυτοι γεγόναμεν] with him in a death like his [τῷ ὁμοιώματι τοῦ θανάτου αὐτοῦ], we shall certainly be united with him in a resurrection like his." The meaning of ὁμοίωμα has been the subject of much debate. Possible meanings center around "image," "likeness," and "form." The real problem is that Paul does not simply speak of being united to the death of Christ, but with some aspect of his death—the ὁμοίωμα of his death. Moo has moved the conversation along by showing that "form" is the best (or least problematic) translation in the context.[19] Along similar lines, C. E. B. Cranfield argues that "the expression σύμφυτος γίνεσθαι τῷ ὁμοιώματι followed by a genitive means simply 'to be assimilated to the form of,' [or] 'to be conformed to.'"[20] This doesn't get us any closer to what the "form" of Christ's death is, but it narrows down the possibilities.

The essential stumbling block for modern interpreters in this question is their search for a *theological* significance to the death of Christ, where Paul assumes a *moral* one. Paul's focus here is not the substitutionary atoning significance of Jesus's death; nor is it on the apocalyptic event of his death as such. The form of Christ's death that Paul assumes here is the moral victory over sin that Jesus accomplished in his death. Just a handful of verses earlier Paul described Jesus's death as the "one act of righteousness [δικαίωμα]" that brought "justification and life for all men" (5:18b) and then went on to refer to it as the "obedience [ὑπακοή]" through which "many will be made righteous" (5:19b). It is not the *fact* of Jesus's death that is in view but that his death perfected his obedience to God. Paul expresses the same idea in Philippians 2:8: "And being found in human form, he humbled himself by becoming obedient [ὑπήκοος] to the point of death, even death on a cross." The same idea of Jesus's obedience in his death as a determinative break with sin is also present in 6:10a: "For the death he died he died to sin, once for all."[21]

---

19. Moo, *Romans*, 368–71.

20. C. E. B. Cranfield, *The Epistle to the Romans*, ICC (Edinburgh: T&T Clark, 1990), 1:308. He adds that this expression is "equivalent to συμμορφίζεσθαι as used in Phil 3.10."

21. Again a text that has proved controversial among those looking for a theological and not a moral significance to Paul's words. Barrett is a notable exception to this trend. "Christ died to sin because he died sinless, because he died rather than sin (by disobeying the Father), and because he died in a context of sin." C. K. Barrett, *The Epistle to the Romans*, 2nd ed., BNTC (Peabody, MA: Hendrickson, 1991), 126. Jesus's death to sin does not come after participating in it or giving allegiance to it but as one who has fought against, resisted, and defeated sin, as the one who "learned obedience through what he suffered" (Heb. 5:8). The same thought is also found in 1 Pet. 4:1–2. See J. de Waal Dryden, *Theology and Ethics in 1 Peter: Paraenetic Strategies for Christian Character Formation*, WUNT 2/209 (Tübingen: Mohr Siebeck, 2006), 181–85.

All this is highly significant because it is the *character* of Jesus's death that Paul says Christians are united to. They not only died with Jesus; they also identify with him in the "form" of his death as a renunciation of sin and its power.[22] The death of Christ carries a moral weight that gives content to what it means to be "united to him in the form of his death" as well as an impetus for Christian obedience. As Chrysostom said, "Paul did not say *in death* but *in a death like his*. For both the first and the second are death but not the death of the same thing. The first is the death of the body, the second is the death of sin."[23] The simple reason why modern interpreters have failed to make this connection is that they have understood Paul to be engaged in a theological discourse, failing to recognize this as a wisdom discourse.[24]

The essential issue here is that traditional interpretations of this passage are forced to claim that Paul is drawing a moral principle (death to sin) from a theological event (the death of Christ) by means of a rhetorical sleight of hand, the result being that Paul draws an inference between two incommensurable fields (like deciding to change my air filters because I like the taste of apples). Paul's real logic draws a *moral* significance (death to sin) from the apocalyptic *moral* event of the death of Jesus, which undoes the sin of Adam in Jesus's fidelity to God and his renunciation of sin and death—the apocalyptic forces that Adam unleashed on the world in his disobedience.

This reading also has important implications for the other perplexing text in this passage, Romans 6:7: "For one who has died [ὁ ἀποθανὼν] has been set free from sin [δεδικαίωται ἀπὸ τῆς ἁμαρτίας]." The two key issues of dispute are (1) how is it that death is meant to set someone free from sin, and (2) does δικαιόω here carry its (classically Pauline) juridical sense of "justify/acquit," or should it be taken as "deliver" or "free from entrapment"?

22. Cf. the paraphrase of Morgan, "United," 301, "If we have died to sin as Christ died and remain so, with the result that death to sin has become inherent in us, we shall certainly also rise as Christ rose, with the result that resurrection will also inhere in us."

23. Chrysostom, *Baptismal Instructions* 10.10, in Gerald Lewis Bray, ed., *Romans*, ACCSNT 6 (Downers Grove, IL: InterVarsity, 1998), 157. Italics original. Cf. the comment of Cyril of Alexandria, "For in that we carry his mortification about in our bodies, we have been buried together with him" (Bray, *Romans*, 154–55).

24. This is, again, an essentially modernist phenomenon. By contrast, the medieval interpreter Peter of John Olivi summarizes Paul's argument as

Christ's grace is so much opposed to sin that it even killed and crucified us to sin. So great is this grace in itself that it has eternally, essentially, and irreversibly established us within the life of Christ, which is completely contrary to our old way of sin. . . . This is clear from the first sacrament of grace, namely, by means of Baptism, which sacramentally conforms us to the death of Christ and his burial, so that, having died to vices, we pass through in the new life of virtues and grace, assimilated in this way to the new life of the risen Christ. (Ian Christopher Levy, Philip D. Krey, and Thomas Ryan, eds., *The Letter to the Romans*, The Bible in Medieval Tradition [Grand Rapids: Eerdmans, 2013], 144)

Most interpreters take this statement as a gnomic principle, with possible roots in ancient Judaism. Some see an allusion to a rabbinic principle that "death pays all debts."[25] Others see a more general principle of "dead men do not sin, because they cannot do *anything*." This second principle is the most common interpretation among commentators.[26] The liability with the first option is simply that the rabbinic principle is irrelevant in this situation because it only applies to human debts. As Cranfield argues, "it is certain that Paul did not think that a man's death atoned for his sins in relation to God, or that a dead man was no longer accountable to God for his sins." He therefore concludes that "the Rabbinic principle is singularly inappropriate as a confirmation of what has just been said."[27]

The second option is equally problematic, primarily because the idea it promotes isn't remotely Christian. Are we to believe, as Käsemann argues, that Paul thinks that "Christians are freed from the power of sin by death"?[28] This seems unlikely given that Paul, in this passage and those that follow, pictures death as both the consequence of sin and its accomplice. If sin is defeated through death, isn't everyone who dies freed from the power of sin? While it is common to read this verse this way, it introduces, *by inference*, a notion that is explicit nowhere else in Paul's writings, has nothing distinctly Christian about it, and defies the internal logic of the passage.

Still, there is a deeper problem with both of these gnomic readings. Both of them, again, assume that this is a "theological" discourse, and therefore the significance of death here is "theological" and so has to pertain to death per se, as an idea. So there has to be something in the nature of death *itself* that brings freedom (or possibly an acquittal) from sin. But as we have seen above, for Paul it is the *moral* significance of the death of Jesus that constitutes victory over sin. Paul sees the death of Jesus as the definitive apocalyptic moral victory over the power of sin.[29]

The most likely interpretation, then, is not to take this statement as a general principle but as a statement about Christians who participate in the death of Christ. As Thomas Schreiner argues, "The reference is not to death in general but to the believer's participation in Christ's death."[30] Both John Murray and Schreiner argue this reading fits better in the context, where the

---

25. See *Šabbat* 151 Baraita, "When a man is dead he is freed from fulfilling the law."

26. E.g., Moo, *Romans*, 376–77.

27. Both quotations from Cranfield, *Romans*, 1:310–11.

28. Käsemann, *Romans*, 165.

29. Cf. Barrett, *Romans*, 124, "Death with Christ is an ethical experience, affecting the relation between man and sin."

30. Thomas R. Schreiner, *Romans*, BECNT (Grand Rapids: Baker Academic, 1998), 319.

theme of participation in the death of Christ is central and is assumed as the protasis of the following verse, "Now if we have died with Christ . . ."[31]

Finally, what does Paul mean by δεδικαίωται ἀπὸ τῆς ἁμαρτίας? This phraseology is not found elsewhere in Paul, which makes it difficult to define.[32] "Acquittal *from* sin" seems an awkward phrase, and the context favors some note of deliverance from the power of sin, not simply acquittal from the guilt of sin. This has led to the common translation practice of taking this phrase in the sense of "freed from sin."[33] As Schreiner says, "The argument seems to be that righteousness necessarily involves freedom from the power of sin." He adds that "this point is crucial for Paul's argument."[34] Why? Because for Paul the righteousness of God is not only revealed in the forgiveness of the sinner but in their moral and spiritual transformation.[35] The foundation of that transformation is a decisive liberty from the power of sin, experienced in union with Christ, and especially in his death as his ultimate act of reverential obedience. As Schreiner concludes, "The use of the verb [δικαιόω] in this context . . . suggests that righteousness is more than forensic in Paul."[36] In this context the verb refers to the righteous activity of God (taking δεδικαίωται as a divine passive)[37] of revealing his righteousness in his people in setting them free from the domain of sin and death and enabling their love and obedience.[38]

This freedom from sin begins with Jesus's own "death to sin," in which Christians participate through their union with Christ, communicated through the sacrament of baptism. As Murray says, "It was by his own dying that he destroyed the power of sin, and in his resurrection he entered upon a state that was not conditioned by sin."[39] It is the Christian's participation in the death and resurrection of Jesus that contextualizes, enables, and motivates the mortification of the "old man" and the vivification of the "new self."

---

31. See John Murray, *The Epistle to the Romans: English Text with Introduction, Exposition and Notes*, NICNT (Grand Rapids: Eerdmans, 1959), 222; and Schreiner, *Romans*, 319.

32. The closest parallel is Acts 13:38–39: "Let it be known to you therefore, brothers, that through this man forgiveness of sins is proclaimed to you, and by him everyone who believes is freed from everything from which you could not be freed by the law of Moses."

33. See Murray, *Romans*, 222; contra Cranfield, *Romans*, 1:311; and Moo, *Romans*, 376.

34. Schreiner, *Romans*, 319.

35. Cf. Adolf Schlatter, *Romans: The Righteousness of God*, trans. Siegfried S. Schatzmann (Peabody, MA: Hendrickson, 1995), 146.

36. Schreiner, *Romans*, 319.

37. This is certainly a better option than saying that death has set them free, especially in Rom. 5–8, where death is always the result of and companion of sin.

38. Cf. Tannehill, *Dying and Rising*, 124, "Man is freed from this situation by God's act of grace in the cross. It is important for Paul that God's grace in the cross not only results in forgiveness for man's past sins but actually breaks the power of sin over man."

39. Murray, *Romans*, 225.

As Hays argues, "Jesus' death is an act of faithfulness that simultaneously reconciles humanity to God and establishes a new reality in which we are set free from the power of sin, able to be conformed to the pattern of his life."[40]

Once more, if we use the Right ARM rubric it will help us to look for the connections in the text between moral actions and theological grounding that supply reasons and motivations. This is a better approach than limiting ourselves to Paul's "theology." As we saw in this case, it is precisely this limited approach that *created* the most difficult exegetical questions in this text. An integrated wisdom approach can "solve" these problems because they are not actually problems in a wisdom hermeneutic.

Galatians

At this point some readers may wonder whether a wisdom reading is fruitful (or possible) for all NT epistles or only suited to some that have an "ethical agenda." Of all Paul's epistles Galatians is the most obvious candidate for a counterexample that seems to resist a wisdom paradigm.[41] The reason for this is that Galatians is primarily theological argumentation focused on Paul's defense of his doctrine of justification and the practical question of gentile circumcision. It is hard to see how this might be classified as a wisdom text. But let's see whether we can make sense of it from that perspective.

To begin with, we need to clarify a few points about the subject matter and purpose of Galatians. It is common, both in scholarly approaches and at a popular level, to understand the text of Galatians (or at least the first four chapters) as a theological exposition of the doctrine of justification and to find a thematic summary of the epistle in 2:16: "Yet we know that a person is not justified by works of the law but through faith in Jesus Christ, so we also have believed in Christ Jesus, in order to be justified by faith in Christ and not by works of the law, because by works of the law no one will be justified." This

---

40. Hays, *Moral Vision*, 32.

41. Hebrews might offer another NT counterexample since it is commonly described as a sermon. However, since we possess no sermons from the first century, the means of identifying Hebrews as a sermon are not historically accessible to us. The only real evidence for Hebrews being a sermon is the evidence against it being an epistle—that it is missing its epistolary greeting. If this is an essential feature for identifying a literary artifact as an epistle, which is the case in the outdated definition of epistle mentioned above, then Hebrews cannot be an epistle. But if we define epistles in terms of function, then Hebrews, as an exhortatory discourse, fits within the definition of paraenetic epistle. In addition, Hebrews adopts rhetorical strategies common to that genre (e.g., exemplars and antitheses founded on conversion). So, even though it is missing an epistolary greeting, functionally Hebrews is a paraenetic epistle, encouraging perseverance and progress evidenced in moral and spiritual practices that reflect core convictions.

approach also understands Paul as writing in response to a theological crisis, where Judaizing Christians have infiltrated the Galatian churches, challenged Paul's authority, and threatened their adherence to justification by faith. So Paul's agenda here is to correct heretical teaching. While this is a common approach, there are several problems with actually fitting the text of Galatians into this paradigm.

The first problem is that Galatians is not primarily concerned with justification but sanctification, specifically how the Galatians will choose to live as Christians in light of the central truths of justification. Even though "justification" is a key word in Galatians, we can easily get tricked by this into thinking that Paul is primarily discussing what we label as the doctrine of justification[42] or the correlate collective boundary conditions tied to circumcision. So, for example, when Paul gets to the point of the matter in 3:2–3, "Let me ask you only this: Did you receive the Spirit by works of the law or by hearing with faith? Are you so foolish? Having begun by the Spirit, are you now being perfected by the flesh?" The key question here is not how they are to become Christians (i.e., justification) but the discontinuity between how they became Christians and how they are pursuing their Christian life (i.e., sanctification). Or, if we return to the thematic verse in 2:16, we find that it occurs in Paul's recounting his confrontation with Peter over his hypocrisy in shunning gentile believers and eating exclusively with Jewish Christians. Paul brings the doctrine of justification to bear to confront Peter for living hypocritically. So the issue is in the area of what we would call sanctification (how a Christian is meant to live), not justification (how someone becomes a Christian).

The second major problem of this common approach is what to do with chapters 5 and 6, which focus on practical (ethical) advice, but do so in a way that seems general and unconnected to the justification/circumcision crisis that prompted the letter. This uncomfortable question has been a persistent thorn in the side of modern interpreters of Galatians. Some have chosen to ignore or downplay these chapters, with some even denying their Pauline origin.[43] Most see it as an ethical appendage to the epistle that, while having good advice for the Christian life, evidences no material connection to the real issues in Galatia. Many interpreters reason that Paul includes this section of the epistle more out of force of habit than out of convictions tailored

---

42. Which is primarily derived from how Paul uses δικαιόω in Romans, but even there Paul's use of this term demonstrates a semantic range that does not directly map onto our technical soteriological understanding of "justification." See Moo, *Romans*, 79–90.

43. For a survey of opinion see John M. G. Barclay, *Obeying the Truth: A Study of Paul's Ethics in Galatians* (Vancouver: Regent College Publishing, 2005), 1–35, 106–45.

to the Galatian churches. According to this approach, our interpretation of Galatians would not materially change if we lost chapters 5 and 6.

But any time we are forced to conclude that Paul did things without a reason, this is usually a sign that his reason is simply hidden to us because he is not thinking like we do. Paul's intentions here are actually not difficult to surmise but are obscured for us by a particular interpretive paradigm that separates theology from ethics and privileges the former over the latter. The problem that modern interpreters have of integrating Galatians 5–6 into the rest of the epistle is illustrative of the shortcomings of such a paradigm.

The key interpretive issue is the presupposition that Paul writes Galatians to deal with a theological crisis, that is, a theological crisis in isolation from any practical or ethical concerns. (Such a presupposition is, as we have seen, unthinkable outside a modernist context.)[44] As we said in the previous chapter, for the writers of the NT, theological heresy always reveals itself in communal dysfunction. The two form one theologico-ethical crisis that needs to be addressed. Paul sees the challenge of gentile circumcision as both a social crisis and a theological crisis in equal measure, without hierarchy. Paul roots his explanation of justification in his Antioch confrontation with Peter. Why? Because this theological heresy tears at the heart of Christian community, just as it did in Antioch, and just as it will in Rome, where Paul will turn again to justification as a foundation to address Jewish and gentile tensions fomented by mutual condescension (Rom. 3:21–30; 14:1–15:9). Paul believes that any acceptance of justification by works creates a system where individuals or groups can elevate themselves above others within the Christian community. This is where the New Perspective on Paul has been incredibly helpful in reminding us that the context for Paul's discussions of justification is, at heart, social conflict.[45]

There are not two problems in Galatia—just one—a theologico-ethical crisis. Paul addresses the short-term practical question of gentile circumcision, not so subtly arguing in the negative. Paul also denounces the "agitators" who are disrupting the lives of these churches. But he also sees other

44. In such a context the religious life is primarily one of either theological rectitude or emotional experience, or some combination of the two. The locus for either (theological reasoning [deriving its coherence from idealism] or emotional experience [deriving its coherence from romanticism]) is human consciousness apart from the faculties of will and action. But biblical models of spirituality understand moral action as the locus of religion and spiritual formation.

45. There is, of course, a tendency to fall off the horse on the other side and define the heart of the gospel only or primarily in terms of sociological markers of inclusion and exclusion. Theological distinctives become pragmatic ciphers for social boundary maintenance and fostering group cohesion. In this context, all human actions are only understandable as they relate to sociological ends, and so all theological predications become ciphers for group survival/cohesion.

negative forces at work that arise not from these outsiders but from within. This is clear enough in 5:15, "But if you bite and devour one another, watch out that you are not consumed by one another." Paul's warning assumes that some level of palpable communal strife is already a reality.[46] Paul points to the natural outcome of the strife that has become normative within the Galatian churches. Once fractious arguments enter into a community, they produce self-justifying antagonistic groups—warring factions. Each feels justified in their stance, even at the expense of their opponents. Paul has to break through the self-justifying logic of factions and point to what it naturally produces—the destruction of communal life and the disintegration of spiritual formation. This unraveling of the community is the natural outcome of the theological heresies that Paul is fighting against. "A little leaven leavens the whole lump" (Gal. 5:9).

These intercommunal dangers are also prevalent in Paul's list of the "works of the flesh" that follow in 5:19–21. This list of vices includes expected items such as drunkenness, sexual immorality, and idolatry. But alongside these standards we find "enmity, strife, jealousy, fits of anger, rivalries, dissensions, divisions," and "envy." More than half of Paul's "works of the flesh" are directly related to communal strife.[47] Paul rhetorically connects "works of the flesh" and being justified by "works of the law" by calling them both "works" (in contrast to the "fruit" of the Spirit in 5:22, or "fulfillment" of the law in 5:14). Theologically, Paul connects them as attempts to privilege oneself on the basis of works. It is clear from his discourse on the fruit of the Spirit, and describing it as a fulfillment of the law, that Paul does not condemn moral agency per se, but a construal of that agency that puts one in a privileged place with God and in relation to others. This is why he contrasts "living by the Spirit" with being "conceited, provoking one another, envying one another" (5:26). Conceit and envy are opposite sides of the same coin of moral

---

46. The grammatical construction εἰ plus the indicative is a conditional protasis that emphasizes the reality of what is stated as an already-present reality or a strong possibility. The context favors the former, but even if Paul is speaking only of an imminent possibility, this is evidence of tensions already present in the community or Paul's expectation of those tensions. Cf. Douglas J. Moo, *Galatians*, BECNT (Grand Rapids: Baker Academic, 2013), 348–49.

47. Virtue and vice lists are a traditional staple in moral discourse, but the particular virtues or vices included in a list are chosen from a large reservoir of tradition. The function of vice lists is not simply to list a group of "bad" things. Their effect is cumulative. The author who utilizes them wants to create a bad association with all these vices. One vice on its own may seem bad, but ten together have a cumulative nauseating effect. Vice lists can also pair obviously bad vices (felonies) with softer ones (misdemeanors), with the intention of transmitting the weight of the felonies to the misdemeanors. This is likely why Paul pairs communal vices such as "dissension" alongside "drunkenness" and "orgies." One's response to the latter pair should be obvious and strong; Paul wants his hearers to transfer that same response to "dissension."

competitiveness used to establish oneself in one's own eyes. This is why Paul warns that "if anyone thinks he is something, when he is nothing, he deceives himself" (6:3). Paul goes on to instruct the Galatians: "But let each one test his own work, and then his reason to boast will be in himself alone and not in his neighbor" (6:4). Seeking to be justified by works of the law necessarily produces comparison, conceit, envy, superiority, dissensions, and strife. Paul is addressing all of this as a single problem with a theological *and* an ethical dimension. Seeking justification "by works of the law" is both a theological and moral vice.

Further evidence of Paul's wisdom agenda in Galatians can be found in his pervasive use of antithetical "two ways" rhetoric. The most obvious examples of this kind of rhetoric are Paul's antitheses between "works of the flesh" and "fruit of the Spirit," and justification "by faith" versus justification "by works of the law," but there are many more, such as Paul's claim that his apostolic authority and gospel come "not from men, . . . but through God" (1:1, 11–12). The same language of antithesis can be found in 2:20: "I have been crucified with Christ. It is no longer I who live, but Christ who lives in me." And again in 3:18: "For if the inheritance comes by the law, it no longer comes by promise; but God gave it to Abraham by a promise." Paul's conclusion in 4:7, "So you are no longer a slave, but a son, and if a son, then an heir through God," is another example. Likewise, Paul trades on the theme of "free" versus "slave," describing preconversion existence in the language of slavery in 4:1–9. He also uses Hagar and Sarah allegorically to represent the same theme of enslavement (to the law), with the conclusion that "we are not children of the slave [Hagar] but of the free woman [Sarah]" (4:31).

What is the point of all these antitheses? They possess a cumulative force of moral persuasion that creates an either/or in a situation the Galatian churches, torn by competing allegiances, experience as bewildering and confusing. The rhetorical staple of the "two ways" provides moral clarity and demands a response. Its purpose is to move its hearers out of complacency and moral confusion. It offers a clear choice, where the options are not only reduced to a duality but where one choice is obviously right and the other wrong. The choice between "free" and "slave" is not a head scratcher. This is what Paul is setting up in 5:1: "For freedom Christ has set us free; stand firm therefore, and do not submit again to a yoke of slavery." So Paul's multiple contrasts serve to contextualize and elicit moral actions, to make them both intelligible and desirable.

Of course some will object that this analysis ignores the "central message" of Galatians: Paul's defense of his apostolic authority and message, especially in chapters 1 and 2. Obviously, if one is looking for the "red meat" of controversy in this letter, then the intensity of these chapters is hard to beat. But the key question still remains: What is Paul *doing* in these chapters? Is the defense of his mission and message an end in itself, or does it serve some other end? If Paul's goal is simply to defend his ministry and to prohibit gentile circumcision, then most of the epistle is simply superfluous. But for Paul the question of gentile circumcision taps into much deeper questions.[48] It is clear from the latter third of the epistle that Paul sees deeper threats to the Galatian churches than simply the presenting problem of gentile circumcision; there are long-term challenges that need to be addressed. This is why Paul connects the Galatian crisis to what may seem like a very general discussion of "works of the flesh" versus "fruit of the Spirit" in Galatians 5:16–25. This is also why, in the middle of a defense of justification, Paul immediately moves to his central image of sanctification: participation in the death and resurrection of Christ. "I have been crucified with Christ. It is no longer I who live, but Christ who lives in me. And the life I now live in the flesh I live by faith in the Son of God, who loved me and gave himself for me. I do not nullify the grace of God, for if righteousness were through the law, then Christ died for no purpose" (Gal. 2:20–21). Paul has bigger fish to fry than defending his apostolic authority and message. These defenses are best understood as *instrumental* in Paul's formative agenda for the Galatian churches. This is the only way to make sense of the epistle as a coherent whole.

Paul confirms this in Galatians 5:6: "For in Christ Jesus neither circumcision nor uncircumcision counts for anything, but only faith working through love." Paul confesses that the presence or absence of circumcision is not the real issue for these churches, but rather it is how the circumcision question chokes the fruit of the Spirit—faith realizing itself in loving actions in community life. Faith produces love because it begins by accepting God's judgment on all idolatrous modes of self-reliance and self-justification, which of necessity create tiers of advantage where some find in themselves a reason to place themselves above others. From this the stares of condescension that destroy communal love are a necessary fruit. It is here that Paul sees justification by faith as the foundation that is able to unite Jews and gentiles with a power that outmatches religious pride and racial prerogatives.

The second element of how faith produces love is simply that faith is the instrument that receives and accepts the love of Christ. As Paul says in Galatians 2:20b, "The life I now live in the flesh I live by faith in the Son of God,

---

48. Cf. Pieter G. R. de Villiers, "Love in the Letter to the Galatians," in *The Bible and Spirituality: Exploratory Essays in Reading Scripture Spiritually*, ed. Andrew T. Lincoln, J. Gordon McConville, and Lloyd K. Pietersen (Eugene, OR: Cascade, 2013), 194–211.

who loved me and gave himself for me." Paul testifies to an agency transformed by the love of Christ, which participates in that love through loving action. The ability to love, understood as the transformative gift of God, comes with a judgment on the sinful self's privileged place in human agency. This is why Paul sees in the crucifixion of Jesus a dual demonstration of love, first as a free gift and second as a judgment of the self's claim to self-determination. So to be united with Christ in love through faith necessarily entails a union with his crucifixion, in which he renounced all self-preservation and selfish prerogatives. This is what Paul means by "I have been crucified with Christ. It is no longer I who live, but Christ who lives in me" (Gal. 2:20a). In the cross Paul sees the testimony of the love of Christ *and* the command to love one's brother. The cross provides the reasons and motivations for loving action in the theological decentering of the self in Christ and the enjoyment of love, both received and offered.

Paul summarizes all this as the transformative free gift of the Spirit in Galatians 5:22–23a: "But the fruit of the Spirit is love, joy, peace, patience, kindness, goodness, faithfulness, gentleness, self-control." The gift of the Spirit is to fill the heart with virtues. This filling also necessarily implies an emptying: "those who belong to Christ Jesus have crucified the flesh with its passions and desires" (5:24). Paul locates this negation of passions and desires in the social sphere: "Let us not become conceited, provoking one another, envying one another" (5:26). But it is not enough to simply recognize these virtues as enabling prosocial behaviors that sustain coherent communal life. The preservation of the community is not a self-justifying good in itself (as is assumed in all social-scientific hermeneutics). The fruit of the Spirit reforms the heart and communicates joy because it enables the realization of the loving righteousness of God in human community. This is a concrete measure of participation in the promised revelation of the eschatological glory of God in the new Jerusalem—the biblical vision of a new humanity enjoying one another, God, and self—the enactment of a redeemed agency in a union of convictions, desires, and actions, all finding their teleological referent in the glory of God. "For neither circumcision counts for anything, nor uncircumcision, but a new creation. And as for all who walk by this rule, peace and mercy be upon them, and upon the Israel of God" (Gal. 6:15–16).

1 John

What about a non-Pauline example? In an echo of Genesis 1:1 and the prologue of John's Gospel, 1 John begins with a christological prologue:

> That which was from the beginning, which we have heard, which we have seen with our eyes, which we looked upon and have touched with our hands, concerning the word of life—the life was made manifest, and we have seen it, and testify to it and proclaim to you the eternal life, which was with the Father and was made manifest to us—that which we have seen and heard we proclaim also to you, so that you too may have fellowship with us; and indeed our fellowship is with the Father and with his Son Jesus Christ. (1 John 1:1–3)

This theologically dense (and grammatically awkward) opening for the epistle signals that at least one of the problems that prompt John to write is christological.[49] It becomes clear later in the epistle (see 3:18–27 and 4:1–5) that certain teachers, whom John calls "antichrists," have introduced some deficient understanding of the incarnation into the churches to which he writes. Determining exactly how these teachers deviated from christological orthodoxy has proven elusive. The emphasis of the verses above is on the material humanity of Jesus. So it is likely that a key element is some form of (proto-)gnostic denial of the true humanity of Jesus. But it is also possible that the divinity of Jesus was also in question. (Both would be the case, for example, in a Platonic demiurge understanding of the incarnation, where Jesus is neither god nor man but an intermediary being.)[50] John stresses the material humanity of Jesus more than his divinity, so perhaps the threat was more palpable in this area.[51]

Much of the history of interpretation has focused on the questions of describing these heretical teachers and their historical origins in western Asia Minor. Who were they? Were there multiple factions? What did they teach? What is their historical connection to Judaism, Hellenism, and the Johannine community? The other major line of inquiry has been on the less speculative question of what John actually teaches in response to this situation. What is John's theological/christological understanding? Along with this comes the genealogical question of where John got his particular brand of Christian convictions.

Of course, theological heresy is not the only threat that concerns John. In addition to the christological controversies, he also addresses divisions and

---

49. See Robert W. Yarbrough, *1–3 John*, BECNT (Grand Rapids: Baker Academic, 2008), 5–15, for a vigorous (and actually plausible) argument for authorship by John the son of Zebedee.

50. Stephen S. Smalley, *1, 2, 3 John*, WBC 51 (Waco: Word, 1984), xxiii–xxv, covers both bases by arguing for two rival groups in the Johannine church: one with Ebionitic tendencies and the other Docetic.

51. It is unclear whether Lieu thinks there were any actual "opponents" that John was responding to, or whether they are simply a socio-rhetorical construct—an antigroup that John uses as a foil to bolster the social cohesiveness of the communities he writes to. See Judith Lieu, *I, II & III John: A Commentary*, NTL (Louisville: Westminster John Knox, 2008), 9–14.

tensions among the members of these churches. This can be seen in the numerous positive teachings on the love of God and intercommunal love (2:10; 3:11, 14a, 16–18; 4:7, 11–12, 21; 5:1–2) as well as numerous denunciations of animosity toward others within the community (2:9, 11; 3:12, 14b–15; 4:8, 20). While these practical ethical issues have historically received less attention in the history of interpretation, recently, as social-scientific approaches have become more dominant, questions of communal identity and boundary maintenance have become more prominent.[52]

As we have seen, approaches that begin by dividing theological and ethical/communal concerns are hampered from the start. If we want to see how these texts function as wisdom, then we need a coherent sensitivity to the intersection of theology and ethics and how they inform each other in the formation of wisdom. We do not get very far into this epistle before this becomes clear. Following the "prologue" of 1:1–4, John introduces what is the programmatic truth for the entire epistle. "This is the message we have heard from him and proclaim to you, that God is light, and in him is no darkness at all" (1 John 1:5). For John this is the theological foundation of all that will be developed later—both theologically and ethically.[53] At the same time, many commentators balk at this verse, puzzled by its possible significance and the reason for its prominent placement here. If we begin with the assumption that John's purpose is to denounce a particular christological heresy, this verse is a curious place to start; it looks off target. Even if it applies to Jesus, it says nothing about incarnational questions or Jesus's relationship to the Father.

It would be easier to take this verse in the direction of a socio-rhetorical statement that uses the language of antithesis to promote communal cohesion. While there is no reason to deny that this is one of the aims of John, the strong tendency in this approach is an implicit denial of any affirmations that move beyond the immanent reality of the community, with the result that this affirmation is drained of its theological force as a statement about the being and nature of God as the one who is all good and all true, without any hint of deception or avarice. As we will see, this theological affirmation is essential for what John is doing in this epistle.

So why does John start in this place? Why does he begin with the message that "God is light, and in him is no darkness at all" (cf. James 1:17)? As Robert Yarbrough rightly argues, "John's frame of reference in the epistle is not dominated first of all by his teaching, his commands, or his encouragement

---

52. Lieu, *I, II & III John*, is a good example.
53. See Georg Strecker, *The Johannine Letters: A Commentary on 1, 2, and 3 John*, trans. Linda M. Maloney, Hermeneia (Minneapolis: Fortress, 1996), 25–28.

to love." Instead, "it is dominated by his vision of God—God's light, his moral excellence and efficacious purity."[54] It is this vision that will animate John's discussions of christological truths and exhortations to brotherly love. How, exactly? The answer is that John sees christological challenges and communal divisiveness not as two challenges but as two expressions of the *same* problem, the failure to comport oneself to the "moral excellence and efficacious purity" of God.

It is no use asking John whether the christological challenge or the communal one is primary or which one comes first. They are both mutually generative and mutually sustaining. And they are both rooted in a failure to live in the presence of the righteous love of God. This is exactly what John means when he says as his follow-up to verse 5 that "If we say we have fellowship with him while we walk in darkness, we lie and do not practice the truth [ψευδόμεθα καὶ οὐ ποιοῦμεν τὴν ἀλήθειαν]" (1:6). The truth that "God is light" is neither an ontological truth nor a moral truth; it is at one and the same time inseparably both (an "onto-ethical" reality).[55]

So what is the connection between this central truth and John's problems with the proto-Docetism of the anti-Christ teachers? First, as we saw, John begins his letter with the incarnational truth that Jesus is the physical embodiment of the "everlasting life" of God, the creator, eternal in glory. As the revelation of the person of God he is also "light" in his "moral excellence and efficacious purity." Jesus's moral character becomes efficacious in the reality of his humanity. If we deny or limit the material humanity of Jesus, then we lose the connection between him and his people, and more critically, the connection between his obedient will and our own. An Apollinarian, or Docetic, demigod Jesus has no connection to our moral experience. This connection is of critical importance to John. We can see this clearly in 2:5b–6: "By this we know that we are in him: whoever says he abides in him ought to walk in the same way in which he walked." John expresses a similar idea in 2:29: "If you know that he is righteous, you may be sure that everyone who practices righteousness has been born of him." Therefore, to know Jesus, to live in communion with him, "to abide in him," necessitates a character revealed in certain actions modeled on the moral life of Jesus as the definitive manifestation of the love and righteousness of God.

This is why, for John, the true test of Christian orthodoxy is love. "Whoever says he is in the light and hates his brother is still in the darkness" (2:9). John says, "This is his commandment that we believe in the name of his Son

---

54. Yarbrough, *1–3 John*, 50.
55. On "onto-ethical" see Dryden, "Immortality in Romans," 299–305.

Jesus Christ and love one another, just as he has commanded us" (3:23). For John these are two coordinate actions—to believe in the Son and to love one another—because "God sent his only Son into the world, so that we might live through him" (4:9).

This again is an example of wisdom that welds certain moral actions to correlate Christian convictions and motivations. "In this is love, not that we have loved God but that he loved us and sent his Son to be the propitiation for our sin" (4:10). John then applies this truth: "Beloved, if God so loved us, we also ought to love one another" (4:11). He places intercommunal acts of love in the context of the revelation of the light of God. This supplies an ideational context for moral actions but also motivations of gratitude along with the desire for deeper communion with God through obedience modeled by Christ. This interweaving of theological and ethical discourse is typical of how 1 John functions as wisdom. Perhaps it will be helpful to look at a concrete example in 1 John 2:1–6:

> My little children, I am writing these things to you so that you may not sin. But if anyone does sin, we have an advocate with the Father, Jesus Christ the righteous. He is the propitiation for our sins, and not for ours only but also for the sins of the whole world. And by this we know that we have come to know him, if we keep his commandments. Whoever says "I know him" but does not keep his commandments is a liar, and the truth is not in him, but whoever keeps his word, in him truly the love of God is perfected. By this we may know that we are in him: whoever says he abides in him ought to walk in the same way in which he walked.

First, we can say that John makes his epistolary intentions clear, "I am writing these things to you [pl.] so that you [pl.] may not sin." John's primary purpose is in shaping the moral life of the community, as a concrete expression of the love of God, that the love of God might be "perfected" (τελειόω).[56] We could describe this as spiritual and moral formation. The obvious import of this verse has historically been lost on various interpreters who understand John's primary purpose as either rebuffing christological heresy or community boundary maintenance. There is little doubt that John is doing both of these, but neither of these activities provides an adequate explanation for the epistle as

---

56. In ancient teleological logic a telos names the goal of philosophic pursuit but also speaks to the process and the participatory enjoyment of the telos in the midst of process, i.e., on the path to the full telos. This corresponds closely to a Christian eschatological already/not yet experience of the enjoyment of the fruits of salvation now as a proleptic participation of salvation in "perfection" in the future. The English term "perfected" only carries the sense of the final state of the perfected thing and does not include any connotation of the process involved.

a whole. John understands the work of Christ as "the righteous one"[57] in the realization of both spiritual and moral freedom, through "abiding" in Christ and communion with God as the undifferentiated pure light. So it is natural for John to expect that the gospel will bring freedom from sin.

At the same time, it does not bring an absolute freedom from sin. As John says earlier, the one who claims to be without sin is self-deceived and denies the truth of God (cf. 1:8, 10). But John reassures us that we have an advocate (ὁ παράκλητος) with the Father, who is the propitiation for our sins, freeing us from guilt, shame, and punishment. John understands this propitiation to restore communion with God and to bring moral freedom by deconstructing the influence of sin in determining the individual's self-understanding and outward movement in moral action. This is the result of "abiding" in Christ, understood as an eschatological communion with God and his righteous will. This is why John's next move is to connect communion with God to obedience to his will: "we know we have come to know him, if we keep his commandments."

At the same time, the juxtaposition of ideas in these verses can be jarring. John moves directly from the gracious provision for sin to an unqualified call for obedience, where assurance of salvation is dependent on that same obedience. "Whoever says 'I know him' but does not keep his commandments is a liar." But whoever claims to be without sin is also a liar. How are we supposed to put these together? Obviously John is making some allowance for the reality of sin, so whatever "keeping his commandments" means, it is *not* moral perfection. But then why doesn't he say that? And how much obedience is enough?

It is no surprise that John loves antitheses, most famously the duality of light and darkness. As we have said before, these dualities describe an absolute ontological and moral antithesis rooted in the nature of God as light. For morally corrupted human agency this light is a revelation of its own short-comings and failures. But at the same time, through the gospel, this light also reorients the hopes and desires of the heart, forming new connections between desire and action that move toward the light. One of John's tools in fostering this kind of formation is to use antitheses of counterbalancing propositions. Taken *on their own* these propositions are dangerous; but taken together they boundary a creative tension that fosters wisdom by exposing and reforming devotions. So here we have statements that demand unqualified obedience, where we are told to "walk as Jesus walked" in obedience to his commands as

---

57. Again, the christological question is not simply an ontological one, as it would become at Nicaea, but a moral one. Jesus's theanthropic union is expressed in his moral obedience and righteousness. According to John 15 it is both an expression of and a means of his relational communion with the Father.

a sign of our real abiding in him. It would be very easy to misconstrue these verses in a perfectionistic way, especially since John places no qualifiers on his demands for obedience. But John counterbalances these demands with the promise of Jesus as our righteous advocate who cleanses us from sin. So it is clear that we do not have to be crushed by moral failures that reveal how far we are from "walking as Jesus walked." At the same time, John writes to free us from sin and moral complacency, so the consolation of a propitiation for our sins is immediately connected to a demand for absolute obedience. There is an intentional, unresolvable dialectic tension here.

Various misunderstandings come from trying to resolve this tension into a formula that always amounts to "just do your best" or "as long as your heart is in the right place." The tension John creates is meant to save us from the errors of perfectionism and moral complacency, but it is also meant to foster the wholehearted pursuit of righteousness as an expression of communion with God. This is why John speaks in the language of unqualified obedience and links that obedience as both an expression of abiding in Jesus and fostering that abiding. This is precisely what we saw in John 15, where abiding produces fruit, and intentional fruit bearing produces abiding. So John can say: "By this we may know that we are in him: whoever says he abides in him ought to walk in the same way in which he walked."

Once again a Right ARM approach to this text saves us from carving it up into "theology" and "ethics," and opens us up to the wisdom intentions of John. This enables us to recognize the necessity of this tension in the ways that it shapes actions, reasons, and motivations. This also means we will be able to resist the temptation to "resolve" this tension and deconstruct how it functions as wisdom.

Conclusion

In these examples we have seen Paul and John engage in paraenetic wisdom discourse to facilitate spiritual formation—remolding the convictions, affections, and actions of Christian communities. They do this in response to communal threats that are at once theological and moral. And so their responses treat theological error and moral vices not as discrete challenges but as one integral threat. They meet this threat in a way that fosters wisdom—a realignment of theological understanding that gives reasons and motivations for moral action.

So, for example, in Romans 6:1–14 we saw Paul understanding the significance of Jesus's death as an apocalyptic moral victory of righteousness over the forces of sin and death. Paul understands this event as having both theological and moral significance. While the implication he draws is a moral one, where participation in the death of Jesus initiates an effective break with the power of sin, the significance of his death is inexorably tied to his resurrection as the eschatological inauguration of the kingdom of God.

The theological and moral cannot be separated without irreparable damage to our understanding of Paul and his understanding of the work of God in Christ.

The agendas of these texts move quickly beyond communicating orthodoxy; they have much deeper concerns in mind. Their purpose is the spiritual formation of God's people as a community that comports itself to the "moral excellence and efficacious purity" of God, revealed in Christ and communicated by the Spirit. From this we can see that reading strategies that carve up epistles into "theology" and "ethics" create distorted interpretations of these epistles that blind us to their formative intentions as wisdom aimed at spiritual formation.

CONCLUSION

Augustine, in a short treatise on homiletics and biblical hermeneutics, famously taught that all scriptural interpretation should yield the fruit of love—the love of God and the love of neighbor. As he says, "Anyone who thinks that he has understood the divine scriptures or any part of them, but cannot by his understanding build up his double love of God and neighbour, has not yet succeeded in understanding them."[1] Augustine built this principle on Jesus's teaching on the "greatest commandment" in Matthew 22:34–40—that the whole of the law and the prophets can be summarized in the commands to love God and neighbor (cf. Rom. 13:8–10).[2]

While Augustine's hermeneutical principle is often cited with approval, it is also, often in the same breath, written off as a sentimental notion of a bygone era, treated like a courtship ritual from the nineteenth century—quaint but irrelevant. We are prone to see Augustine as simply squeezing the Scriptures into a pious mold, drawing a simple moral from a very diverse collection of texts. But the fact that he goes on in the same work to advance

1. Augustine, *On Christian Teaching*, trans. R. P. H. Green, Oxford World's Classics (Oxford: Oxford University Press, 2008), 27. Brenda Deen Schildgen, "Hermeneutics," in *The Oxford Guide to the Historical Reception of Augustine*, ed. Karla Pollmann (Oxford: Oxford University Press, 2013), 1126, refers to this work as "the first fully developed hermeneutics of the Christian era," which "became a guidebook for reading, exegesis, and preaching for a millennium."

2. Very likely Augustine also had Rom. 5:5b, one of his favorite verses, in mind as well: "God's love [ἡ ἀγάπη τοῦ θεοῦ] has been poured into our hearts through the Holy Spirit who has been given to us." Augustine took ἡ ἀγάπη τοῦ θεοῦ as both a subjective genitive (love from God) and an objective genitive (love for God), with the emphasis on the latter. So he saw love for God (and neighbor, as the image of God) as the primary focus of the gift of the Spirit and in this the transformation of the soul proclaimed and effected in the gospel. This understanding is foundational for his hermeneutical expectation that the Scriptures engender love of God and neighbor.

a highly developed and seminal theory of semiotics[3] should give us pause in concluding he is a biblicist simpleton.[4] Augustine understood all Scripture as wisdom—as something that trained convictions and devotions—and that the goal of wisdom is love. As he says: "Scripture enjoins nothing but love, and censures nothing but lust, and moulds men's minds accordingly. . . . By love I mean the impulse of one's mind to enjoy God on his own account; and by lust I mean the impulse of one's mind to enjoy oneself and one's neighbour and any corporeal thing not on account of God. What unbridled lust does to corrupt a person's own mind and body is called wickedness; what it does to harm another person is called wrongdoing."[5]

Augustine believed that the Scriptures "enjoined" love as the central Christian virtue, and so necessarily Scripture's purpose is the moral and spiritual formation of God's people. He understood this as a statement of what the Bible is, not simply a beneficial *use* for it. From this he finds Jesus's summary of the law a cogent summary of a Christian comportment to the Scriptures. Augustine sees a profound hermeneutical principle in Jesus's exegetical argument.[6] Jesus's summary of the law is not only a summary of the *content* of the law but a statement of its *purpose*. This is why Augustine is perfectly serious in believing that the purpose of the Bible is to mold the hearts of God's people to love others and love God. He does not mean that this is what it constantly teaches, but that the primary purpose of the Scriptures is to foster virtue, and especially the virtue of love.

My purpose here is not to defend or promote Augustine's hermeneutical key, but I do hope that this book will at least lend a degree of plausibility to

---

3. Cf. John N. Deely, *Four Ages of Understanding: The First Postmodern Survey of Philosophy from Ancient Times to the Turn of the Twenty-First Century*, Toronto Studies in Semiotics (Toronto: University of Toronto Press, 2001), 215,

> The idea of *sign* as a general notion, which we today take more or less for granted, did not exist before the fourth century AD, when it appeared in the Latin language as a proposal in the writings of Augustine. With Augustine we encounter for the first time the general idea of the sign as applicable equally to natural phenomena like clouds and cultural phenomena like words or buttons. Thus was launched in philosophical tradition a line of speculation that was both the first of the Latin initiatives in philosophy and the one that took the whole of the Latin age to reach maturity. (Cf. Andrea Catellani, "Signs and Semiotics," in *The Oxford Guide to the Historical Reception of Augustine*, ed. Karla Pollmann [Oxford: Oxford University Press, 2013], 1739–45)

4. As in the irresponsible pronouncement that "Augustine knows what Scripture will say before he begins to read it." James J. O'Donnell, "*Doctrina Christiana, De*," in *Augustine through the Ages: An Encyclopedia*, ed. Allan D. Fitzgerald (Grand Rapids: Eerdmans, 1999), 280.

5. Augustine, *On Christian Teaching*, 76.

6. We tend to forget that Jesus is actually making an exegetically based hermeneutical argument, using key elements of the Torah to provide a hermeneutic key to understanding the whole of the Hebrew Bible. Cf. Wolfgang Schrage, *The Ethics of the New Testament*, trans. David E. Green (Philadelphia: Fortress, 1988), 68–87.

his approach, whether we are inclined to adopt it wholeheartedly or partially or not at all. I find Augustine's assumption that the purpose of Scripture is to foster virtue a compelling account of the nature of the Bible and a fruitful interpretive catalyst. I have endeavored to demonstrate in the previous chapters that the Bible is wisdom, aimed at spiritual formation, and that this approach is exegetically fruitful.

Summary: Part One—Tilling the Soil

In part 1 we addressed some foundational questions of particular importance in laying a foundation for developing a hermeneutic of wisdom; our work there involved both critique and construction in the areas of epistemology (knowing and reading), metaphysics (being and doing), and ethics (law and gospel). Our goal in chapter 1 was to form a compelling account of a transformational fiduciary comportment to the biblical text. To get there we needed to recap our common modern and postmodern heritage in the area of epistemology, and especially how these epistemological traditions assume different understandings of the knower and the known—the subject and object in knowing—and how these epistemological comportments translate into biblical hermeneutics as distinctive conceptions of the shared space between reader and text.

We saw that modern conceptions of hermeneutics understand the reader as outside and above the text. Modern epistemology defines the knower as a "sovereign subject" who lives in a self-referential, self-sustaining space, where knowledge is objective, dispassionate, and has no power in itself to affect the knower. In this context understanding entails mastery over a field of inquiry. This translates into hermeneutical methodologies that objectify the text and harvest it as a repository of various forms of information: theological ideas, historical information, and ethical principles. The subject is then in a place to dispose of this information as he or she sees fit: to construct a history of the religion of ancient Israel, a theology of Mark, a Christian ethic, or a NT theology. In NT studies this primarily manifested itself in historical research into the origins of early Christianity and a concern for the genealogy of doctrinal beliefs as they are witnessed to in NT literature. Such research necessarily excludes the questions of how the NT literature might determine the existence of the researcher. Questions of how the text functions as wisdom are excluded from the start by a modern comportment to the text.

While postmodern approaches to biblical research have very different operating principles, they still embody this modernist comportment of treating the text as an object to be mastered. Both modern and postmodern hermeneutics subdue the text's intentionality as a wisdom text and place the reader above the text to determine what in it might be appropriated as valuable. Still, postmodern approaches have a more complex understanding of the space between the reader and the text. Postmodern theories flatly reject the modernist notion of an objective (*wissenschaftlich*) reader who reads objectively and dispassionately. They also reject an understanding of the text as a neutral storehouse of information to be ransacked. Because they understand all knowledge as a social construct, postmodern approaches recognize the agency of the text, primarily within sociological categories of boundary maintenance and community sustainability. Textual intentionality is understood as maintaining a privileged place for an "in-group" over and against multiple "out-groups." Some postmodern projects stop here and, placing one foot back into our modern heritage, understand this sociological picture as something that can be understood as a historical phenomenon from a critical distance. Other postmodern methodologies recognize the agency of both text and reader and actively suppress and redirect textual agency into something more congenial to the agendas of some contemporary community defined by its sexual orientation, race, political affiliation, or other sociological signifier. But as we mentioned above, such operations still give the reader, or reading community, the right to determine the viability, extent, and direction of textual agency.

By contrast a hermeneutic of wisdom seeks to be led by textual agency in a comportment of humility and trust, summarized in the Augustinian/Anselmian formula *credo ut intellegam* (I believe in order to understand). As we saw, this corresponds closely to Gadamer's formulation of the process of hermeneutical understanding. Following Heidegger, Gadamer understands all human experience as historically conditioned and therefore limited in scope. From this he recognized that knowledge is only made possible by judgments of preunderstanding that arrive at understanding from partial knowledge.

The central question in postmodernism is whether this form of understanding should legitimately be called knowledge. Because it is founded on "prejudices" (orienting presuppositions), it is no longer "objective." In contrast with many postmodern philosophers who followed, Gadamer argued that some "prejudices" are legitimate, and understanding is a process of beginning with preunderstandings in an engagement with reality that is open to questioning the necessary starting points provided by preunderstanding. In other words, Gadamer sees the epistemological strategy of *credo ut intellegam* as legitimate and, in fact, the only way to describe human understanding. This does not mean that faith always leads to true understanding but simply that faith is a necessary condition for understanding.

Real understanding, as Gadamer conceived it, is an experience shaped by an inherited habituated comportment, a tradition, in which engagement with reality is *directed* by that tradition but *not determined* by that tradition. In biblical hermeneutics this means that we read from the standpoint of a tradition (most often disclosed in the inherited questions we use to interrogate texts). Gadamer argues that real understanding comes in an engagement with a text that has been generative of traditions but with an openness to the distance between the text and the tradition. An authoritative text has the capacity to interrogate both the reader and the traditions they utilize to read the text. It is this openness to meeting the text as other that Gadamer sees as the touchstone of fruitful, attentive hermeneutical engagement.

The other critical insight of Gadamer was that "application" is never a separate or second phase in the process of understanding a text. Application determines our understanding from the beginning and throughout the process of reading. This is a denial of the modern notion that the meaning of the text is objectively accessible apart from the question of how the text might determine the reader. Gadamer labels all hermeneutical constructs that envision application as a separate final step in interpretation, and the whole separation of "meaning" and "significance," a modern fiction. He rightly understands the methodological separation of being and action in interpretation as naive wishful thinking that does not actually exclude application in practice but merely incorporates it covertly in the interpretive process.

From these elements we can envision a legitimate fiduciary encounter with the text that recognizes its formative wisdom intentionality and seeks to be shaped by it. This recognizes both the nature of the text as wisdom and our historically conditioned access to the text. It also recognizes the nature of the text as a means of grace by which God effectively communicates his gracious presence to his people for the purpose of their spiritual formation.

In chapter 2 we examined a foundational element in the Western intellectual tradition—the dichotomy between being and doing. Going back to Plato and Aristotle, this tradition has located being and knowledge on one side of a fence separating it from action. This distinction was rooted in a theological understanding in which god was identified with self-referential reason. In anthropology this necessarily led to a prioritization of human rationality over human agency,[7] where agency can find *legitimacy* in rationality, but never

---

7. This theological framework not only prioritized reason over actions but problematized emotions and desires, which the doctrine of the aseity of God excluded from the divine nature, and often set emotions over against reason, especially in the Platonic and Stoic traditions.

necessity.[8] This basic antithesis is deeply embedded at a *presuppositional* level in the Western (especially modern) tradition and therefore difficult to access as a belief. But it has given birth to various methodological children characterized by the dichotomies of theology/ethics, indicative/imperative, and meaning/application.

As we saw, the primary liabilities with this antithesis in biblical herme-neutics are, first, that we are approaching a text that is representative of an intellectual tradition that does not recognize or endorse this antithesis. And so our intellectual constructs and reading methodologies necessarily impose dichotomies where none exist and ignore connections that are present. Sec-ond, these connections are vital for understanding how these texts function as wisdom. The goal of wisdom is the restoration of human agency in a will that acts in conformity with redeemed devotions and convictions. And so wisdom operates at the intersection of being and doing. When that connec-tion is severed, the text as wisdom disappears.

The repair of this malady, as Barth understood, can only come in the retrieval of divine agency in the Christian understanding of God and his creative-redeeming agency, revealed in the person of Jesus. This then opens up a space for redefining human agency as a unity of being and doing. This also affords us an opportunity to reassess our hermeneutical presuppositions, to allow for divine agency and to appreciate the function of the biblical text as wisdom encouraging the formation of human agency in a unity of being and action in the habituation of reformed convictions, loves, and actions.

As Gadamer argued, application can never be an independent element or second-level exercise in interpretation. It is not simply that a lack of ap-plication is an incomplete act of interpretation, which it is, but that, because of the nature of the text as wisdom, the naive methodological exclusion of application simply means that questions of application impose themselves covertly on the interpreter who aims to "just say what the text says," which leads to miscontruals of textual intentionality. All of this is simply essential to the historically conditioned nature of both the text and the interpreter and the interpreter's comportment to the intentionality of the text. Gadamer's approach of engaging in a dialectic engagement that recognizes the mutual intentionality of both text and reader, contextualized within a Christian metaphysic that does not separate being and doing, creates the possibility of treating the text according to its nature as wisdom. In this way the text is

8. This is precisely the gulf that Kant, unsuccessfully, tried to breach with his invention of the "categorical imperative." But without a new metaphysic, these imperatives are only moral conventions, not necessary imperatives that must be followed.

freed to operate as a means of grace to communicate the loving righteousness of God to his people.

In the chapter on law and gospel (chapter 3) we saw how a strong antithesis between law and gospel fundamentally undermines the function of the Bible as wisdom. While this antithesis is very good at preserving the fundamental truth that salvation is an unmerited gift of God, it automatically casts suspicion on all attempts at Christian obedience as covert acts of legalistic self-justification. While it proclaims gospel forgiveness, it denies (whether intentionally or not) the gospel's promises of redeemed affections and redeemed agency because it removes all moral demands from the realm of gospel and ascribes them to law. Such an antinomian approach leaves the Christian feeling forgiven, but alienated from the commands of Jesus.

Adolf Schlatter rightly saw that the issue here is not simply carving out a "proper place" for works but a question about the nature of the gospel itself. His insight was to see that in Paul's understanding, especially as formulated in Romans, the gospel proclamation is not only about what the sinner receives from God but about the eschatological revelation of the "righteousness of God" (δικαιοσύνη θεοῦ) and that his righteousness is revealed in his acts of *bringing* judgment and salvation (cf. Ps. 98:1–9). This means that the good news of God is that his salvation restores us to communion with him through, and not in spite of, his righteousness. We are saved *by* the righteousness of God, not saved *from* it. And so our communion with him is not only with his mercy (in forgiveness) but with his righteousness, which establishes communion and demands repentance in the same breath. The gospel is simultaneously and perpetually both gift and call, and if we sever one from the other we have lost a defining tension of the gospel itself. But we have to admit there is a tension here and not attempt to resolve it (cf. Exod. 34:6–7).

We went on to catalog four ways in which this tension often gets "fixed" by severing the necessary connection in the gospel between free grace and acts of obedience. The first, just outlined above, is antinomianism, which takes the justification antithesis of faith/works and universalizes it to all of soteriology. In this context only faith can be good in attaching itself to the promises of forgiveness, but all works are ultimately delegitimized because there can be no necessary link between faith and works. Works are necessarily tied to the demands of the law, from which the gospel frees us.

The modern romantic cousin of antinomianism is authenticity, which prioritizes the integrity of passionate internal motivations as the only necessary mark of genuine moral agency. Like antinomianism, it is suspicious of the demands of the gospel, especially when it understands them as calls to duty (i.e., acts of obedience that do not arise spontaneously from the heart).

Authenticity, then, uses the same law/gospel paradigm to avoid any *necessary* connection between faith and obedience. It is not averse to moral action but only endorses those actions that proceed from authentic feelings.

On the other side of the fence of confusion we saw legalism and moralism. Both of these strategies begin by recognizing that the gospel proclaims and demands something more than an internal psychological state (whether feeling forgiven or feeling authentic); but both implement moral demands in ways that compromise the connection between grace and obedience. Legalism, we saw, is built on a deficient understanding of grace. While legalism is often understood as earning salvation through good works, and it is often thought that the solution to it is grace (often antinomian grace), in fact, legalism can only exist where grace is already present, either promised or presumed. But legalism understands that grace as dormant and in need of a catalyst in order to be realized. In a covenantal context, where laws define the covenantal boundaries of blessing, law keeping becomes the necessary catalyst for salvation. Obedience does not create communion with God, but it makes the promise of God's communion possible; obedience is the necessary condition that makes the release of grace possible. Ultimately, legalism is defined by its ambivalent understanding of grace and its desire to control the grace of God—to limit it and make it accord with our cultural notions of God favoring the good. It inevitably produces what Paul catalogs as the vices of self-importance, conceit, arrogance, and social strife, all built on an inner psychology characterized by shame and rigidity.

In a similar vein, moralism also takes seriously the gospel commands of moral reform, but it severs the link between faith and works by divorcing moral commands from their biblical contexts and gospel motivations. Instead, moralism relies on the logic of modern deontological (Kantian) ethics, which creates a "universal ethic" that consists of a list of self-evident and doable moral duties. Moralism transposes the challenge of the gospel into a program of self-improvement. Like legalism, it also assumes a deficient understanding of grace that ascertains that God is more pleased with us because we have made ourselves polite, hardworking, and financially responsible. Moralism aggrandizes the project of self-improvement and social respectability by labeling it the gift of God. Like legalism, moralism is actually highly ambivalent to the reality of God's grace and places the soteriological locus of control within the grasp of the human moral agent. In this way moralism fatally constrains the call of the gospel that fundamentally decenters the self.

In Jesus's self-identification as the "true vine" in John 15:1–11 we saw that our proper comportment to Jesus is the key to the question of how faith and works are meant to coexist. Jesus's command to his disciples is to abide/remain in him—to pursue the relational proximity and communion that he has established with us. Abiding in Christ is the antidote to legalism and moralism because both are built on a fundamentally deficient understanding of grace as operationalized by works of covenantal obedience or self-improvement. This is why Jesus stresses that fruit bearing is dependent on abiding, as opposed to abiding that is the result of fruit bearing. Abiding is given freely, but also commanded. It is both a gift and a call, simultaneously, not as a sequence.

At the same time, Jesus goes on to teach that abiding is actually a product of fruit bearing. So if you want to abide, you need to bear fruit. Here we find Jesus turning to the errors of antinomianism and authenticity, which are happy to explain abiding in terms of an internal experience of communion with Jesus. But Jesus always teaches that obedience is *necessary*, not only as a fruit of communion but as that which sustains it. Amazingly, Jesus says this is even true of his relationship with the Father: "If you keep my commandments, you will abide in my love, just as I have kept my Father's commandments and abide in his love" (John 15:10). But Jesus still believes that obedience does not create communion, and so it cannot be our starting point. The starting point must be abiding. But there is no abiding apart from obedience. The tension here is deliberate, and the proper understanding of how the grace of God transforms human agency (i.e., the relationship between faith and works) is absolutely dependent on the preservation of that tension. Any move to "resolve" that tension is a failure to understand the gospel as both free gift and uncompromising demand—as the proclamation of the gracious righteousness of God that gives us life.

Summary: Part Two—Planting the Seeds

So then, how can we read the biblical text in ways that preserve this essential gospel tension? We began, in chapter 4, with a theoretical exploration of the genre of gospel and how that genre functions as wisdom in spiritual formation. We found that the gospel genre itself betrays its formative agenda in its affinity with the ancient wisdom genre of βίος. Ancient biography consciously focuses on the virtues of its subjects as formative exemplars for readers on the path of virtue. We argued that this signals not only the expectation that Jesus, as the central character of the narrative, is in some way a formative exemplar for Christian devotions and actions, but it also signals the formative intention of the Gospel narratives per se. This means that we should expect the Gospels to employ multiple narrative tools that facilitate their agenda to shape the affections, convictions, and actions of readers around the person of Jesus out of obedient reverence for him.

The Gospels foster wisdom, where wisdom is understood as a skill of discernment active in moral deliberations to perceive the right course of action by applying general principles within a teleological frame of reference (i.e., something close to the Aristotelian understanding of φρόνησις). One of the ways in which the Gospels do this is in their preservation and transmission of the teachings of Jesus, which are centered on the kingdom of God as the orienting reality for shaping our allegiances and actions. This is the manner in which the Gospels teach wisdom directly.

Of course the canonical Gospels are not simply collections of Jesus's teachings; they are historical narratives with characters, plot, and dialogues. With the help of literary critics, especially Martha Nussbaum, we saw that narratives are actually purposely built for wisdom formation, although the way they do this is more implicit than explicit. The story arc (plot) of a narrative gives a teleological moral vision that drives the narrative toward a conclusion and makes certain choices intelligible and praiseworthy (or agonizing). Whether they want to or not, all narratives (oral, written, or visual) do this. It is inherent in the ways that we interact with narratives in their correspondence to the narrative frame of human experience.

In addition, Nussbaum points to three ways in which narratives participate in and foster wisdom. The first is that narratives are very good at accessing the tensions among incommensurable goods and between incommensurable systems of value. This is at the core of narrative tensions, where characters face moral challenges of having to choose between competing goods or competing allegiances to ways of valuing the good life. This touches on a key Aristotelian insight: that not all goods are commensurable, as though all possible objects for our affection existed on a moral number line that would tell us that friendship is always more important than family or vice versa. Because each moral situation is unique, we need the skill of wisdom (φρόνησις) to discern the right choice in a given set of circumstances. These choices are the engine of narratives and a way in which readers who engage with narratives are schooled in discernment, in how such choices are made well or made poorly.

In addition, Nussbaum argues that narratives form wisdom because they focus on particulars and engage us emotionally. Narratives teach wisdom in their attentiveness to detail, especially in details that guide us in discerning the dispositions and motivations of characters and in sympathizing with the dilemmas they experience in their struggles to live with integrity and pursue what they believe will bring them joy. Even when this pursuit is a miserable failure, narratives form us in our habituated skill of discernment. Narratives do this not through teaching abstract ethical principles but by attending to the particulars that give rise to moral dilemmas. They ask us to experience this in an empathetic way, to feel our way through a dilemma *with* the characters involved. This is important because wisdom is not only a rational faculty but utilizes emotions as moral judgments foundational for moral deliberations. Narratives do not teach us right and wrong as ideas or principles; they teach us to appreciate and admire goodness and to disdain and reject vice. This is critical to the formative function of narratives. Virtue is taking pleasure in and loving the good, not simply a conviction to do what is right. So narratives operate at a subterranean level to shape our moral affections—to value certain objects, pursuits, and character traits, and to desire them for ourselves. At the same time they also ask us to despise certain people because of their mean-spirited, vengeful arrogance (or some other collection of vices).

The Gospels as historical narrative are no different.[9] They ask us to attend to particulars and characters and to sympathize with certain characters and despise others. Some of them face impossible choices of core allegiances and what path they should pursue. At the center of all this action stands Jesus (sometimes tenderhearted, other times hard as stone), rejected by the religious leadership of Israel and followed by fishermen and prostitutes. Some come to him for healing and get more than they are looking for, but no one has a neutral encounter with him. All who encounter him are met with a choice of how that encounter will define their lives, either as followers or haters. And Jesus himself will have his own allegiances ultimately tested in his messianic mission to die for his people. In all these things, the Gospels project a moral space in which certain virtues and actions become intelligible and laudable, while others feel incoherent and sordid. This is how the Gospel narratives function as wisdom.

We put these narratival insights into practice in chapter 5 by looking at a few key texts in an effort to model some exegetical tools that help us access the Gospels as wisdom. We began with Mark 5:21–43, a pericope typical of "one-off" characters who encounter Jesus, where Jairus, a synagogue ruler with a dying daughter, and a nameless woman with a chronic bleeding disorder both meet Jesus. Both come to Jesus in desperate need and with some kind of faith that Jesus can help them. We saw that Mark invites our participatory identification with these characters through our sympathies for them and empathy with them as readers who also come to Jesus in need and with faith. Narratives invite this kind of participation, and Mark uses it to realize his goal of forming the faith of his readers.

---

9. Although, of course, as historical narrative they can be distinguished from fictive narrative by the ways in which they claim historical referentiality.

The unclean woman with the bleeding disorder shows a strong belief in Jesus's power to heal, manages to touch him through the crowd, and is instantly healed of her ailment. Mark describes "power going out from Jesus," and it stops him in his tracks. He asks, "Who touched me?" The woman, who was hoping for a secret healing, comes forward "in fear and trembling," expecting public exposure and derision. Instead Jesus affirms her for her faith and, crucially, as a person with dignity and value, worthy of respect and affection—especially evident in Jesus's addressing her as "daughter." But while all this is going on, Jairus's daughter succumbs to her illness, and messengers arrive with the news that she has died. They pose the rhetorical question, which actually gives us a clue to Jairus's internal state, "Why trouble the teacher any further?" Jesus's response is a mix of compassion and implacable demand: "Do not fear. Only believe." Even though the narrative ends with the raising of the dead girl, Jesus gives no hints or promises of this outcome to Jairus, only a call to fearless dependence on Jesus's benevolence and power.

Mark's agenda for us as readers is to experience how Jesus responds to our faith—with unrestricted enjoyment and uncompromising demands. As we learned, in the Gospel narratives faith is always partial and in process. Jesus celebrates faltering, mustard-seed faith in the same breath that he demands deeper allegiance. There is always room to grow. As we saw, while this duality of Jesus's acceptance and demand may seem inscrutable, in fact it situates faith as a virtue between the vices of perfectionism and sloth, both of which reserve the locus of control for the moral agent. Mark seeks to habituate an understanding of faith that attaches itself to the benevolent rule of Jesus in a move that decenters the self and saves it from self-deceptions and idolatry. This is the kind of spiritual formation the Gospels facilitate as wisdom narratives.

We saw similar dynamics at work in the Lazarus narrative in John 11, which focuses on the interactions of Jesus with Mary and Martha. John begins the narrative by introducing an intractable tension where Jesus, after being asked by the sisters to come and heal Lazarus, waits for Lazarus to die, allegedly because he "loves Martha and her sister and Lazarus" (John 11:5). John purposely creates a scene where Jesus looks callous and indifferent to the suffering of these sisters and brother while telling us he really loves them. John's purpose is to engage not only our faith in Jesus but also our doubts and fears, especially as they arise in the context of suffering and grief.

We can see this clearly in the complaint that Martha immediately brings to Jesus when he finally arrives in Bethany (after Lazarus has been dead for four days). "Lord, if you had been here, my brother would not have died" (John 11:21). Martha is grieving, and Jesus let her down. At the same time, she still has faith. "But even now I know that whatever you ask from God,

God will give you" (John 11:22). She wants her brother back. She wants her problem solved. She has faith in Jesus but also feels ambivalent because she is disappointed. So she doesn't explicitly ask for him to raise her brother. If Jesus really cares he will know what she wants and give it to her. Jesus's response names Martha's desire but also asks her to take a step of faith. "Your brother will rise again." Martha takes the safe option. She makes a general pious remark about Lazarus being raised on the last day. Jesus tries to call her back one last time. "I am the resurrection and the life" (John 11:25). The resurrection is not an idea, hope, or future event; it is Jesus himself. Of course he can give life to Lazarus. Martha confesses what she can affirm in the moment, "I believe that you are the Christ, the Son of God, who is coming into the world." While Martha makes a perfect christological confession by Johannine standards, she simply cannot go where Jesus invites her.

When Mary comes to Jesus she confronts Jesus with the same complaint as Martha, but the tenor of the words has completely changed. Mary does not demand Jesus fix her problem. Her brother is dead, and even though Jesus failed to come and save him, she trusts in Jesus's benevolence. She doesn't understand why her brother is dead or why Jesus didn't heal him, but she doesn't allow this to shake her conviction that Jesus does love her and her brother and sister. Her grief becomes an invitation, and Jesus accepts the invitation. His own grief and anger are visible to all, and they drive him to the tomb to raise Lazarus. Through his engagement with Mary, and in his acceptance of her invitation to enter into her grief, John has managed to create a scene where we actually believe that Jesus does love Mary, Martha, and Lazarus. At the same time, John has no intention of "explaining" why Jesus waited. It is still a mystery, but that mystery is given a new context by the tears of Jesus at the tomb of Lazarus.

Once again, we see a narrative expertly used to form our comportment to the person of Jesus through a process of participatory engagement with characters who encounter him. John wants to form faith in the context of doubts and suffering, and he wants us to see ourselves most likely identifying with Martha in her ambivalence but recognizing something beautiful and desirable about Mary openly bringing her grief to Jesus as an expression of her faith in his love and compassion. And it is actually her grief, along with her fellow mourners' grief, that is the instrument of accessing Jesus's own grief. While John leaves our theodical questions unanswered, he has reshaped our convictions about Jesus's presence in our sufferings and his participation in our grief. Only narratives are capable of this kind of intricate spiritual formation.

We followed this study with an examination of the Beatitudes in Matthew 5:3–12. We saw that interpretations of the Beatitudes and the Sermon on the

Mount have historically been hamstrung by the dichotomies of indicative/ imperative and law/gospel, but we also saw that recognizing the Sermon and the Beatitudes as wisdom discourses moves us past these interpretive logjams. The Beatitudes enumerate and promote central virtues that exemplify the comportment of discipleship in the kingdom of heaven. These virtues are set within an eschatological horizon that makes them intelligible and desirable. This is critically important because the virtues that Jesus extols are both countercultural and counterintuitive because they question cultural idolatries and decenter the self in a repentant move toward God and the realization of his kingdom.

So, for example, Jesus's blessing on "the poor in spirit" and the promise that "theirs is the kingdom of heaven" goes against the common expectation that the favor of God is for the spiritually wealthy: the wealthy, the righteous, the powerful, the well adjusted, and the beautiful. By contrast, Jesus reserves the blessing of God for the spiritually poor: the destitute, the wayward, the sinner, the broken souls who know their desperate and perpetual need for the filling of God. These are truly joyful (μακάριος) because they, and not the rich and righteous, are favored by God and incorporated into his kingdom. (This reversal of the humble being exalted and the proud being under judgment is central to the gospel proclamation of Jesus.) This virtue embodies a disposition that humbles itself before God as the source of and giver of life in a perpetual recognition of our place of need—that we never have an inherent ability to produce or procure life for ourselves.

The counterfeit vice, which tries to imitate spiritual poverty, is the sense of spiritual worthlessness. (As we saw, every virtue has an opposing vice and a counterfeit vice.) Spiritual worthlessness has the appearance of humility but is in reality a shield to guard the self from the gracious righteousness of God. This vice denies the path whereby the sinner can receive the grace of God. Its commitment to its own deep unworthiness is a self-protective pride that is deeply committed to finding security in the sphere of the self. Spiritual worthlessness defines the self as essentially corrupt and irredeemable and therefore beyond the pale of redemption. It is a counterfeit humility that operates as a powerful means of relational control because it only allows for responses of rejection and condemnation.[10]

10. This is a common strategy for those who have suffered relational trauma and betrayal, because it protects the self from future harm (by insulating the self from relational engagement) and possesses huge explanatory power in the realm of relational betrayal. (Betrayals are easier to swallow if they were in some sense "deserved.") Unfortunately, this vice of spiritual worthlessness is oftentimes promoted in the contemporary church as a virtue, and untold spiritual harms have resulted from it.

By contrast, true spiritual poverty finds in the gracious will of God the freedom to bring its sinful, crippled soul into the presence of God with an expectation of embrace, not because God is constrained by our repentance but because it is his pleasure to give life. In this way the virtue of spiritual poverty frees the self to be embraced as it is and to pursue the life of righteousness without the pretensions of perfectionism or a self-authenticating purity of will. Ultimately, this virtue frees us to pursue and enjoy the glory of God as an end in itself, not simply as an instrumental good.

Alongside the disposition of spiritual poverty, we saw the Beatitudes list other virtues: grief, meekness, hungering and thirsting for righteousness, mercy, purity of heart, and peacemaking. As with all ancient understandings of virtues, these dispositions are not reducible to ethical commands, and they are mutually sustaining. These are character traits, instilled in the soul through a reshaping of convictions, desires, and actions. They are habituated through action but never reducible to actions, duties, or mindless habits. From this we can see how the Beatitudes function as a wisdom discourse that supplies a set of virtues along with an eschatological counternarrative that lends intelligibility to these counterintuitive and countercultural virtues.

Chapter 5 concluded with a look at the moral world projected by Mark's Gospel with the aid of categories supplied by Richard Hays. Instead of cataloging the ethical teaching of Mark, Hays's concern is with the moral vision of Mark, a value-laden depiction of the world encoded in the Gospel narrative. Hays summarizes his findings in six propositions:

1. The world according to Mark is *a world torn open by God.*
2. Because the cosmic conflict is under way, *time becomes compressed.*
3. God's apocalyptic invasion of the world has also wrought an inversion: *God has reversed the positions of insiders and outsiders.*
4. Mark's Gospel *redefines the nature of power and the value of suffering.*
5. Mark's vision of the moral life is profoundly *ironic.*
6. Mark's lack of closure calls for *active response* from the reader.[11]

These six propositions provide an excellent summary of Mark's "moral vision" that provides a set of moral norms and practical expectations for the life of discipleship. It does more than teach doctrines or give principles; it fosters a picture of the world that fosters certain dispositions and impels

---

11. See Richard B. Hays, *The Moral Vision of the New Testament: Community, Cross, New Creation, A Contemporary Introduction to New Testament Ethics* (San Francisco: HarperSanFrancisco, 1996), 88–90.

action. It is a value-laden world that demands allegiance or rejection. For example, Hays says, "the world according to Mark is *a world torn open by God.*" This sets the tone for an apocalyptic moral vision in which all social mores and institutions come under judgment, and their prominence in determining responsible agency is immediately relativized. The new rule of the kingdom of God, which John announced and Jesus enacts, supplants all other allegiances and affections and redirects them onto the person of Jesus as both Lord and Christ. This prescribes a moral space in which every human authority and institution can be questioned, not because authorities and institutions are illegitimate per se (as in many postmodern critiques of power) but because the Gospel narratives subordinate all allegiances under allegiance to Christ. That allegiance is the central integrating devotion that decenters the self and allows us to move toward our neighbors in service, both individually and corporately.

In chapter 6 we turned our attention to the NT genre of epistle, with a focus on how this genre functions as wisdom. Research into ancient epistolary genres over the last few decades has concluded that paraenetic epistles provide the best correlate genre to the epistle of the NT both in terms of form and function. Most importantly for us, the genre of paraenetic epistle is widely recognized as a wisdom genre, primarily because it promotes demonstrable moral progress, where mature moral agency reflects core convictions in a coherent marriage of actions, reasons, and motivations.

The genre of paraenetic epistle dates back to Plato and Aristotle but really developed within the Hellenistic philosophical schools. Paraenetic authors developed numerous literary-rhetorical tools along the way, such as the use of moral exemplars, virtue and vice lists, moral commands and maxims, household instructions (*Haustafeln*), an emphasis on conversion as a life-defining choice, and an integration of moral and philosophical teaching. This epistolary tradition focused on promoting progress (προκοπή) and understood the impediments to progress as deeply habituated vices (intellectual, moral, and emotional). In response, paraenesis was conceived as a complex reeducation of the soul in all these areas.

This translates into literary/rhetorical strategies aimed at the inculcation of three core proficiencies: (1) the development of virtuous habits, (2) rehabilitated affective attachments, and (3) the development of φρόνησις (wisdom/discernment). So, while the purpose of a basic tool such as moral commands might seem straightforward as a means of populating a list of rules, for paraenetic authors the function of moral imperatives was always first and foremost formative. As moderns we tend to look at commands as simply prescribing duties (because we interpret them through the categories of Kantian deontological ethics). In ancient paraenesis the picture is much more complex: commands promote moral habits and, with these habits, the transformation of the affections and the development of practical wisdom.

We also saw that paraenetic authors from the schools often referred back to their students' conversions to philosophy as a life-defining moment, drawing stark contrasts between their life before and after their enlightenment. This strategy was utilized as a way of promoting progress in the process of breaking bad habits and instilling new ones. This was done by associating all that characterized preconversion life with vice and connecting postconversion existence with virtue. This was to help students extricate themselves from well-rehearsed vices that still shaped their desires and actions.

We see the same strategy employed by NT epistolary authors, who often speak of conversion in the language of "old self" and "new self" as a means of promoting a definitive break with past vices that did not simply disappear in conversion. This is where we see that the eschatological tension between the "already" and the "not yet" has huge explanatory power for the tension between the process of sanctification and the declarations of a definitive, one-time event of salvation. So, for example, in Romans 6 Paul can declare that we have both "died to sin" (v. 2) and are "set free from sin" (v. 7) in our union with Christ, and then command us: "Let not sin therefore reign in your mortal body, to make you obey its passions" (v. 12), with the obvious implication that we have not *completely* died to sin nor been completely set free from it. Yet Paul still affirms death to sin as the definitive reality that enables the process of freedom from sin, and in so doing it cuts affective ties to former sins while establishing new affective ties to Christian virtues.

These reflections led us to return to the old dichotomy of being and action and how this paradigm is often used to carve up epistles into "theology" and "ethics." We saw that the most pernicious element in this paradigm is its assumption that "theological" elements in the epistle are directed at addressing doctrinal issues and instilling orthodox convictions, while "ethical" elements address social tensions that have no substantive connection to the theological uncertainties addressed in the epistle. Unfortunately, this (all too common) schema deconstructs how NT epistles function as wisdom. It is precisely where "theology" and "ethics" intersect that effective paraenesis is able to shape individuals and communities in coherent lives of desires, actions, and convictions. We saw that NT epistles address a single communal challenge that has theological and moral facets to it but that these are inseparably linked and addressed as a coherent unity. This means that both "theology" and "ethics" serve the paraenetic goals of reshaping convictions, desires, and actions. "Theology" primarily serves to give reasons and motivations that make certain actions reasonable and intelligible. Likewise, "ethics" not only prescribes duties but promotes the development of practical wisdom (φρόνησις) and reeducates affective attachments to God, self, and other.

We put these insights into practice by working through some exemplary texts in chapter 7. We began by looking at a few sample texts from Ephesians, where we found Paul consistently giving theological grounds and motivations for moral actions. This connection is the engine of spiritual formation that aims at an effective and coherent reforming of human agency in heart, mind, and will. Paul's letters cannot be understood apart from this formative agenda, and when we ignore this connection we misconstrue Paul's theology and inevitably appropriate his moral demands through some form of legalism, moralism, antinomianism, or authenticity (or some mixture of these).

In Romans 6:1–14 Paul dives into a discussion of baptism as the sacramental sign of union with Christ and the correlate topic of dying with Christ and being raised with him. All this is to answer the seemingly straightforward question "Are we to continue in sin that grace may abound?" But Paul's rejection of sin is not based on a consequentialist ethic or a deontological appropriation of the Torah. His answer is our profound and mysterious connection to the death and resurrection of Jesus. Before Paul gives his prohibitions in verses 12–13, he grounds his readers in an eschatological vision of communion with Christ and participation in his death and resurrection. Paul is engaged in a paraenetic wisdom discourse, marrying moral actions to a value-laden vision of the manifestation of the righteousness of God in the apocalyptic events of Jesus's death and resurrection, and his focus is on the Roman church's participation in those events through moral and social actions motivated by love for God and allegiance to his righteousness.

We found that appreciating Paul's formative wisdom agenda helped us in unraveling one of the most difficult exegetical challenges in this passage: Paul's declaration in Romans 6:7 that "the one who has died has been set free [δεδικαίωται] from sin." Interpreters looking for a theological significance for death have been forced to conclude that death itself provides a definitive freedom from sin. But this seems incredibly unlikely given the intimate connection Paul depicts between death and sin. From Romans 5:12 onwards death is the result of and malevolent ally of sin, not the instrument of its defeat. The overthrow of sin and death only comes about through the δικαίωμα of Jesus. It is through participation in his death, as the definitive apocalyptic moral event, that this event becomes effective in the life of the Christian community in its freedom from sin. This is obscured by approaches that fail to recognize this as a wisdom text in which Paul is engaged in spiritual formation, grounding the responsibilities of redeemed moral agency in the apocalyptic vision of the saving work of God in Christ. In this Paul effectively marries moral commands to a theological vision that gives reasons and motivations for moral actions, rendering them intelligible and desirable.

On the surface Galatians, with its emphasis on Paul's defense of his ministry and gospel of justification by faith, appears to be an imposing counter-example that resists a wisdom paradigm. What we found, however, is that Paul has deeper agendas in Galatians than addressing the question of gentile circumcision and defending his mission and message and that these elements of the epistle serve an instrumental role in Paul's formative agendas for the Galatian churches. This is clear in Galatians 5:6, "For in Christ Jesus neither circumcision nor uncircumcision counts for anything, but only faith working through love." For Paul the question of circumcision is not an end in itself. His concern is with the fruit of orthodox devotions, not simply defending orthodox ideas. The necessary fruit of the gospel, its τέλος, is love. For Paul love is the test of gospel orthodoxy. Being justified "by works of the law" produces self-satisfaction, conceit, envy, and communal strife, all of which Paul labels as "works of the flesh," which derail the manifestations of the fruit of the Spirit.

As in Romans 6, Paul turns to the theme of dying with Christ as central to Christian self-understanding and moral action. "I have been crucified with Christ. It is no longer I who live, but Christ who lives in me. And the life I now live in the flesh I live by faith in the Son of God, who loved me and gave himself for me" (Gal. 2:20). In the cross Paul finds a demonstration of the love of Christ but also a recasting of the self whereby delusions of self-sufficiency and ambitious desires for self-promotion and self-protection are put to death. In the cross Paul finds the love of Christ but also the call to love his neighbor, and especially his brothers and sisters in Christ. All this is wrapped up in Paul's understanding of what it means to "live by faith in the Son of God." For Paul this is a transforming eschatological vision that determines his response to the Galatian crisis, which threatens the manifestation of the gracious righteousness of God in the Galatian communities. From this it becomes clear that Paul sees the presenting problem of gentile circumcision as a threat to spiritual formation, which needs an answer that addresses both short-term crises as well as long-term communal and spiritual health. The gospel is under threat in these churches, but not only in their confusion over the proper basis for justification. This is clear enough in the connection Paul makes between a denial of justification and the disruption of community in his confrontation with Peter at Antioch (Gal. 2:11–16). What is at stake is the life of the community, which Paul understands not as an end to be sought in itself but as the goal of the gospel proclamation—the presence of the Spirit redeeming human agency as a demonstration of the eschatological love of God, for his praise and glory.

We saw a similar dynamic at work in 1 John, where christological heresy is tearing at communal life. Like Paul, John addresses this as a single, integrated challenge. The preservation of communal life is not an end in itself, just as christological orthodoxy is not an end in itself, nor can the two questions be dealt with in isolation. John subordinates both of these challenges to his deeper agenda of comporting human agency (both collective and individual) to the glory of God. This becomes clear in the programmatic verse for the letter, "This is the message we have heard from him and proclaim to you, that God is light, and in him is no darkness at all [οὐδεμία]" (1 John 1:5; cf. James 1:17). John understands all of Christian duty to be circumscribed by one's comportment to what Yarbrough labels the "moral excellence and efficacious purity" of God.[12] As John says in the next verse: "If we say we have fellowship with him while we walk in darkness, we lie and do not practice the truth" (1 John 1:6).

Here, again, we see wisdom at work, shaping actions to convictions and affections. But the goal here is not simply to produce right actions or to preserve community. The goal is spiritual formation—remolding the self and human agency to enjoy and glorify God—to experience his "efficacious purity" that brings life and redirects the self toward the other in acts of love and service. John understands all christological misunderstandings and communal infighting as challenges to this singular vision. Like Paul, he understands this demonstration of the loving righteousness of God as the τέλος of the gospel proclamation, where genuine love is understood as *the* eschatological manifestation of the Spirit. This is the moral vision that John imprints on his audience as the frame of reference for all moral action.

From all these epistolary examples, the wisdom agenda of Christian paraenesis becomes clear. These texts are written for the purpose of spiritual formation. They certainly have numerous subordinate agendas attached to this purpose, but too often the history of interpretation has concerned itself solely with these subordinate agendas after severing them from their larger purpose. As we saw, this is a necessary consequence of dividing up epistles into "theology" and "ethics." It is precisely where theology and ethics meet that the integrated wisdom agenda of these epistles becomes transparent, but when this link is cut the epistles' formative wisdom intentionality is immediately hidden from us, and we are only left with the subsidiary purposes of supplying theology and ethical principles. But if we

---

12. Robert W. Yarbrough, *1–3 John*, BECNT (Grand Rapids: Baker Academic, 2008), 50.

recognize the wisdom objective inherent in the form of address—paraenetic epistle—this supplies us with an interpretive schema that opens up to us the formative intentionality of the NT epistles to shape the convictions, affections, and actions of the people of God according to a vision of his loving righteousness and demonstrated in charity and justice in the Christian community's service to others.

Reading Texts, Seeking Wisdom[13]

The central claim of this book is that the Bible is a wisdom text. We have made an extended argument about how and why we should accept this designation for the Gospels and epistles of the NT. A more cursory argument that extends this claim to the remainder of the canon can be found in the appendix that immediately follows. We have seen that the Gospels (appropriating the wisdom genre of βίος) and epistles (appropriating the wisdom genre of paraenetic epistle) are wisdom texts whose purpose is the spiritual formation of their recipients. This is both explicit in the texts themselves (e.g., Luke 1:4; John 20:31; Rom. 1:5; 1 Cor. 2:1–15; Eph. 1:15–23; Phil. 2:12–18; 1 Thess. 4:1–12; Titus 2:1–14; 2 Pet. 3:1–2; 1 John 2:1) and implicit in their literary forms, and ought to be uncontroversial. But as we have seen, the various research methodologies of biblical criticism necessarily exclude this wisdom intentionality from their purview. This is true whether the exegete is sympathetic to the formative wisdom intentions of the text or not; it is methodologically excluded.

Unfortunately this means that our research methods are flawed to the degree that they are not shaped by nature of their object,[14] as all good research methodologies ought to be.[15] Gadamer understood this better than anyone

13. This title is taken from a collection of essays that celebrated the five hundredth anniversary of the Lady Margaret's Professor of Divinity chair at Cambridge, at the time held by my postgraduate supervisor Prof. Graham Stanton. David F. Ford and Graham Stanton, eds., *Reading Texts, Seeking Wisdom: Scripture and Theology* (London: SCM, 2003). The collection reflects Graham's commitment to bringing together biblical scholars and theologians for fruitful interchange.

14. Cf. Sandra M. Schneiders, *The Revelatory Text: Interpreting the New Testament as Sacred Scripture*, 2nd ed. (Collegeville, MN: Liturgical Press, 1999), 25, "I want to reexamine the question of what kind of reality the Bible is in hopes that in the answer to that question will be carried the answers, or at least the beginnings of answers, to the questions of what can count for understanding of this reality, what kind of knowledge of it is possible and desirable, and how we can pursue that knowledge with methodological integrity."

15. This is why, for example, chemists and biologists operate on very different principles in their research practices, and oftentimes one finds a certain level of suspicion (or bewilderment) when they are forced to mingle academically.

else in the twentieth century. Engagement in the humanities requires a different set of tools from other forms of human enquiry. He also understood that
research methodologies are ultimately determinative of research outcomes.
As Schneiders notes:

> The point of H.-G. Gadamer's masterwork, *Truth and Method*, is that when
> method controls thought and investigation the latter may lead to accurate data
> but it does not lead to truth. Method, understood as a preestablished set of
> procedures for investigating some phenomenon, in fact not only *attains* its
> object but *creates* its object. In other words, it determines a priori what kind
> of data can be obtained and will be considered relevant. . . . Method not only
> assures a systematic coverage of certain areas of investigation; it also rules out
> of court any data not discoverable by that method.[16]

The substance of this book has sought to not only argue that the Bible is
wisdom but to develop new methodological tools that help us to see and engage with the biblical text as wisdom. We have seen that such methodologies
produce readings that are not only helpful for spiritual formation but also
fruitful in solving some exegetical challenges that are actually products of
our current methodologies.[17] These new reading strategies make the Scripture
available to us as wisdom—not simply as a beneficial by-product or something
that we can "use" the Bible for—through our recognition of the nature of the
biblical text as wisdom and reading it as such.[18] This method respects and is
led by textual intentionality, and recognizes the Bible as a vehicle of the creative agency of God to realize his effective transforming communion with his
people.[19] A hermeneutic of wisdom opens itself to the expectation of God's
presence in and through the attentive reading of his Word and the realization

---

16. Schneiders, *Revelatory Text*, 23–24. She illustrates in the same passage: "If, for example,
my method of investigation is a ruler, the only scientifically reliable datum that can emerge is
linear dimension. If no other methods are employed, over a long period of time I might even-
tually conclude that the only significant datum about reality is linear dimension and that the
essential scientific definition of reality is in terms of physical extension."

17. Cf. J. de Waal Dryden, "Revisiting Romans 7: Law, Self, and Spirit," *JSPL* 5, no. 1 (2015):
129–51.

18. This distinguishes my approach from the common foundation of the various hermeneutic
strategies collectively referred to as theological interpretation of Scripture. As helpful as these
strategies may be, in general they still abide by the principle that "application" is something
that we add to a neutral text, instead of understanding application as the reappropriation of
the illocutionary force of the text itself.

19. See John Webster, *Holy Scripture: A Dogmatic Sketch*, Current Issues in Theology
(Cambridge: Cambridge University Press, 2003), 5, "'Holy Scripture' is a shorthand term for
the nature and function of the biblical writings in a set of communicative acts which stretch
from God's merciful self-manifestation to the obedient hearing of the community of faith."

of its formative intentionality to rehabilitate our convictions and affections and to remold our moral agency in love for both God and our neighbors. In the end, this is very close to the spiritual formation that Augustine prescribed as the litmus test for a healthy and attentive reading of Scripture—that it facilitates a deeper love of God and love of neighbor.

APPENDIX

WISDOM AND
"WISDOM LITERATURE"

Some biblical scholars, especially those who specialize in the study of the OT, will likely be uncomfortable with my loose use of the term "wisdom," since that designation is customarily applied to a small corpus of books from the Hebrew Bible: Proverbs, Job, and Qoheleth (Ecclesiastes), and, in addition to these, often the Apocryphal books of Ben Sira and the Wisdom of Solomon.[1] These literary works have long been considered a distinct genre unto themselves, separate from the Torah, the Prophets, and the Psalms. My classification of certain NT genres as examples of wisdom seems to conflict directly with this traditional distinction, or at least to muddy the waters to the point where the designation "wisdom" is in danger of losing any real significance.

My goal in this appendix is to explain, first, how my understanding of wisdom relates to the traditional designation of a discrete set of texts as Wisdom literature. Second, I will show that the traditional understanding of what is and is not "Wisdom literature" has always been hard to define with any real specificity, and its accuracy and utility have increasingly been called into question in the last few decades. Finally, I will argue (in a somewhat immodest proposal) that the whole of the Bible is wisdom, or more precisely that all the various genres found in the OT and NT are in fact subgenres of

---

I owe a special thanks for the assistance of my friend and OT colleague Scott Jones in the research and writing of this appendix.

1. Cf. Roland E. Murphy, "Wisdom in the OT," *ABD* 6:920.

wisdom, or put another way, as John Collins has suggested, wisdom should be understood as a "macro-genre."[2]

What Is Wisdom?

First we need to distinguish between two senses of the term "wisdom." One refers to a learned skill. In the ancient world this can range from the skill of shipbuilding to the skill of managing an empire. More generally, it is a skill for living life well, where the means for living "well" can be variously understood as the embodiment of particular virtues, and a "skill" is a developed intuition to perceive and desire those virtues. In this sense a person or people can possess wisdom.

The second sense of wisdom refers to the ways a person or group can inculcate this kind of practical intuition in another person or group. This can take various forms but is most generally conceived of as "instruction" in wisdom, as in the staple wisdom motif of a father's instruction to his son. This is the sense in which we speak of wisdom texts or Wisdom literature, but just as often this formative enterprise is simply referred to as "wisdom."[3] It is the second sense that is in view as I try to define what I mean by wisdom or wisdom texts vis-à-vis what has traditionally been referred to as "Wisdom literature."[4]

As we will see below, trying to define wisdom as a genre describing a particular group of texts has proven harder for Wisdom literature than for any other biblical genre. Part of the difficulty lies at the start in trying to define what we mean by a "genre." Here we also have two competing definitions: one is a "traditional" understanding in which a genre is a literary taxonomy that defines literary types according to shared literary features. While still a prominent model among biblical scholars, this way of understanding genres was largely abandoned decades ago by literary critics who work in genre studies.[5] Most contemporary genre theorists think of genres functionally

2. John J. Collins, "Wisdom Reconsidered, in Light of the Scrolls," *DSD* 4, no. 3 (1997): 265.

3. Both senses are summarized well by Nancy deClaissé-Walford: "In the ANE context, wisdom is an umbrella term that encompasses humanity's quest to understand and organize reality, to find answers to basic existential questions, and to pass that information along from one generation to another." Nancy deClaissé-Walford, "Wisdom in the Ancient Near East," *NIDB* 5:863.

4. I have purposely avoided using the term "Wisdom literature" in this book and this appendix except in reference to those works traditionally so designated. I have used the terms "wisdom" and "wisdom text" to refer to works outside that collection that function as wisdom texts as I define them here.

5. Benjamin G. Wright, "Joining the Club: A Suggestion about Genre in Early Jewish Texts," *DSD* 17 (2010): 292. "It does seem . . . that the tack taken by biblical scholars over the years—one

instead of taxonomically. Understood functionally, genres are a means of packaging communication in order to achieve certain social ends. In this way genres are an instrument for encoding intentionality. Certain literary forms tend to be associated with certain generic types simply because those forms are better at realizing the communicative goals of the author. In this context the question of shared literary forms is not discarded but *subordinated* to communicative intent.

So when we talk about wisdom as a genre we have two competing understandings at play. One understands wisdom as primarily circumscribed by a discrete set of literary forms. The other understands the genre of wisdom as primarily described by an intentionality to inculcate wisdom and sees the question of literary forms as highly flexible. My definition of wisdom assumes the latter. As we will see below, the first definition has never proved a workable definition for biblical Wisdom literature because of the diversity of literary forms found in these texts. (The amount of literary diversity is all the more striking given the small sample size of texts on offer.)

I will argue that wisdom is a formative intention that is realized in wisdom texts and that these texts form a genre because of their shared intention of fostering wisdom. What I mean by wisdom is most closely related to the Aristotelian understanding of wisdom as practical reasoning (φρόνησις). While this definition is one of many from the ancient world, it represents something of the shared assumptions of how ancients conceived of what was entailed in possessing wisdom. So, while Aristotle's definition is more developed than some others, his definition, in its general contours, is a typical expression of an ancient understanding of wisdom.

So I would define wisdom (understood as a skill) as a formed intuition that is able to make sound moral judgments and to desire what is good, virtuous, and life giving. Wisdom is more than a body of knowledge that one can transmit or possess; it is a disposition, what Aristotle would have called a virtue.[6] This definition is strikingly similar to how wisdom is understood in the Wisdom literature of the Hebrew Bible. Douglas Miller describes wisdom (חכמה) as "the ability . . . to assess complex situations, determine the issues involved, and

---

that is primarily classificatory or definitional and that relies on lists of features—for the most part has been set aside in contemporary genre studies." He goes on to quote Newsom as support. "Over the past quarter century, however, genre theorists have become increasingly dissatisfied with an approach that defines genres by means of lists of features." Carol Newsom, "Spying Out the Land: A Report from Genology," in *Bakhtin and Genre Theory in Biblical Studies*, ed. Roland Boer, SBL Semeia Studies 63 (Leiden: Brill, 2008), 20.

6. In fact, in Aristotle's understanding, wisdom (φρόνησις) is the central virtue that sustains all the others. See Julia Annas, *The Morality of Happiness* (Oxford: Oxford University Press, 1993), 73–83.

then make the best possible decisions." He continues: "Such a skill, for this too can be acquired, involves gaining information to some extent, but even more it means being the kind of person who can live well in a world of complex challenges. Particularly in the book of Proverbs, wisdom is associated with a variety of life habits—often called virtues—that contribute to the prospect of a successful life."[7] So according to Miller, wisdom as it is understood in the Hebrew Bible is actually quite close to my loosely Aristotelian definition.[8]

Wisdom texts then are texts that foster and sustain the formation of this kind of intuitive skill. These texts challenge and form devotions and practical reasoning, our understandings of who we are and who we ought to be, of what we love and what we ought to love, of what is right versus what is morally convenient.[9] This wisdom agenda is not tied to a single literary form but, as we will see below, finds expression in multiple forms. As Matthew Goff observes, "the range of literature that can be legitimately categorized as wisdom is so broad that one must acknowledge that wisdom is an inductive category based on our reading of ancient literature, rather than a precise class of texts that was rigidly defined by their authors."[10]

The Traditional Understanding of Wisdom Literature

Wisdom literature has traditionally been understood (through form criticism) as a distinct genre of literature in the Hebrew Bible with a distinct ideology, a distinct form, and coming from a distinct social context (*Sitz im Leben*). This

7. Both quotations from Douglas B. Miller, "Wisdom in the Canon: Discerning the Early Intuition," in *Was There a Wisdom Tradition? New Prospects in Israelite Wisdom Studies*, ed. Mark R. Sneed, SBL Ancient Israel and Its Literature 23 (Atlanta: SBL Press, 2015), 89.

8. Cf. Michael V. Fox, *Proverbs: A New Translation with Introduction and Commentary*, AB 18 (New Haven: Yale University Press, 2000–2009), 2:934–45, where he details the close correspondence between Israelite and Socratic wisdom. A similar argument could be made about wider ancient context. Cf. deClaissé-Walford, "Wisdom in the ANE," 5:863, "In terms of content, wisdom has been defined as a way of thinking about and ordering reality that reflects a shared ethos regarding assumptions and expectations about life. Thus wisdom writers attempted to categorize the world, measure human actions, evaluate the relative status of events and movements of life and prescribe paths of life."

9. See William P. Brown, *Character in Crisis: A Fresh Approach to the Wisdom Literature of the Old Testament* (Grand Rapids: Eerdmans, 1996), 1–21. Cf. Roland E. Murphy, "Wisdom in the OT," ABD 6:925. "The approach of wisdom to morality is much broader than that of the Decalogue in that it aims at character formation. It is also deeper in the motivation it supplies. Whereas the Decalogue simply invoked divine authority (thou shalt not!), the sages develop specific motivations, and anticipate temptations. . . . If one may designate the codes in the OT as 'law,' the wisdom rules are better described as 'catechesis,' or moral formation."

10. Matthew Goff, "Qumran Wisdom Literature and the Problem of Genre," *DSD* 17 (2010): 318.

marriage of ideology, form, and context is often referred to as the "wisdom tradition" of ancient Israel.

Historically, it has been easier to say what Wisdom literature is not than to say what it is. This is especially so in discussing the ideology or outlook of Wisdom literature. Many of the themes that dominate other genres of biblical discourse are surprisingly absent, or at least sidelined, in Wisdom literature. As James Crenshaw says: "Within Proverbs, Job, and Ecclesiastes one looks in vain for the dominant themes of Yahwistic thought: the exodus from Egypt, election of Israel, the Davidic covenant, the Mosaic legislation, the patriarchal narratives, the divine control of history and movement toward a glorious moment when right will triumph. Instead, the reader encounters in these three books *a different world*, one that stands apart so impressively that scholars have described that literary corpus as an alien body within the Bible."[11] For these reasons Wisdom literature has customarily been seen as an independent stream of thought that relies on observations of human nature and experience instead of divine revelation. It has often been understood in contrast to (and in conflict with) what Crenshaw labels "Yahwistic thought." So, in terms of its ideology, wisdom represented a distinct and independent school of thought in ancient Israel.

In form criticism, Wisdom literature also represents a *literal* school of thought, not just in contrast with the *ideas* of prophetic Yahwism but as a group in competition with the priests and the prophets. So Wisdom literature is often associated with ancient "sages" who sought their own spheres of influence and produced their literature to further those ends. The *Sitz im Leben* for these sages was likely some combination of royal court and literary school. As Katharine Dell describes it: "As the literature of the educated, wisdom has its natural home in two main environments: the court and the school. While the court context may have been overplayed in the past, it is clear that the king needed an educated circle around him to act as advisors, administrators, and recorders of events. . . . Such a group of sages would have needed education, and a court school based in Jerusalem seems the most likely possibility. We know from Sumerian and Egyptian contexts that wisdom was used in a school context."[12] This professional class of scribes was

---

11. James L. Crenshaw, *Old Testament Wisdom: An Introduction*, rev. ed. (Louisville: Westminster John Knox, 1998), 21. Italics original. Cf. Walter Zimmerli, "The Place and Limit of the Wisdom in the Framework of the Old Testament Theology," *SJT* 17 (1964): 146–58.

12. Katharine J. Dell, "Wisdom in the Old Testament," *NIDB* 5:870; cf. Marvin A. Sweeney, "Form Criticism," in *Dictionary of the Old Testament: Wisdom, Poetry and Writings*, ed. Tremper Longman and Peter Enns (Downers Grove, IL: IVP Academic, 2008), 237, "The presentation of royal characters and elite society in the book, together with sophisticated literary and pedagogical style points to the royal court as the likely setting for the book of Proverbs. Many

the impetus for wisdom, and the Wisdom literature they produced expressed their particular beliefs and furthered their political advantage.

Finally, this group produced literature that embodied their unique outlook in unique literary forms, as distinguished most obviously from historical narratives and prophetic utterances. Crenshaw summarizes these forms: "Formally wisdom consists of proverbial sentence, or instruction, debate, intellectual reflection; thematically, wisdom comprises self-evident intuitions from mastering life for human betterment, gropings after life's secrets with regard to innocent suffering, grappling with finitude, and quest for truth concealed in the created order and manifested in a feminine persona."[13] Crenshaw argues that these literary forms are best suited to communicating the worldview of the wisdom tradition. He famously stated that "When a marriage between form and content exists, there is wisdom literature."[14]

Seen in this way, it is obvious that the Wisdom literature of the Hebrew Bible represents its own theological tradition, distinct from and often in conflict with both the prophetic and priestly traditions, which had their own literature and their own influences on the Hebrew canon. It is also clear from this that speaking of "wisdom" in other parts of the Bible, whether in the OT or NT, is highly implausible within this historical reconstruction of the ideology, social context, and form of Wisdom literature.

The Incoherence of the Traditional Definition

But the coherence of this picture inherited from form criticism has been systematically challenged in recent decades by numerous specialists of Jewish Wisdom literature.[15] The challenge has come on two fronts: the first is the coherence and accuracy of the definition itself, and the second has been

---

speculate that it was produced by a circle of the wise who may have functioned as professional teachers of young students who would aspire for positions of responsibility in the royal court, the temple or elsewhere in ancient Israelite and Judean society."

13. Crenshaw, *Old Testament Wisdom*, 11.

14. Crenshaw, *Old Testament Wisdom*, 11.

15. It is not, however, a recent phenomenon. As Sheppard notes, "The problem of defining 'wisdom' has plagued our work from the very beginning of modern study." Gerald T. Sheppard, "Biblical Wisdom at the End of the Modern Age," in *Congress Volume: Oslo 1998*, ed. A. Lemaire and M. Sæbø, VTSup 80 (Leiden: Brill, 2000), 371. He continues, "In the late eighteenth century and early nineteenth century modern critics began to show convincingly that a historical reconstruction of 'wisdom literature' in ancient Israel was not simply identical with the content of the biblical books editorially associated with Solomon. As an alternative, various historical, comparative, and form-critical criteria seemed to offer a more accurate historical basis for finding and defining vestiges of ancient Israelite wisdom literature preserved, almost accidentally, in various traditions of the Bible" (372).

the recognition that the boundary separating Wisdom literature from other biblical and extrabiblical genres is actually quite porous.

It has long been recognized that the first challenge to defining the Wisdom literature of the Hebrew Bible is that the literary characteristics of Job, Qoheleth, and Proverbs have very little, if any, overlap. This small collection of three books contains elements of narrative, poetry, aphorisms, dialogues, and revelations. As Collins concludes, "There is universal agreement that wisdom does not constitute a *literary* genre, and that it can find expression in various literary forms."[16]

Along with their literary diversity, these three books fail to present a unified teaching on the nature of wisdom and often seem to directly contradict one another. Qoheleth and Job raise deep questions about the viability of the worldview presupposed in Proverbs that the wise and the righteous will flourish, while the fool and the wicked will eat the dust of remorse. In fact, it is precisely *because* of his righteousness that Job is singled out for suffering. As Stuart Weeks says, "It is difficult to group the three closely . . . , not only because they share little in common formally, but also because the attitudes and conclusions of Job and Ecclesiastes are radically different from those of the writers in Proverbs."[17]

So, in terms of literary form and content the Wisdom literature of the Hebrew Bible does not represent, as Crenshaw argues, a coherent "marriage of form and content."[18] In fact these three books actively resist precisely this sort of artificial coherence.[19] Collins summarizes the persistent angst in defining Wisdom literature, which begins with "the widespread intuition that these books in question have *something* in common."[20] But the problem is that "scholars have great difficulty in specifying just what these books have in common."[21]

The problem gets even more difficult if we include, as most wisdom specialists do, Ben Sira and the Wisdom of Solomon, which include theological

16. Collins, "Wisdom Reconsidered," 265. Italics added. Cf. Wright, "Genre in Early Jewish Texts," 291, "Today there still seems to be no general consensus about what constitutes wisdom as a literary genre."

17. Stuart Weeks, "Wisdom in the Old Testament," in *Where Shall Wisdom Be Found? Wisdom in the Bible, the Church and the Contemporary World*, ed. Stephen C. Barton (Edinburgh: T&T Clark, 1999), 27.

18. Cf. Goff, "Wisdom and the Problem of Genre," 325.

19. Cf. Wright, "Genre in Early Jewish Texts," 314, "If the goal is to arrive at a list of features that satisfactorily articulates a definition of the genre *wisdom*, the diversity inherent in the wisdom tradition would seem to overwhelm any attempt at defining such a genre."

20. Collins, "Wisdom Reconsidered," 265. Italics added.

21. Collins, "Wisdom Reconsidered," 265. Cf. Goff, "Wisdom and the Problem of Genre," 319, "The Hebrew Bible contains a diverse range of material encompassed by the macro-label 'wisdom.'"

elements from the Torah not found in the canonical Wisdom literature. With the addition of new materials from Qumran (where it is not uncommon for wisdom to be mixed with apocalyptic) many wisdom specialists have been forced to rethink their understandings of Wisdom literature from the ground up.[22]

This has included questioning the traditional form-critical *Sitz im Leben* of a circle of court sages as the social context for the production and transmission of Wisdom literature. As Weeks contends, "Nobody, except for biblical scholars, seems to assume that Egypt and Mesopotamia has distinct 'wisdom traditions,' except in some purely literary sense, so why should we speak of a wisdom tradition in Israel, and take it to imply a wholly separate school of thought?"[23] As Mark Sneed concludes, "The popular notion that there were distinctive and separate scribal schools of priests, prophets, and sages is not supported by the ancient Near Eastern evidence."[24]

With the coherent picture of ideology, form, and setting called into question, many have been forced to reject the tradition form-critical definition of Wisdom literature. Gerald Sheppard, for example, concludes that "the term 'wisdom' in the phrase 'biblical wisdom literature' does not indicate a genre, but names a corpus of literature within the scriptures."[25]

"Wisdom Influence"

The second way in which the traditional definition of Wisdom literature has eroded has come in the recognition that wisdom shows a consistent habit of "spilling its banks" and finding its way into the other genres of the Hebrew Bible. One classic example of this is Psalm 1, recognized by all but the most stubborn form critics as a "wisdom psalm."[26] (The designation "wisdom

22. Goff, "Wisdom and the Problem of Genre," 335, "In the new landscape of Early Jewish wisdom with all the Qumran scrolls available, wisdom as a literary category, which was somewhat loose to start with, is now even looser." The prototypical, but by no means only, example of this is 4QInstruction. As Wright has noted, "As scholars have recognized about *4QInstruction*, apocalyptic tradition has significantly influenced it, and in several respects it does occupy a spot somewhat along the blurred edge between wisdom literature and apocalypse." Wright, "Genre in Early Jewish Texts," 306. Cf. Lawrence M. Wills and Benjamin G. Wright, eds., *Conflicted Boundaries in Wisdom and Apocalypticism*, SBL Symposium Series 35 (Atlanta: SBL Press, 2005).

23. Weeks, "Wisdom," 30.

24. Mark Sneed, "Is the 'Wisdom Tradition' a Tradition?," *CBQ* 73 (2011): 65. As Weeks says, "There is no compelling evidence in the texts themselves to suggest that all were bred in the same stable" (Weeks, *Wisdom*, 27).

25. Sheppard, "Biblical Wisdom," 396.

26. As Sneed, "Wisdom Tradition?," notes, "Crenshaw becomes very rigid and rejects the possibility of their existence; they are merely instances of psalms that reflect some of the themes in the Hebrew wisdom literature" (67). On the history of "wisdom psalm" research see Simon

psalm" itself is recognition that wisdom moves freely outside what is traditionally understood to be Wisdom literature proper.)[27] Psalm 1 has many traditional markers of a wisdom text: most obviously the dichotomy between the righteous and the wicked and its use in a "two ways" of life antithesis. The obvious problem for a traditional understanding of wisdom is that this is not in Proverbs but the Psalter. Worse still, in the Psalter's final redaction this wisdom psalm was placed first. As Clinton McCann notes, "Scholars almost unanimously agree that Psalm 1 was placed at the beginning of the Psalter to orient the reader on how to approach the entire collection."[28]

If that were not problematic enough, this psalm teaches that the primary devotion of the righteous person is not to be found in the Psalter, or in Proverbs, but in the Torah. So we have a psalm using the vocabulary and themes of wisdom to talk about meditation on the Torah as the primary means of God's blessing. In six verses this psalm manages to deconstruct all our neat distinctions between genres that exist in their discrete theological worlds and social agendas arising from unique *Sitz im Leben*.

Historical Narrative

Another example of this kind of cross-genre fertilization, which at one time was routinely referred to as "wisdom influence" on other genres, can be found in the now-common recognition of wisdom themes and intentions in the historical books of the OT. Von Rad tore down the wall between Torah and wisdom in his famous article on wisdom themes in the Joseph narrative.[29]

Chi-chung Cheung, *Wisdom Intoned: A Reappraisal of the Genre "Wisdom Psalms,"* LHBOTS 613 (London: Bloomsbury T&T Clark, 2015), 2–16.

27. There is a scholarly self-deception in assuming that having created the category of "wisdom psalm" solves the problem of genre, when in reality it only names the problem. Physicists participate in an analogous self-deception when they respond to the challenge of whether light is a wave or a particle by naming it a "wave-particle." This only names the incongruity; it does not solve it.

28. J. Clinton McCann Jr., "'The Way of the Righteous' in the Psalms: Character Formation and Cultural Crisis," in *Character and Scripture: Moral Formation, Community, and Biblical Interpretation*, ed. William P. Brown (Grand Rapids: Eerdmans, 2002), 136.

29. See Gerhard von Rad, *The Problem of the Hexateuch and Other Essays*, trans. E. W. Trueman Dicken (Edinburgh: Oliver & Boyd, 1966), 292–300. He concludes that "the Joseph story, with its strong didactic motive, belongs to the category of early wisdom writing" (299). Fox objects to "the proposition that the Joseph story is a didactic text cued to Wisdom literature" (Michael V. Fox, "Wisdom in the Joseph Story," *VT* 51 [2001]: 26). His criticism of von Rad's thesis is that it is completely based on the presence and absence of particular literary forms associated with Wisdom literature, which we have already seen is problematic. The heart of his criticism is that the narrative, at least at one point, turns on Joseph's gift for interpreting dreams. Fox argues that this is not a characteristic of either Wisdom literature or the proverbial wise man. He concludes that "the concept of wisdom in the Joseph story is affiliated with the

Since then numerous studies have demonstrated that wisdom themes and language are pervasive in OT narratives.[30] In ways very similar to my treatment of Gospel narratives, many scholars have demonstrated the wisdom agendas of these texts, though of course expressed in a style that is more implicit than the apodictic style of Proverbs.[31] In his studies in Genesis, Leon Kass summarizes the central characteristic of these narratives that connects them to a formative wisdom agenda:

> As a result of many readings and rereadings of Genesis, I am increasingly impressed by the leanness of the text and the lacunae in the stories. Little of what we readers might like to know about an event or a character is told to us. Much of what we are told admits of a wide variety of interpretations. Rarely does the text tell us the inner thoughts and feelings of a character. Rarely does the text tell us the meaning of an event. And almost never does the text pronounce judgment on the words or deeds of any protagonist. Why this reticence? What purpose could it possibly serve? . . . The open form of the text and its recalcitrance to final and indubitable interpretations are absolutely perfect instruments for cultivating the openness, thoughtfulness, and modesty about one's own understanding that is the hallmark of the pursuit of wisdom.[32]

---

pietistic and inspired wisdom of Daniel rather than with the ethical and practical wisdom of the Wisdom literature" (40). So he agrees that it is a wisdom text, just not formally "Wisdom literature," but this fails to recognize that the category of Wisdom literature is a hermeneutical heuristic, not a list of formal literary features. Cf. Sneed, "Wisdom Tradition?," 67, "The classification of genres is not etched in stone but is a heuristic device that aids in understanding literatures that resemble each other. . . . Genre criticism today is not primarily a classificatory or taxonomic enterprise, like organizing a mineral collection. Rather, it emphasizes the dynamism of genres and explains how they are an intricate part of the production of meaning."

30. E.g., Gordon J. Wenham, *Story as Torah: Reading the Old Testament Ethically*, OTS (Edinburgh: T&T Clark, 2000); John H. Sailhamer, "A Wisdom Composition of the Pentateuch?," in *The Way of Wisdom: Essays in Honor of Bruce K. Waltke*, ed. J. I. Packer and Sven Soderlund (Grand Rapids: Zondervan, 2000), 15–35; Richard G. Bowman, "The Complexity of Character and the Ethics of Complexity: The Case of King David," in *Character and Scripture: Moral Formation, Community, and Biblical Interpretation*, ed. William P. Brown (Grand Rapids: Eerdmans, 2002), 73–97; Thomas B. Dozeman, "Creation and Environment in the Character Development of Moses," in *Character Ethics and the Old Testament: Moral Dimensions of Scripture*, ed. M. Daniel Carroll R. and Jacqueline E. Lapsley (Louisville: Westminster John Knox, 2007), 27–36; Bruce C. Birch, "Divine Character and the Formation of Moral Community in the Book of Exodus," in *The Bible in Ethics: The Second Sheffield Colloquium*, ed. John W. Rogerson, Margaret Davies, and M. Daniel Carroll R., JSOTSup 207 (Sheffield: Sheffield Academic Press, 1995), 119–35.

31. Cf. John Barton, *Understanding Old Testament Ethics: Approaches and Explorations* (Louisville: Westminster John Knox, 2003), 55–74.

32. See Leon Kass, *The Beginning of Wisdom: Reading Genesis* (New York: Free Press, 2003), 18–19. Cf. Meir Sternberg, *The Poetics of Biblical Narrative: Ideological Literature and the Drama of Reading*, The Indiana Literary Biblical Series (Bloomington: Indiana University Press, 1985), 41–57.

Kass argues that the narrative form itself reveals the wisdom agenda of these historical narratives. For him it is their narrative style, not just narrative in general, that marks them as wisdom. The sparse style, whose lacunae invite the participation of the reader to make informed inferences about the motivations of its protagonists, is essential to how these narratives function in forming wisdom. As Kass points out, the text is silent precisely at the points where we as readers want to understand how and why these characters did what they did. These characters are never simplistic embodiments of ideals but possess a complex psychological realism that makes their actions all the more difficult to discern.[33] At the same time, the narrators of these texts place alongside deliberate lacunae subtle clues of implicit commentary that are the foundations for the readers' forming judgments about the narrative's characters.[34] In this way readers make informed inferences, which is the central intuitive skill that defines wisdom. Through these acts of practical judgment the commitments and affections of readers are formed in wisdom. In addition, Kass also makes the point that this style of storytelling forms certain virtues in its readers, namely openness, attentiveness, moral sensitivity, and humility.[35]

While there are numerous examples of exegesis of OT historical narratives that understands them as fundamentally shaped by wisdom concerns, one excellent example is the work of Walter Moberly on the Akedah narrative (in Gen. 22).[36] This narrative of Abraham's faithful obedience is a dramatic example of what Nussbaum calls the challenge of competing "incommensurable goods," pitting love for a son against the fear of the Lord. Moberly makes a sustained argument for understanding this text in terms of

33. As Brown says, "They are enfleshed with ambiguity and conflict, life and blood. Round characters connote a sense of personal realism with their own appeal and aim in the rhetoric of wisdom. Their task is in part to deconstruct, reform, or reconstruct of [sic] traditional contours of ethical character" (*Character in Crisis*, 17).

34. Cf. V. Philips Long, "Scenic, Succinct, Subtle: An Introduction to the Literary Artistry of 1 & 2 Samuel," *Presb* 19, no. 1 (1993): 32–47.

35. Cf. Robert Alter, *The Art of Biblical Narrative* (New York: Basic Books, 1981), 176,
> What is it like, the biblical writers seek to know through their art, to be a human being with a divided consciousness—intermittently loving your brother but hating him even more; resentful or perhaps contemptuous of your father but also capable of the deepest filial regard; stumbling between disastrous ignorance and imperfect knowledge; fiercely asserting your own independence but caught in a tissue of events divinely contrived; outwardly a definite character and inwardly an unstable vortex of greed, ambition, jealousy, lust, piety, courage, compassion, and much more? Fiction [i.e., narrative] fundamentally serves the biblical writers as an instrument of fine insight into these abiding perplexities of man's creaturely condition."

36. See R. W. L. Moberly, *The Bible, Theology, and Faith: A Study of Abraham and Jesus*, Cambridge Studies in Christian Doctrine 5 (Cambridge: Cambridge University Press, 2000), 71–161.

its formative wisdom intention. This can be seen clearly in his summary of the significance of the Akedah narrative: "In Genesis 22 we have not only a story which is definitive of the meaning of 'one who fears God'; but, given its position as the climactic story in the life of Abraham, the friend of God, Genesis 22 may appropriately be read as a, arguably the, primary canonical exposition of the meaning of 'one who fears God.' For a contemporary faith and theology which is rooted in scripture, this is a passage that will inform, and give a critical edge to, debate as to which people may appropriately be recognized as (in Christian parlance) 'believers'/'people of faith.'"[37]

As an "exposition" of the fear of God, this narrative is informed by and informs the most fundamental wisdom teaching—that "the fear of the Lord is the beginning of wisdom" (Prov. 9:10).

Prophets

Like other OT genres, there is a long history of finding "wisdom influence" in the prophets, recognizing that certain wisdom themes and vocabulary frequently present themselves there.[38] Recently, though, some specialists in prophetic literature have explored not simply wisdom *themes* but wisdom *intentions* in these texts. Specifically, there are many studies now that examine these texts in light of their formative intentions, using prophetic imagery and symbolic actions to form the dispositions of the people of God through practices that enact grief and hope.[39] The work of Jacqueline Lapsley on Ezekiel is characteristic of what is most fruitful and promising about this type of approach.[40] She recognizes that Ezekiel is best understood as a speech-act

37. Moberly, *Bible, Theology, and Faith*, 79. He describes "the fear of God" as "the primary term within the Old Testament for depicting a true and appropriate human response to God." He then adds that this phrase is "a Hebrew equivalent to 'faith' in Christian parlance."

38. See, for example, William McKane, *Prophets and Wise Men*, SBT (London: SCM, 1965); H. G. M. Williamson, "Isaiah and the Wise," in *Wisdom in Ancient Israel: Essays in Honour of J. A. Emerton*, ed. John Day, R. P. Gordon, and H. G. M. Williamson (Cambridge: Cambridge University Press, 1995), 133–41; A. A. Macintosh, "Hosea and the Wisdom Tradition: Dependence and Independence," in *Wisdom in Ancient Israel: Essays in Honour of J.A. Emerton*, ed. John Day, R. P. Gordon, and H. G. M. Williamson (Cambridge: Cambridge University Press, 1995), 124–32; W. McKane, "Jeremiah and the Wise," in *Wisdom in Ancient Israel: Essays in Honour of J.A. Emerton*, ed. John Day, R. P. Gordon, and H. G. M. Williamson (Cambridge: Cambridge University Press, 1995), 142–51.

39. E.g., Kathleen M. O'Connor, "The Book of Jeremiah: Reconstructing Community after Disaster," in Carroll R. and Lapsley, *Character Ethics and the Old Testament*, 81–92; M. Daniel Carroll R., "'He Has Told You What Is Good': Moral Formation in Micah," in Carroll R. and Lapsley, *Character Ethics and the Old Testament*, 103–18.

40. Jacqueline E. Lapsley, *Can These Bones Live? The Problem of the Moral Self in the Book of Ezekiel*, BZAW 301 (New York: de Gruyter, 2000).

aimed at the spiritual formation of grieving exiles. One window into that intention is how Ezekiel deals with grieving itself.

> The Israelites' tendency is to resolve their grief over the temple too easily and only by means of their own ritualized mourning, a mourning in which God is not an active player. Their reduction to an animalistic state allows them to feel their loss with all its attendant pain and without analgesic. The irresolvability of their grief leaves open a space for the radical action of God, space that was previously closed off in the well-ordered culture of ritualized mourning. . . . For Ezekiel, only through a progressive dehumanization can the people be prepared for new life. Nothing of the old nature can be retained. Later in the book (chap. 37), the re-creation of humanity can only be initiated after the people are declared dead; they are brought to new life with nothing of the old life remaining except their bones. The people must be crushed so low that they no longer seek piecemeal solutions for their desperate situation, such as setting their hearts on the temple or mourning its loss in the usual, customary ways. The symbolic ordering of experience (religion, culture) must be violently disturbed before the people can perceive the divine action that ultimately seeks to restore them to their full humanity (in Ezekiel divine salvific action is unilateral; humanity can only receive it). Yet for all its austerity it does not seem far from the mark in terms of the way radical change sometimes happens. The oppressed will only rise up when their oppression becomes unbearable. Slight improvements in policy may have the effect of delaying much-needed, but more radical, change.[41]

Lapsley has a good sense of the shaping of moral and spiritual dispositions through symbolic actions that expose and reconstitute convictions and desires. This is at the heart of how the prophetic literature functions as wisdom.

Psalms

We have already mentioned Psalm 1 as an example of wisdom's incorporation in the Psalter as an indication that, while the Psalter was primarily collected for use in public worship, its purpose was seen, at least in part, as instrumental in the formation of wisdom.[42] This is simply a recognition that liturgical participation through song informs and reinforces fundamental

41. Jacqueline E. Lapsley, "A Feeling for God: Emotions and Moral Formation in Ezekiel 24:15–27," in Carroll R. and Lapsley, *Character Ethics and the Old Testament*, 99.

42. Cf. R. N. Whybray, "The Wisdom Psalms," in *Wisdom in Ancient Israel: Essays in Honour of J. A. Emerton*, ed. John Day, Robert P. Gordon, and H. G. M. Williamson (Cambridge: Cambridge University Press, 1995), 154, "It can also be argued that all liturgical texts have a didactic function in that the confessions of faith which they make are also a kind of self-instruction in which worshippers remind themselves of the articles of that faith."

convictions and devotions, as Gordon Wenham has recently argued.[43] In addition to this, McCann points to the final redaction of the Psalter as evidence of its eudaemonistic wisdom intentionality:

> Given the importance of the final form of the psalter, it is necessary to begin a consideration of the theology of the psalms with Psalm 1–2; even more specifically, with the very first word of the psalter: "Happy" (NRSV). In a real sense, the rest of the psalter will portray the shape of human happiness, and it is clear from the beginning and throughout Psalms that the definition of human happiness is thoroughly God-centered. The "happy" are those who constantly delight in God's "instruction" (תורה tôrâ, Ps. 1:2; NIV and NRSV, "law"). In short, happiness derives from the complete orientation of life to God, including perpetual openness to God's instruction.[44]

McCann summarizes how this happiness becomes defined in terms of a handful of moral and spiritual dispositions. "The definitions of 'happiness' and 'righteousness' in terms of refuge, the fundamental dependence upon God for life and future, makes sense only in the light of the affirmation that lies at what has been identified as the theological heart of the psalter: The Lord reigns (Psalms 93–99)!"[45]

From all this we can see that wisdom in various forms can be found across the whole Hebrew canon. This makes the identification of wisdom as a genre all the more difficult. It also makes the location of wisdom within a self-contained group of sages all the more implausible.

Wisdom Studies after Form Criticism

The traditional definition of Wisdom literature has taken a beating of late, with some suggesting the category be abandoned altogether.[46] Unsurpris-

---

43. Gordon J. Wenham, *Psalms as Torah: Reading Biblical Song Ethically*, STI (Grand Rapids: Baker Academic, 2012).

44. J. Clinton McCann Jr., "The Book of Psalms: Introductory Commentary and Reflections," *NIB* 4:666. He adds, "Not surprisingly, the word for 'happy' (אשרי *'ašrê*) will occur throughout Book I and the rest of the psalter, including as soon as the conclusion of Psalm 2 (see also Pss. 32:1–2; 33:12; 34:8; 40:4; 41:4; 65:4; 84:4–5, 12; 89:15; 94:12; 106:3; 112:1; 119:1–2; 127:5; 128:1; 137:8–9; 144:15; 146:5)." Cf. Robert L. Cole, *Psalms 1–2: Gateway to the Psalter*, Hebrew Bible Monographs 37 (Sheffield: Sheffield Phoenix Press, 2012).

45. McCann, "Psalms," 667.

46. E.g., Weeks, "Wisdom," 30, "Ultimately, I think, the wisdom tradition is something of a phantasm in Old Testament scholarship. . . . None of the wisdom books benefits from attempts to interpret all three in terms of a single, separate tradition, and down that path lie the futile, negative definitions of wisdom literature, as non-historical, non-nationalistic and ultimately

ingly, this has caused something of an identity crisis for wisdom studies and produced some fascinating and deep disciplinary soul-searching. The current state of the discipline of wisdom studies is reflected in the recent collection of essays published under the title *Was There a Wisdom Tradition?*[47] The essays in this volume range from calls for radical reform (Sneed and Kynes), more moderate reform (Dell), to a preservation of traditional categories (Fox and Schellenberg). All these different-tempered articles, however, are unified in recognizing the central tension that Wisdom literature has traditionally been too narrowly defined, but that loosening the category only slightly runs the risk of what Will Kynes calls the "threat of pan-sapientialism," in which the category of wisdom is quickly overwhelmed and drops into the canonical sea. This collection of essays is representative of a growing consensus that incorporates (1) a deep questioning of the nature of genre itself, (2) a declining allegiance to form-critical categories, and (3) a recognition of a circular heuristic involved in beginning with a set list of texts and then defining a genre around them.

The increasing difficulty in defining wisdom as a genre has forced many scholars to ask fundamental questions about the nature of genre itself. (It is important to note that this is something peculiar to wisdom studies; this level of theoretical questioning about genre has not been an issue in the fields of historical narrative or prophetic literature.) While several studies have focused on this question, the most prominent discussion has centered on the distinction between generic realism and generic nominalism. Kenton Sparks says that generic realism "posits that texts are uniquely and intrinsically related to the generic categories in which we place them."[48] As Sneed explains, in this view, "Genres are viewed as static, and the business of genre analysis is primarily about taxonomy."[49] In contrast to this, generic nominalism recognizes genres as inherently flexible communicative conventions that operate as hermeneutic heuristics, not primarily as taxonomies of literary characteristics.[50] The current consensus is moving decidedly away from generic realism to generic nominalism

---

non-Israelite." Cf. Goff, "Wisdom and the Problem of Genre," 325, "The prospects of wisdom as a viable category can seem rather bleak."

47. Mark R. Sneed, ed., *Was There a Wisdom Tradition? New Prospects in Israelite Wisdom Studies*, SBL Ancient Israel and Its Literature 23 (Atlanta: SBL Press, 2015).

48. Kenton L. Sparks, *Ancient Texts for the Study of the Hebrew Bible: A Guide to the Background Literature* (Peabody, MA: Hendrickson, 2005), 6.

49. Mark R. Sneed, "'Grasping After the Wind': The Elusive Attempt to Define and Delimit Wisdom," in Sneed, *Was There a Wisdom Tradition?*, 40.

50. As Sneed, "Wisdom Tradition?," 67, says, "Genre criticism today is not primarily a classificatory or taxonomic enterprise, like organizing a mineral collection. Rather, it emphasizes the dynamism of genres and explains how they are an intricate part of the production of meaning."

and corresponds to my approach to genre as stated above, although this nominalism tends to be more minimalist than my functional definition.[51]

The next characteristic of contemporary wisdom studies is a move away from form-critical categories, especially in the emphasis on a wisdom tradition understood in contradistinction to other movements within ancient Israel. Along with this is an openness to think more in the categories of intertextuality within a common tradition that defined ancient Israel. Form criticism began with the commonplace observation that every text is representative of its social context and is easily misunderstood apart from that social context. From this, form critics derived a historical principle: genres are representative of social contexts, and specific genres were *uniquely* representative of different social contexts. As Sparks puts it: "Gunkel presumed that each piece of literature belonged to only one genre, that each genre stemmed from one unique *Sitz im Leben*, and that the relationship between form and context was essentially inflexible."[52] Today many wisdom scholars are rejecting this identification between genre and *Sitz im Leben* as a historical methodology of wish fulfillment that is too neat and too convenient. With this, it is also common for the whole proposal of a "school" of sages, at least as a politically and theologically independent group, to be put aside.

51. Goff, "Wisdom and the Problem of Genre," 334, is typical of this generic nominalism when he says, "The genre wisdom . . . is a heuristic construct we develop to make a wide range of texts intelligible. This minimalist definition rightly moves away from a taxonomical approach to genre and recognizes the flexibility and fluidity in genres, but it goes too far in its nominalist tendencies. No linguists, as least those who work in linguistic pragmatics and discourse analysis, would agree with the idea that genre is 'in the eye of the beholder.' Genres are shared socio-linguistic constructs necessary for communication." (See Charles Bazerman, "Genre as Social Action," in *The Routledge Handbook of Discourse Analysis*, ed. James Paul Gee and Michael Handford [New York: Routledge, 2012], 226–30.) This means that the texts today labeled "Wisdom literature" were participants in one or more ancient genres. Precisely what these genres may have been is historically inaccessible to us. The truth of what Goff says is that our genre labels are our heuristic constructs derived from seeing common connections. What Goff forgets is that the goal of our genre labels is a correspondence between our constructs and the ancient genres that were utilized in the composition of these texts. Because genre understandings are hermeneutically determinative, if we want to understand texts for what they are and what they say, then we commit ourselves to the ongoing process of refining our genre understandings by shaping them to the texts available to us and testing which genre proposals prove most fruitful. To see genres as only our constructs is to deny the historical aspect inherent in biblical research. As Weeks says, "Genre is not only a matter of classification, but of composition also, and although it is true that works may be assigned to categories which would have been unknown to their authors, it is surely no less true that authors typically rely heavily on genre, and on their readers' recognition of generic conventions." Stuart Weeks, "Wisdom, Form and Genre," in Sneed, *Was There a Wisdom Tradition?*, 163; cf. John Frow, *Genre*, The New Critical Idiom (London: Routledge, 2006), 72–99.

52. Sparks, *Ancient Texts*, 6.

As Sneed argues, "Many of Gunkel's erroneous form-critical assumptions served to predispose biblical scholars to turn priest against prophet and each against sage, as well as each other, and one type of literature against or in competition with another."[53]

Sneed, Kynes, and Dell see this movement away from the categories supplied by form criticism, especially the notion of an isolated wisdom tradition, as a catalyst for understanding wisdom intertextually, where the Hebrew canon represents both common and distinct traditions. They see this as both historically more plausible and exegetically more fruitful. As Dell argues, "What intertextuality seems to highlight is unexpected links between books." She continues:

> These kinds of links emerge where one least expects them once an intertextual approach or inner-biblical approach is taken. The result is more integration across the canon of scripture (in its broadest sense) and less of a piecemeal approach to texts. Perhaps, after all, the literary product that is the Old Testament is ultimately the result of scribal work that seeks to make these links and is a cohesive whole for that reason alone. But this does not nullify the quest for subdivisions and more subtle statements about genres within the whole. The wisdom category is one of these. It has tentacles flowing into many other genres and texts but ultimately it is a useful literary category—and it had real living contexts, however lost to us those may seem now.[54]

Dell is representative of the tension of wanting to recognize and promote intertextual linkages while at the same time preserving a space for something distinct about Wisdom literature.

But what is it that makes Wisdom literature distinct? Sneed's answer "you know it when you see it!"[55] will not satisfy many. Even so, Sneed's answer points to what is now a common confession of wisdom scholars. As Goff admits, "The criteria for defining wisdom are subjective and scholars can reach various conclusions as to which texts should be so classified."[56] Goff's confession here is refreshing in its honesty. He and Sneed both argue that this is simply a reality that wisdom scholars have to get comfortable with. The reason they are willing to embrace what many others are not is that they were

---

53. Sneed, "Grasping After the Wind," 60–61. He adds, "The almost unconscious drive to discern an ever more fractured and dissentious Scripture no doubt ultimately derives from the Enlightenment need to curtail the authority of the Bible" (61–62).

54. Katharine J. Dell, "Deciding the Boundaries of 'Wisdom': Applying the Concept of Family Resemblance," in Sneed, *Was There a Wisdom Tradition?*, 158.

55. Sneed, "Grasping After the Wind," 62.

56. Goff, "Wisdom and the Problem of Genre," 334.

driven to it by reading wisdom texts and by recognizing the circularity inherent in the traditional delineation of a corpus of Wisdom literature in the OT.

Because of the difficulties inherent in defining Wisdom literature, a more
traditional approach simply begins with a discrete group of texts (Proverbs,
Job, Qoheleth, with the possible addition of Ben Sira, Wisdom of Solomon,
and some wisdom psalms) and labels those texts Wisdom literature. (The justification for these texts and not others is simply the honoring of a scholarly
tradition.) Then, utilizing this group of texts, it derives a description of the
genre of Wisdom literature and uses that description to defend the proposal
that these texts form a distinct genre called Wisdom literature. As Kynes points
out, Crenshaw's description of the features of the wisdom genre (cited above)
simply "lists the features of texts in his wisdom corpus." As Kynes concludes,
this operation "proves nothing unassumed from the outset."[57] While Kynes
is critical of the circularity of Crenshaw's traditional definition, he also recognizes it as the only tool that wisdom scholars have to curb the movement
toward pan-sapientialism. So in the end one has a choice between adherence
to a traditional assumption of what constitutes the corpus of Wisdom literature or recognizing that any delineation of a wisdom corpus is a subjective
(though not arbitrary) act.

Reading for Life[58]

My solution to these questions, both untried and unlooked for, is simply to
embrace the "pan-sapientialism" that Kynes and others fear will dilute the
distinct stream of Wisdom literature. It is this fear that has kept wisdom scholars from attending to the possibility that some kind of pan-sapiential theory
might actually be a workable solution. (The problem for wisdom scholars is
that this definition does not answer their primary question, which is, What is
unique about the group of texts customarily labeled "Wisdom literature?"[59])
In its favor, understanding the whole of the OT as some form of wisdom is a
theory that can easily explain all the evidence of "wisdom influence" across
the Hebrew canon. Such a pan-sapiential theory leaves room for the study of

57. Both quotations from Will Kynes, "The Modern Scholarly Wisdom Tradition and the
Threat of Pan-Sapientialism," in Sneed, *Was There a Wisdom Tradition?*, 16.

58. This title has a long intertextual history. I am borrowing from Barton, who borrowed it
from Nussbaum, who lifted it from Dickens's *David Copperfield*. See Barton, *Understanding
Old Testament Ethics*, 62.

59. Wisdom scholars are not trying to answer how Wisdom literature relates to the rest of
the Bible; they are trying to understand what is unique about these particular texts. This is the
case with all biblical subdisciplines that are defined along generic lines.

various genres (understood as subgenres of wisdom) on their own terms while at the same time providing a basis for the kind of innerbiblical intertextual connections that Dell and others see as hermeneutically profitable. But if we are going to look at the whole OT through the lens of wisdom in a constructive way, we are back to our old question of, What is wisdom?

In his struggle to define Wisdom literature Collins focused on what he labels the "instructional" mode that unites these texts. As he says, "The coherence of wisdom literature . . . lies in its use as instructional material rather than in literary form, strictly defined."[60] As Goff explains, "[Collins] points toward *instructional intent*, not form, as the key for understanding the coherence of sapiential literature as a genre."[61] If we follow Collins and take a formative instructional intent as the defining mark of wisdom, then we can quickly see that the boundaries of wisdom in the OT become very expansive. As Goff admits, "Instructional intent is itself much broader than wisdom literature. Thus the most important criterion for defining wisdom literature as a distinct body of literature is not restricted to sapiential texts. Many texts, as Collins observes, are instructional in a broad sense. The Torah itself, as the Hebrew implies, can be considered as 'instruction.'"[62] Understood in this way, the whole of the Hebrew Bible can fit under the umbrella of wisdom.[63] While Kynes sees this as the end of the definition of wisdom and anything hermeneutically fruitful to be derived from it, I contend that this is a very fruitful insight into the nature of the OT, because recognizing all biblical genres as subgenres of wisdom provides a crucial insight into the encoded intentionality of these various texts, which is hermeneutically fruitful—foregrounding the wisdom-forming agenda that unites the OT while also recognizing that this agenda is realized in diverse ways through different types of texts.

What, then, do we do with Proverbs, Job, and Qoheleth? Is there still a special place for these texts if we label the whole of the OT wisdom? I think so. The recent discussion by Cheung on what constitutes "wisdom" provides some helpful categories. He argues that wisdom texts all display (1) a ruling wisdom thrust, (2) a didactic speech intention, and (3) an intellectual tone.[64] The first two elements correspond to Collins's category of "instructional

---

60. Collins, "Wisdom Reconsidered," 281.

61. Goff, "Wisdom and the Problem of Genre," 327. Italics added.

62. Goff, "Wisdom and the Problem of Genre," 327.

63. Cf. John L. McKenzie, "Reflections on Wisdom," *JBL* 86, no. 1 (1967): 2, "This heavy wisdom flavor in the entire collection of Jewish and Christian sacred books suggests that wisdom is much more than a literary form, much more than a way of life, as it has often been called. It was also a way of thought and a way of speech, which was by no means limited to the schools and the writings of the sages."

64. Cheung, *Wisdom Intoned*, 28–37.

intent" and, I would argue, apply to the whole Hebrew canon. The last element of "intellectual tone," however, is something unique to the Wisdom literature.[65] I would describe it as persistent, explicit wisdom discourse. Many texts deal with wisdom themes sporadically and/or implicitly. The distinctive feature of "Wisdom literature" is that it pursues its formative wisdom intent through modes of discourse that deal *explicitly* with wisdom questions and themes on a persistent basis. By contrast, historical narratives pursue their formative wisdom agenda largely implicitly, although at times they may betray their intentions in explicit wisdom terminology or the incorporation of wisdom sayings. (It is at these points that the category of "wisdom influence" has been historically prominent.)

The traditional definition of Wisdom literature began with a small group of texts but has struggled to define what precisely those texts hold in common. It is clear that what they hold in common is not a set of literary characteristics. I would accept the definitions offered by Collins and Cheung as an umbrella that describes these particular wisdom texts, but in turning to the rest of the Hebrew Bible I would simply want to "open" the umbrella (with the exception of Cheung's "intellectual tone" element), recognizing that the genre of wisdom is best described in terms of an "instructional intent" and not by a set of form-critical literary characteristics or particular *Sitz im Leben*.

This theory helps to explain why the question of genre has been so problematic for wisdom studies in a way that is not true for any other biblical genre. When we see "wisdom influence" across the genres of the OT, and in the apocalyptic literature of Qumran, what we are seeing is not simply a general problem of the fluidity and interpenetrations of genres per se.[66] So, it is not the same as the question of historical narrative intruding into prophecy or psalmody. What we see evidence of is the presence of one genre—wisdom— in every other. This is why wisdom specialists have been driven toward both more generalized definitions of wisdom and more nominalist definitions of genre. Given this evidence, it is not an unreasonable suggestion of Collins that wisdom is best understood as a "macro-genre" that encompasses other

65. Cf. Goff, "Wisdom and the Problem of Genre," 327–28, where he describes the distinctive feature of Wisdom literature as its "noetic" level of discourse. He adds that "the other major factor that allows for the identification of wisdom literature is that texts so designated participate to a significant extent in a sapiential discourse."

66. As seems to be assumed by Wright, "Genre in Early Jewish Texts," 303, "If we look at genres analogously to clubs, not only might genres have full participants and affiliates, but some texts might participate in more than one club, perhaps fully in one and as an affiliate of another (or others). Or perhaps one might conceive of the relationships among different genres as more akin to a Venn diagram, where the circles overlap in places, rather than to a series of self-contained circular spaces."

biblical genres.[67] Sneed expresses a similar idea in his appeal to take wisdom as a "mode" and not a "genre."[68]

When combined with the arguments in this book on the NT wisdom genres of gospel and paraenetic epistle, we are (almost) in a place to see the whole of the Bible as engaged in different ways in the formation of wisdom. We could also include Revelation, since studies of Qumran literature have given ample evidence of the mixing of apocalyptic and wisdom,[69] which I would argue is best explained (again) by seeing apocalyptic as a form of wisdom.[70] With this piece in place, it would be possible to make a sustained argument, no matter how radical it may sound to some, that the whole of the Bible operates in a wisdom mode or is made up of a collection of texts that appropriate different wisdom genres (or subgenres). If we follow Collins in defining wisdom primarily in terms of its "instructional intent," then this proposal becomes much less radical. The evidence in favor of this proposal can be found in the last three decades of studies of "wisdom influence" across the Hebrew Bible.[71]

67. Admittedly, what Collins means by "macro-genre" is less expansive than I have in mind. The term "metagenre" might be more appropriate for what I propose.

68. Sneed, "Wisdom Tradition?," 57, "Hebrew wisdom literature should be described as a mode of literature and not strictly a genre. Mode is a broader category than genre, a higher level of abstraction."

69. Two prominent examples being Mysteries and 4QInstruction. As Goff, "Wisdom and the Problem of Genre," 329 says, "*4QInstruction* can be understood as exemplifying another type of sapiential discourse that emerges in the late Second Temple period characterized by extensive engagement with the apocalyptic tradition."

70. See Grant Macaskill, *Revealed Wisdom and Inaugurated Eschatology in Ancient Judaism and Early Christianity*, Supplements to the Journal for the Study of Judaism 115 (Leiden: Brill, 2007). Von Rad may have had the right instinct when he argued for wisdom (and not prophecy) as the incubator of apocalyptic. See Gerhard von Rad, *Old Testament Theology*, trans. D. M. G. Stalker, 2 vols. (Edinburgh: Oliver & Boyd, 1965), 2:301–8. Whether or not the relationship is genealogical, von Rad was noting the deep connections between apocalyptic and wisdom, which he saw as stronger than between apocalyptic and prophecy.

71. Further evidence could also be found in the frequent suggestion of a sapientializing movement in the late stages of the redaction of the OT writings. As Kynes summarizes:

This view has recently been given a new historical explanation in David Carr's arguments that wisdom was at the heart of the enculturation of Hebrew scribes (Carr 2005, 2011). The latter view of later sapiential editing built on a notion that wisdom came to dominate the theology of late Judaism, which is already evident in von Rad's *Old Testament Theology*. . . . Gerald Sheppard (1980, 13) proposed a means through which this thinking seeped back into earlier texts by taking the use of wisdom as a "hermeneutical construct," already recognized in Sir 24 by von Rad (1993, 245), and arguing that it was applied in the editing of texts across the Hebrew Bible. Similar arguments expanding on his thesis soon followed (e.g., Wilson 1992; Van Leeuwen 1993). By attributing the entire canon to "scribal scholars," Sneed combines the school setting with that of scribal editing and conflates wisdom as an early formative influence with the later sapiential editing of texts of other genres. In so doing, he demonstrates the diachronic pincer movement by wisdom has invaded the broader canon. ("Threat of Pan Sapientialism," 22–23)

Finally, despite the worries of Kynes, a "pan-sapiential" understanding of the OT can be very fruitful hermeneutically, opening up new possibilities for both intertextual readings within the OT and studies of particular texts in light of their formative wisdom intentionality.[72]

72. We could add that this proposal also fits more naturally into the broader understanding of wisdom in the ancient Near East. Cf. deClaissé-Walford, "Wisdom in the ANE," 5:863, "A number of scholars maintain, however, that were it not for the wisdom books of the OT, the various texts from Egypt and Mesopotamia now designated as 'wisdom' would not be considered a distinct collection, since their subject matters and forms are far from uniform and univocal. Indeed, the so-called wisdom texts of the ANE include a great variety of forms and subject matters."

BIBLIOGRAPHY

Alexander, Loveday. "Paul and the Hellenistic Schools: The Evidence of Galen." In *Paul in His Hellenistic Context*, edited by Troels Engberg-Pedersen, 60–83. Studies in the New Testament and Its World. Minneapolis: Fortress, 1995.

—————. "What Is a Gospel?" In *The Cambridge Companion to the Gospels*, edited by Stephen C. Barton, 13–33. Cambridge: Cambridge University Press, 2006.

Allen, Diogenes. *Philosophy for Understanding Theology*. Atlanta: John Knox, 1985.

Alston, William P. *Epistemic Justification: Essays in the Theory of Knowledge*. Ithaca, NY: Cornell University Press, 1989.

Alter, Robert. *The Art of Biblical Narrative*. New York: Basic Books, 1981.

Annas, Julia. *The Morality of Happiness*. Oxford: Oxford University Press, 1993.

Aristotle. *Nicomachean Ethics*. 2nd ed. Translated by Terence Irwin. Indianapolis: Hackett, 1999.

Ashton, John. *Understanding the Fourth Gospel*. 2nd ed. Oxford: Oxford University Press, 2007.

Auerbach, Erich. *Mimesis: The Representation of Reality in Western Literature*. Translated by Willard R. Trask. Princeton: Princeton University Press, 1953.

Augustine. *Homilies on the First Epistle of John*. Translated by Boniface Ramsey. The Works of Saint Augustine: A Translation for the 21st Century. Hyde Park, NY: New City Press, 2008.

—————. *On Christian Teaching*. Translated by R. P. H. Green. Oxford World's Classics. Oxford: Oxford University Press, 2008.

Aune, David Edward. *The New Testament in Its Literary Environment*. LEC 8. Edited by Wayne A. Meeks. Philadelphia: Westminster, 1987.

Austin, J. L. *How to Do Things with Words*. Cambridge, MA: Harvard University Press, 1962.

Baird, William. *History of New Testament Research*. 2 vols. Minneapolis: Fortress, 1992.

Barbarick, Clifford A. "The Pattern and the Power: The Example of Christ in 1 Peter." PhD diss., Baylor University, 2011.

Barclay, John M. G. *Obeying the Truth: A Study of Paul's Ethics in Galatians*. Vancouver: Regent College Publishing, 2005.

———. *Paul and the Gift*. Grand Rapids: Eerdmans, 2015.

Barrett, C. K. *The Epistle to the Romans*. BNTC. 2nd ed. Peabody, MA: Hendrickson, 1991.

Barth, Karl. *Church Dogmatics*. 14 vols. London: T&T Clark, 2004.

———. *Ethics*. Translated by Geoffrey W. Bromiley. New York: Seabury, 1981.

Barton, John. *Understanding Old Testament Ethics: Approaches and Explorations*. Louisville: Westminster John Knox, 2003.

Bauckham, Richard. *Gospel of Glory: Major Themes in Johannine Theology*. Grand Rapids: Baker Academic, 2015.

———. *James: Wisdom of James, Disciple of Jesus the Sage*. Edited by John Court. New Testament Readings. London: Routledge, 1999.

———. *Jesus and the Eyewitnesses: The Gospels as Eyewitness Testimony*. Grand Rapids: Eerdmans, 2006.

———. *Jesus and the God of Israel: God Crucified and Other Studies on the New Testament's Christology of Divine Identity*. Grand Rapids: Eerdmans, 2009.

———. *The Testimony of the Beloved Disciple: Narrative, History, and Theology in the Gospel of John*. Grand Rapids: Baker, 2007.

Bayer, Hans F. *A Theology of Mark: The Dynamic between Christology and Authentic Discipleship*. Explorations in Biblical Theology. Phillipsburg, NJ: P&R, 2012.

Bayer, Oswald. *Martin Luther's Theology: A Contemporary Interpretation*. Translated by Thomas H. Trapp. Grand Rapids: Eerdmans, 2008.

Bazerman, Charles. "Genre as Social Action." In *The Routledge Handbook of Discourse Analysis*, edited by James Paul Gee and Michael Handford, 226–38. New York: Routledge, 2012.

Beasley-Murray, George R. *John*. WBC. 2nd ed. Nashville: Thomas Nelson, 1999.

Bennema, Cornelis. *A Theory of Character in New Testament Narrative*. Minneapolis: Fortress, 2014.

Benner, David G. *Spirituality and the Awakening Self: The Sacred Journey of Transformation*. Grand Rapids: Brazos, 2012.

Berger, Peter L., and Thomas Luckmann. *The Social Construction of Reality: A Treatise in the Sociology of Knowledge*. Garden City, NY: Anchor Books, 1967.

Best, Ernest. *A Critical and Exegetical Commentary on Ephesians*. ICC. Edinburgh: T&T Clark, 1998.

Billings, J. Todd. *Union with Christ: Reframing Theology and Ministry for the Church*. Grand Rapids: Baker Academic, 2011.

———. *The Word of God for the People of God: An Entryway to the Theological Interpretation of Scripture*. Grand Rapids: Eerdmans, 2010.

Birch, Bruce C. "Divine Character and the Formation of Moral Community in the Book of Exodus." In *The Bible in Ethics: The Second Sheffield Colloquium*, edited by John W. Rogerson, Margaret Davies, and M. Daniel Carroll R., 119–35. JSOTSup 207. Sheffield: Sheffield Academic Press, 1995.

Bockmuehl, Markus. "'The Form of God' (Phil. 2:6): Variations on a Theme of Jewish Mysticism." *JTS* 48, no. 1 (1997): 1–23.

———. *Jewish Law in Gentile Churches: Halakhah and the Beginning of Christian Public Ethics*. Edinburgh: T&T Clark, 2000.

———. *Seeing the Word: Refocusing New Testament Study*. STI. Grand Rapids: Baker Academic, 2006.

Bonhoeffer, Dietrich. *Discipleship*. Translated by Barbara Green and Reinhard Krauss. Edited by Geffrey B. Kelly and John D. Godsey. Dietrich Bonhoeffer Works 4. Minneapolis: Fortress, 2001.

Booth, Wayne C. *The Company We Keep: An Ethics of Fiction*. Berkeley: University of California Press, 1988.

———. *The Rhetoric of Fiction*. 2nd ed. Chicago: University of Chicago Press, 1983.

———. *A Rhetoric of Irony*. Chicago: University of Chicago Press, 1974.

Boring, M. Eugene. *Mark: A Commentary*. NTL. Louisville: Westminster John Knox, 2006.

Bowman, Richard G. "The Complexity of Character and the Ethics of Complexity: The Case of King David." In *Character and Scripture: Moral Formation, Community, and Biblical Interpretation*, edited by William P. Brown, 73–97. Grand Rapids: Eerdmans, 2002.

Bray, Gerald Lewis, ed. *Romans*. ACCSNT 6. Downers Grove, IL: InterVarsity, 1998.

Brooks, David. *Bobos in Paradise: The New Upper Class and How They Got There*. New York: Simon & Schuster, 2000.

Brown, Gillian, and George Yule. *Discourse Analysis*. Cambridge Textbooks in Linguistics. Cambridge: Cambridge University Press, 1983.

Brown, Jeannine K. *Scripture as Communication: Introducing Biblical Hermeneutics*. Grand Rapids: Baker Academic, 2007.

Brown, Raymond E. *The Gospel according to John: Introduction, Translation, and Notes*. 2 vols. AB 29A–B. Garden City, NY: Doubleday, 1966–70.

———. *An Introduction to the Gospel of John*. ABRL. Edited by Francis J. Moloney. New York: Doubleday, 2003.

Brown, William P. *Character in Crisis: A Fresh Approach to the Wisdom Literature of the Old Testament*. Grand Rapids: Eerdmans, 1996.

Brueggemann, Walter. *Reality, Grief, Hope: Three Urgent Prophetic Tasks*. Grand Rapids: Eerdmans, 2014.

Bultmann, Rudolf. "Das Problem der Ethik bei Paulus." *Zeitschrift für die neutestamentliche Wissenschaft* 23 (1924): 123–40.

———. *The Gospel of John: A Commentary*. Translated by George R. Beasley-Murray. Philadelphia: Westminster, 1971.

———. "New Testament and Mythology: The Problem of Demythologizing the New Testament Proclamation." Translated by Schubert M. Ogden. In *New Testament and Mythology: And Other Basic Writings*, edited by Schubert M. Ogden, 1–43. Philadelphia: Fortress, 1984.

———. *Theology of the New Testament*. Translated by Kendrick Grobel. 2 vols. New York: Scribner, 1951–55.

Burnett, Richard E. *Karl Barth's Theological Exegesis: The Hermeneutical Principles of the Römerbrief Period*. Grand Rapids: Eerdmans, 2004.

Burridge, Richard A. *Imitating Jesus: An Inclusive Approach to New Testament Ethics*. Grand Rapids: Eerdmans, 2007.

———. *What Are the Gospels? A Comparison with Graeco-Roman Biography*. 2nd ed. Grand Rapids: Eerdmans, 2004.

Camery-Hoggatt, Jerry. *Irony in Mark's Gospel: Text and Subtext*. SNTSMS 72. Cambridge: Cambridge University Press, 1992.

Campbell, Douglas A. *The Deliverance of God: An Apocalyptic Rereading of Justification in Paul*. Grand Rapids: Eerdmans, 2009.

Capes, David B. "*Imitatio Christi* and the Gospel Genre." *BBR* 13, no. 1 (2003): 1–19.

Carroll, Robert P. "Poststructuralist Approaches." In *Cambridge Companion to Biblical Interpretation*, edited by John Barton, 50–66. Cambridge: Cambridge University Press, 1998.

Carroll R., M. Daniel. "'He Has Told You What Is Good': Moral Formation in Micah." In *Character Ethics and the Old Testament: Moral Dimensions of Scripture*, edited by M. Daniel Carroll R. and Jacqueline E. Lapsley, 103–18. Louisville: Westminster John Knox, 2007.

Carroll R., M. Daniel, and Jacqueline E. Lapsley, eds. *Character Ethics and the Old Testament: Moral Dimensions of Scripture*. Louisville: Westminster John Knox, 2007.

Carson, D. A. *The Gospel according to John*. PNTC. Grand Rapids: Eerdmans, 1991.

Carson, D. A., Peter Thomas O'Brien, and Mark A. Seifrid, eds. *Justification and Variegated Nomism*. Vol. 1, *The Complexities of Second Temple Judaism*. Grand Rapids: Baker Academic, 2001.

Catellani, Andrea. "Signs and Semiotics." In *The Oxford Guide to the Historical Reception of Augustine*, edited by Karla Pollmann, 1739–47. Oxford: Oxford University Press, 2013.

Charry, Ellen T. *By the Renewing of Your Minds: The Pastoral Function of Christian Doctrine*. Oxford: Oxford University Press, 1997.

Cheung, Simon Chi-chung. *Wisdom Intoned: A Reappraisal of the Genre "Wisdom Psalms."* Edited by Claudia V. Camp and Andrew Mein. LHBOTS 613. London: Bloomsbury/T&T Clark, 2015.

Childs, Brevard S. *Biblical Theology of the Old and New Testaments: Theological Reflection on the Christian Bible.* Minneapolis: Fortress, 1993.

Chisholm, Roderick M. *Perceiving: A Philosophical Study.* Ithaca, NY: Cornell University Press, 1957.

Code, Alan. "Aristotle's Logic and Metaphysics." In *From Aristotle to Augustine*, edited by David Furley, 40–75. Routledge History of Philosophy. London: Routledge, 1997.

Cole, Robert L. *Psalms 1–2: Gateway to the Psalter.* Hebrew Bible Monographs 37. Sheffield: Sheffield Phoenix Press, 2012.

Collins, John J. "Wisdom Reconsidered, in Light of the Scrolls." *DSD* 4, no. 3 (1997): 265–81.

Conway, Colleen M. "Speaking through Ambiguity: Minor Characters in the Fourth Gospel." *BibInt* 10 (2002): 324–41.

Cranfield, C. E. B. *The Epistle to the Romans.* 2 vols. ICC. Edinburgh: T&T Clark, 1990.

Crenshaw, James L. *Old Testament Wisdom: An Introduction.* Rev. ed. Louisville: Westminster John Knox, 1998.

Crites, Stephen. "The Narrative Quality of Experience." In *Why Narrative? Readings in Narrative Theology*, edited by Stanley Hauerwas and L. Gregory Jones, 65–88. Grand Rapids: Eerdmans, 1989.

Culler, Jonathan. "Towards a Theory of Non-Genre Literature." In *Surfiction: Fiction Now and Tomorrow*, edited by Raymond Federman, 255–62. Chicago: Swallow, 1981.

Culpepper, R. Alan. *Anatomy of the Fourth Gospel: A Study in Literary Design.* FFNT. Philadelphia: Fortress, 1983.

Davies, William David, and Dale C. Allison. *A Critical and Exegetical Commentary on the Gospel according to Saint Matthew.* 3 vols. ICC. Edinburgh: T&T Clark, 1988.

deClaissé-Walford, Nancy. "Wisdom in the Ancient Near East." In *NIDB*, 5:862–65.

Deely, John N. *Four Ages of Understanding: The First Postmodern Survey of Philosophy from Ancient Times to the Turn of the Twenty-First Century.* Toronto Studies in Semiotics. Toronto: University of Toronto Press, 2001.

Deidun, T. J. *New Covenant Morality in Paul.* AnBib 89. Rome: Biblical Institute Press, 1981.

Dell, Katharine J. "Deciding the Boundaries of 'Wisdom': Applying the Concept of Family Resemblance." In *Was There a Wisdom Tradition? New Prospects in Israelite Wisdom Studies*, edited by Mark R. Sneed, 145–60. SBL Ancient Israel and Its Literature 23. Atlanta: SBL Press, 2015.

———. "Wisdom in the Old Testament." In *NIDB*, 5:869–75.

Dennison, William D. "Indicative and Imperative: The Basic Structure of Pauline Ethics." *CTJ* 14, no. 1 (1979): 55–78.

Derrida, Jacques. "The Law of Genre." *Critical Inquiry* 7 (1980): 55–81.

de Villiers, Pieter G. R. "Love in the Letter to the Galatians." In *The Bible and Spirituality: Exploratory Essays in Reading Scripture Spiritually*, edited by Andrew T. Lincoln, J. Gordon McConville, and Lloyd K. Pietersen, 194–211. Eugene, OR: Cascade, 2013.

Dibelius, Martin. *A Fresh Approach to the New Testament and Early Christian Literature*. London: Nicholson & Watson, 1936.

———. *James: A Commentary on the Epistle of James*. Translated by Michael A. Williams. Hermeneia. Philadelphia: Fortress, 1976.

Dillenberger, John, ed. *Martin Luther: Selections from His Writings*. Garden City, NY: Doubleday, 1961.

Dintaman, Stephen F. *Creative Grace: Faith and History in the Theology of Adolf Schlatter*. American University Studies Series VII: Theology and Religion 152. New York: Peter Lang, 1993.

Dodd, C. H. *Gospel and Law: The Relation of Faith and Ethics in Early Christianity*. Bampton Lectures in America. Cambridge: Cambridge University Press, 1951.

———. *Historical Tradition in the Fourth Gospel*. Cambridge: Cambridge University Press, 1963.

———. *The Interpretation of the Fourth Gospel*. Cambridge: Cambridge University Press, 1953.

Dozeman, Thomas B. "Creation and Environment in the Character Development of Moses." In *Character Ethics and the Old Testament: Moral Dimensions of Scripture*, edited by M. Daniel Carroll R. and Jacqueline E. Lapsley, 27–36. Louisville: Westminster John Knox, 2007.

Dreyfus, Hubert L. *Skillful Coping: Essays on the Phenomenology of Everyday Perception and Action*. Oxford: Oxford University Press, 2014.

Dryden, J. de Waal. "Immortality in Romans 2:6–11." *JTI* 7, no. 2 (2013): 295–310.

———. "Revisiting Romans 7: Law, Self, and Spirit." *JSPL* 5, no. 1 (2015): 129–51.

———. *Theology and Ethics in 1 Peter: Paraenetic Strategies for Christian Character Formation*. WUNT 2/209. Tübingen: Mohr Siebeck, 2006.

Dunn, James D. G. "The Embarrassment of History: Reflections on the Problem of 'Anti-Judaism' in the Fourth Gospel." In *Anti-Judaism and the Fourth Gospel*, edited by R. Bieringer, D. Pollefeyt, and F. Vandecasteele-Vanneuville, 41–60. Louisville: Westminster John Knox, 2001.

———. *The New Perspective on Paul*. Rev. ed. Grand Rapids: Eerdmans, 2005.

———. "The Pauline Letters." In *The Cambridge Companion to Biblical Interpretation*, edited by John Barton, 276–89. Cambridge: Cambridge University Press, 1998.

———. *Romans*. 2 vols. WBC 38A. Dallas: Word, 1988.

———. *The Theology of Paul the Apostle*. Grand Rapids: Eerdmans, 1998.

Eco, Umberto. *The Role of the Reader: Explorations in the Semiotics of Texts*. Advances in Semiotics. Bloomington: Indiana University Press, 1979.

Edwards, James R. *The Gospel according to Mark*. PNTC. Grand Rapids: Eerdmans, 2002.

Engberg-Pedersen, Troels. *Paul and the Stoics*. Edinburgh: T&T Clark, 2000.

Engberg-Pedersen, Troels, and James M. Starr. *Early Christian Paraenesis in Context*. BZNW 125. Berlin: de Gruyter, 2004.

Epictetus. *Discourses*. Translated by W. A. Oldfather. 2 vols. LCL 131–32. Cambridge, MA: Harvard University Press, 1961.

Fewster, Gregory P. "The Philippians 'Christ Hymn': Trends in Critical Scholarship." *CurBR* 13, no. 2 (2015): 191–206.

Fish, Stanley. *Is There a Text in This Class? The Authority of Interpretive Communities*. Cambridge, MA: Harvard University Press, 1980.

Fitzmyer, Joseph A. *Romans: A New Translation with Introduction and Commentary*. AB 33. New York: Doubleday, 1993.

Ford, David F., and Graham Stanton, eds. *Reading Texts, Seeking Wisdom: Scripture and Theology*. London: SCM, 2003.

Fowl, Stephen. "Some Uses of Story in Moral Discourse: Reflections on Paul's Moral Discourse and Our Own." *Modern Theology* 4, no. 4 (1988): 293–308.

Fowler, Alastair. *Kinds of Literature: An Introduction to the Theory of Genres and Modes*. Cambridge, MA: Harvard University Press, 1982.

Fox, Michael V. *Proverbs: A New Translation with Introduction and Commentary*. 2 vols. AB 18. New Haven: Yale University Press, 2000–2009.

———. "Wisdom in the Joseph Story." *VT* 51 (2001): 26–41.

France, R. T. *The Gospel of Mark: A Commentary on the Greek Text*. NIGTC. Grand Rapids: Eerdmans, 2002.

Freeman, Samuel. "Deontology." In *Encyclopedia of Ethics*, edited by Lawrence C. Becker and Charlotte B. Becker, 391–96. London: Routledge, 2001.

Frei, Hans W. *The Eclipse of Biblical Narrative: A Study in Eighteenth and Nineteenth Century Hermeneutics*. New Haven: Yale University Press, 1974.

Frow, John. *Genre*. The New Critical Idiom. London: Routledge, 2006.

Furnish, Victor Paul. *Theology and Ethics in Paul*. NTL. Louisville: Westminster John Knox, 2009.

Gadamer, Hans-Georg. *Truth and Method*. Translated by Joel Weinsheimer and Donald G. Marshall. 2nd rev. ed. New York: Continuum, 2004.

Gammie, John G. "Paraenetic Literature: Toward the Morphology of a Secondary Genre." *Semeia* 50 (1990): 41–77.

Gathercole, Simon J. *Where Is Boasting? Early Jewish Soteriology and Paul's Response in Romans 1–5*. Grand Rapids: Eerdmans, 2002.

Gee, James Paul, and Michael Handford, eds. *The Routledge Handbook of Discourse Analysis*. Oxford: Routledge, 2012.

George, Stephen K., ed. *Ethics, Literature, and Theory: An Introductory Reader*. 2nd ed. Lanham, MD: Rowman & Littlefield, 2005.

Gibson, Andrew. *Postmodernity, Ethics, and the Novel*. London: Routledge, 1999.

Gioia, Luigi. *The Theological Epistemology of Augustine's De Trinitate*. Oxford Theological Monographs. Oxford: Oxford University Press, 2008.

Goff, Matthew. "Qumran Wisdom Literature and the Problem of Genre." *DSD* 17 (2010): 315–35.

Gorman, Michael J. "'Although/Because He Was in the Form of God': The Theological Significance of Paul's Master Story (Phil 2:6–11)." *JTI* 1, no. 2 (2007): 147–69.

———. *Apostle of the Crucified Lord: A Theological Introduction to Paul and His Letters*. Grand Rapids: Eerdmans, 2004.

———. *Cruciformity: Paul's Narrative Spirituality of the Cross*. Grand Rapids: Eerdmans, 2001.

Gregory, Marshall. "Ethical Criticism: What It Is and Why It Matters." In *Ethics, Literature, and Theory: An Introductory Reader*, edited by Stephen K. George, 37–61. Lanham, MD: Rowman & Littlefield, 2005.

———. *Shaped by Stories: The Ethical Power of Narratives*. Notre Dame, IN: University of Notre Dame Press, 2009.

Grene, Marjorie G. *The Knower and the Known*. London: Faber & Faber, 1966.

Griffiths, Paul J. *Intellectual Appetite: A Theological Grammar*. Washington, DC: Catholic University of America Press, 2009.

Grondin, Jean. *Introduction to Philosophical Hermeneutics*. Translated by Joel Weinsheimer. Yale Studies in Hermeneutics. New Haven: Yale University Press, 1994.

Guelich, Robert A. *Mark 1–8:26*. WBC 34A. Dallas: Word, 1989.

Gundry, Robert H. "Grace, Works, and Staying Saved in Paul." *Bib* 66 (1985): 1–38.

Hagner, Donald A. *Matthew 1–13*. WBC 33A. Dallas: Word, 1993.

Hakola, Raimo. "The Burden of Ambiguity: Nicodemus and the Social Identity of the Johannine Christians." *NTS* 55 (2009): 438–55.

Hays, Richard B. "A Hermeneutic of Trust." In *The Conversion of the Imagination: Paul as Interpreter of Israel's Scripture*, 190–201. Grand Rapids: Eerdmans, 2005.

———. *The Moral Vision of the New Testament: Community, Cross, New Creation, A Contemporary Introduction to New Testament Ethics*. San Francisco: HarperSanFrancisco, 1996.

Heidegger, Martin. *The Basic Problems of Phenomenology*. Translated by Albert Hofstadter. Studies in Phenomenology and Existential Philosophy. Bloomington: Indiana University Press, 1982.

———. *Being and Time: A Translation of* Sein und Zeit. Translated by Joan Stambaugh. SUNY Series in Contemporary Continental Philosophy. Albany: State University of New York Press, 1996.

———. "The Onto-Theo-Logical Constitution of Metaphysics." Translated by Joan Stambaugh. In *Identity and Difference*, 42–74. New York: Harper & Row, 1969.

Henderson, Suzanne Watts. *Christology and Discipleship in the Gospel of Mark.* SNTSMS 135. Cambridge: Cambridge University Press, 2006.

Hoitenga, Dewey J. *Faith and Reason from Plato to Plantinga: An Introduction to Reformed Epistemology.* Albany: State University of New York Press, 1991.

Hood, Jason B. *Imitating God in Christ: Recapturing a Biblical Pattern.* Downers Grove, IL: InterVarsity, 2013.

Hooker, Morna D. *The Gospel according to St. Mark.* BNTC. Edited by Henry Chadwick. Peabody, MA: Hendrickson, 1991.

Horsley, G. H. R., ed. *New Documents Illustrating Early Christianity.* Vol. 4, *A Review of the Greek Inscriptions and Papyri Published in 1979.* North Ryde, NSW: The Ancient History Documentary Research Centre Macquarie University, 1987.

Howard, Thomas A. *Protestant Theology and the Making of the Modern German University.* Oxford: Oxford University Press, 2006.

Inwood, M. J. *A Heidegger Dictionary.* The Blackwell Philosopher Dictionaries. Oxford: Blackwell, 1999.

Iser, Wolfgang. *The Implied Reader: Patterns of Communication in Prose Fiction from Bunyan to Beckett.* Baltimore: Johns Hopkins University Press, 1974.

Isocrates. *Demonicus.* In *Discourses I*, translated by George Norlin. 3 vols. LCL 209. Cambridge, MA: Harvard University Press, 1928.

Jauss, Hans Robert. *Toward an Aesthetic of Reception.* Translated by Timothy Bahti. Theory and History of Literature. Minneapolis: University of Minnesota Press, 1982.

Jüngel, Eberhard. "Law and Gospel." Translated by Garrett E. Paul. In *Karl Barth: A Theological Legacy*, 105–26. Philadelphia: Westminster, 1986.

Käsemann, Ernst. *Commentary on Romans.* Translated by Geoffrey W. Bromiley. Grand Rapids: Eerdmans, 1980.

———. "A Critical Analysis of Philippians 2:5–11." *JTC* 5 (1968): 45–88.

———. *Exegetische Versuche und Besinnungen.* 2 vols. Göttingen: Vandenhoeck & Ruprecht, 1960.

Kass, Leon. *The Beginning of Wisdom: Reading Genesis.* New York: Free Press, 2003.

Keener, Craig S. *A Commentary on the Gospel of Matthew.* Grand Rapids: Eerdmans, 1999.

———. *The Gospel of John: A Commentary.* 2 vols. Peabody, MA: Hendrickson, 2003.

Kierkegaard, Søren. *Concluding Unscientific Postscript to Philosophical Fragments.* Translated by Howard Vincent Hong and Edna Hatlestad Hong. 2 vols. Kierkegaard's Writings 12. Princeton: Princeton University Press, 1992.

———. *Upbuilding Discourses in Various Spirits*. Translated by Howard Vincent Hong and Edna Hatlestad Hong. Kierkegaard's Writings 15. Princeton: Princeton University Press, 1993.

Knight, Mark. "*Wirkungsgeschichte*, Reception History, Reception Theory." *JSNT* 33, no. 2 (2010): 137–46.

Köstenberger, Andreas J. *John*. BECNT. Grand Rapids: Baker Academic, 2004.

———. *The Missions of Jesus and the Disciples according to the Fourth Gospel: With Implications for the Fourth Gospel's Purpose and the Mission of the Contemporary Church*. Grand Rapids: Eerdmans, 1998.

Kynes, Will. "The Modern Scholarly Wisdom Tradition and the Threat of Pan-Sapientialism." In *Was There a Wisdom Tradition? New Prospects in Israelite Wisdom Studies*, edited by Mark R. Sneed, 11–38. SBL Ancient Israel and Its Literature 23. Atlanta: SBL Press, 2015.

Lapsley, Jacqueline E. *Can These Bones Live? The Problem of the Moral Self in the Book of Ezekiel*. BZAW 301. New York: de Gruyter, 2000.

———. "A Feeling for God: Emotions and Moral Formation in Ezekiel 24:15–27." In *Character Ethics and the Old Testament: Moral Dimensions of Scripture*, edited by M. Daniel Carroll R. and Jacqueline E. Lapsley, 93–102. Louisville: Westminster John Knox, 2007.

Levy, Ian Christopher, Philip D. Krey, and Thomas Ryan, eds. *The Letter to the Romans*. The Bible in Medieval Tradition. Grand Rapids: Eerdmans, 2013.

Lewis, C. S. *The Abolition of Man, or, Reflections on Education with Special Reference to the Teaching of English in the Upper Forms of Schools*. New York: Macmillan, 1955.

———. *Till We Have Faces: A Myth Retold*. London: G. Bles, 1956.

Lieu, Judith. *I, II & III John: A Commentary*. NTL. Louisville: Westminster John Knox, 2008.

Lincoln, Andrew T. *Ephesians*. WBC 42. Dallas: Word, 1990.

———. *The Gospel according to Saint John*. BNTC. London: Continuum, 2005.

———. "The Spiritual Wisdom of Colossians in the Context of Graeco-Roman Spiritualities." In *The Bible and Spirituality: Exploratory Essays in Reading Scripture Spiritually*, edited by Andrew T. Lincoln, J. Gordon McConville, and Lloyd K. Pietersen, 212–32. Eugene, OR: Cascade, 2013.

Locke, John. *A Letter concerning Toleration*. Great Books in Philosophy. Buffalo, NY: Prometheus, 1990.

Long, V. Philips. "Scenic, Succinct, Subtle: An Introduction to the Literary Artistry of 1&2 Samuel." *Presb* 19, no. 1 (1993): 32–47.

Luther, Martin. *Lectures on Galatians 1535: Chapters 1–4*. Translated and edited by Jaroslav Pelikan. Luther's Works. St. Louis: Concordia, 1963.

———. "Treatise on Good Works." Translated by W. A. Lambert. In *The Christian in Society*, 21–114. Luther's Works. Philadelphia: Fortress, 1966.

Luz, Ulrich. *Matthew 1–7: A Commentary*. Translated by James E. Crouch. Hermeneia. Rev. ed. Minneapolis: Fortress, 2007.

Macaskill, Grant. *Revealed Wisdom and Inaugurated Eschatology in Ancient Judaism and Early Christianity*. Supplements to the Journal for the Study of Judaism 115. Leiden: Brill, 2007.

———. *Union with Christ in the New Testament*. Oxford: Oxford University Press, 2013.

Macintosh, A. A. "Hosea and the Wisdom Tradition: Dependence and Independence." In *Wisdom in Ancient Israel: Essays in Honour of J. A. Emerton*, edited by John Day, R. P. Gordon, and H. G. M. Williamson, 124–32. Cambridge: Cambridge University Press, 1995.

MacIntyre, Alasdair C. *After Virtue: A Study in Moral Theory*. 2nd ed. London: Duckworth, 1985.

———. *Whose Justice? Which Rationality?* Notre Dame, IN: University of Notre Dame Press, 1988.

Malherbe, Abraham J. "Hellenistic Moralists and the New Testament." In *Aufstieg und Niedergang der römischen Welt: Geschichte und Kultur Roms im Spiegel der neueren Forschung*, edited by Wolfgang Haase, 267–333. Hellenistic Moralists and the New Testament. Berlin: de Gruyter, 1992.

———. *The Letters to the Thessalonians: A New Translation with Introduction and Commentary*. AB 32B. New York: Doubleday, 2000.

———. *Moral Exhortation: A Greco-Roman Sourcebook*. LEC 4. Philadelphia: Westminster, 1986.

Malina, Bruce J., and Richard L. Rohrbaugh. *Social-Science Commentary on the Gospel of John*. Minneapolis: Fortress 1998.

Martin, Ralph P., and Brian J. Dodd, eds. *Where Christology Began: Essays on Philippians 2*. Louisville: Westminster John Knox, 1998.

Martyn, J. Louis. *History and Theology in the Fourth Gospel*. NTL. 3rd ed. Louisville: Westminster John Knox, 2003.

McCann, J. Clinton, Jr. "The Book of Psalms: Introductory Commentary and Reflections." In *NIB*, 4:641–1280.

———. "'The Way of the Righteous' in the Psalms: Character Formation and Cultural Crisis." In *Character and Scripture: Moral Formation, Community, and Biblical Interpretation*, edited by William P. Brown, 135–49. Grand Rapids: Eerdmans, 2002.

McDonald, James I. H. *Kerygma and Didache: The Articulation and Structure of the Earliest Christian Message*. SNTSMS 37. Cambridge: Cambridge University Press, 1980.

McGrath, Alister E. *The Making of Modern German Christology: From the Enlightenment to Pannenberg*. 2nd ed. Grand Rapids: Zondervan, 1994.

McKane, W. "Jeremiah and the Wise." In *Wisdom in Ancient Israel: Essays in Honour of J. A. Emerton*, edited by John Day, R. P. Gordon, and H. G. M. Williamson, 142–51. Cambridge: Cambridge University Press, 1995.

———. *Prophets and Wise Men*. SBT. London: SCM, 1965.

McKenzie, John L. "Reflections on Wisdom." *JBL* 86, no. 1 (1967): 1–9.

Metzger, Bruce Manning. *The Canon of the New Testament: Its Origin, Development, and Significance*. Oxford: Clarendon, 1987.

Milbank, John. "Knowledge: The Theological Critique of Philosophy in Hamann and Jacobi." In *Radical Orthodoxy: A New Theology*, edited by John Milbank, Catherine Pickstock, and Graham Ward, 21–37. New York: Routledge, 1999.

Miller, Douglas B. "Wisdom in the Canon: Discerning the Early Intuition." In *Was There a Wisdom Tradition? New Prospects in Israelite Wisdom Studies*, edited by Mark R. Sneed, 87–113. SBL Ancient Israel and Its Literature 23. Atlanta: SBL Press, 2015.

Moberly, R. W. L. *The Bible, Theology, and Faith: A Study of Abraham and Jesus*. Cambridge Studies in Christian Doctrine 5. Cambridge: Cambridge University Press, 2000.

Moo, Douglas J. *The Epistle to the Romans*. NICNT. Grand Rapids: Eerdmans, 1996.

———. *Galatians*. BECNT. Grand Rapids: Baker Academic, 2013.

Morgan, Florence A. "Romans 6,5a: United to a Death Like Christ's." *ETL* 59, no. 4 (1983): 267–302.

Murphy, Roland E. "Wisdom in the OT." In *ABD*, 6:920–31.

Murray, John. *The Epistle to the Romans: English Text with Introduction, Exposition and Notes*. NICNT. Grand Rapids: Eerdmans, 1959.

Nadler, Steven. "Conceptions of God." In *Oxford Handbook of Philosophy in Early Modern Europe*, edited by Desmond M. Clarke and Catherine Wilson, 525–47. Oxford: Oxford University Press, 2011.

Naugle, David K. *Reordered Love, Reordered Lives: Learning the Deep Meaning of Happiness*. Grand Rapids: Eerdmans, 2008.

Neuer, Werner. *Adolf Schlatter: A Biography of Germany's Premier Biblical Theologian*. Translated by Robert Yarbrough. Grand Rapids: Baker Books, 1996.

Newsom, Carol. "Spying Out the Land: A Report from Genology." In *Bakhtin and Genre Theory in Biblical Studies*, edited by Roland Boer, 19–30. Society of Biblical Literature Semeia Studies 63. Leiden: Brill, 2008.

Neyrey, Jerome H., and Richard L. Rohrbaugh. "'He Must Increase, I Must Decrease' (John 3:30): A Cultural and Social Interpretation." *CBQ* 63 (2001): 464–83.

Nolland, John. *The Gospel of Matthew: A Commentary on the Greek Text*. NIGTC. Grand Rapids: Eerdmans, 2005.

North, Wendy E. S. *The Lazarus Story within the Johannine Tradition.* JSNTSup 212. Sheffield: Sheffield Academic Press, 2001.

———. "'Lord If You Had Been Here . . .' (John 11:21): The Absence of Jesus and Strategies of Consolation in the Fourth Gospel." *JSNT* 36 (2013): 39–52.

Nouwen, Henri J. M. *Spiritual Formation: Following the Movements of the Spirit.* Edited by Michael J. Christensen and Rebecca J. Laird. New York: HarperOne, 2010.

Nussbaum, Martha C. "Aristotle." In *A Companion to Metaphysics,* edited by Jaegwon Kim and Ernest Sosa, 24–31. Blackwell Companion to Philosophy. Oxford: Blackwell, 1995.

———. *The Fragility of Goodness: Luck and Ethics in Greek Tragedy and Philosophy.* Cambridge: Cambridge University Press, 1986.

———. *Love's Knowledge: Essays on Philosophy and Literature.* Oxford: Oxford University Press, 1992.

———. *The Therapy of Desire: Theory and Practice in Hellenistic Ethics.* Martin Classical Lectures. Princeton: Princeton University Press, 1994.

———. *Upheavals of Thought: The Intelligence of Emotions.* Cambridge: Cambridge University Press, 2001.

Oberman, Heiko Augustinus. *The Harvest of Medieval Theology: Gabriel Biel and Late Medieval Nominalism.* Rev. ed. Grand Rapids: Baker Academic, 2000.

O'Connor, Kathleen M. "The Book of Jeremiah: Reconstructing Community after Disaster." In *Character Ethics and the Old Testament: Moral Dimensions of Scripture,* edited by M. Daniel Carroll R. and Jacqueline E. Lapsley, 81–92. Louisville: Westminster John Knox, 2007.

O'Donnell, James J. "*Doctrina Christiana, De.*" In *Augustine through the Ages: An Encyclopedia,* edited by Allan D. Fitzgerald, 278–80. Grand Rapids: Eerdmans, 1999.

O'Donovan, Oliver. *Resurrection and Moral Order: An Outline for Evangelical Ethics.* Grand Rapids: Eerdmans, 1986.

Onesti, K. L., and M. T. Brauch. "Righteousness, Righteousness of God." In *DPL,* 827–37.

Parker, David. *Ethics, Theory, and the Novel.* Cambridge: Cambridge University Press, 1994.

Parry, Robin. "Narrative Criticism." In *Dictionary for Theological Interpretation of the Bible,* edited by Kevin J. Vanhoozer, Craig G. Bartholomew, Daniel J. Treier, and N. T. Wright, 528–31. Grand Rapids: Baker Academic, 2005.

Penner, Todd C. *The Epistle of James and Eschatology: Re-reading an Ancient Christian Letter.* JSNTSup 121. Sheffield: Sheffield Academic Press, 1996.

Pennington, Jonathan T. *Reading the Gospels Wisely: A Narrative and Theological Introduction.* Grand Rapids: Baker Academic, 2012.

———. *The Sermon on the Mount and Human Flourishing: A Theological Commentary.* Grand Rapids: Baker Academic, 2017.

Perdue, Leo G. "The Social Character of Paraenesis and Paraenetic Literature." *Semeia* 50 (1990): 5–39.

Peters, James R. *The Logic of the Heart: Augustine, Pascal, and the Rationality of Faith*. Grand Rapids: Baker Academic, 2009.

Plato. *The Republic*. Translated by Desmond Lee. New York: Penguin, 1974.

———. *Theatetus*. Translated by Robin Waterfield. New York: Penguin, 1987.

Plutarch. *How a Man May Become Aware of His Progress in Virtue*. In *Moralia I*, translated by Frank Cole Babbitt. 14 vols. LCL 197. Cambridge, MA: Harvard University Press, 1927.

Polak, Frederik Lodewijk. *The Image of the Future: Enlightening the Past, Orientating the Present, Forecasting the Future*. Translated by Elise Boulding. European Aspects: A Collection of Studies Relating to European Integration Series A: Culture. 2 vols. Leyden: A. W. Sythoff, 1961.

Polanyi, Michael. *Personal Knowledge: Towards a Post-Critical Philosophy*. Chicago: University of Chicago Press, 1962.

Popkes, Wiard. "Paraenesis in the New Testament." In *Early Christian Paraenesis in Context*, edited by James Starr and Troels Engberg-Pedersen, 13–46. BZNW 125. Berlin: de Gruyter, 2005.

Rad, Gerhard von. *Old Testament Theology*. Translated by D. M. G. Stalker. 2 vols. Edinburgh: Oliver & Boyd, 1965.

———. *The Problem of the Hexateuch and Other Essays*. Translated by E. W. Trueman Dicken. Edinburgh: Oliver & Boyd, 1966.

Räisänen, Heikki. *Paul and the Law*. Philadelphia: Fortress, 1986.

Raschke, Carl A. *The Next Reformation: Why Evangelicals Must Embrace Postmodernity*. Grand Rapids: Baker Academic, 2004.

Reath, Andrews. "Categorical and Hypothetical Imperatives." In *Encyclopedia of Ethics*, edited by Lawrence C. Becker and Charlotte B. Becker, 189–94. London: Routledge, 2001.

Reed, Jeffrey T. *A Discourse Analysis of Philippians: Method and Rhetoric in the Debate over Literary Integrity*. JSNTSup 136. Sheffield: Sheffield Academic Press, 1997.

Ricoeur, Paul. *Oneself as Another*. Translated by Kathleen Blamey. Chicago: University of Chicago Press, 1992.

———. *Time and Narrative*. Translated by Kathleen Blamey and David Pellauer. 3 vols. Chicago: University of Chicago Press, 1984–88.

Ridderbos, Herman N. *The Gospel according to John: A Theological Commentary*. Translated by John Vriend. Grand Rapids: Eerdmans, 1997.

———. *Redemptive History and the New Testament Scriptures*. Translated by H. De Jongste. Biblical and Theological Studies. Phillipsburg, NJ: P&R, 1988.

Rohrbaugh, Richard L. *The New Testament in Cross-Cultural Perspective*. Matrix: The Bible in Mediterranean Context. Eugene, OR: Cascade, 2007.

Rowe, C. Kavin. *One True Life: The Stoics and Early Christians as Rival Traditions*. New Haven: Yale University Press, 2016.

Rutherford, Donald. "Innovation and Orthodoxy in Early Modern Philosophy." In *The Cambridge Companion to Early Modern Philosophy*, edited by Donald Rutherford, 11–38. Cambridge: Cambridge University Press, 2006.

Sailhamer, John H. "A Wisdom Composition of the Pentateuch?" In *The Way of Wisdom: Essays in Honor of Bruce K. Waltke*, edited by J. I. Packer and Sven Soderlund, 15–35. Grand Rapids: Zondervan, 2000.

Sanders, E. P. *Paul and Palestinian Judaism: A Comparison of Patterns of Religion*. Philadelphia: Fortress, 1977.

Sandys-Wunsch, John, and Laurence Eldridge. "J. P. Gabler and the Distinction between Biblical and Dogmatic Theology: Translation, Commentary, and Discussion of His Originality." *SJT* 33 (1980): 133–58.

Schildgen, Brenda Deen. "Hermeneutics." In *The Oxford Guide to the Historical Reception of Augustine*, edited by Karla Pollmann, 1126–30. Oxford: Oxford University Press, 2013.

Schlatter, Adolf. *Romans: The Righteousness of God*. Translated by Siegfried S. Schatzmann. Peabody, MA: Hendrickson, 1995.

———. "The Theology of the New Testament and Dogmatics." In *The Nature of New Testament Theology: The Contribution of William Wrede and Adolf Schlatter*, edited by Robert Morgan, 117–66. SBT. London: SCM, 1973.

Schnackenburg, Rudolf. *God's Rule and Kingdom*. Translated by John Murray. New York: Herder and Herder, 1963.

———. *The Gospel according to St. John*. Translated by Cecily Hastings and Kevin Smyth. 3 vols. New York: Seabury, 1968–82.

Schneiders, Sandra M. "The Gospels and the Reader." In *The Cambridge Companion to the Gospels*, edited by Stephen C. Barton, 97–118. Cambridge: Cambridge University Press, 2006.

———. *The Revelatory Text: Interpreting the New Testament as Sacred Scripture*. 2nd ed. Collegeville, MN: Liturgical Press, 1999.

Schrage, Wolfgang. *The Ethics of the New Testament*. Translated by David E. Green. Philadelphia: Fortress, 1988.

Schreiner, Thomas R. *Romans*. BECNT. Grand Rapids: Baker Academic, 1998.

Schulenburg, Sigrid, ed. *Briefwechsel zwischen Wilhelm Dilthey und dem grafen Paul Yorck v. Wartenburg, 1877–1897*. Halle: M. Niemeyer, 1923.

Schüssler Fiorenza, Elisabeth. *Rhetoric and Ethic: The Politics of Biblical Studies*. Minneapolis: Fortress, 1999.

Searle, J. R. *Speech Acts: An Essay in the Philosophy of Language*. Cambridge: Cambridge University Press, 1969.

Seneca. *Moral Epistles*. Translated by Richard M. Gummere. 3 vols. LCL 75–77. Cambridge, MA: Harvard University Press, 1925.

Shepherd, Tom. *Markan Sandwich Stories: Narration, Definition, and Function*. Andrews University Seminary Studies Dissertation Series 18. Berrien Springs, MI: Andrews University Press, 1993.

———. "The Narrative Function of Markan Intercalation." *NTS* 41 (1995): 522–40.

Sheppard, Gerald T. "Biblical Wisdom at the End of the Modern Age." In *Congress Volume: Oslo 1998*, edited by A. Lemaire and M. Sæbø, 369–98. VTSup 80. Leiden: Brill, 2000.

Sherman, Nancy. *The Fabric of Character: Aristotle's Theory of Virtue*. Oxford: Oxford University Press, 1989.

Simonetti, Manlio, ed. *Matthew 1–13*. ACCSNT 1A. Downers Grove, IL: InterVarsity, 2001.

Singer, Peter, and Renata Singer. *The Moral of the Story: An Anthology of Ethics through Literature*. Oxford: Blackwell, 2005.

Smalley, Stephen S. *1, 2, 3 John*. WBC 51. Waco: Word, 1984.

Smith, Christian, and Melinda Lundquist Denton. *Soul Searching: The Religious and Spiritual Lives of American Teenagers*. New York: Oxford University Press, 2005.

Sneed, Mark. "'Grasping After the Wind': The Elusive Attempt to Define and Delimit Wisdom." In *Was There a Wisdom Tradition? New Prospects in Israelite Wisdom Studies*, edited by Mark R. Sneed, 39–67. SBL Ancient Israel and Its Literature 23. Atlanta: SBL Press, 2015.

———. "Is the 'Wisdom Tradition' a Tradition?" *CBQ* 73 (2011): 50–71.

———, ed. *Was There a Wisdom Tradition? New Prospects in Israelite Wisdom Studies*. SBL Ancient Israel and Its Literature 23. Atlanta: SBL Press, 2015.

Sparks, Kenton L. *Ancient Texts for the Study of the Hebrew Bible: A Guide to the Background Literature*. Peabody, MA: Hendrickson, 2005.

Starr, James. "Was Paraenesis for Beginners?" In *Early Christian Paraenesis in Context*, edited by James Starr and Troels Engberg-Pedersen, 73–111. BZNW 125. Berlin: de Gruyter, 2005.

Stein, Robert H. *Mark*. BECNT. Grand Rapids: Baker Academic, 2008.

Steiner, George. *Martin Heidegger*. Chicago: University of Chicago Press, 1978.

Sternberg, Meir. *The Poetics of Biblical Narrative: Ideological Literature and the Drama of Reading*. The Indiana Literary Biblical Series. Bloomington: Indiana University Press, 1985.

Stowers, Stanley Kent. *Letter Writing in Greco-Roman Antiquity*. LEC 5. Philadelphia: Westminster, 1986.

Strecker, Georg. *The Johannine Letters: A Commentary on 1, 2, and 3 John*. Translated by Linda M. Maloney. Hermeneia. Minneapolis: Fortress, 1996.

Stuhlmacher, Peter. *Paul's Letter to the Romans: A Commentary.* Translated by Scott J. Hafemann. Edinburgh: T&T Clark, 1994.

Stump, Eleonore. *Wandering in Darkness: Narrative and the Problem of Suffering.* Oxford: Clarendon, 2010.

Swancutt, Diana M. "Paraenesis in Light of Protrepsis: Troubling the Typical Dichotomy." In *Early Christian Paraenesis in Context,* edited by James Starr and Troels Engberg-Pedersen, 113–53. BZNW 125. Berlin: de Gruyter, 2005.

Sweeney, Marvin A. "Form Criticism." In *Dictionary of the Old Testament: Wisdom, Poetry and Writings,* edited by Tremper Longman III and Peter Enns, 227–41. Downers Grove, IL: IVP Academic, 2008.

Talbert, Charles H. *Reading John: A Literary and Theological Commentary on the Fourth Gospel and the Johannine Epistles.* Reading the New Testament Series. New York: Crossroad, 1992.

———. *Reading the Sermon on the Mount: Character Formation and Decision Making in Matthew 5–7.* Columbia: University of South Carolina Press, 2004.

Tannehill, Robert. "The Disciples in Mark: The Function of a Narrative Role." In *The Interpretation of Mark,* edited by William Telford, 169–95. Studies in New Testament Interpretation. Edinburgh: T&T Clark, 1995.

———. *Dying and Rising with Christ: A Study in Pauline Theology.* Beiheft zur Zeitschrift für die neutestamentliche Wissenschaft und die Kunde der Älteren Kirche 32. Berlin: Töpelmann, 1967.

Taylor, Charles. *A Secular Age.* Cambridge, MA: Belknap Press of Harvard University Press, 2007.

———. *Sources of the Self: The Making of the Modern Identity.* Cambridge: Cambridge University Press, 1989.

Taylor, Mark C., ed. *Deconstruction in Context: Literature and Philosophy.* Chicago: University of Chicago Press, 1986.

Thomas, Johannes. "The Paraenesis of the *Testament of the Twelve Patriarchs.*" In *Early Christian Paraenesis in Context,* edited by Troels Engberg-Pedersen and James M. Starr, 157–89. BZNW 125. Berlin: de Gruyter, 2004.

Treier, Daniel J. *Introducing Theological Interpretation of Scripture: Recovering a Christian Practice.* Grand Rapids: Baker Academic, 2008.

Turner, David L. *Matthew.* BECNT. Grand Rapids: Baker Academic, 2008.

Van Cleve, James. "Kant, Immanuel." In *A Companion to Epistemology,* edited by Jonathan Dancy and Ernest Sosa, 230–34. Oxford: Blackwell, 1992.

Vanhoozer, Kevin J. *The Drama of Doctrine: A Canonical-Linguistic Approach to Christian Theology.* Louisville: Westminster John Knox, 2005.

———. *First Theology: God, Scripture and Hermeneutics.* Downers Grove, IL: InterVarsity, 2002.

Verhey, Allen. *The Great Reversal: Ethics and the New Testament*. Grand Rapids: Eerdmans, 1984.

Volf, Miroslav. *Exclusion and Embrace: A Theological Exploration of Identity, Otherness, and Reconciliation*. Nashville: Abingdon, 1996.

———. "Johannine Dualism and Contemporary Pluralism." In *The Gospel of John and Christian Theology*, edited by Richard Bauckham and Carl Mosser, 19–50. Grand Rapids: Eerdmans, 2008.

Wallace, Daniel B. *Greek Grammar beyond the Basics: An Exegetical Syntax of the New Testament*. Grand Rapids: Zondervan, 1996.

Webster, John B. *Barth's Moral Theology: Human Action in Barth's Thought*. Edinburgh: T&T Clark, 1998.

———. "Christology, Imitability and Ethics." *SJT* 39 (1986): 309–26.

———. *Holy Scripture: A Dogmatic Sketch*. Current Issues in Theology. Cambridge: Cambridge University Press, 2003.

Wedderburn, A. J. M. "The Soteriology of the Mysteries and Pauline Baptismal Theology." *NovT* 29, no. 1 (1987): 53–72.

Weder, Hans. *Die "Rede der Reden": Eine Auslegung der Bergpredigt heute*. 2nd ed. Zürich: Theologischer Verlag, 1987.

Weeks, Stuart. "Wisdom, Form and Genre." In *Was There a Wisdom Tradition? New Prospects on Israelite Wisdom Studies*, edited by Mark R. Sneed, 161–77. SBL Ancient Israel and Its Literature 23. Atlanta: SBL Press, 2015.

———. "Wisdom in the Old Testament." In *Where Shall Wisdom Be Found? Wisdom in the Bible, the Church and the Contemporary World*, edited by Stephen C. Barton, 19–30. Edinburgh: T&T Clark, 1999.

Weima, Jeffrey A. D. *Paul the Ancient Letter Writer: An Introduction to Epistolary Analysis*. Grand Rapids: Baker Academic, 2016.

Wenham, Gordon J. *Psalms as Torah: Reading Biblical Song Ethically*. STI. Grand Rapids: Baker Academic, 2012.

———. *Story as Torah: Reading the Old Testament Ethically*. Old Testament Studies. Edinburgh: T&T Clark, 2000.

Westphal, Merold. *Overcoming Onto-theology: Toward a Postmodern Christian Faith*. Perspectives in Continental Philosophy. New York: Fordham University Press, 2001.

Whitehead, Alfred North. *Process and Reality: An Essay in Cosmology*. New York: Harper, 1960.

Whybray, R. N. "The Wisdom Psalms." In *Wisdom in Ancient Israel: Essays in Honour of J. A. Emerton*, edited by John Day, Robert P. Gordon, and H. G. M. Williamson, 152–60. Cambridge: Cambridge University Press, 1995.

Williamson, H. G. M. "Isaiah and the Wise." In *Wisdom in Ancient Israel: Essays in Honour of J. A. Emerton*, edited by John Day, R. P. Gordon, and H. G. M. Williamson, 133–41. Cambridge: Cambridge University Press, 1995.

Wills, Lawrence M., and Benjamin G. Wright, eds. *Conflicted Boundaries in Wisdom and Apocalypticism*. Society of Biblical Literature Symposium Series 35. Atlanta: SBL Press, 2005.

Wilson, Walter T. *The Hope of Glory: Education and Exhortation in the Epistle to the Colossians*. NovTSup 88. Leiden: Brill, 1997.

Wolterstorff, Nicholas. *Divine Discourse: Philosophical Reflections on the Claim That God Speaks*. Cambridge: Cambridge University Press, 1995.

———. *Justice in Love*. Emory University Studies in Law and Religion. Grand Rapids: Eerdmans, 2011.

———. *Practices of Belief: Selected Essays*. Vol. 2. Cambridge: Cambridge University Press, 2010.

Wrede, William. *Paul*. Translated by Edward Lummis. London: Philip Green, 1907.

Wright, Benjamin G. "Joining the Club: A Suggestion about Genre in Early Jewish Texts." *DSD* 17 (2010): 289–314.

Wright, N. T. *After You Believe: Why Christian Character Matters*. New York: HarperOne, 2010.

Yarbrough, Robert W. *1–3 John*. BECNT. Grand Rapids: Baker Academic, 2008.

Zimmerli, Walter. "The Place and Limit of the Wisdom in the Framework of the Old Testament Theology." *SJT* 17 (1964): 146–58.

SCRIPTURE INDEX

AUTHOR INDEX